The Practitioner Inquiry Series

Marilyn Cochran-Smith and Susan L. Lytle, Series Editors

Inquiry as Stance: Practitioner Research for the Next Generation
MARILYN COCHRAN-SMITH & SUSAN L. LYTLE

Building Racial and Cultural Competence in the Classroom: Strategies from Urban Educators
KAREN MANHEIM TEEL & JENNIFER OBIDAH, EDITORS

Re-Reading Families: The Literate Lives of Urban Children, Four Years Later
CATHERINE COMPTON-LILLY

"What About Rose?" Using Teacher Research to Reverse School Failure
SMOKEY WILSON

Immigrant Students and Literacy: Reading, Writing, and Remembering
GERALD CAMPANO

Going Public with Our Teaching: An Anthology of Practice
THOMAS HATCH, DILRUBA AHMED, ANN LIEBERMAN, DEBORAH FAIGENBAUM, MELISSA EILER WHITE, & DÉSIRÉE H. POINTER MACE, EDITORS

Teaching as Inquiry: Asking Hard Questions to Improve Practice and Student Achievement
ALEXANDRA WEINBAUM, DAVID ALLEN, TINA BLYTHE, KATHERINE SIMON, STEVE SEIDEL, & CATHERINE RUBIN

"Is This English?" Race, Language, and Culture in the Classroom
BOB FECHO

Teacher Research for Better Schools
MARIAN M. MOHR, COURTNEY ROGERS, BETSY SANFORD, MARY ANN NOCERINO, MARION S. MACLEAN, & SHEILA CLAWSON

Imagination and Literacy: A Teacher's Search for the Heart of Learning
KAREN GALLAS

Regarding Children's Words: Teacher Research on Language and Literacy
BROOKLINE TEACHER RESEARCHER SEMINAR

Rural Voices: Place-Conscious Education and the Teaching of Writing
ROBERT E. BROOKE, EDITOR

Teaching Through the Storm: A Journal of Hope
KAREN HALE HANKINS

Reading Families: The Literate Lives of Urban Children
CATHERINE COMPTON-LILLY

Narrative Inquiry in Practice: Advancing the Knowledge of Teaching
NONA LYONS & VICKI KUBLER LABOSKEY, EDITORS

Learning from Teacher Research
JOHN LOUGHRAN, IAN MITCHELL, & JUDIE MITCHELL, EDITORS

Writing to Make a Difference: Classroom Projects for Community Change
CHRIS BENSON & SCOTT CHRISTIAN WITH DIXIE GOSWAMI & WALTER H. GOOCH, EDITORS

Starting Strong: A Different Look at Children, Schools, and Standards
PATRICIA F. CARINI

Because of the Kids: Facing Racial and Cultural Differences in Schools
JENNIFER E. OBIDAH & KAREN MANHEIM TEEL

Ethical Issues in Practitioner Research
JANE ZENI, EDITOR

Action, Talk, and Text: Learning and Teaching Through Inquiry
GORDON WELLS, EDITOR

Teaching Mathematics to the New Standards: Relearning the Dance
RUTH M. HEATON

Teacher Narrative as Critical Inquiry: Rewriting the Script
JOY S. RITCHIE & DAVID E. WILSON

From Another Angle: Children's Strengths and School Standards
MARGARET HIMLEY WITH PATRICIA F. CARINI, EDITORS

Unplayed Tapes: A Personal History of Collaborative Teacher Research
STEPHEN M. FISHMAN & LUCILLE MCCARTHY

continued

Inquiry as Stance

Practitioner Research
for the Next Generation

Marilyn Cochran-Smith & Susan L. Lytle

Teachers College
Columbia University
New York and London

Published by Teachers College Press, 1234 Amsterdam Avenue, New York, NY
10027
Copyright © 2009 by Teachers College, Columbia University

Library of Congress Cataloging-in-Publication Data

Cochran-Smith, Marilyn, 1951–
  Inquiry as stance : practitioner research for the next generation / Marilyn
Cochran-Smith and Susan L. Lytle.
     p. cm. — (The practitioner inquiry series)
  Includes bibliographical references and index.
  ISBN 978-0-8077-4970-8 (pbk. : alk. paper)
  ISBN 978-0-8077-4971-5 (hardcover : alk. paper)
     1. Action research in education—United States. I. Lytle, Susan L. (Susan
Landy), 1942– II. Title.
  LB1028.24.C62 2009
  370.7'2—dc22   2009000125

ISBN (paper): 978-0-8077-4970-8
ISBN (hardcover): 978-0-8077-4971-5

Printed on acid-free paper

Manufactured in the United States of America

16   15   14   13   12   11   8   7   6   5   4   3   2

Contents

Part III. Practitioners' Voices   343

Preface

Inquiry as Stance: Practitioner Research for the Next Generation is the sequel to *Inside/Outside: Teacher Research and Knowledge*, which we published in 1993. In *Inside/Outside*, we made what was then a radical argument: The knowledge needed for teachers to teach well and to enhance students' learning opportunities and life chances could not be generated solely by researchers who were centrally positioned outside of schools and classrooms and imported for implementation and use inside schools. This argument challenged then-prevalent knowledge and power hierarchies by positioning practitioners as knowers at the same time that it rejected transmission models of teaching and learning for both K–12 schools and teacher development. One of the intentions of *Inside/Outside* was to call for renegotiation of the boundaries of research and practice and reconfiguration of relationships inside and outside schools and universities, all in the interest of school and social change.

The arguments we made in our previous book are the groundwork for its sequel. As is the case with many movie sequels, however, the landscape and scene for *Inquiry as Stance* have changed dramatically over the 15 years since the first book was published. The disparities in learning opportunities and outcomes among students from differing racial, cultural, linguistic, and socioeconomic backgrounds have continued and become even more urgent in many places. Exacerbated by annual school progress requirements and narrow ideas about evidence-based education, school dropout rates have increased and teacher-proof curricula have reemerged. In short, the larger educational landscape is now dominated by narrow views of science (even scientism). It is assumed that policy drives reform, and the schools are controlled to a great extent by test-based accountability regimes. At the same time, it is now considered self-evident that the primary purpose of education is to produce the nation's workforce and preserve its place in the competitive global market. Within this context, educational practitioners (especially teachers) are assumed to be the central determining factor in school success, and thus they are also blamed for school failure. Pay-for-performance and other schemes that assume teachers have the ability but not the will to "teach better" are touted as the new solution to what ails the schools.

Inquiry as Stance offers a radically different view of the relationships of knowledge and practice and of the role of practitioners in educational change. It explores what it means to take an inquiry stance for the next generation. It is our hope, of course, that unlike many movie sequels, this new book will match or surpass its predecessor in challenging prevailing notions about teaching, research, and knowledge and in interrupting dominant viewpoints about what it takes to make educational resources and outcomes more just and equitable. A central purpose of this book is to conceptualize inquiry as stance as a challenge to the current arrangements and outcomes of schools and other educational contexts and to call for practitioner researchers in local settings across the country and the world to ally their work with others as part of larger social and intellectual movements for social change and social justice.

We debated and carefully selected each of the words in the title of this book. The term *inquiry as stance*, which we coined in the late 1990s and which we and others have used in many articles and chapters since that time, is intended to signify the idea of inquiry as perspectival and conceptual. To say that we regard inquiry as a stance is to suggest that we see this as a worldview and a habit of mind—a way of knowing and being in the world of educational practice that carries across educational contexts and various points in one's professional career and that links individuals to larger groups and social movements intended to challenge the inequities perpetuated by the educational status quo. This stands in sharp contrast to other commonly held ideas about inquiry (or teacher research or action research or teacher learning communities) as a teacher training or teacher development strategy, a sequence of steps for solving classroom or school problems based on assessment data, or a skill to be demonstrated by beginners to show competence. Our ideas about inquiry as stance are illustrated and threaded throughout every chapter in this volume, including the eight chapters in Part II of this book, which were written by differently positioned practitioners who explore the variety of meanings of an inquiry stance in the context of a wide range of educational practice, and also including the readers' theatre script in Part III. We focus specifically on the notion of inquiry as stance in Chapter 5, considering its promise and reality in the current context, in which policy is seen as the driver of school practice and test scores are the synecdoche for learning, accountability, and progress.

In this book, we use the phrase *practitioner research* as an umbrella term to encompass multiple genres and forms of research (including action research and self study, among several others that we describe in some detail in Chapter 2) where the practitioner is simultaneously a researcher who is continuously engaged in inquiry with the ultimate purpose of enriching students' learning and life chances. We use *practitioner research* and *practitioner inquiry* more or less interchangeably throughout this book. However, for the book's title, just as we did with the title of *Inside/Outside*, we use *research* rather than the somewhat softer word *inquiry* to signal that practitioner research is not simply a beneficial, but benign, form of professional development for individuals and groups (which it can be). Rather, we suggest that it is also a valuable mode of critique of the inequities in schools and society and of knowledge hierarchies, which have implications within as well as beyond the local context. This means that our decision to use *research* in the title is as much a political and strategic decision as it is a semantic one.

With this book, we want to make it very clear that we find untenable the concepts of a *knowledge base* for teaching and of *evidence-based education*, if and when these terms are understood to be grounded in scientific (or scientistic) research on educational practice carried out solely by those outside of the contexts of schools and other sites of practice and with the intention of discovering universally applicable practices that will reform the work inside them. We very intentionally use *practitioner research* here instead of *teacher research*, as we did in *Inside/Outside*. We realized many years ago, as we worked with differently positioned educators after the publication of our first book, that the term *teacher* unnecessarily and inaccurately narrowed the scope of the work. Thus in this new book, we use *practitioner* in an expansive and inclusive way to mean a wide array of education practitioners, including teachers to be sure, but also including school and school district administrators and other leaders, teacher candidates, teacher educators, community college instructors, university faculty members and administrators, adult literacy and language program practitioners, community-based educational activists, parents, and others who work inside educational sites of practice.

This book is "next generation" in the sense that it is a sequel to our earlier book, as mentioned above. It elaborates and interrogates many of the questions and conceptual frameworks we have developed for understanding, critiquing, and using research and inquiry carried out by practitioners during the two decades since we worked on the ideas in the previous book. The book also outlines the currently much broader sweep of practitioner research, especially its prominence in programs, projects, networks, communities, and partnerships all over the globe, which are often connected to one another through new virtual and real communications channels. Chapter 1 provides an overview of the expansive scope and reach of the practitioner research movement, identifying five major themes that have emerged and, in many cases, continued the trends we had identified in the previous decade.

This book is also "next generation" in the sense that its chapters theorize and portray what it means to take seriously the premises of practitioner research during a time when education politics and policies are radically different from those of the previous era. Chapter 1 introduces this idea by highlighting the major features of the current policy/political context, especially the heavy emphasis on test-based accountability, education science, and the identification of teacher quality as the linchpin in education reforms of all kinds. Chapter 3 extends this point, in particular connecting practitioner research with policy by using some of the major premises of practitioner research as lenses for critical analysis of NCLB legislation.

This book has three parts. Part I is a set of five lengthy essays in which we theorize inquiry as stance and its role for the next generation of practitioner research by taking up the questions posed in the paragraphs above as well as other epistemological, methodological, ethical, and policy issues. Part II is a set of eight chapters written by eight practitioners who are engaged in practitioner research in K–12 schools or teacher education. The authors of these chapters are our colleagues, associates, co-presenters, co-authors, students, and former students; some of these chapters are based on practitioner research dissertations or drawn from work undertaken in practitioner research courses. For all of these chapters, "working the dialectic," which we describe in some detail in Chapter 4, is the mode of inquiry, which refers to the reciprocal and recursive relationships of research and practice (or of theorizing and doing), as well as the dialectic of generating local knowledge of practice while also making that knowledge accessible outside the local context. Part III offers a unique format for exploring inquiry as stance for the next generation—a readers' theatre script that includes 20 "practitioners' voices," which are juxtaposed and comingled in a performance-oriented format, followed by commentary from two practitioners who edited the script.

We are delighted that this book is being published as part of the Practitioner Inquiry Series, which we developed and have edited for Teachers College Press for more than a decade. This series publishes both books *by* practitioner researchers and books *about* practitioner inquiry and its role in teaching and learning, teacher education, curriculum development, professional development, school reform, alternative forms of assessment, social change initiatives, and community-based education. Many of the books in the series blur the boundaries between theory and practice by providing rich insider accounts of the complex, day-to-day work of educational practice as well as how practitioners theorize and understand their work from the inside. To our knowledge, the Practitioner Inquiry Series is the only series of its kind in the world. Its books offer rich local knowledge of practice in particular contexts but also speak to practice, policy, and research at a more general and public level. The books in the series take up many of the most important educational issues of the day. What makes them different from others on these same topics is that they provide compelling insider accounts of the complexities of teaching, learning, and schooling in today's increasingly globalized and test-based culture at the same time that they provide rich and generative conceptual frameworks for understanding that complexity. It is our hope that *Inquiry as Stance* will continue the tradition of the nearly three dozen series books now in publication or in press.

★ ★ ★

In the last paragraph of the preface to *Inside/Outside*, we quoted a favorite line from Mary Catherine Bateson (1990), who suggested in *Composing a Life* that "writing a book with someone is a curious kind of sharing in the creation of a new life, an intimacy that establishes a permanent link even when one moves on to other interests" (p. 89). Bateson's insight has turned out to be more fitting and relevant to our work together than we first imagined. For more than 30 years now, we have been friends and colleagues. For 20 of those years, we have talked, thought through, written, wrestled with, critiqued, read, connected, and jointly constructed our ideas about practitioner inquiry as research genre, movement, way of knowing, and social educational critique. We wrote our first paper on the topic in 1987, and, as this book goes to press, it is 2009. Along the way, our children grew up, our family lives changed, and our career paths converged but also diverged. Over these years, we researched and wrote individually as well as with many other collaborators about a variety of different topics, but we also regularly wrote together about practitioner research.

During all of the years of our work together as co-authors, co-editors, and co-presenters, we comingled the professional, the personal, and the political. Of course, we sometimes disagreed. More often than not, however, we brought fresh perspectives to bear on each other's work and lives, and our different knowledges, experiences, theoretical frameworks, problems, and contexts were complementary and synergistic rather than dissonant. Working at different universities in different cities for the last dozen years, we have nonetheless maintained the intellectual intimacy born in the creation of the papers that turned into the chapters of our first book—in part because we also maintained our joint interests in practitioner research and our shared beliefs in the fundamental ideas about teaching, practice, inquiry, community, equity, social justice, and the purposes of education that are central to practitioner research. During the spring of 2008, although at different universities and different cities, we each taught a similar course on practitioner inquiry during the same semester for the first time ever in our somewhat parallel academic careers. This created a new occasion for shared ideas, new questions, and deliberations about the fundamental assumptions of practitioner research within the culture of the research university and in the context of the broader world of education policy and politics.

We continue to think that the bonds and energy that come from close collaborative work—for us as co-authors, for practitioners who are members of educational communities, and for anyone who struggles alongside others to bring about educational change—are central to ongoing efforts to redistribute resources, recognize the knowledge traditions of differently positioned individuals and groups, and renegotiate school–university relationships. We do not believe that making inquiry a stance is the panacea for the problems of practitioner development or school change or knowledge generation. But we do see it as a way of life and a worldview that has a powerful influence on all of these and also has the potential to help build larger alliances among practitioner researchers and others who are part of larger social and intellectual movements committed to school and social change.

REFERENCE

Bateson, M. C. (1990). *Composing a life*. New York: Plume.

Acknowledgments

We would like to thank the many practitioner groups, inquiry communities, students in graduate courses, and colleagues, both locally and beyond, who have made this book possible. In particular, we want to thank the 21 writers whose work comprises the chapters and readers' theatre script in Parts II and III of this book. Their insights, commitments, and critiques greatly expand the ways we think about practitioner research in the next generation, and their contributions here are invaluable.

We also want to thank our editors at Teachers College Press—Brian Ellerbeck, Carole Saltz, and former editor Carol Collins—for their ongoing enthusiasm and support of the Practitioner Inquiry Series. Their foresight in recognizing practitioner research as an emerging field and their willingness to sponsor many first-time authors have helped to create a unique resource for the educational community. In addition, we want to thank the members of the advisory board of the Practitioner Inquiry Series. For many years, they have worked on behalf of this book series and have provided creative leadership for the field.

We are grateful for the assistance of Katrina Bartow, Jennifer Lytle, Tracy McMahon, Christine Power, and Moira Raftery, who helped us organize and prepare the final manuscript. We could not have completed the book without them. We also want to thank Rebecca Akin and Gerald Campano for editing and writing about the script. Their perspectives, insights, and compelling prose bring new dimension to the book and make clear how important it is to theorize practitioner inquiry from the inside.

Finally, we both want to thank our families—Larry, Brad and Lindsey, Michael, and Karen as well as Torch, Sarah and Jacob, Jenny and Joe, and Caleb and Eli—for their love, interest, and sense of humor in supporting the seemingly endless process of creating this book.

Part I

THEORIZING AND CONTEXTUALIZING PRACTITIONER RESEARCH

It is now broadly assumed by nearly everybody interested in improving the schools—researchers, policymakers, school-based leaders, politicians, parents—that teachers and other practitioners are the key to educational change. Indeed, many educational leaders now believe that good practice, or what is referred to more commonly as "best practice," has the capacity to overcome the impact of factors and forces outside of school, including failed social policies, poverty, and racism as well as a system of schooling in which low expectations and outcomes for certain groups and subgroups of students are endemic. Along with the identification of teachers as the linchpin of educational reform, there has also been increased emphasis on teacher learning. Indeed, there are now many initiatives to establish school-based professional learning communities and other practitioner groups as the most efficacious sites of educational reform. Consequently, more and more practitioners are now expected to be the gatherers and interpreters of school and classroom data as part of larger initiatives to improve school achievement.

Recognizing that teachers and other practitioners are critical to the success of all efforts to improve education is clearly an idea whose time has come—or should have come long ago. We agree with many others in the larger educational community that reshaping schools as places that support practitioner learning is a project well worth pursuing, and it is certainly right to recognize the importance of teachers' work and the sometimes dramatic impact a single teacher can have on the learning and lives of students. But it is also important to note that despite these supposedly new assumptions about teachers, beneath the surface of prevailing educational policy and behind many (but not all) of the initiatives spawned by that policy are the same assumptions about teachers, teaching, and learning that were in operation decades ago but were subsequently rejected by scholars and practitioners from many different perspectives.

What we mean is that behind the current educational regime is a kind of back-to-the-future enterprise that, despite its rhetoric, makes certain assumptions: teachers are primarily technicians; the goal of teacher learning initiatives is to make teachers more faithful implementers of received knowledge and curriculum; subject matter is a more or less static object to be transmitted from teachers to students; the purpose of educational systems, which are the bellwether of the health of the economy, is to produce the nation's workers; and students' learning can be adequately assessed through standardized tests. The new twists of this revived regime are the development of tightly controlled accountability systems with high-stakes tests at their center and strong penalties for failure to meet required goals, and the idea that recognizing the importance of teacher learning translates into programs to train teachers to use assessment data to determine best practices for their schools and classrooms.

The chapters in this book are united by their grounding in a core of radically different assumptions about teachers, teaching, learning, school leadership, educational change, and the purposes of education in a democratic society. Explored in a variety of different ways across the five chapters that comprise Part I, these core premises include the idea that practitioners are deliberative intellectuals who constantly theorize practice as part of practice itself and that the goal of teacher learning initiatives is the joint construction of local knowledge, the questioning of common assumptions, and thoughtful critique of the usefulness of research generated by others both inside and outside contexts of practice. In addition, this book assumes that subject-matter knowledge is fluid and dynamic, constructed in the interactions of all participants within learning communities; part of what it means to learn subject matter, then, is to critique its meanings and sources, including whose knowledge perspectives are left out. We see the purpose of educational systems as improving learning and enhancing the life chances of all students so that they have genuine choices about meaningful work, continued education, and civic engagement. Finally, we assume that accountability for students' learning goes far beyond what can be measured on tests and is influenced by the interaction of many complex, systemic, and historical factors; the focus of accountability includes academic learning, social and emotional development, and preparation for participation in a diverse democratic society in an increasingly cosmopolitan world.

Grounded in these core assumptions, the five essays in Part I theorize and contextualize practitioner inquiry as educational movement, research genre, political and policy critique, challenge to university culture, and lifelong stance on teaching, learning, schooling, and educational leadership. Chapter

1 locates practitioner research in terms of broader educational policy and political contexts. Here, we suggest that despite the emergence of an acutely conservative political climate and an accountability system focused almost exclusively on test scores, the practitioner research movement has survived and thrived over the last two decades in the United States and in many other parts of the world. To illustrate its power and reach, we explore five major themes in the movement. In Chapter 2, we describe the multiple genres of practitioner research, suggesting that, despite differences, these share several key features. From another angle, however, we also contrast the practitioner research movement with the recent emphasis on professional learning communities as a lever for school reform, identifying commonalities but also pointing to critical—and worrisome—differences. Chapter 3 uses a practitioner research framework to unpack and critique the images of teaching, teachers, and teacher learning that are central to NCLB policy, arguing that in many ways these are retrograde and dangerous, especially given the astonishingly comprehensive mandates and regulations of the policy. Chapter 4 turns inward, focusing on what it means to take seriously the premises and assumptions of practitioner research within the culture of research universities. Here, we suggest that these premises interrupt many traditional assumptions about research and teaching in ways that are constructive and challenging.

Finally, in Chapter 5 we turn specifically to the title idea of this book—the concept of inquiry as stance on teaching, learning, schooling, and school leadership—as opposed to inquiry as project, as sequence of steps for solving a particular problem, or as skill to be demonstrated. We argue that "inquiry as stance" is what critical theorists have called a counterhegemonic notion in that it challenges the ideas about teaching, learning, learners, diversity, knowledge, practice, expertise, evidence, school organizations, and educational reform that are implicit or explicit in the dominant educational regime. At the same time, however, there is a paradox. Unlike the term *counterhegemonic*, inquiry as stance is decidedly not a byproduct of the distanced and sometimes impenetrable theorizing of those outside of schools and other contexts of practice who develop critical perspectives about what is going on inside. Rather the idea of inquiry of stance has emerged—and, we suspect, this is why it has resonated with so many others—out of the dialectic and synergy of inquiry, knowledge, and practice and from the intentional conceptual blurring of theory and practice, knowing and doing, conceptualizing and studying, analyzing and acting, researchers and practitioners, and public and local knowledge. Inquiry as stance begins with the idea that all of these are joined dialectically rather than being discrete phenomena that must then later be translated into one another or sutured together. This makes inquiry as stance much more than a counterhegemonic or oppositional notion that engenders trenchant critiques of the current educational regime and fosters new insights that counteract narrow notions of test-based accountability and practitioners as implementers. Even more importantly, in Chapter 5 we theorize inquiry as stance as a powerful affirmative and constructive idea that repositions the collective intellectual capacity of practitioners and suggests a framework for aligning it with other larger social and political movements that aim for radical transformation of teaching, learning, and schooling.

Taken together, the five essays that comprise Part I of this book provide a generative conceptual framework for considering practitioner inquiry for the next generation. They also serve as a call for new alliances among the many communities of educators who reject current dominant notions about knowledge, practice, and the role of practitioners in educational change.

Chapter One

Practitioner Inquiry in Trying Times

Some 20 years ago, we began writing about the reemergence of practitioner research as a promising way to conceptualize the critical role of teachers' knowledge and actions in student learning, school change, and educational reform. Arguing that neither process–product nor interpretive research on teaching recognized teachers' roles in the generation of knowledge, we pointed to some of the consequences of this omission, including teachers' ambivalence about academic research and the field's lack of information about classroom life from an emic perspective. We also recognized that it was difficult for the university-based community to acknowledge the potential of teacher research. To make this happen, we argued that there would need to be incentives, supportive networks, reform of school organizations and the cultures of teaching, and ways of dealing with the hierarchical power relationships that characterized much of schooling and (as we would argue later) the cultures of university life as well (Cochran-Smith & Lytle, 1990).

Nearly a decade later (Cochran-Smith & Lytle, 1999a), we tried to take stock of what had happened to these ideas, arguing that part of what had made teacher research into a movement (and not just an educational fad) was that it stemmed from several different but compatible intellectual traditions and educational projects. We described five significant trends in the U.S. teacher research movement: its prominence in teacher education, professional development, and school reform; the development of a number of conceptual frameworks and theories of teacher research; the dissemination of this work beyond local settings; the emergence of critiques related to knowledge, methods, and purposes; and the transformative potential of teacher research for some aspects of university culture (Cochran-Smith & Lytle, 1999a).

Despite these positive trends, we ended our 1999 essay on a decidedly sober note. The educational climate of the late 1990s seemed vastly different from the prevailing sentiments of the late 1980s and early 1990s, when calls for the professionalization of teaching, enlarged roles for teachers, and enhanced teacher leadership were surfacing across the nation. Instead, the educational discourse of the time was dominated by the standards movement, the intensification of pressures for accountability, the emerging rhetoric of best practices, and the increasing prominence of outsiders designing plans for whole-school improvement. All of these developments, which de-emphasized local contexts, local knowledge, and the role of teachers as decision makers and change agents, seemed to us to be antithetical to the heart of the teacher research movement.

At that time we suggested that the future of the movement was uncertain, and we foretold serious challenges in the form of narrowed outcomes, prespecified curriculum, high-stakes tests, and cooptation of teacher communities for the implementation of federal, state, and district policies. At the same time, however, we also predicted that the central ideas of the movement would remain deeply compelling to many teachers, teacher educators, researchers, and other practitioners and thus that practitioner research would be sustained as a viable framework for improving the school lives and life chances of students.

To begin this book, we highlight what has happened to practitioner research over the last 10 years, since we wrote our 1999 essay. We identify five major themes that build on but also differ from what was happening a decade ago. These developments represent very promising directions for maintaining and adding to the strength of the movement, and taken cumulatively, the message is a decidedly hopeful one: Despite all of the forces working against it, teacher research and the larger practitioner inquiry movement continue to flourish in the United States and many parts of the world. Many educators still believe that deep and significant changes in practice can only be brought about by those closest to the day-to-day work of teaching and learning. And across myriad contexts, practitioner research initiatives are proliferating, often "pushing back" against constraining policies and mandated practices and opening up spaces for practitioners to articulate and enact deep beliefs about the fundamental purposes of education (see Figure 1.1.).

It is important to point out that our account of the current state of practitioner research is necessarily partial. This chapter is not intended as a comprehensive literature review. Instead, we have identified what we regard as significant themes and have provided selected references to illustrate those themes. We know that much of the work of practitioner research remains radically local, generated and sustained by those who do not privilege publication and dissemination over trying to practice better, thus doing work that is consequential but invisible, except to its immediate participants. In addition to a considerable number of recent publications based on or related to practitioner research, then, there is an enormous amount of activity that exists under the radar of even the most energetic synthesizers. Some unpublished work is widely circulated among teachers and teacher educators, and many of the "outcomes" of participation in inquiry communities are palpable and relevant only to those who are in them: people who teach differently, who advocate for students, who take leadership roles in their schools or districts or universities, and who question current assumptions and taken-for-granted practices.

Figure 1.1. Practitioner Research in Trying Times.

Educational Policy/Political Climate		
Education Directly Linked to National Economic Status	Dominance of Test-Based Accountability	Elevation of Science of Education

↓ ↓ ↓

Negative Impact on Practitioner Research		
Focus on Means, Not Ends of Education	Reemergence of Transmission Models of Teaching and Learning	Exclusionary Views of Knowers and Knowledge

⇩ ⇩ ⇩

Nevertheless . . .

The Practitioner Research Movement Is Thriving Worldwide

and it is

Pushing Back Against Constraints

⇧ ⇧ ⇧

Five Current Themes in Practitioner Research
• Taking on Issues of Equity, Engagement, and Agency • Developing Conceptual Framework • Inventing and Reinventing Communities of Inquiry • Shaping School Reform and Educational Policy • Re-Forming Research and Practice in Universities

There are also demographic issues involved in taking stock of the movement. Some of the prominent leaders in inquiry communities have changed positions and are carrying their inquiry stances into their day-to-day work as school leaders, mentors, or college or university faculty members. Some are at or approaching retirement. And some versions of practitioner research have been brought into line with technical views of teaching and educating in sync with the prevailing business and neoliberal climate of the day.

Furthermore, what is going on now in the practitioner research movement is far from monolithic. Because there are so many different initiatives informed by a range of purposes, contexts, epistemologies, methods, resources, and consequences, various actors in and around the movement necessarily represent it using different information and different frameworks. These differences are in fact one of the reasons the movement is dynamic, not dormant, "alive and well" in spite of—or perhaps in resistance to—the dominant discourses of the day.

THE CURRENT POLICY/POLITICAL CLIMATE IN U.S. EDUCATION

We begin by setting our "telling" of the practitioner research movement over the last 10 years within the context of the current policy/political climate. We point to dimensions that seem especially toxic to its core elements.

Education and the Economy

In much of the discourse about public education, it is now considered self-evident that the nation's place in the global economy depends on the quality of its educational system. Policymakers, pundits, and others demand that the schools produce students who have the array of knowledge and skills needed to thrive in the new "knowledge society" wherein low-level work is done by machines or outsourced to the lowest bidder, and "developed" nations compete for high-paying jobs that require sophisticated intellectual skills and strategies. Consistent with this view is the assumption that the primary purpose of education is to produce a workforce that can meet the demands of the competitive global market and preserve—or, better yet, boost—the nation's place in that market.

The shift to a knowledge economy has also shifted the locus of education policymaking in the United States from low-profile state agencies and local decisions to the highest levels of government and business (Oakes, Lipton, Rogers, & Renee, 2006), including presidents, governors, federal legislators, corporate CEOs, and major philanthropists. Overwhelmingly, they have concluded that the current educational system in the United States is failing to produce the workforce needed and that the nation urgently needs major reforms—or a complete overhaul—of the education system.

What do these ideas about education's inextricable link to the economy mean as a backdrop for practitioner research? First, it is important to note that from this perspective, what we (Cochran-Smith & Lytle, 1998) once called the "ends question" in education (i.e., debates about the purposes of teaching, learning and schooling) is closed. In other words, the complicated string of assumptions and values that support the idea that preparation for economic roles is the central purpose of schooling is taken for granted and regarded as straightforward.

In contrast, at the heart of practitioner inquiry is problematizing the ends question. Practitioner researchers question the fundamental goals of teaching, learning, and schooling: What purposes—besides academic achievement as indicated by test scores—are important in the schools? What about teaching toward the democratic ideal, deliberation and debate, and challenging inequities? Practitioner researchers also raise questions about power and authority: Who makes decisions about purposes and consequences? How do school structures, assessment regimes, and classroom practices challenge or sustain the status quo? What are the consequences for students' learning and their life chances? What part do practitioners play in broader social and intellectual movements?

Emphasis on Accountability

It is eminently clear that the accountability movement now dominates the discourse about reforming education in the United States and elsewhere. The testing requirements put into place by No Child Left Behind (NCLB), along with its annual requirements concerning pupils' and schools' progress, now drive most district, state, and school-level initiatives regarding curriculum, graduation and promotion policies, and practices related to test preparation. There is also a major focus on accountability systems in teacher preparation, professional development, selection of teaching materials, and whole-school initiatives.

The accountability emphasis is reflected in the recurring language of outcomes, results, effectiveness, evidence, monitoring systems, test scores, adequate yearly progress, and bottom lines. Words like these have been used so consistently in everyday discourse and at every level of schooling that they are now fully normalized and neutralized. This is exacerbated, we suspect, by the fact that many young educators either do not know about or do not remember a time without high-stakes accountability.

From this perspective, it is assumed that teaching is the transmission of agreed-upon knowledge, learning is the demonstration of that knowledge in high-stakes contexts, and differences in local settings and capacities are unimportant. In contrast, when practitioners engage in inquiry, they typically work from expanded rather than narrow views of teaching and learning. This includes conveying knowledge to students, to be sure, but it also includes representing complex knowledge in accessible ways, asking good questions, co-constructing curriculum, forming relationships with students and parents who have widely varying abilities and backgrounds, collaborating with other professionals, interpreting multiple data sources, and posing and solving problems of practice.

The accountability movement assumes there is consensus across society about what it means to be educated, whose knowledge and values are of most worth, and what counts as effectiveness. Yet even as teaching becomes more and more public, it remains, at its heart, radically local—embedded in the immediate relationships of students and teachers, shaped by the cultures of schools and communities, and connected to the experiences and biographies of individuals and groups.

Evidence, Science, and Scientism

The third influential aspect of the policy climate is the current emphasis on evidence and the elevation of science. The notion of "scientifically based research" and its complement, "evidence-based education," reflect renewed confidence in the power of science to solve social and educational problems. The presumption here is that today's rich data sources, powerful analytical techniques, and increasingly sophisticated researchers permit the verification of scientifically based practices and policies that increase achievement, improve teaching and the schools, and solve the problems involved in providing universal education to a large and diverse population.

What do these ideas mean as part of the backdrop for practitioner research? First, many of the most important issues that have been contested throughout the history of educational research are assumed to be beyond debate: the purpose of research, the questions that should be asked, the relationship between the researcher and the "objects" of research, the methods employed, standards for reporting research results, and relationships between research and practice. Clearly, this has devastating implications for the funding and dissemination of practitioner inquiry, not to mention the many other forms of research this devalues and essentially discounts.

At the base of this devaluation is a narrow and exclusionary view of knowledge and knowers. In our analysis of images of teachers, knowledge, and teaching in NCLB documents (see Cochran-Smith & Lytle, 2006; Chapter 3 in this volume), we found that "good teachers" were consistently characterized as wise consumers of products and selectors of research-based strategies to boost students' achievement. Throughout NCLB rhetoric, we found that teachers' implementing practices based on scientifically based research and doing "what works" were valorized and contrasted with learning through trial and error, relying on theory, following educational fads, or employing "unproven" practices based on ideological rather than empirical grounds. There is no question that the current regime of scientifically based research and evidence-based education positions practitioners as the recipients of other people's knowledge.

TAKING STOCK: MAJOR THEMES IN TEACHER INQUIRY/PRACTITIONER RESEARCH

Despite all of the forces seemingly working against it, teacher inquiry and the larger practitioner research movement appear to be flourishing in the United States and in many other parts of the world. There are multiple indicators that many teachers, teacher educators, school leaders, university-based teachers and researchers, and other stakeholders are engaged in the admittedly uphill struggle to democratize the locus of knowledge and power that determines the quality and quantity of educational opportunities afforded to children. These indicators include single and collaboratively authored accounts, documentation of the work of networks, the reports of myriad conferences and professional organizations, and Internet-based communities and resources that support practitioner inquiry. In the remainder of this chapter, we highlight five themes in the corpus of practitioner research over the last 10 years: (1) the emphasis on issues of equity, engagement, and agency; (2) the development of new conceptual frameworks; (3) the continued growth and reinvention of inquiry communities; (4) the use of practitioner research to shape school and district reform and educational policy; and (5) the persistence of efforts to alter the relationships of research and practice in universities. For each theme, we provide examples to emphasize the continuity of this work with previous efforts (Cochran-Smith & Lytle, 1999a) and to highlight what we regard as some of the most promising new directions in the movement. Given the limitations of space, we draw mainly from teacher research/practitioner research in the United States but with some reference to cross-national and international work as well.

Theme I: Taking on Issues of Equity, Engagement, and Agency

Over the last decade, the body of published practitioner research reflects a distinctive commitment to investigating issues of equity, engagement, and agency in classrooms and schools across the country. In stark contrast to remedies prescribed by No Child Left Behind, many teachers and students have embraced the challenge of providing access to quality education by defining equity more broadly and complexly than through performance on high-stakes tests. In addition to compelling practitioner studies in their local sites, many educators in schools and universities have documented inquiry-based curricula that put students at the center of investigating topics of concern to them in their own lives and communities.

Classroom-, School-, and Program-Based Investigations. A considerable number of published accounts of practitioner research explicitly address concerns related to equity. Taking up a range of overlapping issues in specific local contexts, this work provides valuable cases with potential significance to wider audiences. What is notable here is the publication of so many books about equity in just a few years. Unlike the other sections of this chapter where we briefly elaborate a few texts, here we list the topics or foci in bulleted form, each with selected examples.

- Issues of language and cultures (Ballenger, 2004; Fecho, 2004)
- Language and literacy in multilingual and multicultural early-childhood classrooms (Meier & Henderson, 2007)
- Critical literacies, critical pedagogies (Aaron et al., 2006; Duncan-Andrade & Morrell, 2008; Morrell, 2007; Vasquez, 2004)
- Immigrant students' cultural resources and narratives for literacy education (Campano, 2007)
- Turn-around pedagogies as literacy interventions (Comber & Kamler, 2005)
- Imagination in elementary literacy learning (Gallas, 2003)
- Narrative inquiry and the special needs of children (Hankins, 2003)
- Adult literacy education in community colleges (Wilson, 2007)
- Discourses of queer youth (Blackburn, 2005; Blackburn, Clark, Kenney, & Smith, in press)
- Curriculum genres and classroom inquiry (Pappas & Zecker, 2001a, 2002b)
- Action research for equitable classrooms across one district (Caro-Bruce, Flessner, Klehr, & Zeichner, 2007)

- Families, literacy, and culture (Compton-Lilly, 2003, 2007; Gonzalez, Moll, & Amanti, 2005)
- Gender in urban education (Ginsberg, Shapiro, & Brown, 2004)

Conducted and published concurrently with the era of No Child Left Behind, together the inquiry-based texts, focusing on issues of equity, suggest more complex and nuanced interpretations of this concept among practitioner researchers.

Other practitioner-based classroom and school-based studies focus on student engagement through improving content-area pedagogy and curricula in subjects such as science and mathematics (e.g., Feldman, Konold, & Coulter, 2000; Langrall, 2006; Masingila, 2006; Smith & Smith, 2006; van Zee, 2005; Van Zoest, 2006) and TESOL (Allwright, 2005; Borg, 2006; Cunningham Florez, 2001). Many of the volumes cited here represent efforts by teacher researchers to grapple with issues of social justice in their particular schools, classrooms, and communities over time. Some of this work takes place within communities and/or networks that have organized purposely to foreground social justice issues.

Networks and Cross-Network Initiatives. Many of the prominent teacher networks, including the National Writing Project and The Bread Loaf Teacher Network, have put issues related to equity front and center. Because networks often connect geographically dispersed and distinctive local sites, equity issues vary considerably from site to site even within the network. The Philadelphia Writing Project, for example, convened a group of parents, teachers, and students to form a participatory inquiry group to study school reform from their diverse perspectives. Known as TAPAS (Teachers and Parents and Students), the group was funded by the Consortium for Policy Research in Education and supported by Research for Action to conduct systematic inquiry into the then-current systemic reform initiative in urban Philadelphia, with a particular focus on parent leadership in school reform and parent–educator relationships (Gold, Rhodes, Brown, Lytle, & Waff, 2001). Other networks have focused on gender equity in education, such as the Gender Awareness Through Education program in Philadelphia (Ginsberg et al., 2004) in which teams of teachers, parents, and administrators engaged in practitioner inquiry to consider gender in relation to other social issues, including race, class, religion, sexual orientation, and (dis)ability.

The Teacher Research Collaborative (TRC), a 3-year alliance among teachers, teacher educators, and staff from the Bay Area Coalition for Equitable Schools, the Bay Area Writing Project, the Coalition of Essential Schools, and the National Writing Project, also took up issues of equity through inquiry. The TRC project was based on the pursuit of local answers to fundamental questions about the nature of equity, how it relates to teaching and working in schools, and the role of equity in teacher research/action research. In *Working Toward Equity: Writings and Resources from the Teacher Research Collaborative* (Friedrich, Tateishi, Malarkey, Simons, & Williams, 2005), the authors explain that their project aimed "to establish an ongoing presence for equity-focused teacher inquiry, to develop and articulate strategies for using inquiry to improve student learning and achievement, and to share resources that its members had found useful to educators leading teacher inquiry with an equity focus" (p. 1). Project participants were educators from urban and suburban communities across the United States who together explored the complex and sometimes contested intersections among equity, inquiry, and leadership. One of the most challenging aspects of their work was figuring out why and how to make equity an explicit focus in teacher inquiry despite the risks, complexities, and resistance to change that this would likely churn up.

Students as Researchers and Social Actors. The third section in this first theme on issues of equity emphasizes a key facet of teacher research/ practitioner inquiry from its inception: the close connection between teacher inquiry and student inquiry (Branscombe, Goswami, & Schwartz, 1992). Many of the published volumes mentioned above engage students directly in the inquiry process. Practitioner research as social inquiry or critical action research has long entailed collaborations among teachers, students, and other key stakeholders. In the past several years, however, new initiatives have focused directly on inventing curricula with students as a means toward more equitable and democratic educational opportunities. Here, co-construction of curriculum provides a context for students to change their relationships to their schools and communities and to affect the broader social, cultural, and political milieu. Some of this work essentially creates a new genre, as in Linda Christensen's *Reading, Writing, and Rising Up: Teaching About Social Justice and the Power of the Written Word* (2000). Rather than illustrating how teachers empower students, this recent work reveals how inquiry conducted with and by students allows learners to empower themselves to take different stances toward their education, acting as agents for change in their schools and communities.

Some of this work links writing, community, public engagement, and social action. In New Orleans, for example, a Students at the Center Writing Project (linked to Bread Loaf and teamed with The Algebra Project) supported students and teachers using radio, filmmaking, and writing to develop, in Dixie Goswami's words, students' "powerful literacies" (personal communication). Bread Loaf projects foreground students' writing, as in the recently released *HIP DEEP: Opinion, Vision, and Essays by American Teenagers"* (Young, 2006), which contains essays, speeches, and poems by 50 young rural and urban writers. *Writing to Make a Difference: Classroom Projects for Community Change* (Benson & Christian, 2002), another edited volume associated with Bread Loaf, provides striking examples of students' action research on such subjects as fighting racism, investigating environmental hazards, and teenage health risks.

The National Writing Project has also sponsored a number of equity-focused initiatives that support students as social activists. In *Writing for Change: Boosting Literacy and Learning Through Social Action* (Berdan et al., 2006), for example, teachers and students merged literacy education and community problem solving in their schools, communities, and lives. Written in collaboration with the Centre for Social Action in England and involving students K–12, the book tells the stories of a robust kind of service learning that encourages students to work together on their chosen problems, carry out projects, and reflect on their solutions.

In *Writing America: Classroom Literacy and Public Engagement* (Robbins & Dyer, 2005), the authors also link classroom-based social literacy with avenues for contributing to the larger community. The book describes a multiyear student–teacher curriculum development project, funded by the National Writing Project (NWP) and the National Endowment for the Humanities, that merged community research, school literacy, and writing. A companion volume, *Writing Our Communities: Local Learning and Public Culture* (Winter & Robbins, 2005), translated this inquiry-based curriculum into resources for teachers. Both projects emanated from the Kennesaw Mountain Writing Project in rural Georgia, which provided the infrastructure and intellectual community for teachers to pursue curriculum development as inquiry. Similarly, *Literacies in Place: Teaching Environmental Communications*, edited by Comber, Nixon, and Reid (2007), represents the work of a group of primary educators in Australia who participated in "rethinking the potential relationship between literacy and environmental studies in the light of changes that informational and communications technologies (ICT) are bringing to our understandings of literacy" (pp. 11–12). The teachers focused on redesigning curricula so that primary school students might become environmental activists within and beyond their local communities.

Inquiry-oriented work in which students position themselves as researchers provides an edgy and palpable means for disrupting the current policy/political climate, in which teachers are consistently positioned as the transmitters of others' knowledge and students as the recipients. A recent volume, *Revolutionizing Education: Youth Participatory Action Research in Motion* (Cammarota & Fine, 2008), argues that adults cannot predict the issues young people face or will face in the future and how they will be encouraged to interrogate them. Based in the tradition of participatory action research, the Youth Participatory Action Research (YPAR) project involved many young people who would be classified in the traditional sense as "marginalized" and "at risk." The project gives new meaning to the concept of education as "something students do—instead of something done to them" (p. 10). Under this first theme of post-2000 practitioner research that emphasizes equity, engagement, and agency, we have shown a noteworthy array of efforts by individuals, inquiry communities, and various collectives to make equity mean something real and palpable in specific contexts. This recent work also makes visible the strong linkages between practitioner inquiry and student inquiry and the significant symmetries in learning that accrue when they are intentionally co-constructed. This array also reveals the power of practitioner networks to deepen local work and link various locals to spread innovative ideas across settings.

Theme II: Developing Conceptual Frameworks

From the beginning, participants in, supporters of, and commentators on the practitioner inquiry movement have described, theorized, and critiqued this approach to inquiry. Until relatively recently, however, most of the literature *about* practitioner research was written by university-based researchers, and only some of it drew explicitly on the published texts of teacher practitioner inquiry (Lytle, 2000). Since 2000, a wider range of participants in the movement has been involved in the development of conceptual frameworks that draw on their emic understandings of the practice of teaching and emanate from practitioners' constructions of their diverse experiences in classrooms and within and across communities.

Theorizing the Practice of Teaching. Various insiders to the movement have offered new and extremely rich accounts of teaching that talk back to the reductive views of children, schools, and standards that dominate today's educational landscape. A key example is Patricia Carini's collection of essays, *Starting Strong: A Different Look at Children, Schools and Standards* (2001), which is a companion volume to *From Another Angle: Children's Strengths and School Standards* (Himley & Carini, 2000). The latter explored the documentary processes developed at The Prospect School in North Bennington, Vermont, now widely used in teacher inquiry communities across the country. As Joseph Featherstone writes in the Foreword to *Starting Strong*:

> [F]rom the 1960s on, Carini and many others opened up a host of new and critical perspectives on education: promoting qualitative and alternative modes of scholarship, attacking the cult of omniscient educational research, reminding an educational world too often managed by male big shots that teachers and children are the real voices and characters in the educational drama. The heart of this movement has been its insistence over a very long haul on the root of educational reality: that children and teachers are shapers of meaning and interpreters of experience. (p. xii)

Exploring what makes us "human," Carini articulated what it means to be exquisitely attentive to children's thoughts and meanings and to the thoughts and meanings of adults who have responsibility for the education of children. Carini's philosophical writing both derived from and informed Prospect's unique approaches to oral inquiry as a form of practitioner research. These recent volumes illuminate the power and complexity of descriptive processes for understanding and acting on students' strengths in the era of standards and standardization.

There are many others whose theorizing of *teaching* has added new momentum to the teacher research movement. Notable among them are two recent volumes by Sonia Nieto, *What Keeps Teachers Going* (2003) and *Why We Teach* (2005). By learning from teachers about what inspires them, how they relate to their students, how they create learning environments that make time and space for thoughtful, engaged work, and what they value about being educators in these times, Nieto's respectful accounts offered an emic perspective on frameworks that teachers who stay in the classroom use to guide their teaching. Along different but related lines, Weinbaum and colleagues' (2004) volume on *Teaching as Inquiry* built a conceptual framework linking teacher and student learning through case studies of inquiry conducted under the auspices of three leading educational organizations.

Theorizing Practitioner Research. Over the past decade, some new conceptualizations and some refinements of previous frameworks for practitioner inquiry have emerged. For example, Gerald Campano's *Immigrant Students and Literacy: Reading, Writing and Remembering* (2007), which is based on the immigrant, refugee, and migrant narratives of his 5th-grade students in Stockton, California, posed the question: "What would it mean to develop curricula that acknowledges our students' unique social identities, not as problems, but as profound sources of knowledge that could help

us illuminate aspects of our shared world and inform the ways we conceptualize our pedagogies?" (p. 16; also see Chapter 13 in this volume). Now a
professor at Indiana University, Campano suggested that a major challenge
for urban teachers is to "create an environment in which all children and
young adults feel empowered to reflect critically and draw upon the realities of their lives. What it takes to create such an environment is not simply
a matter of setting the conditions for knowledge to occur, but is a type of
knowledge *in and of itself*" (p. 16, emphasis in original). Campano theorized
the identity of teacher researcher as:

> an emergent professional and activist identity . . . [that] involves stretch-
> ing the ideas of *social location and inquiry stance*. . . . As urban teacher re-
> searchers *collaboratively* inquire into their own practices in a wide variety
> of settings *over time*, they may begin to notice salient patterns, recurrent
> themes, similar concerns, and observations that resemble one another and
> that, when conceptualized together, begin to have explanatory power and
> general relevance. Despite the differences in teaching contexts and between
> researchers, these features point to aspects of a shared phenomenology. (p.
> 115, emphasis in original)

Another example of practitioner-generated theorizing occurs in *Teacher
Research for Better Schools* (Mohr et al., 2003), where Marion Mohr and her
colleagues spoke explicitly to the generation of theories about how students
and teachers learn, how teaching and learning are related, and how schools
change. These conceptual frameworks derived primarily from their research
as teachers over time.

In their recent book *Funds of Knowledge: Theorizing Practices in Households, Communities, and Classrooms*, Norma Gonzalez, Luis Moll, and Cathy
Amanti (2005) showed vividly how teachers can document the competence and knowledge from life experiences held by families and use this
knowledge embedded in communities within their teaching. Gordon Wells
(2001, 2003) analyzed the affinities of teaching and research, the centrality
of communities of inquiry, and the ways "dialogic inquiry" builds sociocultural theory. Patti Stock (2001, 2004) explored alternative genres of
teacher research, encouraging the critical analysis and conceptualization of
the practitioner inquiry movement by teacher researchers themselves.

In addition, debates regarding the foundational theories underlying practitioner inquiry have been widely disseminated. For example, a recent issue of
Educational Action Research published in the United Kingdom (Brennan et al.,
2005) provided a retrospective analysis of Carr and Kemmis's seminal *Becoming Critical* (1986), focusing on questions about the use of critical social science

theory and its current relevance to action research. Other university-based researchers have explored relationships between practitioner research/action research, participatory action research and feminist theory (McGuire, 2001; Brydon-Miller, McGuire, & McIntyre, 2004), as well as specific approaches such as participatory action research (Kemmis & McTaggart, 2005).

Epistemologies, Methodologies, and Methods. An indication of the robustness and inherent optimism of the practitioner inquiry movement is the proliferation of guides and handbooks intended to support new practitioner researchers (see, for example, Burnaford, Fischer, & Hobson, 2001; Chiseri-Strater & Sunstein, 2006; Falk & Blumenreich, 2005; Fox, Martin, & Green, 2007; Lankshear & Knobel, 2004; Rymes, in press). These reflect an interesting and provocative array of epistemologies, methodologies, and methods drawn from disciplines such as composition studies, technoliteracy and critical theory, technology, linguistic anthropology, health and human sciences, as well as education.

Lankshear and Knobel's *A Handbook for Teacher Research: From Design to Implementation* (2004), for example, grew from the authors' initial engagement with the Primary English Teaching Association (PETA) in Australia and was transported to and expanded in Mexico. The authors disputed the notion that teacher research is inherently nonquantitative and that it exclusively involves direct research in classrooms. Instead, they argued that teachers learn by researching a variety of topics, including "policy, communities, social class, the work world, [and] nonstandard language varieties" and by engaging in "historical, anthropological, sociological or psychological studies and theoretical work conducted in other places and/or at other times" (p. 7). We single out Lankshear and Knobel's book to indicate that each of the so-called how-to books on practitioner research contains an argument about the nature, purposes, participants, forms, outcomes, and consequences of various approaches to teacher research, in much the same way that the field of qualitative research has expanded to include multiple varieties. The steady production of such books suggests that, within the movement, there is a deep and useful conversation taking place that includes many teachers—school- and university-based—who have a stake in shaping its directions and practices.

Ethical Considerations. A substantial part of the current conceptual work regarding practitioner research focuses on the complex and somewhat unique ethical issues involved. In Jane Zeni's *Ethical Issues in Practitioner Research* (2001), for example, practitioner research was defined broadly and spun out in distinctive ways by differently positioned educators. The individual chapters offered local and vivid accounts of different aspects of these projects, but they also functioned as "telling cases" (Mitchell, 1984) for those engaged in related work in other contexts. Drawing from her own long and deep experience with school- and university-based practitioners, Zeni explored the critical ethical issues and dilemmas that come with the territory of insider research in the increasingly politicized arena of educational change projects. As classroom teachers, administrators, parents, community members, school staff, district leaders, and university faculty work together to construct relationships that make traditional boundaries more porous and negotiable, it is no surprise that the relationships among the many participants are more complicated and that the ethical issues are intensified.

Campbell and Groundwater-Smith's *An Ethical Approach to Practitioner Research* (2007) represents a cross-national foray into this territory. While primarily focused on a comprehensive range of ethical issues in the United States, Australia, and Europe, this volume acknowledged similar challenges faced by others in professional practice, such as legal, nursing, and social care contexts. In taking up ethical dilemmas related to practice-based inquiry, the book focused on roles for academic researchers, consultants, teachers, students, and children. It also paid particular attention to the relationships of "field-based" researchers and academic researchers and to the concerns of various "consequential stakeholders," as well as to difficult epistemological issues and competing knowledge interests. These texts and other recent articles considered the vulnerable and consequential relationships among various constituencies in the practitioner inquiry movement (e.g., Fecho, 2003), underlying ethical principles and practices (Nolen & Putten, 2007), and the relationship of practitioner inquiry to the practices of institutional review boards (Pritchard, 2002).

A decade ago we suggested that efforts to theorize teacher research focused on social inquiry, on ways of knowing in communities, and on practical inquiry (Cochran-Smith & Lytle, 1999a). These approaches have been augmented over the last decade by practitioners' own theorizing and by theories of teaching that respond to the challenges of the current policy and political climates. In addition, a proliferation of publications have explored practitioner research epistemologies and methods as well as ethical issues that come with this territory.

Theme III: Inventing and Reinventing Communities of Inquiry

From the late 1980s until the late 1990s, there was rather broad institutional support for forming communities that embodied the core concepts of the teacher research movement: teaching as a deliberative (not technical) profession, knowledge generation for practice from practice, and the value of local questions and uncertainties in grappling successfully with issues of teaching and learning at all levels. As we noted earlier, however, when the accountability movement accelerated, the focus shifted to an almost singular emphasis on student outcomes as demonstrated on high-stakes tests. The notion that practitioners could identify questions for systematic inquiry and that teachers and students could co-construct curricula contrasted dramatically with compliance with mandated, "research-based" curricula that promised to deliver particular outcomes. This in turn affected the availability of federal, foundation, state, and local resources to support teacher inquiry communities as opposed to narrow teacher training centered on preset curricula and assessment.

Despite this shifting policy emphasis, many practitioner networks continued to support inquiry communities. However, they also acknowledged the need to address standards-based and policy-driven pedagogy, curricula and assessment. Although teacher networks like Bread Loaf and The National Writing Project, for example, intentionally maintained and even deepened their support for inquiry communities, shifts in the makeup, design, activities, and purposes of inquiry communities are now perceptible, and some groups are struggling to retain their identities while managing top-down regimes of accountability.

Affordances of New Technologies. During the last decade, even well-established inquiry networks have needed to become inventive in supporting established lines of work. The Bread Loaf Teacher Network, for example, has used the web-based "Breadnet" to link rural and urban teachers for intensive study of language and literacy connected to joint classroom-based curriculum development based on research by teachers and students in classrooms. From its inception, Bread Loaf made teaching with technology a central focus. But the explosion of Internet possibilities during the past decade or so has now created affordances for reinventing community at a whole new level. As Dixie Goswami wrote about the uses of Breadnet:

> Computer networking provides teacher researchers (and their student collaborators) with an important source of data not previously available. . . . Studying the discourse informs and changes the online communication and at the same time generates new questions about language and learning and new approaches to research design for systematic, intentional studies. (Goswami, personal communication)

Over the last decade, the Bread Loaf Teacher Network magazine has reported myriad variations on cross–school and school–university virtual networking that in turn create new relationships across boundaries of place, ethnicity, race, culture, and language. This has spawned investigations into topics such as "what it means to be bilingual," for example, an inquiry conducted virtually among two U.S. high school teachers in Arizona and Massachusetts in collaboration with a university faculty member from South Africa, a primary school head from England, and their students (Lewis, Guerrero, Makikana, & Armstrong, 2002). Funded by a grant from the Spencer Foundation, this collaborative inquiry surfaces narratives of language acquisition from bilingual adults and adolescents to reveal the specific ways that acquiring a language is at once personal, social, and academic.

The resources of technology have not only enabled new inquiry communities to form and communicate online but also spawned innovative uses of technology for sharing inquiries and classroom practices with audiences that extend beyond those involved in creating the online representations. A prominent example is the Carnegie Foundation's CASTL Program for K–12 teachers and teacher educators, which was continued in Carnegie's CASTL Program, Goldman-Carnegie Quest Project, and The Teaching and Learning Commons, under the conceptual umbrella of the "scholarship of teaching and learning" (http://carnegiefoundation.org/programs). Each of these initiatives was designed to create a space for an interactive intellectual community where distal educators can participate in enriching and inventing the documentation of teaching and learning practice. Beginning with face-to-face communities that brought participants from across the country for intensive institutes, the Carnegie projects now make widely accessible the practices of teachers and teacher educators through multimedia technology. (See http://carnegiefoundation.org/programs; Hatch, 2006; Hatch et al., 2005; Hatch & Shulman, 2005).

Another example of the affordances for practitioner inquiry of new technologies is an online teacher community that enables access to national discourses on key educational issues and thus provides a kind of infrastructure for inquiry of various kinds. The Teacher Leaders Network (TLN; www.teacherleaders.org) is a virtual community launched by the Center for Teaching Quality in 2003 based on the assumption that society currently underestimates the potential and the complexity of teachers' work and that "good teaching" is currently being defined by people and institutions other than teachers. While not specifically aligned with the practitioner research movement, this opportunity for dialogue and information gathering through virtual connectivity enables learning across a diverse group of local, committed educators and makes "learning as a teacher" a more collegial, agentive, and public process.

Online teacher networks such as TLN are essentially without boundaries and uncontrollable by the hierarchies of schools or districts or the intrusions of federal education policy. The Internet permits user-generated forms of sharing, collaboration, and support that are fast and fluid. While many uses of the Internet for lesson planning and information sharing are not based on teacher research or practitioner inquiry, there are now quite a number of inquiry groups that use digital technologies to share classroom and school data sources and analyses to an extent inconceivable only a short number of years ago. Furthermore, putting teachers and other educators' work on the web contributes to what we see as the growing "publicness" and visibility of teaching, giving teachers and teacher educators more access to and images of the daily work of others, up close and personal. Along with this access, however, come consequential questions about who is framing these images and what messages these representations are sending about the profession of teaching. The web not only connects local work with wider conversations but also makes possible the commercialization, control, and the "selling" of teaching rather than interrogating it in order to improve it.

Local Groups with National Reach. The practitioner research movement continues to thrive in part because local communities are making public and accessible the distinctive processes and findings of their work. The Philadelphia Teachers Learning Collaborative (PTLC) exemplifies the powerful possibilities of local groups with national connections and national reach to support local knowledge generation in other locations. Closely linked to the Prospect School's Patricia Carini and to the North Dakota Study Group, the PTLC has met every week in urban Philadelphia for more than 30 years to use structured oral inquiry processes to improve students' learning, teachers' lives, and the institutions in which they work. Much of this research has been against the grain of the traditional labels, practices, and accountability systems of schools and schooling (Abu El-Haj, 2003).

A number of PTLC and/or Prospect members have contributed to a series of books that explore the power of descriptive processes for understanding and acting on students' strengths. These practitioner researchers subscribe to a highly theorized norm of accountability that holds teachers accountable for observing, knowing, and teaching children in ways that are diametrically different from the notions of accountability explicit in NCLB and other policy tools. PTLC and Prospect members have several books either in press or in preparation, including Margaret Himley and Pat Carini's *Jenny's Story* (in press) and Lynne Strieb's *Inviting Families* (in press), based on her 30-year history of working with parents. Both of these texts draw on the phenomenological perspectives developed at The Prospect School and its spin-offs in Philadelphia, New York, and other cities. Along somewhat similar lines, the Brookline Teacher Researcher Seminar has been very influential beyond its local impact. In the edited volume *Regarding Children's Words: Teacher Research on Language and Literacy* (2004), Cynthia Ballenger and colleagues provided thoughtfully documented case studies that highlighted the distinctive ways these practitioners had developed to collect and analyze classroom data as the group evolved over time.

Some local practitioner groups are smaller than those described above. They may be limited to two or three teachers and yet, by virtue of their connections to national organizations, have venues to disseminate their work. For example, Mary Klehr and two other experienced practitioner researchers in Madison, Wisconsin, have created an inquiry community to study their own practices of arts integration and arts-based research. Supported by a "Communities of Inquiry" grant from the National Council of Teachers of English (NCTE), they formed a small collective to foreground their use of aesthetic texts such as visual imagery, performance, poetry, and storytelling. Klehr explained the effort this way:

> Our collaborative process involves developing and refining aesthetic techniques. . . . Each of us is responsible for introducing a number of arts-based methods such as poetry, theater, visual and sonic collage, and film to the group, around which we develop short informational and exploratory sessions. We combine various of these methods with more familiar data such as field notes, interviews, and analysis of student work, in order to shed new light on specific questions and classroom practices. (personal communication)

This community, along with others funded by NCTE grants, illustrates the kinds of grassroots initiatives that reveal the heart of the practitioner research movement, offering compelling evidence for its value to practitioners and hence its perpetuation.

Cross-National Communities. Another promising trend for the future of the practitioner inquiry movement are the cross-national communities that are flourishing in many places throughout the world. In the United States, the American Educational Research Association (AERA) has special interest groups devoted to Teacher as Researcher, S-STEP (Self Study of Teacher Education Practices), and Action Research. Several annual conferences feature practitioner research, such as the Ethnography in Education Research Forum at University of Pennsylvania, the CRESS Center conferences at the University of California at Davis, and the bi-yearly International Teacher Research Conference (ITRC) held after AERA. A recent edited volume by Clarke and Erickson (2003), for example, based on presentations at ITRC, contains 45 pieces from practitioner researchers all over North America and the United Kingdom, and represents its contents as a key resource for teachers, teacher educators, and policymakers.

A growing network of Bread Loaf teachers in Nairobi, Mumbai, Tanzania, and Bulgaria study what students know about culture. Inquiry related to the teaching of English as a second language is going on at Lancaster University and the University of Leeds in the United Kingdom. Brian Street and colleagues at Kings College in London and elsewhere are researching—in collaboration with Indian educators—how teacher researchers in India infuse ethnographic approaches to numeracy and literacy as social practices in South Asia (Street, Rogers, & Baker, 2006; Nirantar, 2007). There are also major international practitioner research conferences sponsored by the Collaborative Action Research Network (CARN) in the United Kingdom and other organizations that represent collaborations across countries and continents. Many of these projects are reinventing the concept of inquiry communities and increasingly depending on the Internet and web-based technologies for connecting and collaborating.

Grassroots, National Professional Organizations, and Foundations. Sustaining and deepening the work of practitioner research communities require sources of support, including visible and accessible sites for collaboration, publication, and dissemination. A number of new grassroots efforts to support and spread action research are in development. The North American Action Research Alliance (NAARA), for example, encourages exchanges between people doing action research and others in fields, including health and human services around such foci as alternative epistemologies, collaborative subversion, and the politics of social justice (http://naara.ed.uiuc.edu). A critical dimension of this initiative relates to the expansion of inquiry communities within and beyond education.

Among national professional organizations and foundations, there is evidence that some previous sources of support for practitioner research are being sustained while new ones continue to emerge. NCTE, for example, awards work related to teacher research, provides grants for teacher-initiated studies, and supports a large school-based network of inquiring teachers called CoLEARN (see www.ncte.org/profdev/online/colearnwi; Donnelly et al., 2005; Fleischer & Fox, 2003; Stock, 2004). The National Council of Teachers of Mathematics (NCTM) has a series of four practitioner inquiry–based volumes with 90-some authors, each devoted to teaching and learning at different grade levels (Langrall, 2006; Masingila, 2006; Smith & Smith, 2006; Van Zoest, 2006). The International Reading Association (IRA) supports teacher research groups and publishes both practitioner research and books about practitioner research. Over the last decade, the Teachers College Press Practitioner Inquiry Series has published new and established authors' work, with more than three dozen books now in print or preparation. The Chicago Foundation for Education gives grants to promote action research as a way to improve instruction and inform district policy, with the explicit aim of giving teachers a voice in making policy (Temkin, 2005). The Spencer Foundation's website indicates it will support practitioner-generated research. As professional organizations, TESOL, NCTE, NCTM, and the Center for Applied Linguistics all favor practitioner research as professional development and publish articles in their professional journals. Somewhat further afield, the website of the National Health Museum introduces science and health teachers to teacher research.

In describing efforts during the last decade to invent and reinvent social structures to support practitioner research, we emphasize the importance of the collaborative nature of this work and the desirability of having configurations at many levels. This includes small, practitioner-initiated projects at the local level; school-based, out-of-school, and cross-school groups; and virtual networks or major commitments by professional organizations and foundations. It is important to note, however, that there are sometimes radical differences between the various iterations of practitioner research and the now-widespread phenomena of professional learning communities; we explore some of these in Chapter 2.

Theme IV: Shaping School Reform and Educational Policy

A decade ago, we described the ways practitioner research had been aligned with inquiry-based alternatives to traditional transmission models of professional development; curriculum innovations in writing, literacy, science, math, and social studies; alternative forms of assessment; and the creation of a professional discourse around race, gender, and schooling. We also expressed concern, however, that as practitioner research was being linked to an ever-widening range of educational agendas, it could become both trivialized and marginalized, or co-opted into educational change initiatives antithetical to its purposes. The current era, as we have argued above, represents such a challenge. The fourth theme we identify in the current practitioner research movement involves efforts to disrupt the new master narratives of evidence-based decision making and accountability by reframing reform initiatives and making schools and districts more permeable to alternate epistemologies and ways of constructing teacher and student learning.

Schools as Sites of Change. Recent work in practitioner research at the school level continues the theme of teachers "studying their own schools" (see the new 2007 edition of Anderson, Herr, & Nihlen's classic volume) and making teacher research in school and district-based networks the primary mode of professional development (Mohr et al., 2003). While these enterprises can be envisioned as bumping up against the current educational climate, as we have noted, school-based "inquiry" can also be co-opted and turned into top-down, step-by-step processes. As Anderson and colleagues (2007) put it, action research in schools can be "a popular name for merely poring over test scores" (p. xvii).

Collaborative inquiry looking at student work currently figures prominently in many school reform agendas, but much of it depends almost exclusively on the data from high-stakes tests and outsiders' agendas, protocols, and goals (Boudett, City, & Murnane, 2005; McLaughlin & Talbert 2006; Wood, 2007), as we discuss in Chapter 2. An exception clearly grounded in teacher agency was the work of the National Study Group, established to compare efforts across schools to support systematic inquiry into student work (Weinbaum et al., 2004). The participants in the Study Group—the Academy of Educational Development in New York City, the Coalition of Essential Schools, and Project Zero—were highly visible organizations investigating school-based efforts to take an inquiry stance (Cochran-Smith & Lytle, 2001) on improving teaching and learning. Their investigations built on Stokes's (2001) analysis of what three different types of inquiry engaged in by teachers at a California elementary school enabled them to learn and do. Weinbaum and her colleagues (2004) constructed detailed case studies of inquiry projects at four different schools, revealing the variability of entry and the inextricable connections between teacher learning and student learning and between inquiry and equity.

Project SOULL (A Study of Urban Learning and Leading) was designed to investigate how teacher leaders in urban secondary schools define, enact, and assess leadership in relation to school change (Lytle, 2006; Lytle, Portnoy, Waff, & Buckley, 2009). The evolution of the project reflected teachers' urgency about finding a context to struggle openly with day-to-day issues and support each others' efforts in a time of fundamentally destabilizing conditions.

As the project evolved, it expanded to include not only inquiry into how teachers lead, primarily from the classroom, but also how they intervene at various levels of the system in the service of social justice and equity for urban students and communities. Projects and study groups that construct professional development as inquiry (see, for example, Calliari, Rentsch, & Weaver, 2005; Tachibana, 2007) allow teachers to co-labor around dealing with the challenges and fundamental uncertainties of their daily practice.

Organizing to Inform Policy. As we show above, many educators from different locations and for different audiences are constructing research as concerted action to bring about change and, more specifically, to influence educational policy. In *Teachers Organizing for Change: Making Literacy Learning Everybody's Business* (2000), Cathy Fleischer, who has been a leader in practitioner inquiry over many years, re-imagined teachers as community activists who are part of the public discourse in education. Fleischer argued for a focus on one's own community, drawing strategies from the work of community organizers in public health, environmental advocacy, and social justice.

It is important to note that in a certain sense, all of the work described above is intended to inform policy by affirming and acting on beliefs that run counter to the current images of teachers and teaching in the present climate (Cochran-Smith & Lytle, 2006). But some teacher networks make bringing teachers' voices into the policy arena via teacher action research an explicit goal. A prominent example is the Teachers Network Policy Institute and the Teachers Network Leadership Institute, described by Frances Rust and Ellen Meyers in several recent monographs and articles (MetLife Fellows, 2008; Meyers & Rust, 2003; Rust & Meyers, 2006). These depicted the work of a national network of teacher researchers designed to position teachers' classroom- and school-based research in relation to educational policy, with the aim of bridging the chasm "between classrooms and statehouses" and "enabl[ing] teachers as individuals to enter policy discussions in their schools and their local communities and as a network to affect decision-making at local state and national levels" (Rust & Meyers, 2006, p. 70). Drawing on Cobb, McClain, deSilva Lamberg, and Dean (2003), Rust and Meyers described the movement of teacher research into the policy arena as a "*boundary encounter*," a time when members of one community "engage in activities with members of another community" (p. 80). The network strategy aimed to show policymakers what happens when their policies are translated into practice.

Along somewhat similar lines are students' efforts to talk back to practices or policies that constrain their learning, which is a predictable consequence of encouraging students to inquire into their own schools and school systems, as we discussed in Theme I above. One example involved the inquiries carried out by students, parents, and teachers in an effort called "writing to be heard." This work was sponsored by Research for Action (RFA), a not-for-profit group working with Youth United-for-Change, an organization dedicated to providing young leaders in Philadelphia with training and tools to improve the quality of their education and communities. In a project about building respectful communities, high school students (Crosby, George, Hatch, Robinson, & Thomas, 2006) examined adult–student relationships in their three new small schools. Conducting interviews, informal conversations, and observations, the students authored their own report, which made recommendations for district and school leaders, teachers, and community groups.

In our discussion of the fourth theme in the practitioner research movement, we have pointed to ways practitioner research is positioned to take a critical stance on current change initiatives that diminish the role of teachers as decision makers. Many of the initiatives we described in the first three themes are also aimed to impact school reform and, in some cases, educational policy. Affecting policy is admittedly very difficult, however, as policymakers have been increasingly enamored of research and evidence that "proves" what practice should look like rather than illuminates its complexities. How to accumulate meaningful findings from case studies, the primary genre of practitioner research, represents an ongoing challenge to the movement.

Theme V: Re-Forming Research and Practice in Universities

In this final theme, we consider the practitioner inquiry movement's explicit efforts to alter relationships of knowledge, practice, and power in universities and to rethink hierarchical connections between teaching and research. As we suggested in our article a decade ago (Cochran-Smith & Lytle, 1999a), practitioner research has the potential to collide with the long-standing tradition of universities to privilege research while holding teaching and service in relatively low regard and with the tendency of universities to call for changes in schools without altering the cultures of their own institutions. We argued then that there was increasing evidence that involvement with practitioner research can have a transformative effect on aspects of university culture.

Here we point to some of the ways practitioner research has surfaced in the academic literature of education, informed teacher education, and influenced education dissertations and advising during the last decade. We discuss briefly how practitioner research has continued to be a subject of academic research and teaching and has been embedded in school–university partnerships. (We take up some of these issues in more detail in Chapter 4.)

   Visibility of Practitioner Research in the Academic Literature. In the last decade, a number of handbooks and monographs entirely focused on exploring practitioner research have been published, including *Participatory Action Research* (McIntyre, 2008), *The SAGE Handbook of Educational Action Research* (Noffke & Somekh, in press), the *Handbook of Action Research: Participative Inquiry and Practice* (Reason & Bradbury, 2001, 2008), *On Teacher Inquiry: Approaches to Language and Literacy Research* (Goswami, Lewis, Rutherford, & Waff, in press), and the *International Handbook of Self-Study of Teaching and Teacher Education* (Loughran, Hamilton, LaBoskey, & Russell, 2004). In addition, in many handbooks and research syntheses on teaching and other education-related subjects, there are now one or more chapters devoted to practitioner research, including Zeichner and Noffke's (2001) chapter on practitioner research in *The Handbook of Research on Teaching*; Fecho and Allen's (2002) chapter on teacher inquiry into literacy, social justice, and power in *The Handbook of Research on Teaching the English Language Arts*; Fecho, Allen, Mazaros, and Inyega's (2006) chapter on teacher research in writing classrooms in *Research on Composition: Multiple Perspectives on Two Decades of Change*; Kemmis and McTaggart's (2005) chapter on participatory action research in *The SAGE Handbook of Qualitative Research*; Lytle's (2000) chapter on teacher research and reading research in the *Handbook of Reading Research*; and Fries and Cochran-Smith's (2005) chapter on teacher research on classroom management in the *Handbook of Research on Classroom Management*. Furthermore, a recent edition of the *Handbook of Research on Teaching Literacy Through the Communicative and Visual Arts* (Flood, Heath, & Lapp, 2008) includes in each of its major sections a number of pieces under the heading "Voices from the Field," designed to balance the perspectives of differently positioned participants in the conversations representing major topics. Another indicator of the vibrancy of practitioner research is the lively debate in academic journals, such as *Educational Researcher,* about what it means for practitioners in graduate school to "become researchers" and the role of practitioner research in the university's canon (e.g., Anderson, 2002; Labaree, 2003; Metz & Page, 2002).

   Preservice teacher education is another area in which practitioner research continues to play a prominent role at the university level. There is a growing literature on the promises and problems of inquiry in teacher education, including Celia Oyler's (2006) volume, *Learning to Teach Inclusively: Student Teachers' Classroom Inquiries,* written with her preservice inclusion study group;

Marilyn Cochran-Smith and colleagues' efforts to construct inquiry as both process and legitimate outcome of teacher education (Barnatt, Cochran-Smith, Friedman, Pine, & Baroz, 2007; Cochran-Smith, 2003a, 2003b) and Linda Valli and Jeremy Price's analyses of the intended and unintended consequences of encouraging preservice teachers to engage in action research (Price, 2001; Price & Valli, 2005; Valli, 1999; Valli & Price, 2000). In addition, there are a number of studies of the role of inquiry in the development of preservice teachers' ideas and beliefs about teaching, learning, and diversity (e.g., Hyland & Noffke, 2005; Levin & Rock, 2003; Rock & Levin, 2002) and about the relationships of inquiry and reflection, identity, and learning in various teacher education settings, including professional development schools (e.g., Crocco, Bayard, & Schwartz, 2003; Freese, 2006; Mule, 2006; Schultz & Mandzuk, 2005). Some alternative teacher education programs located at universities, such as Teach for America, have also become sites that encourage new teachers' inquiries (Lytle et al., 2009).

Academic Research and Teaching. The current educational policy/political climate has profoundly impacted the agendas of many research universities, resulting in both acceptance and resistance to stipulations about the purposes of schooling, accountability, and "scientifically based research." At the same time, many faculty have become involved in practitioner research, seeking to work out research agendas that involve practitioners in equitable roles and relationships and that aim to influence practice. Programs in language and literacy, teaching and curriculum, higher education, and leadership have begun offering formal preparation in using practitioner methodologies and practitioner questions to drive the design of doctoral dissertations. Herr and Anderson's *The Action Research Dissertation* (2005), for example, provided guidance on developing doctoral dissertations based on the realities of everyday practice. Many graduate students who pursue praxis-oriented degrees are electing to conduct practitioner research for their EdD and PhD dissertations as well. Courses in teacher research, action research, participatory action research, and other related genres are proliferating in graduate schools. In addition, local sites of the National Writing Project at nearly 200 colleges and universities across the country have professional development efforts that reflect a commitment to practitioner inquiry.

Many academics, including ourselves, have engaged in long-term field-based projects working with local teachers and school and community leaders aimed at addressing social justice issues through various kinds of inquiry in classrooms, schools, and districts (e.g., Aaron et al., 2006; Anderson, Herr, & Nihlen, 2007; Caro-Bruce et al., 2007; Ginsberg et al., 2004; Meier

& Henderson, 2007; Nieto, 2003, 2005). A number of uniquely constructed inquiry communities also flourish at universities. Steve Fishman and Lucille McCarthy, for example, have conducted research in Fishman's college philosophy class for 20 years (Fishman & McCarthy, 1998, 2000, 2002, 2007), contributing not only to Dewey scholarship but also imagining new ways compositionists and philosophers can conduct interdisciplinary inquiry aimed at deepening our understanding of learning and teaching.

School–University Partnerships. A wide range of school–university partnerships (as well as many strong practitioner inquiry groups and networks not affiliated with universities) are discussed in the sections above. As we have noted, in the United States collaborations such as the National Writing Project and Bread Loaf Teacher Network have used the synergies of schools and universities to support inquiries by teachers and other practitioners, sometimes in collaboration with university-based faculty. We want to focus here on one additional example, however, because it highlights both the positive and problematic aspects of the role of the university in practitioner research: a United Kingdom project described in *Researching Schools: Stories from a School–University Partnership for Educational Research* (McLaughlin, Black-Hawkins, Brindley, McIntyre, & Taber, 2006). McLaughlin and his colleagues provided a forthright account of what happened when the two worlds of school practitioner and university-based research attempted a merger. This is a largely untold tale, partially because of the complexities and controversies in the academic and educational policy arena around what counts as knowledge useful for educational improvement.

Researching Schools is based on a 6-year partnership between the University of Cambridge Faculty of Education and eight secondary schools in the United Kingdom. The story is unusual because it was based both in the (British) tradition of teacher research and the concept of schools as researching organizations. Across the participating schools, there were key roles for teacher research coordinators, student voice coordinators, head teachers, members of the project steering group, project directors, a faculty research officer, partnership coordinators, and critical friends. The project saw its challenge as understanding:

> how [university] staff and school staff within the partnership find ways and means of working together on research issues and questions of mutual interest in order to create a systemic research culture within and across the partnership schools. One problem (of perhaps many) posed by this challenge will be to find ways in which the research process and outcomes can have utility for teachers in terms of their front-line accountabilities, at the

same time as meeting the different accountability pressures upon [university] personnel. (McLaughlin et al., 2006, p. 14)

Not only was the focus of the project on researching the partnership itself, but the intention was also to move beyond individual teachers as researchers to authentic collaboration on and orchestration of the broader research endeavor. This complex agenda yielded considerable debate about the role of the teacher as researcher.

Across the schools in the partnership, however, classroom action research was the most common form of knowledge generation, while knowledge generation as a school and as a network were more difficult to achieve. Many, if not most, of the teachers saw the value of their research as chiefly for their own practice and themselves as the audience, although there was evidence of teachers engaging *with* research (echoes of Stenhouse, 1975). The authors commented that the policy climate in England had not been supportive of researching schools or partnerships but at the same time had been enamored of practice being informed by evidence. They urged recognition of the complexity of teaching and suggested rethinking teachers' workloads to allow them to devote time to doing research that would translate evidence to more effective practice. We include this example because it contains so many of the significant design features, challenges, and contradictions that can be endemic to serious efforts to re-form relationships of knowledge and practice, within and beyond the university.

In highlighting some of what has occurred since 2000 in colleges and universities that supports and extends the practitioner inquiry movement, we are suggesting that the institutionalization of practices and debates around the relationships of inquiry, knowledge, and practice are alive and well at the postsecondary level. In Chapter 4 of this volume, we describe in some detail how our own experiences with practitioner inquiry have led to the "constructive disruption" of university culture in our own institutions and provoked many questions, some not answered, about what it means to live lives that foreground practitioner knowledge in a university context.

LOOKING BACK, LOOKING AHEAD, AND MOVING FORWARD

We have been suggesting throughout this chapter that the practitioner research movement appears stronger and more persistent than would be expected in the current climate. Among the vast array of practitioner inquiry–related projects and programs, many are intentionally pushing back against top-down mandates and expanding narrow definitions of what constitutes a "good" education. Considerable evidence shows that, during the last decade, despite all the forces working against it, the practitioner research movement has continued to thrive in parallel with other initiatives that aim to democratize the locus of knowledge and power and thereby directly influence the educational opportunities afforded to children in urban, rural, and suburban districts and other educational institutions across the country.

That said, we hope this book will support ongoing efforts to imagine what can sustain and expand practitioner research in the next generation. Clearly there are many challenging and coexisting realities. The powerful accountability regime that currently dominates the policy and the political contexts of education creates exceedingly trying times for practitioners and others who are addressing the concerns of policymakers differently and who persist in asking a different set of questions.

For example, at the same time that schools exist where teachers are allowed to teach something only if it will improve test scores, there are schools where groups of teachers meet regularly to look closely and descriptively at students' work. At the same time that teachers are writing books about their efforts to teach in ways that truly embrace equity and access to meaningful learning activities, there are children and schools labeled "failing" because of high-stakes test results. At the same time that school systems are promoting teacher collaboration toward predetermined ends, there are vast virtual networks where teachers and learners from radically different cultural contexts read common texts and investigate questions about the environment and its impact on families and communities.

One of the purposes of compiling the literature of and about practitioner inquiry—and indeed, of reading it—is to come to understand the crucial questions it raises for the practitioner inquiry movement and for the field of education more broadly. In the final section of this chapter, we name just a few of these issues, anticipating that readers will have generated many of their own.

Looking ahead to the next generation, we ask many questions: How should those of us invested in practitioner research take this fragmented reality (and the powerful messages it sends to teachers and students, parents and academics) into account? How do we respond to work that calls itself teacher research or action research or participatory inquiry and yet is very much in line with narrowed policies that co-opt the language of practitioner research to marshal participants' energies in opposite directions? Certainly, we are not suggesting here that all practitioner research should look the same across contexts or that there is a singular "we" in this diverse, multifaceted movement. Such a stance would undermine its radically local character and diverse lineage. But how is it possible to sort out what is genuinely and productively disruptive of the neoliberal language and mind-set that maintains the status quo from what even unintentionally works to maintain it?

The considerable range and variation of practitioner research have contributed to its richness and vitality but, at the same time, perhaps undermined its coherence as an intellectual and social movement with a palpable impact on emerging policies. Related to this is the lack of "lateral citations" (Franke, 1995) in documentation of the work of practitioner research and the relative lack of effort to connect the work of different individuals, communities, networks, and institutions through webs of citations. Another concern is what it means to affirm efforts to integrate practitioner inquiry with professional development but also to remain committed to the role of practitioner research in generating local and public knowledge to inform wider social change and educational equity. What would it mean for prominent networks to align deliberately with one another and other related social movements? The prospects for practitioner research as a movement going forward into the next decade likely depends in part on orchestrated efforts to preach beyond the choir and to make the value of this work more obvious to the gatekeepers, policymakers, and politicians who control the discourse about what counts, who knows, and what we should do about it.

That the practitioner research movement continues to survive and even flourish does not mean that there are not deep issues *within* that merit attention. How do we understand the needs of teachers and other practitioners to be cosmopolitan, globally informed intellectuals while maintaining the critical focus on the local? Does the movement need to be more discriminating and vigilant about the quality of the work, and if so, how does that happen? What are the most pressing issues of quality and value, and how does a broad, dispersed movement develop criteria and methods for assessing them in differently positioned initiatives? What do we (and who, indeed, is the "we"?) think about the possibility that some practitioner research exists "under the radar" and thus has little or no accountability to a wider public or community? Is it possible that projects without any public scrutiny may circulate less-than-thoughtful practices or have troubling blind spots about what is "best" for children and their families?

Many members of the larger practitioner research community believe that questioning central assumptions is of quintessential importance. Who within and beyond the practitioner research movement can be the "others" who maintain a critical focus on that responsibility? The freedom to imagine, the existentialist Maxine Greene (2008) tells us, comes from encountering

and resisting obstacles. How can these trying times push the work of practitioner inquiry to new depths and perhaps more self-critique—and at the
same time cultivate what Greene has called restlessness and unease as sources
of optimism, power, and possibility? In the chapters that follow, we take up
some of these issues. Our hope is to provide grist for others within and beyond the practitioner research movement to debate, invent, and act on these
and other salient questions in the next generation.

Chapter Two

Practitioner Inquiry: Versions and Variance

In Chapter 1, we portrayed the current landscape of practitioner inquiry as complex, dynamic, and healthy. In short, our message was this: Despite (and perhaps in part because of) the acutely conservative educational climate in the United States and many other places, the practitioner inquiry movement is alive and thriving in programs, projects, networks, communities, and partnerships all over the world. Many of these are connected to one another and to other social groups through print, face-to-face, and electronic channels. We pointed out that practitioner inquiry is now part of, and sometimes center stage in, many local, regional, national, and international meetings, conferences, and publications that are intended to transform teaching and schooling by strengthening its democratic vision and challenging inequities.

But practitioner inquiry has multiple historical and epistemological roots and serves many agendas, which have evolved over time and in different places. For the most part, the multiple roots of practitioner inquiry have been a source of power and strength, and, as we argued in *Inside/Outside*, have helped to make it a movement, not just another trend or a discrete method. It is impossible—and, of course, undesirable—to regard practitioner inquiry as a monolith in the face of its widespread and far-flung development. Despite its variety, however, most versions of practitioner inquiry share a sense of the practitioner as knower and agent for educational and social change. This is a perspective that resonates with many agendas and affirms a commitment deeply felt by many of the people involved with practitioner inquiry around the world. Many of the variants of practitioner inquiry also foster new kinds of social relationships that assuage the isolation of teaching and other sites of practice. This is especially true in inquiry communities structured to foster deep intellectual discourse about critical issues and thus to become spaces where the uncertainties and questions intrinsic to practice can be seen (not hidden) and can function as grist for new insights and new ways to theorize practice.

There are a number of possible approaches to sorting out and making sense of the many versions, variants, hybrids, and genres of practitioner inquiry. In the first part of this chapter, we take up two of these. First we focus on the commonalities shared by the major genres of practitioner inquiry, suggesting that, despite differing epistemological traditions and roots, these genres share a number of important features that unify the versions and variants. We describe eight of these features. We also make the case, however, that—not surprisingly— these same features that cut across multiple versions of practitioner inquiry and make it possible to talk about it in a somewhat unified way also simultaneously divide practitioner inquiry from many traditional forms of educational research. Thus, our second take on the versions and genres of practitioner inquiry is to look closely at the dividing lines that separate practitioner research from most forms of both qualitative and quantitative research on practice. We do this by examining the major critiques of practitioner research. Concentrating on the uniting and the dividing lines of practitioner inquiry allows us to take up what we think are the most interesting and important questions about the relationships of inquiry, knowledge, and practice as well as recurring tensions about method, methodology, epistemology, and ethics in practitioner inquiry.

Following our discussion of uniting and dividing lines, we then take this chapter in a different direction. We compare practitioner inquiry with a related, but different, current trend in educational reform—professional learning communities, which have been developed and promoted in the United States, the United Kingdom, and elsewhere over the last decade and a half, as a lever for school reform and educational improvement. Here, we suggest that the language and rhetoric of professional learning communities and the language and rhetoric of practitioner inquiry resemble one another in many ways. In fact, we think that the resemblances are so strong that they can easily mask important differences in goals and traditions and in ultimate consequences for students, teachers, and other practitioners in educational settings. Drawing on the literature and on our experience over 20-some years as university practitioners and researchers trying to take seriously the underlying premises of practitioner inquiry, we explain what these similarities and differences are, what they mean, and why they matter for the larger project of improving teaching, learning, and leadership for social change.

PRACTITIONER INQUIRY

As we noted in the Preface, we use *practitioner inquiry* and *practitioner research* as conceptual and linguistic umbrellas to refer to a wide array of educational research modes, forms, genres, and purposes (Cochran-Smith & Lytle, 2004). Zeichner and Noffke (2001) and Anderson and colleagues (1994, 2007) have also used the term *practitioner research* in a similar encompassing sense. In using practitioner inquiry as an umbrella, it is not our intention to blur important ideological, epistemological, and historical differences, implying that all terms for practitioner inquiry are synonymous and all forms of practitioner research are the same. On the contrary, we hope to illuminate important differences at the same time that we clarify commonalities. Figure 2.1 portrays practitioner inquiry as an overarching category of research with five major genres (the umbrella shape at the top of the figure with five connected rectangles beneath it), eight features that unite these genres (the box in the middle of the figure connected to the genres with downward arrows), and six critiques that divide practitioner inquiry from many traditional forms of research about educational practice (the bottom rectangle with solid arrows pointing upward).

Major Genres and Versions

Arguably, the major genres and versions of practitioner inquiry in the current discourse of educational research include action research, teacher research,

Figure 2.1. Practitioner Inquiry: The Issues That Unite and Divide

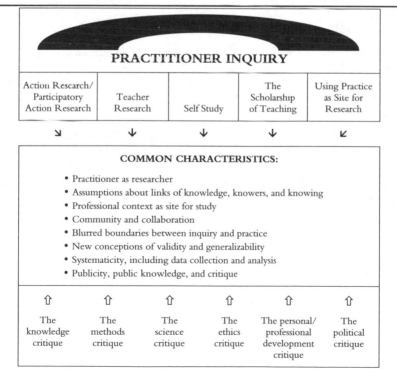

self study, the scholarship of teaching and learning, and the use of teaching as a context for research. Many scholars, ourselves included, have provided in-depth discussions of one or more of these and how they relate to some of the others. In this chapter, we simply name each of the five genres and state its major aim. *Action research* in education is commonly used to describe collaborations among school-based teachers and other educators, university-based colleagues, and sometimes parents and community activists. The efforts of action researchers center on altering curriculum, challenging common school practices, and working for social change by engaging in a continuous process of problem posing, data gathering, analysis, and action (e.g., Carr & Kemmis, 1986; Herr & Anderson, 2005; Noffke, 1997; Zeichner & Noffke, 2001). Similar in some ways, but different in others, *teacher research* refers to the inquiries of K–12 teachers and prospective teachers, often in collaboration with university-based colleagues and other educators. Teacher researchers work in inquiry communities to examine their own assumptions, develop local knowledge by posing questions and gathering data, and—in many versions of teacher research—work for social justice by using inquiry to ensure educational opportunity, access, and equity for all students (e.g., Cochran-Smith & Lytle, 1993, 1999b; Goswami & Stillman, 1987; Meyers, Rust & Paul, n.d.; Stenhouse, 1985).

The term *self study* is used almost exclusively to refer to inquiries at the higher education level by academics involved in the practice of teacher education, broadly construed. Often drawing on biographical, autobiographical, and narrative forms of data collection and analysis, self study works from the postmodernist assumption that it is never possible to divorce the "self" either from the research process or from educational practice (e.g., Hamilton, 1998; Loughran et al., 2004). The term *the scholarship of teaching* was originally coined in 1990 by Ernest Boyer, then president of the Carnegie Foundation for the Advancement of Teaching, as part of a report on new priorities of the professoriate (Boyer, 1990). Later, Lee Shulman and colleagues at Carnegie (Hatch & Shulman, 2005; Hutchings, 2000; Shulman, Lieberman, Hatch, & Lew, 1999) built on this idea and supported higher education faculty across disciplines who were engaged in sustained inquiry into their teaching practices and their students' learning. They suggested that the scholarship of teaching and learning should be public, accessible to critique by others, and exchangeable in the professional community. Along somewhat similar lines, the final genre of practitioner inquiry we include here is carried out by university-based researchers who take on the role of teacher in K–12 settings for a specific period of time in order to conduct research on the intricate complexities involved in theorizing and working out problems of practice (e.g., Dudley-Marling, 1997; Lampert, 1990, 2001; Lampert & Ball, 1998).

Shared Features

Although the genres and forms we have just described do not encompass the whole of practitioner research, we find that they account for the general landscape and point to many of the intricate ethical, epistemological, and political issues involved in the next generation of practitioner inquiry. Despite its many forms, we have found several important features that most of these forms share, which lend unity, but not uniformity, to practitioner inquiry. As we show, however, these same shared features also divide practitioner inquiry from many traditional forms of educational research.

Practitioner as Researcher. One feature that every form of practitioner inquiry has in common is that the practitioner himself or herself simultaneously takes on the role of researcher. Duality of roles enables the classroom teacher, the student teacher, the school principal, the school district superintendent, the teacher educator, the professional development leader, the community college instructor, the university faculty member, the adult literacy program tutor, the fieldwork supervisor, and many other educational practitioners to participate in the inquiry process as researchers, working from the inside. This is quite different from most research on teaching or school leadership, where practitioners are the topics of study, the objects of someone else's inquiry, or the informants and subjects of research conducted by outsiders. In some versions of practitioner inquiry, "researchers" also include participants who are not practitioners in the professional sense but rather are significant stakeholders in the educational process, such as parents, community members, and families.

Community and Collaboration. Although some practitioner research is conducted by individuals working more or less by themselves, in most versions, collaboration among and across participants is a key feature. These collaborations take many forms—they may be inquiry communities of new and experienced teachers across several schools working together with teacher educators to generate local knowledge; university- and school-based educators working collectively with community-based activists and parents to change the conditions of a particular school or neighborhood; faculty members from different disciplines and research paradigms working together to interrogate the assumptions and values that underlie their practices and programs; or small groups of teachers preparing for advanced certification working with university-based facilitators to make visible, document, and critique beliefs and practices. In most forms of practitioner inquiry, the role of the local community is critical, since this is the context in which knowledge is constructed and used, and it is also the context in which knowledge is initially made public and opened up to the scrutiny of others.

Knowledge, Knowers, and Knowing. A third key feature that unites the various versions and variants of practitioner research is the assumption that those who work in particular educational contexts and/or who live in particular social situations have significant knowledge about those situations. This means that all of the participants in inquiry communities are regarded as knowers, learners, and researchers. Most varieties of practitioner inquiry challenge the idea that knowledge can be generated in one site and directly and unproblematically generalized and transmitted to another. Unlike the knowledge generated by outside researchers, the knowledge generated through practitioner inquiry, which often takes the form of enhanced conceptual frameworks, altered practices, and/or reconstructed curricula, is intended primarily for application and use within the local context in which it is developed. With action research (Carr & Kemmis, 1986; Noffke, 1997), the major emphasis is action and social change, not knowledge generation. Nonetheless, some of those who have conceptualized practitioner inquiry, ourselves included, have suggested that local knowledge can often also function as public knowledge by informing practice and policy beyond the immediate context (Cochran-Smith & Lytle, 1993; Meyers et al., n.d.).

Professional Context as Inquiry Site/Professional Practice as Focus of Study. A fourth common feature is that the professional context is taken as the site for inquiry, and problems and issues that arise from professional practice are the focus of study. This means that a variety of educational contexts at different levels of organization become research sites. Although many of these are also common as sites for research on teaching and teacher education conducted by researchers from outside, it is the combination of the practitioner as researcher with the professional context as research site that is critical. Here, questions emerge from day-to-day practice and from discrepancies between what is intended and what occurs. These are often highly reflexive, immediate, and referenced to particular students or situations. But they also have to do with how practitioners theorize their own work, the assumptions and decisions they make, and the interpretations they construct. The unique feature of the questions that prompt practitioners' inquiry is that they emanate from neither theory nor practice alone but from critical reflection on the intersections of the two.

Blurred Boundaries Between Inquiry and Practice. The boundaries between inquiry and practice blur when the practitioner is a researcher and the professional context is a site for research. This is particularly clear when university faculty are engaged in practitioner inquiry. Over the years, many university-based teacher educators have blurred these boundaries, prompting a rethinking of the meanings of research and practice, the roles of researchers and practitioners, and the distinctions between conceptual/theoretical scholarship, on one hand, and empirical research, on the other. As faculty members, a number of teacher educators have learned to make their professional work a strategic site for inquiry by focusing some of their research and grant-getting efforts on the work they do with others in inquiry communities as well as on their own courses and programs (e.g., Cochran-Smith et al., 1999; Loughran et al., 2004). In Chapter 4, we describe some of our own work as practitioner researchers within the university setting, as does Rob Simon in Chapter 10. In addition, some arts and science faculty members have also studied their own teaching, particularly by engaging in the scholarship of teaching and learning (Hutchings, 2000, 2002). In the university context, blurring boundaries and roles allows for innovative programs of research and new kinds of knowledge as well as new tensions and professional dilemmas. In contrast, when school-based practitioners take on roles as researchers, different kinds of tensions and problems emerge, including the concern that research steals time and energy away from the more important activity of teaching.

Validity and Generalizability. An important feature shared by many forms of practitioner inquiry is that notions of validity and generalizability are quite different from the traditional criteria. With some forms of practitioner inquiry, notions of validity are similar to the idea of trustworthiness that has been forwarded as a way to evaluate the results of qualitative research (Lincoln & Guba, 1990; Mishler, 1990). Following Mishler (1990), for example, Lyons and LaBoskey (2002) suggest that with narrative inquiry, validity rests on concrete examples (or "exemplars") of actual practices presented in enough detail that the relevant community can judge trustworthiness and usefulness. In their discussion of self study research, Bullough and Pinnegar (2001) refer to significance, quality, grounding, and authority as criteria of quality. They suggest that because self study borrows from several different scholarly traditions and also introduces the subjectivity of "self" as its central aspect, criteria for assessing quality have yet to be clearly established. Along somewhat different lines, Anderson and colleagues (1994, 2007) make a distinction between practitioner inquiry intended to produce knowledge for dissemination in traditional outlets, on the one hand, and action research intended to transform practice, on the other. For the former, they suggest that common notions of validity are appropriate, but when practitioner research is intended to be transformative, they call for ways of valuing and establishing validity that break with traditional epistemologies (e.g., Clandinin & Connelly, 1990; Cunningham, 1983; Lather, 1986; Watkins, 1991). Anderson and colleagues posit new criteria for practitioner research, including democratic validity (honoring the perspectives and interests of all stakeholders), outcome validity (resolving the problems addressed), process validity (using appropriate and adequate research methods and inquiry processes), catalytic validity (deepening the understandings of all the participants), and dialogic validity (monitoring analyses through critical and reflective discussion with peers).

Systematicity. Most forms of practitioner research share the feature of systematicity and intentionality. Stenhouse's (1985) definition of inquiry as "systematic" and "self critical" emphasized this idea early on. In some instances, systematic documentation resembles the forms of data collection used in other qualitative studies (e.g., observation, interviews, and document/artifact collection). Like those, a strength of practitioner inquiry is that it entails multiple data sources that illuminate and confirm, but also disconfirm, one another. What distinguishes the inquiries of practitioners, however, is that in addition to documenting classroom practice and students' learning, they also systematically document from the inside perspective their own questions, interpretive frameworks, changes in views over time, dilemmas, and recurring themes. Ideas about what count as data and analysis in practitioner research are often different from those of traditional modes. Autobiographical and narrative inquiry (e.g., Cole & Knowles, 1995; Florio-Ruane, 2001; Lyons & LaBoskey, 2002), for instance, treats stories as data and certain kinds of narratives as interpretation. Broader notions of what counts as data are in keeping with some postmodernist perspectives about the nature of knowledge that are more akin to the traditions of the humanities than the social sciences. Practitioner inquiry's new forms and frameworks of analysis as well as new forms of data may be unfamiliar to those accustomed primarily to traditional modes of research. For example, in some forms of practitioner researcher, such as oral inquiry, the analysis of data sources is primarily oral and constructed in the social interactions of particular groups or communities of practitioners (Carini & Himley, 1991; Himley & Carini, 2000). What sets this apart from other forms is that analysis is collectively constructed by practitioners committed to long-term and highly systematic observation and documentation of learners and their sensemaking.

Publicity, Public Knowledge, and Critique. Most descriptions of practitioner inquiry emphasize making the work public and open to the critique of a larger community. As noted, Stenhouse (1985) defined research as systematic inquiry "made public" to others, and much of the current North American teacher research movement features inquiry communities working together to generate "knowledge of practice" (Cochran-Smith & Lytle, 1999a). There are two important issues here—the role of peers and other inside participants in critiquing the analyses of practitioner researchers, on one hand, and making practitioner knowledge public beyond the immediate local context, on the other. With self-study research, Loughran and Northfield (1998) point out that others' perspectives are critical to developing knowledge informed by personal experience. Shulman (1999, 2000) suggests that to become useful and credible to others, the scholarship of teaching must be accessible—transformed, essentially, into community property—which makes possible both peer scrutiny and generativity. A hallmark of many forms of practitioner inquiry is the invention of new ways to store, retrieve, code, and disseminate practitioners' inquiries in the form of CD-ROMs, websites, and other electronic innovations.

Making practitioner inquiry public and accessible beyond the immediate local community raises issues about generalizability and purpose. We have suggested that teachers' work in inquiry communities generates local knowledge that may also be useful more publicly and generally in that it may suggest new insights about teaching and learning; new knowledge about teacher inquiry, teachers' learning, and professional growth; and new knowledge about the relationships among teacher inquiry, knowledge, and school reform (Cochran-Smith & Lytle, 1993).

Critiques of Practitioner Inquiry

On the previous pages, we identified eight salient features shared by most forms of practitioner research. Interestingly, however, in elaborating the assumptions and features that different modes of practitioner inquiry have in common, we also began to point to some of the basic issues that divide practitioner inquiry from more traditional forms and paradigms of educational research.

This is apparent in many of the language markers used to describe practitioner inquiry. These provide useful detail about the genre, but they also tend in certain ways to separate practitioner research from what some critics would call "regular" or "real" research. By virtue of the marker *teacher*, for example, the term *teacher research* suggests that research is not part of what is generally considered the normal work of teaching and calls attention to the fact that research about teaching is an activity usually carried out by someone than other a teacher. Similarly, the prefix *action* in the phrase *action research* seems to suggest that "regular" research resides in the realm of theory or abstraction and is separated from the world of action. Combining the term *self* with *study* calls attention to self study's particular and uncommon focus on the subjectivity of the self and the indivisibility of self and knowledge. Finally a term like the *scholarship of teaching* carries with it the point that teaching has not traditionally been considered scholarly activity in the sense of rigorous or systematic knowledge work. All of these language markers signal divisions between practitioner inquiry and more traditional modes of academic educational research and foreshadow the issues underlying the major critiques of practitioner inquiry that we discuss below.

The most common critiques of practitioner inquiry revolve around issues related to epistemology, methodology, and politics. As we have said, all of these are tied in important ways to the features that define practitioner inquiry, particularly to notions of knowledge generation and use, its validity and generalizability, and to appropriate roles of researchers and sites of research. The critiques are also tied to fundamental ideas about what counts in the first place as research, data, knowledge, evidence, and effectiveness, and who in the final analysis can legitimately be regarded as a knower about issues related to teaching, learning, and teacher development.

There are at least six major critiques of practitioner inquiry, which we have spelled out elsewhere (Cochran-Smith & Lytle, 1999b, 2004) and thus only briefly describe here. What we have called the "knowledge critique" and the "methods critique" of practitioner inquiry have to do with what kind of knowledge—if any—is generated when practitioners do research about their own schools, classrooms, courses, programs, and other contexts of practice (e.g., Fenstermacher, 1994; Richardson, 1996) and whether or not practitioners have the skill to carry out such research adequately (e.g., Huberman, 1996). At the heart of these critiques of practitioner inquiry is criticism of the use of the word *knowledge* itself and of the assertion that practitioners can generate knowledge (as opposed to wisdom or experience) about teaching and teacher education based on their perspectives inside professional contexts. Huberman argues that just because teachers may have intimate insider information about teaching does not negate the need for them to use rigorous and objective research methods. The "science critique" is a subset of the knowledge and methods critiques, which is especially relevant to the current emphasis in the United States and many other places on evidence-based educational practice. Here, the critique is that practitioner inquiry is not scientific in that it is "idiosyncratic" to a particular context and a particular researcher and thus does not permit cross-site generalization and application (e.g., Wilson, Floden, & Ferrini-Mundy, 2001).

The "ethics critique" has to do primarily with the dual roles taken on when the practitioner is also a researcher. In contrast to those who see these blended roles as an advantage and a potential window into rich and enhanced insights about practice, others caution that when practitioners (especially teachers) are engaged in research, they inevitably face conflicts of interest that jeopardize the best interests of their students. The argument here is that this renders informed consent and freedom from coercion about research participation extremely difficult (e.g., Hammack, 1997). The "political critique" of practitioner inquiry has to do with its purposes and ends as well as its political or ideological bases. From one perspective, the political critique says that practitioner inquiry is too benign in that many of its current-day advocates misunderstand its historical roots in critical social action and thus dilute its intended political edge (Elliot, 2005; Kincheloe, 1991; Noffke, 1997, 2005). In contrast, however, some of the more political versions of practitioner inquiry are critiqued by traditional researchers precisely because they do have a political agenda related to equity or social justice. These are dismissed by critics as advocacy rather than research, which is assumed to be apolitical and objective. Finally, the "personal/professional development critique" also has two strands that relate to two different sets of issues. The first is that when practitioner inquiry is primarily aimed at professional development, it is instrumental and reinforcing rather than challenging of the status quo (Anderson, 2002). The other is that certain forms of practitioner inquiry, particularly self studies and those with autobiographical stances, are much too personal in that they focus on the person in an ego-centered or narcissistic sense (Bullough & Pinnegar, 2001; Cole & Knowles, 1998).

As this brief discussion shows, some critiques of practitioner inquiry focus on epistemological and methodological issues, while others focus on political or professional and ethical issues. Often these critiques are combined and overlapping with one another, depending on the context of discussion and the stakes involved. In certain ways, all of these critiques are related to basic assumptions about the nature of inquiry and knowledge and their roles in interpreting and improving practice and policy regarding teaching, learning, and schooling. Most of them are intended to safeguard traditional approaches to knowledge generation and teacher development and preserve the hegemony of outside expertise.

PROFESSIONAL LEARNING COMMUNITIES/
TEACHER LEARNING COMMUNITIES

So far in this chapter, we have focused on the features that both unite various versions of practitioner inquiry and, at the same time, divide practitioner inquiry from much university-based and other research on practice in which the researcher is positioned outside of practice itself. In reviewing the land-scape of practitioner inquiry, however, we think it is also important to look closely at variances that exist among projects and initiatives that occupy the same territory (or at least seem to do so). With this perspective in mind, we turn to "professional learning communities," also known as "teacher learning communities" and "school-based teacher learning communities," which have been developed and promoted in the United States, the United Kingdom, and elsewhere over the last 10 to 15 years as a potential lever for educational reform. In many ways, the features and discourses of professional learning communities resemble the discourses and features of practitioner inquiry. In fact, as we show in the discussion that follows, the resemblances between the two are powerful enough that they can obscure important differences in purposes, frameworks, and assumptions.

Features of Professional Learning Communities

The current emphasis on professional learning communities is based on the argument that many teachers today lack the capacity to teach in ways that meet the demands of the knowledge economy and meet the learning needs of diverse student populations. From this perspective, teacher learn-ing in school-based communities that systematically use assessment and other kinds of student data to take collective responsibility for students' achievement is assumed to be the linchpin of school reform (e.g., Blankstein, Houston, & Cole, 2008; Boudett, City, & Murnane, 2005; DuFour & Eaker, 1998; Hord, 2004; McLaughlin & Talbert, 2006). Milbrey McLaughlin and Joan Talbert (2002) directed the Bay Area School Reform Collaborative, which funded teacher learning communities in 87 California schools. They suggest that teacher learning communities are different from most other professional development efforts, which are episodic and removed from the school site, and also different from most other school reform initiatives, such as state cur-riculum frameworks and school size reductions, which fail to acknowledge the culture of the school as the central problem in American education. With teacher learning communities, the assumption is that practitioners' capacity and commitments grow when they examine assessment data showing that stu-dents' learning is falling short of expectations. McLaughlin and Talbert (2006) argue that because teacher learning communities are positioned between the larger school system level and the realities of individual teachers' classrooms, they can "manage from the middle" (p. 5) to connect teachers' work to larger district and state contexts more effectively and efficiently.

The Inquiry Cycle. Today's professional learning communities come in many shapes and sizes, but—according to the sizable and growing literature written about them—they all have this in common: teachers working collaboratively in school-based groups to examine student and school data in order to take collective responsibility for students' learning. In much of the literature, the "inquiry process" or "inquiry cycle" is regarded as the central driver of school reculturing and reform. McLaughlin and Talbert (2002), for example, describe a six-step "cycle of inquiry" intended to close the achievement gap, beginning with the identification of problems, location of data, and identification of measurable goals, and continuing with building an action plan, taking action, and analyzing data results. Harvard researchers working with Boston Public School administrators and teachers (Boudett et al., 2005; Boudett & Steele, 2007) advocate what they call the "data wise improvement process," which has nine steps divided into three major chunks—preparation, inquiry, and action. WestEd, which is a U.S. regional research and development center, advocates "using data to drive reform" through a five-step inquiry cycle—getting ready to use data, organizing and analyzing data, investigating the factors that impact student achievement, determining effective practices and writing a plan, and implementing and evaluating the plan (WestEd, 2006). Hord and Hirsh (2008) describe the work of professional learning communities through six overlapping steps that include identifying problems, studying solutions and adopting new practices, planning for professional learning, monitoring implementation, revising based on assessment, and reflecting.

Shared Values and Beliefs. In most of the literature about professional learning communities, although professional inquiry or reflective dialogue is named as a central feature of effective communities, the primary emphasis is on creating school cultures (or "reculturing" schools) so there is shared vision and collective commitment to learning (Louis, 2008). As Louis and Kruse (1995) point out, this focus signifies an intentional move away from teaching as a private act reflecting the individual values and practices of an individual teacher—and away from the empowerment of individual teachers. The move is toward the idea that "deprivatizing" teaching practice and developing a sense of shared responsibility for students' learning are linked to a greater sense of collective efficacy and satisfaction with teaching (Kruse, Louis, & Bryk, 1995). This idea is reflected in DuFour and Eaker's (1998) practical guide for school leaders, *Professional Learning Communities at Work: Best Practices for Enhancing Student Achievement*, one of the many how-to guides now available on this topic from the Association for Supervision and Curriculum Development (ASCD) and other professional organizations. DuFour and Eaker assert that "the *sine qua non* of a learning community is shared understandings and common values. What separates a learning community from an ordinary school is its collective commitment to guiding principles that articulate what the people in the school believe and what they seek to create" (p. 25). Along these lines, Stoll, Bolam, McMahon, Wallace, and Thomas (2006) closed their review of the professional learning communities literature in the United States and the United Kingdom with the conclusion that effective professional learning communities are characterized by shared values and vision, with collective responsibility for students' learning based on reflective professional inquiry.

The Literature on Professional Learning Communities. Just as there are many versions and variants of practitioner inquiry, there is also diversity among professional learning communities. It is impossible to paint a picture of the landscape of *professional learning communities* and *teacher learning communities* with just one brush or one color. In fact, the literature on this topic is multicolored and burgeoning. A quick check of amazon.com, for example, reveals some three dozen books—and multiple dissertations and articles—with the phrases professional learning community or teacher learning community in their titles. These volumes are different from one another. Some are intended to conceptualize the theory of school reform behind learning communities by drawing on the related empirical literature or by analyzing multiple case studies of school-based efforts to establish learning communities (e.g., Louis, 2008; Louis & Kruse, 1995; McLaughlin & Talbert, 2006; Stoll & Louis, 2007; Weinbaum et al., 2004). Others—and there are many in this category—offer practical advice, cases, stories, and step-by-step instructions for practitioners and other school leaders who want to set up communities or use data effectively in their own schools (e.g., Boudett et al., 2005; Boudett & Steele, 2007; DuFour & Eaker, 1998; DuFour, Eaker, & DuFour, 2005; Gregory & Kuzmich, 2007; Hord, 2004; Mandinach & Honey, 2008).

There is also a growing body of empirical research, both qualitative and quantitative, that examines the processes, possibilities, and variations of teacher communities in specific schools (e.g., Achinstein, 2002; Little, 2002; McLaughlin & Talbert, 2002; Westheimer, 1999; Wood, 2007). Another body of work uses large national databases or major regional surveys to examine correlations between teachers' sense of professional community and/or collective responsibility, on one hand, and teachers' motivation and students' achievement, on the other (e.g., Bryk, Camburn, & Louis 1999; Yasumoto, Uekawa, & Bidwell, 2001: Lee & Smith, 1996).

Whole-School Communities. Despite these important differences, all of the literature on professional learning communities contributes to a growing sense in the United States, the United Kingdom, and a number of other nations that in order to improve the schools and close persistent achievement gaps, reform efforts need to focus on the collective learning capacity of teachers and need to identify the school—rather than, say, preservice education, non-school-based professional development, restructuring initiatives, or standards-based initiatives—as the critical unit of change. The conclusion of a U.K. task force (Bolam et al., 2005) charged with determining whether school-based professional learning communities were a feasible and useful vehicle for school reform in the United Kingdom reflects this viewpoint. Based on a comprehensive review of the literature, surveys of nearly 400 schools, case studies in 16 schools, and three working conferences, the task force concluded:

> To deal with the impact of globalization and rapid change, new ways of approaching learning seem to be required. Learning can no longer be left to individuals. To be sure in a changing and increasingly complex world, it is suggested that whole school communities need to work and learn together to take charge of change, finding the best ways to enhance young people's learning. (pp. 221–222)

One book of practical advice for principals who want to set up learning communities in their own schools (Hord, 2004) draws on experiences from successful groups in 22 schools in five states in the south and southwest regions of the United States. The advertising blurb on the back of the book reaches the same conclusion as the U.K. task force but adds a point about cost advantages:

> Increasingly the education world is recognizing that the development of learning communities is an effective means for improving schools without increasing the budget or adding new programs. (Hord, 2004)

A few recent discussions of professional learning communities have questioned whether the whole-school community is a large enough unit to bring about effective and sustainable change. Stoll and Louis (2007), for example, suggest that professional learning community membership should be broadened to include staff, networks of schools, parents, and others in order to expand the knowledge bases available to the communities. Along similar lines, Jackson and Temperley (2007) suggest that the school has become too small a unit for professional learning communities; rather, they need to become networked learning communities in order to connect to others and expand the fields of knowledge available.

The Practitioner Inquiry Movement and Professional Learning Communities

As our description so far makes clear, school-based professional learning communities share a number of key ideas and terms with the practitioner inquiry movement. However, it is even more important to point out that these ideas and terms also vary in significant ways. One important caveat here is that there is a great deal of variation among professional learning communities and the literature that describes them, just as there is variation among examples of practitioner inquiry and its descriptions. For heuristic purposes, however, and at the risk of oversimplifying, we treat these two— the practitioner inquiry movement and professional learning communities as a vehicle for school reform—as more or less coherent groups in the sections that follow.

A Venn-diagram kind of thinking may be helpful here to point out shared features as well as differences between the practitioner inquiry movement and the professional learning communities school reform initiative. Figure 2.2 is made up of two circles, the left enclosed with double lines and the right with a single line, which represent practitioner inquiry and professional learning communities, respectively. These share a number of features, which are represented by the words in italics within the overlapping section of the two circles. The differences between practitioner inquiry and professional learning communities are highlighted by the paired terms, from top to bottom, in the nonoverlapping parts of the two circles.

Common Features. Practitioner inquiry and professional learning communities have a number of important features in common:

- Inquiry, or question and problem posing as a central way to know about and improve teaching, learning, and schooling
- The data of practice, including many forms and formats for representing students' and teachers' work, which transforms teaching practice from a private activity with many of its aspects invisible and implicit and thus inaccessible to others into a locally public activity, with many of its aspects visible and explicit and thus open to discussion and critique by others
- Communities of new and experienced teachers, administrators, and colleagues working together over time around joint goals and purposes

Figure 2.2. Practitioner Inquiry and Professional Learning Communities

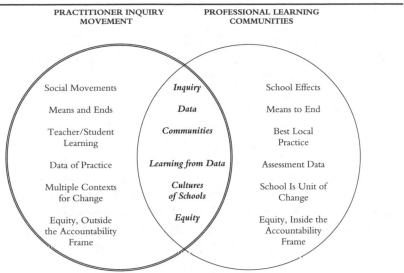

One of the most important ideas underlying both practitioner inquiry and professional learning communities is that they recognize the central role of teachers and other practitioners in shaping the life of schools and as agents in transforming the work of schools. From our perspective, all initiatives intended to make meaningful changes to schools so they are organized to support teachers' and students' learning are moves in the right direction. The differences between and among these efforts, however, are also very important.

Roots and Traditions of Inquiry. The roots of practitioner inquiry, as we and several others have characterized it over the past two decades, are located in several social movements and research traditions (Anderson et al., 1994, 2007; Cochran-Smith & Lytle, 1990, 1993, 1999a, 1999b, 2004; Herr & Anderson, 2005; Hollingsworth & Sockett, 1994; Noffke, 1997; Zeichner & Noffke, 2001). These include the British and North American teacher research movements, the participatory action research movement in Latin

- The cultures of schools as complex webs of norms, expectations, relationships, and layers of history that mediate and shape teachers' interpretive frameworks, practices, and strategies
- An equity agenda, or a commitment to improving the learning experiences and outcomes of those traditionally least likely to have quality learning opportunities and most marginalized by the system

America, the development of critical action research in Australia, a variety of efforts by progressive educators committed to social responsibility to construct alternative ways to solve teaching and learning problems, the paradigm shift in research on teaching and learning that evolved during the 1970s and 1980s (including the use of methods borrowed from ethnography), and challenges to the idea that the "knowledge base for teaching" failed to account for the knowledge generated by teachers (Cochran-Smith & Lytle, 1990).

Although there is some overlap between the traditions mentioned above and those noted in discussions about the background of professional learning communities, the two literatures are remarkably distinct, with very few of the same citations and references. The major roots of the professional learning communities initiative are quite different from the roots of practitioner inquiry. The roots and research traditions of professional learning communities are in the sociology of the workplace, school effects research, organizational theory, and, to a lesser extent, philosophical and sociological theories of communities (e.g., Bryk et al., 1999; Louis, 2008; Westheimer, 1999). Much of the work on professional learning communities is concerned with how school structures influence teachers' work and how the organization of teachers' work shapes teachers' practices and students' outcomes. The emphasis is on school production, or the processes through which schools generate academic achievement and other desired outcomes for which they are responsible. In particular, the literature that emphasizes data-driven improvement more than communities draws explicitly from business models of organizational reform and/or from systems thinking (e.g., Bertfield & Merrill, 2008; Mandinach, Honey, Light, & Brunner, 2008; Reeves, 2007). A different impetus for the current emphasis on professional learning communities is the growing body of evidence, based on large-scale surveys and case studies, that there is a link between a strong collegial or community focus in schools and students' performance on standard measures of achievement (Bryk et al., 1999; Lee & Smith, 1996; McLaughlin & Talbert, 2002, 2006; Yasumoto et al., 2001).

Communities as Means and Ends. Not surprisingly, these differences in the roots and traditions of practitioner inquiry and professional learning communities are connected to differences in the ways inquiry communities are conceptualized in terms of means and ends. From the perspective of practitioner inquiry, communities are understood as both means toward larger goals and as ends in themselves. In other words, communities are regarded as both important contexts within which teachers and other practitioners identify the issues they see as important and as one of the major vehicles that support their representations of their ideas. In inquiry communities, teachers jointly build knowledge by examining artifacts of practice, but they also interrogate their own assumptions, construct new curricula, and engage with others in a search for meaning in their work lives. There is a grassroots aspect here, and some of the longest-lived inquiry communities are teacher initiated and led (e.g., Carini, 2001; Himley & Carini, 2000; Philadelphia Teachers Learning Cooperative, 1984) or become so over time. With practitioner inquiry, the individual does not disappear into the collective and the publicness of practice does not diminish the individual qualities of practice. Rather, as Westheimer (1999) points out in his analysis of two middle schools, the community becomes a site for the merger of the personal and the professional, and the intrinsic value of the community in its own right is acknowledged.

In much of the literature on professional learning communities, on the other hand, there is more of an instrumental view of community, which is understood to be a lever for school reform and for increasing students' performance on achievement tests, decreasing absenteeism, or producing other desired school outcomes (Westheimer, 1999). This probably explains why there are so many books available for principals who want to establish communities in their schools—in part because they are facing enormous pressure to ensure that students perform adequately on tests and they are interested in doing whatever works, including trying to create communities with shared values and beliefs in order to increase achievement. The subtitles and chapter titles of some of the books related to professional learning communities make this instrumental focus clear, as these two examples show—*Data Wise: A Step-by-Step Guide to Using Assessment Results to Improve Teaching and Learning* (Boudett et al., 2005) and *Professional Learning Communities at Work: Best Practices for Enhancing Student Achievement* (DuFour & Eaker, 1998). Jackson and Temperley (2007), who call for professional learning communities to be networked to one another, also make the instrumental purpose clear: "Networks have as their intermediate aim improving teaching practices and as their key outcome, raising pupil achievement" (p. 57).

We are certainly not opposed to professional communities focusing on students' achievement nor to groups of professionals using students' progress to guide decisions about teaching, curriculum, and schooling. But when professional communities are urged to use assessment data and are strongly outcomes-oriented, they tend to focus on quick fixes and short-term goals. They mesh neatly with the current rhetoric and reality of school reform and fit easily inside the dominant test-based accountability regime. A few of those who write about professional learning communities have begun to raise questions along these lines. Louis (2008), for example, cautions that when groups of teachers are assigned to analyze data and focus on test score improvement, they may lose sight of what should be the core emphasis of communities—improving the link between teachers' practice and their students' learning by building trusting relationships and developing norms of shared problem solving. Hargreaves (2007, 2008) also raises questions along these lines, suggesting that there are many versions of communities, only some of them empowering for professionals. He cautions that rather than enriching students' learning, some communities become vehicles for simply boosting test scores or for surveillance of teachers and monitoring their compliance with school and district mandates.

The Data of Practice. Issues surrounding data—what counts as data, what data are privileged, and who decides or selects data for consideration by individuals and communities—reflect further differences between practitioner inquiry and professional learning communities, but they also reveal many important cleavages within the larger group of various initiatives that are termed professional learning communities or teacher learning communities. It is here that the idea of a continuum of approaches and perspectives within the current discourse about professional learning communities is most important. With practitioner inquiry, there is a very broad and some would say rather loose definition of data, which includes students' work of all kinds (from test scores to drawings, from dramatic play to college essays), but it also includes observations of students in and out of school, practitioners' plans as well as their journals and other self-reflective accounts of daily life among children and adolescents, school and classroom artifacts such as report cards and textbooks, and the talk that occurs among practitioners and among practitioners, parents, and others.

When practitioners take their work as a site for inquiry, all sorts of questions emerge from all sorts of data and artifacts that not only represent but also shape and embody that work. From this perspective, practitioners are regarded as generators of knowledge that is usable in, and often beyond, the local context—by other practitioners, policymakers, higher education faculty—and many other contexts.

Like those engaged in practitioner inquiry, some of the teacher learning communities described by McLaughlin and Talbert (2006) also draw on an array of data, especially a variety of representations of students' learning, from test scores to student work. At the other end of the continuum of professional learning communities, however—the end furthest away from the roots of the practitioner inquiry movement, as we are characterizing it here—there is an almost exclusive emphasis on assessment data, particularly tests. The "data wise improvement process," (Boudett et al., 2005; Boudett & Steele, 2007), for example, focuses almost entirely on strategies for teaching practitioners to use assessment results to improve achievement by building a "data culture" wherein working with tests and other assessments is broken into manageable steps, such as learning the difference between norm- and criterion-referenced tests or what test reliability means for schools. Similarly, the *Developing an Effective School Plan* project (Van Houten, Miyasaka, Agullard, & Zimmerman, 2006), created at WestEd, features data mentoring workshops wherein elementary teachers learn how to disaggregate test results, identify patterns in the data, and then adjust instruction in keeping with these results. In these examples of professional learning communities, practitioners are taught how to generate questions about test data and how to rectify discrepancies or close gaps between the achievement levels of subgroups. Similarly, the data-driven approach to school improvement described in Mandinach and Honey's (2008) edited volume focuses on helping teachers and other school-based personnel use test data and other progress-monitoring tools to continuously assess students' achievement. In these situations, the focus is on teachers learning to be better collectors and users of assessment data.

School Culture/Local Context. With both practitioner inquiry and professional learning communities, there is emphasis on local contexts and local cultures, which are recognized as inevitable mediators of change and shapers of practice. The work of practitioner inquiry assumes that practitioners generate local knowledge of practice by taking an inquiry stance on both the knowledge generated by those outside the local context and the knowledge constructed through the joint efforts of practitioners working together in inquiry communities.

With practitioner inquiry, however, communities are not necessarily school-based. In fact, as we showed in Chapter 1, practitioner inquiry communities are defined and constituted in a wide variety of ways. They are school-based, cross-school, and cross-urban or rural sites. They are made up of teacher candidates, experienced teachers, teacher educators, social science researchers, content-area scholars, school administrators, adult literacy instructors, parents, and community members. They are neighborhood, regional, national, and international. They are real and virtual, their borders expanding and becoming more permeable as technology creates ever-increasing possibilities. Practitioner inquiry's theory of change centers on the idea that teaching and learning are local and relational, but it does not assume that teacher learning is place-based or instrumentally related to specific practices. Rather there are many ways and contexts within which practitioners deepen their understandings of how children learn, interrogate their own assumptions and practices, and rethink practice, which includes, but goes well beyond, the specific strategies teachers use in classrooms. And there are many sources that help to broaden practitioners' strategies and conceptual frameworks, including a wide array of theory and research from other practitioners as well as university-based and other researchers.

With professional learning communities, on the other hand, as McLaughlin and Talbert (2006) point out, schools are regarded as the fundamental unit of change, and it is assumed that meaningful reform must take place at the school level. Here the assumption is that in order for effective changes in curriculum and instruction to occur, students' learning needs must be held up to the yardstick of standards and expectations by all of the members of a school community, not just by some. Both commitment and capacity are assumed to increase when data reveal that measured learning does not meet standards and expectations. From this perspective, much of the work of professional learning communities is to analyze data and then develop local "best practices" by closely examining classroom practices in the light of assessment data. With the "data wise" project (Boudett et al., 2005) and its sequel, "data wise in action" (Boudett & Steele, 2007), for example, the focus was explicitly on what teachers could control and do within the contexts of their own classrooms, with other factors that influence students' learning, such as students' background or resources, explicitly put aside.

Equity and Accountability. We use this final issue—equity and accountability—to consider what all this adds up to or what the bigger picture is. As we noted earlier, both practitioner inquiry and professional learning communities work from an equity agenda in that they are intended to improve the education of those who have been marginalized by the educational system. But there are critically important differences here. With practitioner inquiry, the larger project is *not* making schools into communities so test scores will go up and classroom practices will be more standardized. The larger project is about generating deeper understandings of how students learn—from the perspective of those who do the work. The larger project is about enhancing educators' sense of social responsibility and social action in the service of a democratic society. Practitioner inquiry, with its roots in critical research movements, grassroots teacher groups, and initiatives intended to deepen educators' sense of social responsibility, is often explicitly linked to larger movements for social justice and social change. Even when not overtly linked to these political movements, however, the larger project of practitioner research is based on a deep and profound sense of accountability for students' learning and life chances.

With the more instrumental focus of many professional learning communities and teacher learning communities, on the other hand, inquiry and communities are located inside the prevailing accountability frame. Here the equity agenda is defined as closing the gap in achievement scores between various groups and subgroups of students. The emphasis is on test outcomes rather than on learning more expansively defined. To a certain extent, then—and depending on the communities themselves, of course— some professional learning communities and teacher learning communities retain many of the existing structures of power and privilege and may reify rather than challenge dominant epistemologies and values about the purposes of schooling, the relationships of researchers and the objects of research, and the educational questions that are most worth asking.

CONCLUSION: UNPACKING THE DISCOURSE, UNMASKING DIFFERENCES

Our intention in this chapter is not to valorize or romanticize practitioner inquiry—"it's all good"—and at the same time reject professional learning communities—"they're all bad." To the contrary, as we have tried to make clear, we think professional learning communities are moves in the right direction that resemble practitioner inquiry in many important ways and share some important features. Along with many of those who write about practitioner inquiry, we believe that working on the school as an organization and considering how it can be retooled as a place that supports community and inquiry is a project well worth pursuing. When comparing and contrasting perspectives, there is always the danger of oversimplification and of creating unhelpful dichotomies—dangers we hope we avoided in this chapter. But we also think it is important to unmask the very real differences that exist among projects and initiatives that use the same language—here, the language of inquiry and inquiry stance, community, the data of practice, and school culture.

We made a similar point a number of years ago (Cochran-Smith & Lytle, 1999a) when we argued that just because a teacher education program or a professional development project featured things called "teacher research" or "reflection" or "collaboration" did not mean they were connected to the same larger social and political agendas or that they were constructed to serve the same purposes. We pointed out then, as we do now, that the salient differences among these are not in their language, or even in the structures they use, but in their roots and branches—that is, their broader intellectual and social traditions as well as their assumptions about knowledge and knowers, teachers' work, the activity of teaching, and the larger purposes of schooling in a democratic society.

Chapter Three

Troubling Images of Teaching in No Child Left Behind

So far in this book, we have been describing and theorizing "the next generation" of practitioner research. In Chapter 1, we described the current landscape of practitioner research, which is now the centerpiece of many educational initiatives and larger projects around the world and in cyberspace. Here, our intention was to portray both the depth and breadth of practitioner research and to argue—admittedly optimistically—that the movement is alive and well despite the acutely conservative political climate in the United States and elsewhere and notwithstanding the increasing number of education policies intended to circumscribe, rather than capitalize on and expand, teachers' work. In Chapter 2, we looked more closely at the notion of practitioner research itself, analyzing the common features of its multiple versions and identifying points of convergence, but also divergence, between practitioner research and professional learning communities, a widely advocated school reform initiative that bears a strong resemblance to practitioner inquiry. With Chapter 2, our intention was to open a critical discourse about the potential of inquiry communities for good and ill by raising many questions and suggesting that the differences beneath the surface of many look-alikes may well be more important than their apparent similarities.

As we have shown in some detail in the preceding chapters, despite its variations, practitioner research is unified by certain fundamental assumptions about research, teaching, and teacher learning, all of which emphasize teacher agency and knowledge generation in the interest of social change and social justice. In this chapter, we take a different tack by closely examining the dramatically different assumptions about research, teaching, and teacher learning that are the building blocks of No Child Left Behind, the groundbreaking education policy that has redefined the politics of education for this decade and perhaps for many decades to come.

Chapter 3 is the only chapter in this book that presents previously published work. With the exception of editing for length, this chapter appeared as it is here as one of a collection of papers about *No Child Left Behind* in a special issue of the 2007 volume of the *Harvard Educational Review*. We accepted the opportunity to write an analysis of the precedent-setting NCLB legislation for the *Harvard Educational Review* precisely because the legislation was (and is) precedent setting and, as we say below, because of its "astonishingly comprehensive" reach into nearly every aspect of teaching, learning, and schooling in this nation. We also took on this task because we believed at the time (and continue to believe) that many of NCLB's operating assumptions about research, teaching, and teachers are wrong-headed and dangerous.

Readers will note that the overall tenor of this chapter is different from our cautiously optimistic tone in Chapter 1 and our respectfully critical tone in Chapter 2. We took great pains in this chapter to base our critique on completely transparent and directly cited evidence from NCLB itself and its accompanying policy tools. However, we fully acknowledge that we are sharply critical in this chapter—some would say, excoriating—of NCLB's ideas and assumptions about teachers, teaching, and the knowledge teachers need to teach well. We take this position because we, and so many others across the nation, are deeply troubled about the potentially devastating impact of NCLB's perspectives and policies on American public education—and on both our understandings of the nature of teaching as an activity and a profession and of the nature of students' learning experiences as future participants in a democratic society.

TROUBLING IMAGES OF TEACHING IN NCLB

Not since *A Nation at Risk* (National Commission on Excellence in Education, 1983) likened the country's "rising tide of mediocrity" to an invasion by a foreign power have such emotional rhetoric and "sensational metaphors" (Fuhrman & Lazerson, 2005, p. xxvii) been used to describe a federal education effort. Like *A Nation at Risk*, the No Child Left Behind Act (NCLB) (P.L. 107-110, 2002) makes a clear connection between education and the economy; also like its predecessor, NCLB has provoked powerful responses. Shortly before its passage, for example, the National Conference of State Legislators to Congress ("State Groups Call," 2001) called it "an egregious example of a top-down, one-size-fits-all federal reform," sharply questioning the idea that annual statewide testing in multiple subjects was necessary for an effective state accountability system. On the other hand, Rod Paige, then the secretary of education, referred to groups and organizations that complained that NCLB was an unfunded mandate as "enemies of equal justice" and "apologists for failure" (quoted in Schemo, 2002) and likened resisting NCLB to maintaining apartheid (Paige, 2003). Meanwhile, President Bush (2002) rebuked those who questioned the ability of schools and teachers alone to raise test scores for their "soft bigotry of low expectations." Along similar lines, when spokespersons for the National Education Association questioned the tenets of NCLB, Paige referred to the group as a "terrorist organization" (quoted in Pear, 2004).

Despite enormous debate about its short- and long-term impacts and its intended and unintended consequences, NCLB has been broadly recognized as an unprecedented entry by the federal government into matters of education previously left to the states and school districts. Spokespersons for the Bush administration now claim victory for the policy, pointing to rising test scores and narrowing achievement gaps (*Harvard Educational Review*, 2005). On the other hand, skeptics and critics point to skyrocketing dropout rates (Orfield, Losen, & Wald, 2004), the growing number of schools deemed in need of improvement (Olson, 2004), and the unreasonableness of "adequate yearly progress" goals (Linn, 2003). Others say the jury is still out.

It is clear that there are many questions about what the ultimate legacy of this landmark legislation will be. What there is no question about, however, is that it is students—and the teachers and school-based administrators who serve them—who are bearing the brunt of NCLB and who are most affected by it on a day-to-day basis.

In this chapter, we offer a critique of NCLB that is somewhat different from other critiques. We focus explicitly on what NCLB says, assumes, and implies about teachers, teaching, and the role of teacher learning in educational improvement. We do so for two reasons. First, NCLB is astonishingly comprehensive. Its mandates and definitions coupled with its explicit accountability procedures and penalties are overtaking practice and policy related to virtually every aspect of teaching—recruitment, preparation, certification, induction, licensure, assessment, professional development, school and curricular change, and all sorts of education research related to teachers and teaching. At the same time that it is comprehensive, much of the discourse about NCLB is couched in the unassailable—and persuasive—language of fairness, equity, and high standards for America's schools, its teachers, and its children. This language masks some of the most negative fallout of NCLB, which needs to be exposed. Our second reason for undertaking this analysis is that we believe NCLB's conceptions of teachers and teaching are flawed—linear, remarkably narrow, and based on a technical transmission model of teaching, learning, and teacher training that was rejected more than 2 decades ago and that is decidedly out of keeping with contemporary understandings of learning. Our analysis is intended to provide readers with a lucid and organized way to discern the major problems with images of teachers and teaching that are endemic to NCLB and that have implications for the continuing development of the practitioner research movement.

TRAINING/TESTING AS THE KEY TO SCHOOL REFORM

During the mid- to late 1990s, "teacher quality" became the watchword of school reform. Despite nearly unanimous agreement that teacher quality was important, however, there was no agreed-upon definition. Debates notwithstanding, NCLB cemented into law a particular perspective on teacher quality—one that targets training and testing as the bottom lines of the educational process and stubbornly ignores the fact that many issues related to knowledge and teaching are contested. In this chapter, we analyze the assumptions about teachers, teaching, and teacher quality that are either implicit or explicit in NCLB. To do this, we use a framework we developed in the late 1990s (Cochran-Smith & Lytle, 1999a) to expose differences among various teacher learning and inquiry initiatives in terms of their major images and underlying assumptions about teachers and teaching. As Figure 3.1 indicates, the framework focuses on the following:

- Images of knowledge (i.e., assumptions about what teachers need to know and do in order to teach well; what forms of knowledge they need and what its sources are; how teachers' knowledge is related to teachers' practice and to pupils' learning)
- Images of teachers and teaching (i.e., assumptions about how, when, and what teachers do; what is assumed about the nature of the activity of teaching; what assumptions are made about the purpose of teaching in schooling and society)
- Images of teacher learning (i.e., assumptions what, how, when, and from whom teachers should learn over time; what supports and constrains their continued learning)

We use the term *images* here to mean the central common conceptions that are symbolic of basic attitudes and orientations to teaching and learning. To conduct our analysis, we reviewed the text of the NCLB act itself as well as major policy tools that accompanied and supported it (e.g., annual reports to Congress on teacher quality issued by the secretary of education), NCLB implementation guidelines (e.g., letters from the secretary of education to chief state school officers), and public statements related to NCLB (e.g., public addresses by President Bush and Secretary of Education Paige or Spellings that referred specifically to NCLB as the centerpiece of federal education policy). Following our analysis of each of the three images, we offer a critique of each.

Figure 3.1. Unpacking NCLB: Perspectives on Teachers and Teaching

IMAGES OF . . .	EMPHASIS of NCLB and Its Policy Tools
KNOWLEDGE	
What is assumed about:	Subject–matter knowledge
What teachers need to know and do in order to teach well	Knowledge of scientifically based teaching techniques
What forms of knowledge they need and what its sources are	Knowledge of pedagogy and supervised practice not important
How teachers' knowledge is related to teachers' practice and to pupils' learning	
TEACHERS AND TEACHING	
What is assumed about:	Teachers as determining factor in students' achievement
How, when, and what teachers do	
The nature of the activity of teaching	Teaching as selecting correct techniques
The purposes of teaching in schooling and society	Purpose of teaching as preparing nation's workforce
TEACHER LEARNING	
What is assumed about:	Teacher preparation through alternative routes
How, when, and from whom teachers learn over time	
What supports and constrains their continued learning	Professional development based on scientific research
The contexts in which teachers learn	Teacher learning "on the job"

NCLB: Images of the Knowledge Teachers Need to Teach Well

According to NCLB, teachers must have knowledge in two areas in order to teach well—subject matter and the techniques of teaching that rigorous scientific research has shown to be effective.

Subject-Matter Knowledge. Throughout Title II of NCLB, there are assertions about the need to improve teachers' academic subject–matter knowledge. Section 2113, for example, specifies that state funds received through NCLB may be expended so that:

(A)(i) teachers have the necessary subject matter knowledge and teaching skills in the academic subjects that the teachers teach; and
(ii) principals have the instructional leadership skills to help teachers teach and students learn;
(B) teacher certification (including recertification) or licensing require-

ments are aligned with challenging State academic content standards; and (C) teachers have the subject matter knowledge and teaching skills, including technology literacy, and principals have the instructional leadership skills, necessary to help students meet challenging State student academic achievement standards. (P.L. 107-110, 2002, section 2113)

In this section of Title II, which is only 79 words in length, subject-matter knowledge, academic subjects, or academic content standards are mentioned five separate times. This heavy emphasis on subject-matter knowledge is repeated in all of the documents and speeches that accompanied the unveiling and implementation of NCLB. The rationale for this is clear in Secretary of Education Rod Paige's first report to Congress on teacher quality: "Teachers with strong academic backgrounds in their subjects are more likely to boost student performance" (U.S. Department of Education, 2002, p. vii).

NCLB offers two funding programs to enhance teachers' content knowledge: the Teaching American History grants, which focus on improving teaching and learning of "traditional" history content, and the Science and Math Partnership grants, designed to upgrade teachers' knowledge and skill. In addition, all of the secretary's reports to Congress on teacher quality promote alternate routes into teaching that bypass university-based teacher preparation. The stated rationale is that alternate routes attract into teaching persons with strong subject-matter knowledge and work experience even though they have not taken education courses.

There are two important ideas in NCLB's emphasis on subject matter. The first, which is conveyed in a consistent rhetoric of school failure, has a three-step chain of reasoning: (1) What it takes to teach is subject matter; (2) many American teachers are not competent in subject matter; (3) teachers are not competent because existing teacher preparation and licensure systems do not work. In Paige's first report to Congress, under the heading "A Broken System," the report concluded that schools of education and formal teacher training programs were failing to produce highly qualified teachers because of states' low academic standards for teachers coupled with high barriers that kept out qualified prospective teachers without teacher preparation. The report called for changes in certification requirements with more "rigorous academic content [and] eliminating cumbersome requirements not based on scientific evidence" (p. viii).

The second point has to do with the kind of knowledge NCLB indicates teachers do not need—knowledge of pedagogy and the knowledge gained from teaching practicums. As noted above, the NCLB rhetoric is quite specific about this:

By adding strict new mandates about "highly qualified" teachers, Congress indicated the importance of teacher quality in improving the nation's schools. By focusing its definition of "highly qualified" teachers on preparation in content knowledge, as opposed to components such as pedagogy or teaching practicums, it expressed its opinion of what matters most. (U.S. Department of Education, 2002, p. 6)

The secretary's report indicates that this conclusion is based on "the best available" scientific research.

Knowledge of Scientifically Based Research Techniques. In addition to knowledge of subject matter, NCLB makes it clear that teachers need to have knowledge about the techniques of teaching that rigorous scientific research has "proven" effective. The emphasis on scientifically based research (SBR) is unmistakable in all of the documents and tools accompanying NCLB, including *NCLB: A Toolkit for Teachers* (U.S. Department of Education, 2004a), which is a booklet for teachers available on the NCLB website or in hard copy, Braille, large print, audiotape, or computer diskette. The *Toolkit* lays out NCLB's four "commonsense" pillars for fixing the schools, one of which is the use of educational programs and techniques that have been clearly demonstrated to be effective on the basis of SBR. NCLB documents emphasize that employing practices based on SBR and doing "what works" is very different from learning through trial and error, relying on theory, following educational fads, or employing unproven practices based on ideological rather than empirical grounds. The *Toolkit* points teachers to the What Works Clearinghouse website to determine which programs actually work.

The emphasis on teachers' knowledge of scientifically based classroom techniques is especially clear in discussions about teaching reading. The *Toolkit* tells teachers: "In recent years, scientific research has provided tremendous insight into exactly how children learn to read and the essential components for effective reading instruction" (p. 30). The *Toolkit* also asserts that these components of reading instruction work for everybody: "Research has consistently identified the critical skills that young students need to learn in order to become good readers. Teachers across different states and districts have demonstrated that scientifically based reading instruction can and does work with all children" (p. 29). Along similar lines, during White House remarks on the implementation of NCLB, President Bush (2002) commented:"[It] requires a curriculum that works if you want every child to read. They don't want fancy theories, or what may sound good. Science is not an art—I mean, reading is not an art; it's a science. We know what works."

Critique of NCLB's Images of Knowledge. NCLB's unambiguous position—that in order to teach well, what teachers must know is subject matter and proven teaching techniques—is problematic for a whole host of reasons. We mention just two of these here: the narrow and outdated view of subject-matter knowledge as an agreed-upon object that can be transmitted from one party to another and the problematic notion that there is a scientifically proven body of knowledge about educational techniques and programs.

As noted above, as part of its first pillar of accountability, NCLB requires that all teachers have solid academic content knowledge in the "core" subject areas they teach. NCLB asserts that this is common sense. And of course it is in some ways. No one disputes the claim that teachers should have solid content knowledge in the areas they teach. No one disagrees with the conclusion that teachers teaching subjects "out of field" is, usually, a serious problem. And no one argues with the conclusion that some teachers in some schools, especially in schools that are hard to staff and with large numbers of students traditionally not well served by the educational system, are deficient in some areas of content knowledge.

However, the premise that subject-matter knowledge is a kind of object that can be given more or less directly by one party to another is not in keeping with current understandings about learning based on research in the cognitive sciences and other fields (National Research Council, 2000). Nevertheless, an objectified image of knowledge and a transmission view of teaching and learning are implicit in nearly all of the official discourse promoting NCLB. It is also clear in NCLB discourse that teachers, in turn, are supposed to "give" subject-matter knowledge to their students. The idea that knowledge is an object to be transmitted from outside experts to teachers, who then transmit it to students—with testing at the end to be sure there were no foul-ups in the transmission process—is not in keeping with how we understand learning today. Decades of research have shown that learning is a process of developing usable knowledge (not just isolated facts) by building on previous knowledge and experience, understanding and organizing information in a conceptual framework, and monitoring progress toward learning goals (National Research Council, 2000). The transmission model of knowledge that is implicit in NCLB is out of date and insufficient.

Furthermore, it takes only a cursory reading of the educational literature to arrive at the conclusion that subject-matter knowledge (i.e., what one needs to know in a given discipline, such as history or mathematics) as well as epistemology (i.e., what it means to "know" in a given area, such as knowing how to read) are historically fluid, contestable, and—currently—highly contested rather than "given" and static, as NCLB presumes. Neither the language of NCLB itself nor any of its policy tools acknowledge current debates about "core" academic areas or the politics of knowledge.

Like its notion of subject-matter knowledge, NCLB's notion of SBR is represented in the discourse as an unproblematic idea despite the fact that SBR and its complement, "evidence-based education" (EBE), have been widely debated and critiqued in the research community in the United States and elsewhere (Cochran-Smith, 2005; Erickson, 2005; Hammersley, 2000; Lather, 2004; Trinder & Reynolds, 2000). Critiques notwithstanding, SBR and EBE are ubiquitous in NCLB and all of its policy tools, and these notions are integrated in the federal education apparatus, including the Reading First grants, the Institute of Education Sciences, and the What Works Clearinghouse. Perhaps even more problematic, the premises about the nature of knowledge that underlie SBR and EBE have been stitched so seamlessly into the discourse about how to improve teaching that they are now nearly imperceptible.

The biggest problems with SBR and EBE are their shared assumptions that knowledge related to teaching is universal and generalizable and that the teacher's job is to know that knowledge and apply it with fidelity. The importance of local knowledge and the idea that teachers and other practitioners have the capacity to generate local knowledge of practice through their own classroom and school inquiries are antithetical to the premises of NCLB. As we have argued previously (Cochran-Smith & Lytle, 1999b), from the perspective of local knowledge, both knowledge generation and knowledge use are inherently problematic:

> That is, basic questions about knowledge and teaching—what it means to generate knowledge, who generates it, what counts as knowledge and to whom, and how knowledge is used and evaluated in particular contexts— are always open to question. Further . . . [knowledge is] regarded as not existing separate from the knower. Rather, from this perspective, knowledge-making is understood as a pedagogic act—constructed in the context of use, intimately connected to the knower, and although relevant to immediate situations, also inevitably a process of theorizing. From this perspective, knowledge is not bound by the instrumental imperative that it be used or applied to an immediate situation but rather that it may also shape the conceptual and interpretive frameworks teachers develop to make judgments, theorize practice, and connect their efforts to larger intellectual, social, and political issues as well as to the work of other teachers, researchers, and communities. The basis of this knowledge-practice conception is that teachers across the professional life span play a central and critical role in generating knowledge of practice by making their classrooms and schools sites for inquiry, connecting their work in schools to larger issues, and taking a critical perspective on the theory and research of others. (pp. 272–273)

A number of scholars (e.g., Anderson, Nihlen, & Herr, 1994; Noffke, 1997; Stenhouse, 1985) have theorized forms of inquiry grounded in practice, such as practitioner inquiry, teacher research, action research, and others. These forms of knowledge generation are intended to alter the relationships among knowledge, practice, and power that are implicit in concepts such as SBR and EBE and are designed to interrupt the assumption that knowledge generated by outsiders can be transported directly to schools and applied by insiders to solve problems of practice. In this era of accountability, however, where a narrow and, some would say, a nonscientific view of science has been elevated as the one and only way to generate knowledge about teaching, local knowledge is more likely to be regarded as anecdote or fad than it is to be seen as a legitimate way of knowing about schools and classrooms.

NCLB: Images of Teachers and Teaching

NCLB makes it clear that teachers are expected to play the primary role in improving student achievement. NCLB's assumptions about the nature of teachers' work and its significance are tied directly to testing, accountability, and scientifically based research as the key to improving the quality of what teachers do.

The Central Importance of Teachers. NCLB-related statements and activities consistently position teachers as the critical players in improving student achievement across all grades and subject areas. This is clear in Secretary Paige's (U.S. Department of Education, 2004b) many references to teachers as key determinants of student success and to teaching as a factor that can overcome all other factors. In addition to focusing on teachers' experience and knowledge of subject-matter content, NCLB constructs an image of teachers that links their verbal and cognitive abilities directly to student outcomes. William Sanders's Tennessee research (Sanders, 1998; Sanders & Horn, 1994; Wright, Horn, & Sanders, 1997) on the value that effective teachers add to students' achievement is frequently used to buttress this argument and to show that individual teachers can make an enormous difference in school outcomes. According to the Institute of Education Sciences's (IES) director Russ Whitehurst (2002), one of NCLB's goals is to improve the quality of teaching by being more selective about the cognitive abilities of teachers selected to enter the field and removing conventional "barriers" to becoming a teacher; these barriers include master's degrees and pedagogical coursework.

In the preface to the first report to Congress on teacher quality, President Bush referred to the power of teachers, asserting that "we give them great responsibility: to shape the minds and hearts of our children" (U.S. Department of Education, 2002, p. iii). Similarly, at the NCLB summit in Philadelphia, Secretary of Education Margaret Spellings (2006a) returned to this refrain, saying:

> All of us know that the hard work of educating our students happens in classrooms, not in the superintendent's office, the state legislature, the U.S. Capitol, or, for that matter, in the Education Secretary's office. (np)

In an earlier interview, Spellings ("Newsmaker: Margaret Spellings," 2005) argued that NCLB's success in closing the achievement gap could be attributed to "annual measurement, to paying attention to every child, every year, and to prescribing a cure, an instructional cure if you wish" so that students get to grade level on the timetable required by the law. Spellings's medical image of teachers as the healers or fixers of deficits who prescribe "instructional" cures for ailments underlines the importance attributed to teachers and justifies NCLB's rationale for new initiatives related to teacher training, recruitment, retention, incentives, and other programs.

Conceptions of Good Teaching. According to NCLB and related documents, successful teaching has several dimensions. The first is that good teachers are consumers of certain products as well as confident and selective in deciding what to do in their classrooms to foster student achievement. The *Toolkit for Teachers* (U.S. Department of Education, 2004a), for example, suggests that as teachers prepare lessons for their students, they are faced with three essential questions:

- How do I know what works?
- What intervention is best to support a student who lacks certain skills?
- How do I analyze a program's or intervention's effectiveness? (p. 31)

Framed this way, the teacher's task is to select among a proliferating set of educational interventions that claim to be supported by evidence. To mitigate this problem, the *Toolkit* refers teachers to a U.S. Department of Education (2003) guide entitled *Identifying and Implementing Educational Practices Supported by Rigorous Evidence* and to the What Works Clearinghouse (http:// whatworks.ed.gov/). Therein teachers will find information to guide their selection and implementation of curriculum and instructional strategies for their classes, as well as guidance in identifying interventions that have promise for working with students lacking particular skills.

The NCLB canon identifies another crucial dimension of good teaching: teachers' uses of test data to make decisions. The *Toolkit* describes the how's and why's of data-driven decision making as follows:

> Effective teachers use data to make informed decisions and are constantly improving classroom practice to better serve their students. One of the most important aspects of good teaching, as most teachers know, is the ability to discern which students are learning and which are not, and then to tailor instruction to meet individual learning needs. (p. 45)

In a certain sense, this quotation suggests NCLB's recognition of the importance of individualizing instruction. However, the recommended strategy is heavily, if not wholly, dependent on standardized test data. NCLB and its accompanying policy documents make it clear that tests are the primary sources of information for teaching and the principal route to informed decisions about instruction. In response to complaints that frequent testing undermines quality educational processes rather than supports them, President Bush (2002) retorted:

> I've heard people say: You test too much . . . if testing determines whether you can read, too bad that we test. As a matter of fact, it's to your advantage that we test. How do you know if you don't give people a chance to show us? How do you know? It's the systems that don't test are those that quit on kids. (np)

This logic and the seeming "common sense" of this proposition are consistent across the many speeches and interviews explaining NCLB and its intentions: Tests are how we know about what students are learning, and good teaching entails raising test scores. As Spellings pointed out, "What gets measured gets done. Amen" (*Harvard Educational Review*, 2005, p. 371).

Throughout NCLB, it is clear that good teaching requires focusing on students' weaknesses or their lack of skills, which are identified by tests. Teachers are instructed to zero in on those weak areas, or, as Paige (2004) suggested in reference to one particular population that often has difficulty with tests: "We need to remediate the heck out of these special needs kids" (np).

Purposes of Teaching and Its Role in Schooling and Society. Throughout the NCLB law and its accompanying rhetoric, the improvement of educational outcomes is directly and consistently linked to global competitiveness. Speaking before the House Committee on Science, for example, Spellings

(2006b) made the case that education is critical to our economic and national security. Even before NCLB became law, Paige (2001), in a speech at the Summit on the 21st Century Workforce, argued that the effort to improve educational outcomes is about producing the labor force we need: "We need to prepare our children for the work force of the 21st century" (np). Paige argued that schools must be held accountable and school success must be measured by performance, not by spending—by outputs, not by inputs: "Every publicly traded company in this country reports results to its investors every quarter. Is it not asking too much for our schools to report annually on their results?" (np). The logic in Paige's remarks and throughout the NCLB rhetoric is clear: When the "output" of excellent teaching is understood as raised scores on high-stakes tests, then students, who are the "products" of that teaching, can take their rightful (and needed) place in a strong, competitive workforce.

Critique of NCLB's Images of Teachers and Teaching. NCLB's perspective on the goals or ends of teaching as boosting scores on high-stakes tests and the means of teaching as using scientifically certified knowledge about best practices has been roundly critiqued from many quarters, including classroom teachers and educators who work closely with teachers (e.g., Bracey, 2004; Meier & Wood, 2004; Poetter, Wegwert, & Haerr, 2006). In our critique in this chapter, we focus on three of the most problematic aspects: the heavy loading of responsibility and accountability on the shoulders of teachers without acknowledging the need for changed policies that deal with school cultures and complex societal problems; the distorted and reductionist conception of teaching practice and the work of teachers; and the narrowing of the purposes of teaching and schooling resulting in an impoverished view of the curriculum and the broader social and democratic goals, processes, and consequences of education.

There is considerable agreement in the educational community and among the public that teachers should be primary actors in improving educational outcomes and that the quality of teaching is a critical factor in student achievement. However, there is also widespread awareness that placing the full responsibility for student learning on teachers ignores the many other salient factors that have contributed to the inequality of educational opportunity. NCLB's construction of the problem forces attention to state compliance with federal law, district compliance with state standards and testing programs, and local district and school efforts to prepare for and administer high-stakes tests. Others have written compelling critiques of NCLB's not-so-hidden agenda around privatization and the redefinition of education in terms of national priorities construed in market terms (Acker, 1996; Apple, 2006; Smyth, 2001).

Here we wish to point to the ways that making the teacher "the answer" to the problems of education distracts attention from underresourced schools and other systemic factors such as poverty and racism. As Cochran-Smith (2005) explains, quality teachers alone cannot fix the schools:

> To do so will take simultaneous investments in resources, capacity building, and teachers' professional growth, not to mention changes in access to housing, health, and jobs. Acknowledging that the problems of the nation's schools include, but go far beyond, teachers, and that the problems of the nation include, but go far beyond schools, is not an excuse. It reflects categorical acceptance of the goal of equal and high quality education for all students and flat out rejection of the idea that holding teachers and teacher preparation accountable for everything will fix everything, while meanwhile letting everybody else off the hook. (p. 11)

Ironically, the notion of "highly qualified" teachers at once underscores and undermines teachers' public image and thus contributes—positively or negatively—to the public trust so essential for building parental and community support for schools. By calling for teacher tests to screen out those who are not "fit to teach" by virtue of their intelligence and cognitive abilities, for example, and by legislating top-down control of teacher's work, NCLB contributes to the paradox that teachers are taken to be both the problem and the solution to what is wrong with schools (Cochran-Smith, 2005; Cohen, 1995; Fullan, 1993). While NCLB rhetoric ostensibly elevates teachers and makes them the standard bearers for high expectations for students, the discourse of teacher deficits—fueled by increased monitoring and surveillance of daily practice—has never been more prevalent (Lytle, 2006).

Making teachers the centerpiece of NCLB reform has been accompanied by new forms of regulation that buttress the image of teaching practice as a fundamentally technical, instrumental, certain, and decontextualized activity. Many teachers are now expected to teach to state standards by following district-made scripts, selecting among research-based programs according to criteria specified by governmental publications, and choosing interventions based on diagnosis of student weaknesses derived from results of high-stakes tests. Teachers are being compelled to reduce their practice to teaching a narrow set of skills that increasingly bypass the kinds of professional judgments about and knowledge of students and communities that many regard as the distinguishing features of excellent practice (e.g., Allington & Johnston, 2001; Pressley et al., 2001).

Analyzing the conditions of teachers' work in Australia, which has striking parallels to our current situation, Smyth (2001) describes what happens when the language of teaching is transformed through market and business metaphors:

> First, a discourse about the work of schooling is constructed that becomes unassailable. For example, we naturalize the discourse so that we need "skill profiles" and "task analyses" in order to produce "needs statements," against which to produce highly structured "performance objectives" so that "outcomes" can be measured against "standards." Presumably the intent (although it is not put this way) is to produce labor that is more compliant. Opposition to this line is branded as being deviant, old-fashioned, or just out of touch. (pp. 81–82)

By privileging subject matter over pedagogy and by taking most of the important decisions out of the hands of teachers, NCLB's images of teaching are deceptively simple and instrumental, governed by a tight logic reminiscent of diagnostic-prescriptive frameworks that required teachers to attend primarily to student deficits rather than their strengths. When Secretary Spellings referred to teaching as "prescribing an instructional cure," she explicitly invoked a scientific or medical metaphor wherein students are the unhealthy patients who are ailing from lack of skills and need the "treatments" of teachers to become healthy and "proficient."

It is telling that NCLB and its accompanying documents and websites do not use the term *professional practice* to refer to what teachers do. This language signals a very different set of assumptions and conjures up very different images of teaching from those prevalent in NCLB. We and many others have written about teaching as a complex, deliberative, inherently uncertain, contextual, social, cultural, and political process. We and many others have depicted the daily work of teachers as wrestling with the complexity of classroom life and with the constant dynamic challenge of building instruction on the cultural and linguistic resources children and adolescents bring to school (e.g., Ballenger, 1998; Campano, 2007; Cochran-Smith & Lytle, 1993; Hargreaves, 2003; Nieto, 1999). The messy realities of teaching do not lend themselves simply to the selection and implementation of curricula and methods produced by experts from afar. Ambiguities, uncertainties, and unpredictably are the substance of teaching. For many teachers, as Dudley-Marling (1997) points out, "uncertainty is not a threat to their professional identities, but an occasion for reflection and growth" (p. 252).

In his recent sociological study of who controls teachers' work, Ingersoll (2003) points out that how one defines the job of teaching is extremely important. Schools are not just organized to deliver academic learning but also function as primary means for the socialization of children and youth. Describing the nature of teaching, he says:

> Teaching is interactional work. The production process calls for employees to work not with raw materials or objects, but with other individuals. Moreover, the individuals with whom teachers work are neither mature, socialized adults nor voluntary participants. . . . For all these reasons, teaching is an inherently ambiguous, unpredictable, and fluid craft. Teaching requires flexibility, give-and-take, and making exceptions, and it can present formidable and unusual challenges. . . . Regulations often don't work well for irregular work. . . . Rules can never cover all the contingencies in work like teaching, where there is little consensus and much ambiguity surrounding means and ends. (pp. 140, 142)

Ingersoll argues that trying to improve schools by imposing more accountability on teachers reflects a lack of knowledge on the part of those who would fix the schools. Apple (2006) makes the related point that in order to fix the schools,

> we need to listen to a much broader array of voices, including . . . the voices of the thousands of teachers (most of whom were and are women) and community activists within the multiple oppressed communities within this nation who struggled to build an education that was responsive to the lives and hopes of their students. (p. 121)

By requiring that teachers concentrate on raising scores in a limited set of school subjects, the law virtually assures a narrowing of the curriculum with conspicuous inattention to the broader social and democratic goals of education. Many critiques of NCLB by differently situated scholars and advocates have publicly expressed concerns about the negative effects of high-stakes testing on children, teachers, schools, and communities. Implemented as intended, the law crowds out many important subjects, limits teachers' repertoires, and, ironically, given the rhetoric of the law, diminishes the likelihood that teachers will fulfill their social commitments, especially teaching for a truly knowledgeable, well-informed, caring, and productive citizenry.

NCLB: Images of Teacher Learning

NCLB does not use the language of "teacher learning" per se, but the law and its documents are quite specific about two enterprises that are intimately linked to teacher learning—teacher preparation and professional development for teachers. There are detailed descriptions of preferred models of teacher preparation as well as detailed criteria for teachers' professional development.

Teacher Preparation. As noted above, when it comes to teacher preparation, NCLB rhetoric has consistently challenged schools of education as a rightful location for teacher preparation programs and instead championed alternate routes into teaching. NCLB names a number of alternate routes as innovative approaches for streamlining teacher preparation and improving teacher quality. The legislation also specifies that prospective teachers who are enrolled in, but have not completed, alternate certification programs or who obtain certification by passing a state-approved teacher test in states that have test-only certification channels are fully eligible to be counted as "highly qualified teachers."

The federal preference for alternate entry routes is also clear in the secretary of education's annual reports, which measure the progress of states—at least in part—by whether or not they offer alternate routes that streamline certification and often bypass universities. The first of the secretary's reports (U.S. Department of Education, 2002) asserted that "traditional teacher-training programs" (p. 13) failed to attract talented prospective teachers because of lack of rigor, rigidity of training, and lost opportunity costs for candidates. Although later reports softened this conclusion somewhat, the first report concluded: "Alternate routes to certification demonstrate that streamlined systems can boost the quantity of teachers while maintaining—or even improving—their quality. . . . [Thus] a model for tomorrow would be based on the best alternate route programs of today" (p. 19).

NCLB's approach to teacher preparation is also apparent in its emphasis on the American Board for Certification of Teacher Excellence's (ABCTE) new "Passport to Teaching." This newly developed teacher test, which is touted in the secretary's reports and public addresses, was initially funded with a $35 million discretionary grant from the federal Department of Education. Described on the ABCTE website as the "premier alternative route to teacher certification" (American Board for Certification of Teacher Excellence, 2006), the "Passport" is a national teaching examination, designed to assess subject area and professional teaching knowledge and now recognized as a route to teaching certification in five states.

Professional Development. According to NCLB (P.L. 107-110, 2002), highly qualified teachers must receive high-quality professional development based on SBR in order to raise pupils' achievement levels. Title IX, which spells out NCLB's definitions of key terms, defines "professional development" as activities that:

(i) improve and increase teachers' knowledge of the academic subjects the teachers teach, and enable teachers to become highly qualified;

(ii) are an integral part of broad school wide and district wide educational improvement plans;

(iii) give teachers, principals, and administrators the knowledge and
    skills to meet . . . student academic achievement standards;
(iv) improve classroom management skills;
(v)(I) are high quality, sustained, intensive, and classroom-focused in
    order to have a positive and lasting impact on classroom instruction
    and the teacher's performance in the classroom; and
    (II) are not 1-day or short-term workshops or conferences. (Section
    9101)

The Title IX definition goes on to specify that professional development should advance teachers' strategies based on SBR in direct alignment with state standards, give teachers knowledge and skills to provide instruction for limited English proficient children and children with special needs, and include instruction in the use of data and assessments to inform practice (Section 9101).

The NCLB *Toolkit for Teachers* (U.S. Department of Education, 2004a) addresses the question "Who determines what is high-quality professional development?" in terms of federal, state, and local responsibilities (p. 49). The federal role is described exactly as listed above, while the state is responsible for reporting this to the federal government and monitoring the state's expenditure of Title II funds. At the local level, districts are charged with conducting needs assessments and using achievement data to decide the professional development needed.

There are a number of important points about teachers' learning implicit in discussions about teacher preparation and professional development in the NCLB documents. First, it is clear that teacher preparation should be streamlined—with subject-matter knowledge paramount and the rest picked up on the job. Second, only "high-quality" professional development, based on scientific research and designed to boost achievement, is valuable—and funded. Third, the proof of all this is test scores. "Scientifically designed studies" are now under way at IES to establish empirically which teacher preparation and professional development "delivery models" are most effective based on pupils' measured achievement (U.S. Department of Education, 2005). In addition, the Improving Teacher Quality state grants provide funds for professional development based on a "review of scientifically based research and an explanation of why the activities are expected to improve student academic achievement" (section 2112). In one interview ("Interview: U.S. Secretary of Education," 2005), Spellings referred to this increasing press to measure teacher education and professional practice in terms of teachers' ability to raise students' achievement as "a shift toward a culture of achievement" (p. 372).

Critique of NCLB's Images of Teacher Learning. NCLB's image of teacher learning and teacher development is one that would be considered by many scholars, ourselves included, as "training" rather than "learning." The distinction we make here is between the technical and behavioral aspects of teachers' work, divorced from their decision-making processes, ideas, beliefs, theorizing, and analyses. NCLB implies that early on, teacher training is the attainment of subject-matter knowledge through a college-level major in a subject area and/or through on-the-job experience in an area related to subject-matter (e.g., a position in civil or military engineering is assumed to enhance subject-matter knowledge related to mathematics and science teaching and thus equip one to be a teacher). Once on the job, teacher training is presumed to occur through participation in periodic professional development sessions that upgrade and update teachers' skills in keeping with the latest scientifically proven techniques. NCLB's assumptions and assertions about teacher preparation and professional development are problematic for many reasons, three of which we discuss: a limited and narrow view of knowledge as something that can be given to teachers to give to their students; the assumption that beyond subject matter, what new teachers need to know can be picked up on the job; and the idea that teachers' ongoing development is a matter of training and retraining rather than learning.

We have already critiqued NCLB's problematic notion of subject-matter knowledge as an object that teachers are charged with transmitting to students. As we noted, with the knowledge transmission model of teaching, testing is used to ensure that transmission has occurred or to penalize teachers and schools when it has not. Given these views, it is not surprising that NCLB and its policy tools imply a knowledge delivery model of teacher training parallel to its model of students' learning, with teacher tests constituting the accountability mechanism more or less parallel to the annual student tests now required in grades 3–8. The only problem with teacher tests, according to the secretary's reports, is that their cut scores are too low. For example, the fourth annual report (U.S. Department of Education, 2005) lauded the fact that all but one state had quality standards regulating all teaching fields and grade levels and noted that 39 states and outlying areas required a content-specific bachelor's degree for teacher certification. The report criticized the typical current 95 percent pass rate on state teacher tests and decried the fact that states had still not raised minimum passing scores.

The second problem with NCLB's view of teacher development as training is its assumption that beyond subject matter, new teachers can get what they need by learning on the job. For example, one of the "brighter" notes mentioned in the Spellings report was that 85 percent of states had established alternate pathways into teaching. Although these vary considerably, with many alternate routes, candidates take on classroom responsibility prior to their completion of coursework and without the benefit of supervised, school-based practicum experience. This means that many alternate-route teachers are thrust into a situation where they must learn about the processes, activities, and problems of teaching on the job. Granted, all new teachers do some learning on the job. And, in fact, learning from teaching over the course of the entire professional life span is a hallmark of what many educators would consider good teaching. However, learning on the job without the benefit of coursework and supervision is quite different from the learning on the job that all teachers do.

With many alternate routes, the challenges all new teachers face are exacerbated by the fact that participants are placed in high-poverty classrooms in urban, rural, and other areas where schools are hard to staff and where there is high teacher turnover. As has been pointed out repeatedly, it is precisely the students in these schools, who have not traditionally been well served by the system, who need the best teachers but who often end up with teachers who are least prepared (Darling-Hammond & Sclan, 1996) and who have not had the benefit of specific preparation related to teaching diverse populations, teaching English language learners, or working with students with special needs. With regard to Teach for America (TFA), which is often a poster child for alternate routes and a favorite of Laura Bush, there have been a number of studies intended to explore whether TFA teachers are as or more effective than other teachers. These have had mixed results. A recent national study examined whether TFA teachers improved "or at least [did] not harm student outcomes relative to what would have happened in their absence" (Decker, Mayer, & Glayerman, 2004, p. ix). The study did not ask whether TFA teachers were effective; in fact, the students of both TFA and the control-group teachers in this study scored poorly. Rather the study asked whether TFA teachers did any harm to pupils by making their achievement scores any worse than they would have been anyway, given the reality that high-poverty schools often have to hire poorly educated, uncertified, and unqualified teachers.

The do-no-harm kind of question points to a major problem with cost–benefit studies of on-the-job approaches to teacher preparation and reflects the underlying failure of NCLB to take responsibility for genuinely changing the educational status quo. The purpose of these studies is to identify models of teacher preparation and entry routes that will not worsen things in high-poverty, hard-to-staff, and minority schools because the teachers are "good enough" to maintain or slightly increase existing very low levels of achievement. This approach ignores the issue of investing in programs and entry routes that interrupt the cycle of inadequate resources, low expectations, and poor achievement.

A third problem with NCLB's view of teacher development is its direct embrace of training–retraining as the way to provide competent teachers for the nation's schools. President Bush (2002) used the language of training in White House remarks on implementation of NCLB during its first year. In praising work in the state of Alabama, he commented: "[In Alabama] they have retrained 2,500 teachers. Retraining is the right word; they've been trained once. Now they're being trained in a curriculum that will work" (np). The implication in Bush's remarks is that however teachers in Alabama were "trained" in the first place was both insufficient and faulty. With NCLB in place, however, as Bush asserted, teachers can be "retrained"—and get it right this time.

The model of teacher development as training and retraining is retrograde and inconsistent with contemporary understandings of teaching and learning. As Cochran-Smith and Fries (2005) argued in their analysis of the history of research on teacher education, "training" was the focus during the 1960s and 1970s when researchers and teacher educators identified the most effective procedures for training teachers to display specific teaching behaviors that had been validated as effective ways to raise pupils' test scores. With this approach, teaching was regarded largely as a technical transmission activity, and teaching and learning were assumed to be related in a linear way. Teacher behavior was the beginning point and pupil learning the endpoint of classroom exchanges. Building on these premises, the assumption was that teacher training was also a technical transmission activity and that teacher training and teacher behavior were related linearly.

During the 1980s, the technical view of teaching and the training view of teacher development were to a large extent rejected, in large part because of their overly simplified view of teaching and learning that ignored not only teacher cognition but also the dynamic, social, moral, and political aspects of teaching. New ideas about teachers and teaching were influenced by the development of cognitive science, the application to education of research perspectives from anthropology and other interpretive traditions, new relationships between educational research and practice, and the shift from a linear to a systemic view of how research influenced policy (Lagemann, 2000). During this time, teacher development generally shifted from teacher training to teacher learning, which meant examining the kinds of knowledge, attitudes, and beliefs teachers brought with them to teacher preparation and professional development opportunities (as well as how these changed over time);

how teachers learned (and generated) the knowledge, skills, and dispositions needed to teach; how they made professional decisions inside and outside the classroom; how they learned about their students and their cultures; and how they interpreted and connected their experiences in courses, workshops, and learning communities to their work in schools and classrooms. NCLB policy reflects none of these shifts in perspectives.

TROUBLING IMAGES OF TEACHING

As we have shown, there is much that is troubling about the images of teachers and teaching in NCLB. The law and its supporting documents create the false expectation that if all teachers were "highly qualified," they could fix everything that is wrong with public schools. NCLB emphasizes a narrow version of subject matter, for students and teachers as well—one that omits much that is known about the contested nature of content knowledge and epistemology. NCLB emphasizes teaching as transmission using empirically proven methods, universally applied to the education of students and to the "training" of teachers.

A Matter of Truth and Consequences

The professional knowledge and understanding teachers derive from their local experiences and relationships with students are missing in the NCLB equation. NCLB's aura of certainty has little resonance with experienced teachers who know firsthand and day-to-day the complexities of working with diverse groups of students in varying school cultures and communities. Back-mapping the curriculum from high-stakes tests and using frequent benchmark assessments to maintain control over instruction dramatically narrow the purposes of education and put forward an impoverished view of teaching, learning, curriculum, and schooling. The overall effect is both seductive and confusing. In a certain way, NCLB policies seem to be motivated by unassailable assumptions about equity and equality of educational opportunity. At the same time, however, NCLB undermines the broader democratic mission of education.

It is important to be clear here. Regardless of individuals' views and critiques of NCLB, there is no question about the impact the law and its federal, state, and local implementation mechanisms are having on the conduct of American public education. NCLB is changing how we—the educational community, the policy community, and the public—think about teachers and teaching. Like it or not, diverse stakeholders in the educational process are coming to regard teachers as technicians, student learning as test performance, and teacher learning as training about "what works." NCLB is pervasive and strategic in its reasoning, using simple direct language and repetition to present an impermeable logic about how to fix the schools by fixing teachers and teaching.

Using marketplace, military, and business concepts of alignment and the reduction of variation as its code metaphors, NCLB has narrowed the meaning of teaching and is already having severe effects on teachers and student learning. A recent survey by the Center on Education Policy (2006), for example, found that "71% of the nation's 15,000 school districts had reduced the hours of instructional time spent on history, music and other subjects to open up more time for reading and math" (np). This has led in some instances to resistance from teachers and administrators and to worries that there will be serious costs for speaking out about what is going on in public schools as a consequence of NCLB (Bracey, 2003; Darling-Hammond, 2004; Edelsky, 2005). Furthermore, because of the authoritarian structure of NCLB, some teachers are compelled to adhere to strict forms of implementation, but not because they believe they are enhancing students' engagement with school or because they see dramatic changes in learning and achievement.

In a recent study of teacher resistance to mandated policies, for example, Achinstein and Ogawa (2006) analyze the experiences of two new teachers working within "prescriptive instructional programs and control-oriented educational policies" (p. 30). Achinstein and Ogawa argue that the cases illustrate resistance driven by teachers' adherence to professional principles, not, as is often assumed in the literature, by psychological deficiency related to refusal to change. Achinstein and Ogawa (2006) define teachers' professional principles in the following way:

> Professional principles are conceptions about teaching and professionalism in which teachers view themselves as professionals with specialized expertise, who have discretion to employ repertoires of instructional strategies to meet the individual needs of diverse students, hold high expectations for themselves and students, foster learning communities among students, and participate in self-critical communities of practice. (p. 32)

The authors argue that the system exercises both technical and moralistic control over teachers and teaching by limiting dissent and debate, constraining professional discourse, and ultimately contributing to teacher attrition.

Along similar lines, in a case study of urban teachers' learning and leadership, Lytle (2006) argues:

> Teachers [in this study] do not oppose standards, the need for highly quali-
> fied teachers, the assessment of outcomes, or policies that seek to rectify
> long-standing inequities in the system. What they resist is the gross over-
> simplification of the complexity of the task at hand, the proliferation of
> policies and high stakes tests that fail to take into account that teaching is
> not fundamentally technical work, but rather what many have regarded as
> a highly complex, deliberative, and adaptive process. (p. 275)

Lytle suggests that repetitive presentation and testing of material is not the
primary way to improve student performance and is unlikely to engage urban adolescents who themselves often have studied resistance to business as
usual in schools. As we have alluded above, arguments for democratic education make a clear case for the relationship between teachers' active participation in the cultures of teaching and schooling and the lessons learned by
students who observe their teachers being and becoming agents of change
(Fuhrman & Lazerson, 2005). Much of the scripted curricula and high-stakes
testing routines being cemented into place through NCLB have the intent
of altering the face of teaching as a profession. Yet, as Susan Moore Johnson
(Moore Johnson & The Project on the Next Generation of Teachers, 2004)
points out, evidence is accumulating that the next generation of those who
elect to teach will come expecting to have opportunities to grow in (not to
be contained by) the profession—and thus to exercise influence within and
beyond the classroom.

Toward a Different Image: Teaching and Teachers' Roles in Educational Improvement

To improve student learning and to retain qualified teachers, we need
to unpack and critique the images of teachers and teaching that are creeping
into the national psyche. We offer an alternative image of teaching as a complement to broader critiques of the social, political, and cultural context in
which NCLB is failing to solve the central issues at play in public education
(see, for example, recent work by Anyon, 2005; Apple, 2006; Berliner, 2006;
Hursh, 2006; Lipman, 2003; Oakes, 2005). Building from the literatures
of critical feminism, anti-racist pedagogy, and the work of social justice–
oriented educators, we believe this different image of teachers and teaching
is actually congruent with the basic goals of NCLB in the sense of improving the education of all children. It parts company with NCLB, however, in
that it offers a much richer notion of teaching, one that holds considerable
promise as a framework for discussion by teachers, teacher educators, school
administrators, and policymakers. This image is one of opening (rather than
closing) the training/testing loop and of embracing (rather than denying) the

myriad complexities and uncertainties of practice that, when acknowledged and acted on, improve the likelihood of actually doing the job better. We are offering here a different vision of teaching, one that emphasizes that teachers need to have a transformed and expanded view of practice that goes far beyond what teachers do when they stand in front of students. Rather than using strategies certified by so-called scientifically based research, teaching requires the intentional forming and re-forming of frameworks for understanding practice. This means that teaching is about how students and their teachers construct the curriculum, co-mingling their experiences, their cultural and linguistic resources, and their interpretive frameworks. Teaching also entails how teachers' actions are infused with complex and multilayered understandings of learners, culture, class, gender, literacies, social issues, institutions, herstories and histories, communities, materials, texts, and curricula. A critical dimension of teaching is how teachers work together to develop and alter their questions and interpretive frameworks informed not only by thoughtful consideration of the immediate situation and the particular students they teach and have taught, but also by making sense of the multiple social, economic, political, and cultural contexts within which they work.

The notion of teaching that we are contrasting here with the images of NCLB is consistent with what we and many others have posited for decades (Apple, 1987; Giroux, 1988; Popkewitz, 1991). Our image is also consistent with provocative new conceptualizations that attend, for example, to the global cosmopolitan teacher (Luke, 2004), to the need for "deliberative pedagogies" in the service of democratic education (Simon, 2005), and to the importance of teachers as public intellectuals in the current conservative era where teaching is increasingly controlled (Apple, 2006). We are arguing throughout this book that embracing this more transformative view of teaching means that teachers at all levels, of all subjects, take *an inquiry stance* on practice. We need teachers who do research about their own work, teachers who assume roles as co-constructors of knowledge and creators of curriculum. Now more than ever we need teachers who assume a teacher identity that entails becoming theorizers, activists, and school leaders. In contrast to the limiting and even atrophied images of teachers promulgated through NCLB, this image of practice encompasses expanded responsibilities to children and their families, transformed relationships to teacher colleagues and other professionals in the school setting, and deeper and altered connections to communities, community organizations, and school–university partnerships.

All of these relational dimensions of teaching are central to creating the conditions for meaningful student learning. Rather than defining teaching as accountability for student scores on tests, teaching, from this perspective, requires a more complex and deeper understanding of what it means to be educated. This different stance requires a parallel shift in professional development, so that teachers have access to many resources but do not relinquish their prerogatives to generate knowledge from their own practice and to make reasoned choices among alternatives. There are critical relationships between teacher learning and student learning. When teachers learn differently, students learn differently; when teachers at all levels of experience are encouraged to ask questions, their students are more likely to find themselves in classrooms where their own questions, not rote answers, signal active and consequential engagement with ideas. In our troubled democracy, there is no more significant outcome for educational institutions, and we cannot afford to cultivate an image of teachers and teaching that promises less.

Chapter Four

Constructive Disruption: Practitioner Research and University Culture

As we have suggested throughout this book, for more than 2 decades, we have been among those who have attempted to theorize teacher research and other forms of inquiry that contribute to the current practitioner research movement. At the same time, we have worked with others to develop inquiry–centered projects, programs, and assessments related to teacher education, teacher development, educational leadership, and school reform. Over the years, in many of our articles and chapters about practitioner inquiry and the practitioner research movement, and in our earlier book, *Inside/Outside* (Cochran-Smith & Lytle, 1993), we have argued that, when taken seriously, practitioner research represents a radical challenge not only to the cultures of schools and other educational contexts but also to the cultures of universities. Along these lines, we have asserted that when practitioners do research, they dramatically realign their relationships to the brokers of knowledge and power not only in schools but also in universities. We have also argued that the transformation of schools and programs into centers for inquiry has far-reaching implications for, and indeed requires, the parallel and reciprocal transformation of universities. And we have criticized the long-standing tendency of those who work at universities to call for school transformation without parallel self-examination and restructuring.

Despite all our claims and critiques, however, we have seldom written explicitly—from the perspective of our own experiences at research universities—about how the larger project of practitioner research changes both the people who do it and, to a certain extent, the institutions where they work. Although there is now a substantial literature about the role of practitioner research in schools and in school–university partnerships, there is very little that focuses on the university, particularly on the contradictions that are generated when practitioner research brushes up against, and sometimes collides with, what has traditionally been valued and rewarded in university culture. In this chapter, our purpose is to explore what it has meant over more than 2 decades for us to take seriously and try to live by the premises that are central to the project of practitioner research while simultaneously working within the cultures of large research universities.

In a number of ways, this chapter is different from the other chapters in Part I of this book. This chapter looks inward at the culture of universities, as opposed to focusing on the broader national and international contexts in which practitioner research is thriving or on K–12 schools and other educational settings that are outside of the university context. In and of itself, this posture is somewhat unusual. Wisniewski (2000) suggests, for example, that the literature on higher education, including much of the rhetoric about innovative and exciting campus directions, conveys the impression that "academic change is rampant." Wisniewski asserts that this is not the case and that, to the contrary, "organizational gridlock" (p. 5) with very limited genuine change is a more accurate description of the culture of universities. In light of this, Wisniewski calls for studies of change in the academy, which, although sorely needed, are avoided by most university researchers, who prefer to "direct their gaze" at K–12 school change rather than at their own settings and interactions with students, administrators, and colleagues.

A second way this chapter departs somewhat from the others in the book is that it shifts slightly in style and voice and is more autobiographical in nature. In this chapter, we draw on our own experiences at universities to explore and illustrate a process we call "working the dialectic" of inquiry and practice within the culture of research universities, which is different in many ways from the cultures of K–12 schools and other educational settings. Finally, this chapter is more about raising questions than positing answers or putting forward assertions. In particular, we have tried to problematize our own experiences to raise questions about university expectations and norms for research, teaching, and service and the potential of practitioner research to disrupt these—constructively.

We begin this chapter by tracing the roots of our interest in practitioner research and explaining what we mean by "working the dialectic." Then we turn to six dimensions of university culture that are to a certain extent disrupted when we take seriously the premises and assumptions of practitioner research. We loosely group these six under two broad headings, one related to research and the other related to teaching. Taken together, and in relation to the connections of both research and teaching to service, these speak to many of the intersections, divides, and enduring epistemological, methodological, and ethical issues related to professional work within the culture of research universities.

TRACING OUR ROOTS

We trace our emerging interest in practitioner research to the early and mid-1980s and to our increasing dissatisfaction with business as usual at the university. Like many university-based practitioners and researchers at the time, we were deeply concerned about the significant disparities in the distribution of educational opportunities, resources, achievement, and positive outcomes between minority and/or low-income students and their White, middle-class counterparts. But we were also concerned about the way practitioners were being positioned in the discourse about teacher education and professional development and with the way university-generated knowledge was assumed to encompass everything there was to know about teachers, teaching, and reforming the schools.

Innovative Programs as Strategic Research Sites

During this time, we worked closely with new and experienced urban teachers at the University of Pennsylvania to develop innovative preservice and professional development projects and programs, particularly the preservice program Project START (Student Teachers as Researching Teachers), which existed at Penn for more than a decade, and the school–university collaborative PhilWP (the Philadelphia Writing Project), an urban site of the National Writing Project, which continues. Throughout all our time working at research universities, we have never been solely practitioners or solely researchers. Rather, we see ourselves as negotiating the borders of educational practice and scholarship by wrestling with the daily dilemmas of practice and simultaneously theorizing the emerging domain of practitioner research.

We regarded all of the projects in which we were involved as strategic sites for both research and practice, in particular for rethinking fundamental assumptions about the intellectual activity of teaching and for reconstructing practice as inquiry across the professional life span. In the beginning, it was our close work with teachers that heightened our awareness of the gap between university discourse and the reality of daily life in schools and made us reject the claim that those located at universities or external research agencies could be the primary agents of enduring change inside schools and classrooms. Early on we realized that external researchers were not the only actors who had developed critical perspectives about the social and political arrangements of schools and schooling. On the contrary, we found many of the urban practitioners with whom we were collaborating (including members of the Philadelphia Teachers Learning Cooperative, Teacher Educators for Social Responsibility, and those who had worked with Patricia Carini and others at the Prospect School and the North Dakota Study Group) had for many years been researching their work with students and linking this to practice-based critical perspectives on the larger sociopolitical contexts of school and society.

Jointly with these and many other teachers, student teachers, teacher educators, and school leaders, we used practitioner research as a way to rethink practice, question our own assumptions, and challenge the status quo—not only in the schools and other sites of professional practice but also in the university. Over time we came to use the term *teacher research*, and a bit later the more inclusive terms *practitioner research* and *practitioner inquiry*, as a kind of shorthand for a larger set of premises, briefly listed here but also mentioned in the Preface and elaborated in Chapter 5. Although practitioner research is certainly not a monolith, as we make very clear in Chapters 1 and 2, the following premises are central to the larger enterprise: Practitioners are legitimate knowers and knowledge generators, not just implementers of others' knowledge; school–university relationships are (or ought to be) reciprocal and symbiotic, not unilateral or top-down; educational practice is relational, theoretical, and political as well as practical—it is not simply a technical or instrumental activity; variously configured inquiry communities have the potential to be the central contexts in which practitioners learn and the major sites for imagining and enacting change over the course of the professional career; schooling is a deeply cultural, political, and historical process that tends to reinforce existing structures of power and privilege and construct inequitable learning opportunities and life chances for students; and practitioner research—understood as a stance, rather than an individual project—has the potential to shape an activist agenda and thus be part of larger social movements for school reform, societal change, and social justice that directly confront and are intended to change existing structures and opportunities.

Working at the Intersection of Two Worlds

Although the inception of Project START and PhilWP in 1985–1986 was central to the genesis of our interest in practitioner research, we actually trace the roots of this interest to a time long before then. Both of us began our work at the university having been K–12 teachers, and then we served as part-time instructors, supervisors of student teachers, and lecturers for a number of years at the university. Later, after we had completed our doctorates at Penn in the early 1980s, we continued as lecturers or adjunct faculty until we eventually obtained tenure-track assistant professor positions at the university.

Throughout this time, we were actively involved in all aspects of the academic programs at the university and also engaged in scholarly and professional work, both before and after we were "officially" faculty members. Despite the important opportunities these positions gave us to teach and to learn, it is also clear that, like many women who worked directly with teachers at research universities at this point in time historically, we were to a certain extent marginalized as members of the faculty in the early years of this work. Because of our close association with teachers and student teachers, we were identified more with practitioner-oriented issues than with "real" research. This was the case in part because at many schools of education at research universities during the early 1980s, an individual's status roughly mapped to her closeness to or distance from the daily practice of schools and other educational programs. This kind of hierarchy distinguished those who "did social science" (i.e., they engaged in scholarship about education broadly construed and/or closely identified with the concerns of a particular discipline, such as psychology, history, or economics) from those who identified themselves as both practitioners and scholars who were working directly in the field of education (i.e., they were involved primarily in teacher education, professional development, school leadership, or other work that focused directly on teaching, learning, and schooling).

In retrospect, we realize that our unwillingness to privilege either scholarship or practice in those early years also pushed us to try to construct a critical integration that connected our more grassroots work with teachers and other practitioners to our teaching and research at the university. This desire to locate our work at the intersection of two worlds deeply informed and continuously called into question our perspectives on collaboration and power, voice and representation, culture and difference, the purposes of teaching and teacher education in terms of social change and social justice, and the interrelationships of inquiry, knowledge, and practice.

Interestingly, part of the reason we were able to work at the intersection of these two worlds even though we were at a major research university was the relatively small size of our programs in preservice teacher education and in reading, writing, and literacy. In addition, in those early days, both of us had a great deal of autonomy and what we now realize were unusually rich opportunities to invent new program structures, imagine new relationships with school-based colleagues, and figure out how to make our projects sites for critical inquiry. Commenting on our apparent freedom to pursue these ideas, a colleague from another university once pointed out that during this time, many administrators and faculty at the university appeared for the most part "mercifully uninterested" in what was going on in our programs, even though we were by then writing about them and beginning to draw attention to the political dimensions of this work as going "against the grain" of common practice and being "risky business" in the world of schools (Cochran-Smith, 1991; Lytle, 1993).

Shifting Viewpoints about Teachers and Research

Our early ideas about teacher research were consistent with the emerging view of the teacher as knower and researcher that was part of the paradigm shift in researching, teaching, and assessing writing that evolved during the 1970s and 1980s (e.g., Atwell, 1987; Berthoff, 1987; Bissex & Bullock, 1987; Goswami & Stillman, 1987; Heath, 1983; Mohr & MacLean, 1987; Myers, 1985; Wells, 1986). At roughly the same time, in critical and democratic social theory, there was an emerging focus on the role of teachers in research conceptualized as a form of social change (e.g., Beyer, 1988; Carr & Kemmis, 1986; Elliot, 1985; Kemmis & McTaggart, 1988; McNiff, 1986; Stenhouse, 1983; Stenhouse in Rudduck, 1985). These ideas were also in sync with the growing interest at Penn's Graduate School of Education in ethnographic and qualitative research. Beginning in the mid-1970s, the University of Pennsylvania was at the forefront of exploring and fostering ethnographic research as a legitimate mode of inquiry into educational problems and issues. Led over the years by well-known researchers from anthropology, linguistics, and literacy, including Dell Hymes, David Smith, Shirley Heath, Frederick Erickson, Bambi Schieffelin, and Nancy Hornberger, Penn was among the first to offer an array of courses in ethnographic and qualitative research methodology and to permit and indeed encourage doctoral dissertations that relied on these approaches to data collection and analysis. Much of this work examined the cultures of schools and classrooms and attempted to represent educators' knowledge from their own perspectives inside schools; it also explored and began to unpack many inequities in the structures, opportunities, and outcomes of teaching, learning, and schooling for various groups and subgroups of students, based on race and culture as well as socioeconomic, linguistic, and experiential backgrounds.

Efforts of this kind were intensified and made public via the university's Ethnography in Education Research Forum, which began in the late 1970s and continues annually. This conference, which we participated in from the beginning, has been known over time for promoting conversations about ethnographic and qualitative research among an unusually wide range of participants—local, national, and international—including graduate students, school- and program-based teachers and administrators, and university faculty. Ours and many others' ideas about practitioner research were first made public at "Teacher Research Day," a special event we initiated with teachers and student teachers at the Forum in 1986. Since that time, what is now informally known as "Practitioner Research Day" has attracted practitioner researchers and inquiry communities locally and from around the world as well as featured speakers who help to conceptualize and disseminate the notion of practitioner research as a mode for knowledge generation, professional development, and activism for school and social change. As collaborators and co-authors, we used the Forum as a context for sharing our emerging ideas about what it means to make inquiry central to teaching, learning to teach, and leadership in schools and other educational settings. From 1987 through 1997, we had the privilege of presenting almost a dozen keynote talks that introduced Teacher Research Day by positing conceptual frameworks at once firmly rooted in our ongoing projects and programs and also intended to suggest generative questions and issues for the larger field. Over these same years, our student teachers and our school- and program-based teacher and administrator colleagues also presented their work at the Forum and at a growing number of regional and national conferences related to teacher education, language and literacy, leadership and urban education. Much of this work was published in a variety of forms in educational journals, professional newsletters, and in-house publications, and some of it eventually became part of the text for *Inside/Outside* (Cochran-Smith & Lytle, 1993).

Together and separately, for teachers, administrators, student teachers, school leaders, and university faculty, engaging in research on our own practice (broadly construed) became the central way of knowing for the growing inquiry community in the Philadelphia area. In 1996, our paths as university colleagues diverged somewhat, as Cochran-Smith went to Boston College to direct the doctoral program in Curriculum and Instruction and lead the university's programs in teacher education, and Lytle remained at Penn to continue to direct PhilWP as well as the Reading, Writing and Literacy program and eventually to chair the Language and Literacy in Education Division. During the next decade, both of us did research, taught courses, served as editors, took on leadership roles in education nationally and internationally, and collaborated with many different co-authors to explore a wide range of topics related to teaching and teacher education research, policy and practice, professional development, urban school leadership, literacy and language, and teacher development.

Throughout this time, we also continued to collaborate with each other to analyze and theorize many aspects of practitioner research, including the various relationships of inquiry, knowledge, and practice that are implicit or explicit in teacher development initiatives and policies; trends in the practitioner research movement within the context of the emerging accountability era; practitioner researcher as a way to identify and challenge school and social inequities; the notion of inquiry as stance on teaching, learning, and schooling; the ethical dilemmas involved in fostering and engaging in practitioner research; the construct of practitioner research as an umbrella term for multiple genres and variations of inquiry that share key features and challenge traditional assumptions about knowers, knowledge and research; the contradictions and potential of practitioner research in the context of the university; the purposes and ends of practitioner research as professional development, knowledge generation, and, especially, school and social change that challenges the status quo, in particular current definitions of educational accountability and responsibility; critiques of practitioner research; and the epistemological status of knowledge generated by practitioners. (Many of these topics are further analyzed in the chapters of this book.)

WORKING THE DIALECTIC

As noted above, there were multiple traditions that influenced the development of the current practitioner research movement. All of these had in common a construction of the teacher as knower and agent in the classroom and in larger educational contexts. They also had in common a critique of prevailing concepts of the teacher as technician, consumer, receiver, transmitter, and implementer of other people's knowledge as well as a critique of many of the prevailing social and political arrangements of schools and schooling that reinforce existing systems of power, privilege, and inequity. Although practitioner research has been influenced by several theories and intellectual movements, as we noted in Chapter 2, we see it as a theoretical hybrid grounded more deeply in the dialectic of critical inquiry and practice than in one particular theoretical tradition or framework.

The Dialectic of Inquiry and Practice

For many years now, we have endeavored to theorize and take seriously the concept of practitioner research (along with its underlying premises about knowledge, teaching, schooling, and power) and to instantiate and act on those premises in our daily university work as well as in various partnerships and collaborative contexts in K–12 schools and in community-based settings. We think of these efforts collectively as "working the dialectic." (See Figure 4.1.) Here the term *dialectic* refers to the tensions and presumed contradictions between a number of key ideas and issues that have to do with research,

Figure 4.1. Practitioner Research and University Culture: Dimensions

WORKING THE DIALECTIC OF INQUIRY AND PRACTICE   (capitalizing on the tensions between research and practice, researcher and practitioner, conceptual and empirical research, local and public knowledge)

RECOUNTING RESEARCH (rethinking what counts as research)	**RECASTING TEACHING** (reinventing university courses and programs)
Professional Work as Research Site (blurring the boundaries among research, teaching, and service)	**Inquiry as Pedagogy, Pedagogy as Inquiry** (generating and investigating questions)
Researching and Writing with Teachers and Others (exploring the tensions of collaboration and critique)	**Inquiry as Content** (collaboratively constructing knowledge)
Practitioner Research as Dissertation (questioning knowledge generation and use, school–university power relationships)	**Inquiry as Outcome** (developing and working from an inquiry-based worldview on educational problems and issues)

practice, and knowledge. The first, and perhaps most important of these, is the assumed dichotomy between research and practice; the second is the twin of the first—the assumed disjuncture between the role of the researcher and the role of the practitioner. When research and practice are assumed to be dichotomous, then analysis, inquiry, and theorizing are understood to be part and parcel of the world of research, while action, experience, and doing are considered integral to the world of practice.

In contrast, practitioner research is defined, at least in part, by turning these dichotomies on their heads. With practitioner research, the borders between inquiry and practice are crossed, and the boundaries between being a researcher and being a practitioner are blurred. Instead of being regarded as oppositional constructs, then, inquiry and practice are assumed to be related to each other in terms of productive and generative tensions. From this perspective, inquiry and practice are understood to have a reciprocal, recursive, and symbiotic relationship, and it is assumed that it is not only possible, but indeed beneficial, to take on simultaneously the roles of both researcher and practitioner. This means that when university- or school-based educators "work the dialectic" of inquiry and practice, there are not distinct moments when they are only researchers or only practitioners. Rather, these activities and roles are integrated and dynamic.

A third dialectic that is integral to the notion of practitioner research is a challenge to the assumption that conceptual research in education is something that is quite distinct from empirical research in education, with the former presumably based on theory and logic and the latter based on evidence and data. Practitioner research challenges—and intentionally muddies—this distinction. The research carried out by practitioner researchers does not fit neatly into the categories of either solely empirical or solely conceptual research; instead, it is best understood as a hybrid based on the dialectic of the two. To be sure, some practitioner research leans more toward the conceptual, and some leans more toward the empirical. But by definition, practitioner research is grounded in the identification and empirical documentation of the daily dilemmas and contradictions of practice, which then become grist for the development of new conceptual frameworks and theories. In turn, these new distinctions and concepts guide new understandings and improvements in practice in the local site, as well as more broadly. The result is an epistemological hybrid, which is perhaps best represented by a new hyphenated label that describes this research—conceptual-empirical inquiry or empirical-conceptual inquiry.

Finally, practitioner research bumps up against the assumed distinction between local knowledge, which is often devalued because of its allegedly parochial and limited use, and some other kind of knowledge, sometimes labeled "formal," which is presumed to be more generalizable, more widely usable, and more broadly or publicly applicable. To be sure, practitioner research is usually prompted by questions and issues that arise from a local context, and it is indeed intended to generate knowledge that is useful locally. However, from the perspective we take here, practitioner research generates what we have called "local knowledge of practice" (Cochran-Smith & Lytle, 1999b) that is intended to influence local action but also includes interpretive frameworks and theories of practice that are useful and usable in other contexts. Our perspective on local knowledge is somewhat different from some other descriptions of practitioner research, particularly action research (Noffke, 1997), which explicitly state that the end goal is local action, not knowledge production. Our notion of local knowledge of practice challenges the view of knowledge production as something disembodied from the knower and the context and therefore untenable.

We argue instead that the interpretive frameworks, conceptions, theories, and strategies generated by practitioner researchers in one local context are often pertinent to the work of educators working in other local contexts. (These ideas are elaborated in Chapter 5.)

The Dialectic and University Culture

When we refer to "working" the dialectic, we mean capitalizing on, learning from, and mining the dialectic described above as a particularly rich resource for the generation of new knowledge. Clearly, this occurs when we study and theorize our practice as university-based faculty members and teacher educators. But in addition to this, in our teaching and in our efforts to evaluate programs, we also highlight and learn from the work of those who have engaged in practitioner research. Thus, for example, in the construction of reading lists for courses or in synthesizing research on particular topics for scholarly publications, we recognize practitioners as legitimate knowledge generators and thus feature in our reviews the inquiries of school-based practitioners and university-based teacher educators. We also "work" the dialectic by collaborating with others to support and learn from the inquiries of student teachers, new and experienced school-based teachers and administrators, university-based fieldwork supervisors, mentors and teacher educators, community program–based educators, and many other educational colleagues and collaborators.

In our case, as university-based faculty members, working the dialectic has been an especially productive way to invent and direct teacher education, professional development, and leadership projects and, at the same time, to theorize and analyze many aspects of those projects. Based on this work, we have tried to theorize practitioner research through a series of empirical-conceptual essays presented and published over a period of 20 years. In each essay we have written about practitioner research, we have addressed a particular question or set of questions that were problematic in our daily work as teachers, teacher educators, and researchers. Thus, in a very real sense, the contradictions in our own practice have oriented our research just as much as our reading of the wider literature related to teacher learning, inquiry, school leadership, language and literacy, social justice, research methodology, and many other topics has. In this sense, we have been working the dialectic in our scholarly publications by writing in what we think of as an intentionally hybrid genre that blurs the conceptual and the empirical.

At the same time, the distinctions we have made in our writing have provided new lenses on our practice and on our interpretation of the literature. For example, an early essay we wrote on the multiple genres of teacher research grew out of our extensive reading of the varied forms in which teachers wrote about their daily work and also out of our participation with teachers in a range of written and oral documentary processes. These experiences contributed to our growing discontent with the assumption that research by school-based teachers should be expected to follow the conventions of method and presentation developed in the university. The conceptual framework we developed based on these experiences in turn influenced us to formalize and rethink the kinds of inquiry opportunities available in our programs and projects. A second example is from years later when we wrote a conceptual-empirical essay on the ethics of practitioner research. This was prompted by our many complicated dealings with institutional review boards and by our analysis of the issues that had emerged over time dealing with the process of informed consent. These experiences, as well as our reading of the literature on research ethics, heightened the significance of the fact that with practitioner research, practitioners are clearly not the objects of study carried out by someone else outside of the research site, although this is implicitly assumed in the regulations governing human subjects research. We discuss this more fully in the next section of this chapter.

It is important to point out that working the dialectic is a decidedly nonlinear process. Rather, in our own work, as we theorized the relationships of inquiry, knowledge, and practice based on critical analysis of others' work as well as systematic inquiry into our own practice, we saw many ways to reinvent practice, which prompted further nuances in our theoretical frameworks and posed new questions to analyze. These, in turn, suggested new approaches to practice as well as revised interpretive frameworks and questions. Over the years, working the dialectic changed our work, changed who we are, changed what we do and how we do it. We believe that inquiry changes the people who do it, and for us, in our location at the university, it also challenges—or "constructively disrupts," as we suggest in the remainder of this chapter—many of the formal and informal rules universities live by. It has been our experience that taking practitioner research seriously at the university creates issues and tensions that are at once disruptive and productive. These have to do with dilemmas and contradictions about positions and relationships, about research conventions and practices, and about the broader meanings of scholarly activity. At times, this can make working within the university context difficult; however, it can also be generative—suggesting new questions and prompting further critique about school–university relationships. We take up a number of these issues in the remainder of this chapter.

DISRUPTING UNIVERSITY CULTURE

Schools of education at universities have long been under fire for their historical efforts to distance themselves from issues of practice while garnering academic respectability by imitating the standards and paradigms of the arts and sciences (e.g., Clifford & Guthrie, 1988; Cunningham, 2008; Judge, 1982; Shen, 1999). This has resulted in the persistent dominance of paradigms and programs that elevate basic over applied research and research over teaching and service. This critique is not unique to schools of education and educational research; it extends to broader critiques of social science as disconnected from the real problems of the social world (Reason & Rowan, 1981; Sherman & Torbert, 2000). Along these lines, for example, anthropologists Greenwood and Levin (2007) claim that current social science research practices undermine the possibility that universities can fulfill their socially meaningful missions.

Fortunately, however, over the last 20 years, there have been a number of productive (and sometimes controversial) efforts by people in education and in the arts and social sciences to rethink and redo the work of universities, particularly in relation to the communities in which they are located. Many differently positioned university-based faculty members and administrators have been working with many school-based and other educational colleagues to imagine different relationships among inquiry, knowledge, and practice, and to reconsider what the contributions of universities should be to real-world educational and social problems. This has resulted in provocative and innovative projects that link schools and universities in new ways, such as university-assisted schools, courses and programs that infuse academic learning with service learning in the community, professional development schools and centers for pedagogy, national and international networks linking scholars and practitioners, efforts to redefine the EdD degree in education as a practice-centered scholarly degree, and ongoing debates about ways of knowing and the role of practitioners' knowledge in educational research and scholarship. Although different, all of these projects and innovations disrupt (or attempt to disrupt) certain aspects of university culture and interrupt (or attempt to interrupt) traditional assumptions about knowledge, learning, and communities that segregate the university world from the broader world of social and educational problems. They have in common a critique of traditional academic ways of knowing that have failed to change and, some would argue, have even contributed to enduring social problems and to the overall failure of the educational system to serve large segments of the population. In contrast with initiatives like those mentioned above, scholars and their many colleagues and partners are actively involved in inventing and using more transformative ways of knowing that are capable of challenging common school practice and policy, as well as developing new approaches grounded in the sociocultural and historical experiences of individuals and groups. In a general sense, practitioner research is located within the context of these broader intellectual and social movements, and it is part of larger efforts to reconceptualize the ways we conduct and represent research for, with, and about teaching, learning, and schooling.

There are multiple, complex, and inevitable tensions endemic to interrupting the historical relations of knowledge and power between schools and universities. In the remainder of this chapter, we scrutinize some of these tensions by exploring what it has meant for us to work within the cultures of research universities while also taking seriously the central premises of practitioner research. We group these tensions into two broad categories that address research and teaching, arguably the two central activities engaged in by university-based educators, both of which are connected to what most universities label "service." The first of these we refer to as "recounting research" and the second, "recasting teaching."

Recounting Research

Research and publication are clearly at the heart of the work of university faculty members, particularly at research universities. But when we take the premises of practitioner research seriously over a long period of time, many traditional aspects of research and publication are disrupted. We use the phrase *recounting research* as our heading here, intentionally invoking and intertwining the two meanings of the word *recount*—to narrate or tell the story and details of something and to recalculate or tote up what is considered a legitimate member of a category. In this section, we discuss what it means and what it disrupts in the culture of research universities when (1) we make our own professional work a site for research, (2) we work with teachers and other practitioners as co-authors and writing partners, and (3) we sponsor and supervise the dissertation research of graduate students who take their own schools, classrooms, and other contexts of professional education as sites for research.

Professional Work as Research Site

In Chapter 2, we suggested that with practitioner inquiry, the practitioner simultaneously takes on the role of researcher, the professional practice context functions as the site for research and the focus of study, and the boundaries between inquiry and practice and between the role of researcher and the role of practitioner are blurred. What does this mean at a research university?

As university faculty members, we have explored the complex relationships of inquiry, knowledge, and professional practice by drawing on data collected from multiple sites in two different university contexts, including preservice teacher education programs, urban professional development collaboratives, and university and/or field-based leadership programs. Working the dialectic of inquiry and practice, we have explored the ways we and our students and colleagues co-constructed knowledge; investigated issues of language, culture, and literacy; and analyzed the contexts that support inquiry communities and practitioner learning over the professional career.

Within this general program of research, we have tried to understand how teachers and other practitioners raise questions, collect classroom and school data, generate analyses and interpretations, and alter students' learning opportunities. More specifically, we have looked at how prospective teachers reconcile the issues of race, culture, and diversity with the demands of high standards, content coverage, and test-based accountability while they are initially learning to teach. We have investigated how experienced teachers understand race, culture, and diversity as dimensions of leadership in an urban school district undergoing dramatic change. We have compared the literacies of women in a university program, women in a community college, and women who are homeless in order to explore how individuals differently positioned in terms of gender and schooling construct their learning "herstories." We have traced the attempts of a large teacher education faculty group from different disciplinary and methodological backgrounds to grapple with what it means to do teacher education for social justice. We have studied the practitioner research of educational leaders to try to understand the relationships of leadership and inquiry. We have explored the characteristics of preservice and inservice courses and teacher inquiry communities as environments that support ongoing learning in the face of continuous societal and educational change. And we have explored what it means to create a "culture of evidence and inquiry" in a large teacher education program with a stated social justice agenda and a mandate to produce evidence of effectiveness.

Although many of these questions could be explored by researchers outside of their own professional contexts, we have found that something different results when one's own professional work is the research site and one's own emerging issues and dilemmas are the grist for systematic study. As noted above, when university-based faculty members intentionally work the dialectic of inquiry and practice, a hybrid genre of research emerges that braids the strands of empirical and conceptual scholarship and blurs the demarcation between research and teaching as well as teaching and service. In contrast, the university triumvirate of research, teaching, and service has long been assumed to make clear distinctions among these three as a way to parse and evaluate the productivity and overall worth of faculty at research universities.

When university instructors make a university course the site for research and when they explore how the students in that course understand the issues and co-construct meanings, they intentionally disrupt university distinctions. Does this work count as teaching or research? If it is possible that teaching and researching a course is simultaneously research *and* teaching, does that mean it counts as both, and if so, does this lead to "double counting" in the annual calculus of university productivity? On the other hand, if a university course is taught within the context of a school–university partnership and a university faculty member is a co-teacher or co-leader along with school-based colleagues, does this mean that from the university perspective, the faculty member's participation counts as teaching or as service? Taking the premises of practitioner research seriously inevitably blurs the boundaries of research, teaching, and service, and thus disrupts the culture of universities by opening these distinctions to question.

The most common—and perhaps most important—question about how efforts like these should be "counted," however, is not about double dipping or double counting. Rather, the central question within the culture of universities is whether or not this kind of scholarship counts (or should count) at all in the realm of "real" research. This question emerges because making one's professional work the site for research collides with traditional research conventions regarding the distance and objectivity of the researcher vis-à-vis the object of his or her research. Practitioner research diametrically contradicts these conventions, since there is no distance at all between the researcher and the "subjects" or "objects" of study—they are one and the same. From the perspective of practitioner inquiry, the insider status of the researcher is regarded as an asset to be capitalized on and mined, given the emic perspective, the unique insight, and the longitudinal viewpoint the researcher brings to the topic of study. None of these qualities of practitioner research are considered a limitation or a drawback of the genre any more than the outside perspective of a researcher conducting research in the context of other people's classrooms would be considered a drawback. These are simply characteristics of this genre of research.

Taking one's own professional work as the site for research also disrupts many conventional norms regarding the ethics of educational research. Indeed, some critics have suggested that "ethical practitioner research" is basically an oxymoron since a practitioner, such as a K–12 school-based classroom teacher or a university-based course instructor, could not possibly engage in research about his or her own teaching without directly or indirectly coercing students to participate (e.g., Hammack, 1997). Given that freedom from coercion is considered a seminal aspect of ethical practice when human subjects are participants in social science research, the very idea of practitioner research and the supposed conflicts of interest this poses are called into question. Many of these questions have to do with what are considered to be the proper purposes and goals of educational research and the assumed neutrality and impartiality of researchers in relation to those purposes. Practitioner research does not begin with the assumption that research purposes are neutral, nor does it assume that the good researcher is studiously agnostic about the questions or outcomes of research. Rather, it is a hallmark of much of practitioner research that the ultimate goal is challenging inequities, raising questions about the status quo, and enhancing the learning and life chances of students. Emancipatory goals like these are anathema to traditional views about research purposes, which prompts some university critics to dub practitioner inquiry as advocacy rather than research.

Researching and Writing with Teachers and Others

For many years we have focused much of our conceptual–empirical research as well as our writing and grant-getting efforts on the work we do with others in various communities of practitioner researchers. Making this work genuinely collaborative has involved the development of close and equitable working relationships with school-based practitioners and others not directly affiliated with the university, as well as with student teachers, cooperating teachers, supervisors, graduate students, and other university faculty members who are teacher education practitioners. We have also collaborated with field-based educators whose positions do not fit neatly into the usual categories. These varied relationships have made it possible to explore the design, facilitation, governance, and assessment of practitioner research–related activities at many organizational levels and across a wide range of formats.

These collaborations disrupt the culture of the university in that conversations about policies and programs become more inclusive and decisions once made unilaterally by university people are jointly negotiated. These collaborations also generate a number of tensions and contradictions. One set of tensions occurs when collaborative relationships are nested within graduate degree programs—here students are invited to "collaborate" with faculty who also grade them, and supervisors are invited to "collaborate" with faculty who also hire and fire them. Other contradictions occur in school–university partnerships where so-called collaboration may actually perpetuate existing hierarchies or, in contrast, may be interpreted by teachers as abdication of university responsibility. Still other contradictions occur in inquiry groups of teacher educators where there are marked differences in rank, status, and purpose among those at different points in their university careers. The potential for silencing and the emergence of issues of power and control come with the territory of collaboration around practitioner research.

There are particular challenges related to researching and writing with K–12 teachers and other school-based practitioners, which interrupt the norms of research and writing by university faculty. In our own co-authored writing, we have tried to theorize practitioner research by drawing on projects that involved countless other people over multiple years. Here we have built our understandings and arguments out of the work of communities and explicitly used many examples of other people's writing. In many cases, we have represented the work of local communities through our own perspectives as university-based teachers and researchers, and none of the disclaimers we have always included indicating that we were using others' words with their permission have altered the fact that we garnered much of the credit for this work in the academic community and directed much of the writing to an academic audience.

Over the years, we also frequently wrote collaboratively with many university practitioners, school-based teachers and researchers, graduate students, consultants, and others. Trying to represent complex relational work in ways that do justice to all participants and their diverse perspectives generates a number of very palpable dilemmas: How do differently positioned participants select or allocate responsibilities for facilitation, design, and documentation of the research process? What kinds of questions do practitioners raise and value, and how do these shape the collaboration and research on the collaboration? What conventions of writing, what audiences, and what modes of data collection and analysis are ultimately privileged, even when the explicit intention is not to perpetuate the dominance of the university? How do various collaborators participate in conceptualizing, drafting, revising, and editing, and what does collaboration really mean, when sometimes, in the final product, we retain for ourselves the "last word" or the shape of the "final draft"? How and when are alternatives to traditional writing and publishing venues that may align with the agendas of some participants in the collaboration more than others pursued, and by whom? When is action *without writing* the preferred outcome of a collaborative practitioner research project, and how can that be negotiated?

At the heart of many of these decisions are issues about how collaborative groups—in which we as university educators are simply members, although, in a certain sense, never simply members—negotiate priorities in purposes for writing about joint work. Even deciding what to disclose and what to obscure or omit entails very different risks and consequences for the differently positioned writers in the group. What is troubling is that as university researchers, we tend to argue for pushing boundaries and writing about unsettling subjects. But we are also much more likely to get credit for doing this and much less likely than some of our school-based colleagues to have to deal directly with the fallout of our choices.

A particularly dicey dilemma is how, when, and whether it is appropriate in our writing (when we are writing alone or when we write with other practitioners and school-based colleagues) to include examples from inquiry communities that reflect negatively on the participants, or on the group as a whole, or on the students who are being represented. There is enormous tension around critique in collaborative inquiry: Who can critique whom? When is this appropriate and when is it destructive of what are sometimes the fragile strands of collaborative relationships? Are private contexts for critique more appropriate than public ones, or do these simply force underground a discourse that could make visible the very issues the group most needs to engage? These issues around critique in writing are complexly related to the alliances and loyalties that structure our lives in both universities and schools—the culture of silence about the work of one's colleagues; the culture of social groups based on bonds of gender, race, class, and ethnicity; and the culture of seniority and experience that makes longevity in a group and sometimes age, rank, or other markers of prior status the passports for full participation for some while at the same time inhibiting others' contributions.

One final challenge in doing collaborative research and writing that disrupts university culture relates to the university's regulations for human subjects research. Sometimes it is extremely difficult, even impossible, to conceptualize the meanings of "informed consent" in ways that represent accurately the complicated relationships of participants in a collaborative research project. Because participants in these projects are in so many complicated ways both the researchers and the researched, the university's categories often do not fit: Who indeed are the "human subjects" in this research, and who signs off on whom? Who is entitled to write about whom, and who "owns" the data? How can the concept of *a priori* consent be applied to research processes that are largely evolutionary and require the building of trust over time to determine how the design, methods of data collection, and analyses and interpretation of findings will be respectfully and fairly orchestrated?

Practitioner Research as Dissertation

As we noted in our discussion about taking one's professional work as the site for research, there is a concern at research universities about whether practitioner research counts as "real" research. Advising EdD and PhD practitioner research dissertations disrupts university culture, in that it calls into question many traditional assumptions and requires that advisers and researchers negotiate relationships that differ significantly from the norm. With practitioner dissertations, it is *not* assumed that practitioners must shed their consciousness and experience as practitioners in order to assume the role of researchers. On the other hand, it *is* assumed that practitioner dissertations ought to do some meaningful work in the world of schools and classrooms. Both of these assumptions fly in the face of conventional university understandings about what it means to do a dissertation, which is arguably the central experience that socializes doctoral students into the culture of educational research and the norms of research universities.

Over time, we have supervised a considerable number of practitioner research studies, including those written by teachers, librarians, specialists, and school leaders at public and independent elementary, middle, and secondary schools; district central offices; postsecondary settings, including community colleges, college, and university programs; and community-based education and adult literacy settings. Topics have ranged from critical literacy and literature, assessment, writing, and the use of media texts to classroom control, co-teaching, academic identity, learning to teach, participatory practice, and family education. With many of these topics, issues of race, culture, language, sexual orientation, and/or religious identity have been central threads. As it becomes more common for doctoral students to embark on practitioner dissertations, new questions and dilemmas about the nature of research within and outside of the academy emerge. As we noted in Chapter 1, this is especially complex in an era when the norms for quality research have narrowed and determinations of what counts as research-based or evidence-based practice have been made primarily by those outside of the profession.

Advising practitioner research dissertations creates a thorny, albeit rich, context for interrogating some of the questions in the larger debate about the nature of research, the nature of practice, and relationships between the two: Is practitioner research "real" research? If so, what kind of research is it? Is there some unique contribution it can make to educational theory and practice? How does an altered stance on knowledge generation relate to an altered stance on practice? According to whose criteria should practitioner research be evaluated?

Many practitioner research dissertations call into question deeply entrenched assumptions about knowledge generation and use and about power relationships in school and university cultures. When practitioners do research, for example, they may dramatically realign their relationships to the brokers of knowledge and power not only in schools but also in universities. They may write about collaborative work with teachers, school leaders, families, and community members in ways that add considerably to the complexities of authorship, ownership, and authority that inhere in traditional dissertations. With the exception of Herr and Anderson's (2005) book about action research dissertations, there has been little attention in the literature to rethinking the multifaceted relationships of faculty members as mentors and research advisers to practice-based projects.

Here we want to call attention to what we have experienced as challenges, contradictions, and dilemmas in this work in our own contexts. Not only have we been receptive to developing the practitioner research genre with teachers, but we have also introduced this concept into doctoral courses and programs for mid-career educational leaders, teacher educators, and informal educational programs. The process of mentoring practitioner research dissertations has raised serious questions about expectations for dissertation rigor and relevance as well as issues about accountability and epistemology. These include questions about "the significance" of practitioner studies, which is often established as a consequence of the research process rather than fully predetermined at the proposal stage; the emergent and contextual nature of practitioners' research questions and methods, which reflect their legacies and positionalities as well as their personal, professional, and institutional commitments; the stated purpose of practitioner dissertations as the generation of local and public knowledge, which feeds back into the system as the practitioner advocates for change among multiple audiences; and the relationship of the research to ways of knowing in classroom, school, and community contexts. As we have evolved our own pedagogies for advising practitioner dissertations, we have been conscious of doing so in the context of our institutions' (and the field's) standards and expectations. But we have also been continuously instructed by practitioners' interpretations of those standards and the possibilities they see for change.

We have found that a central dimension of advising practitioner dissertations is listening to the practitioner and being aware that this work disrupts and reinvents certain traditional practices. The impulse to "trouble" what is expected and to challenge what is required by dissertations has been a consistent feature of most of the dissertation work we have done with practitioners. In a certain sense, it is not really surprising that doctoral students (and their dissertation advisers) struggle with some of the expectations of university culture. This happens not because practitioners resist change or socialization into a new environment but because they bring strong commitments to their own epistemologies and beliefs about what it means inside and outside the university to do research about practice.

Over the years, we have learned that it is important not to assume that the commitments of practitioners need to be reframed or redirected in order to generate dissertations. Practitioners' questions emerge from important and immediate concerns, engagements, and commitments to their professional settings, even though these questions may not be perceived by others as significant for building knowledge in the field. Practitioners' questions may come in part from the literatures encountered in their graduate program, but their intent is not originality. Rather, as our colleague Elizabeth Cantafio expresses it, the point is to "make the familiar more familiar."

The closeness of practitioners to their data sources is often pointed out by critics as a way to question the credibility and validity of their findings. Labaree (2003), for example, calls for a corrective on myopia because practitioners are "too close" to issues of practice and need to "step back." To counter this kind of critique, feminists and others suggest that there is great value in "disciplined subjectivity" or "critical distance" or in students' "critical subjectivity" (Herr & Anderson, 2005). Interrogation of researchers' own assumptions, beliefs, values, practices, and theories of practice is essential, but figuring out the mentor's role in these processes is neither obvious nor simply transferable from one situation to another.

We see practitioner dissertations as a site of generative struggle and the mentoring process as a "pedagogy of not-knowing" (Lytle & Cantafio, 2007). This speaks to the profound reciprocity of the mentoring process, an organic relationship that intentionally disrupts the expert–novice distinction and, from its inception, displaces the hegemony of the university. Mentoring practitioner dissertations, then, becomes a form of learning that is more than paying close attention to graduate students. It involves reimagining and renegotiating both the dissertation and relationships with dissertation writers in ways that destabilize the fixed boundaries of research and practice and create spaces for radical realignment and redefinition.

Recasting Teaching

In addition to research and publication, teaching is one of the central activities of most university faculty members at research universities, although, as we noted above, it has traditionally been secondary to research. Many aspects of university teaching are disrupted when we take seriously and put into practice the central premises of practitioner research. We use the phrase *recasting teaching* as the heading for this section of the chapter. Here, as we did with the notion of *recounting research* in the previous section, we play off two meanings of the word *recast*—to change the form or shape of something and to re-create or regenerate a sense of uncertainty or doubt. We invoke these two meanings to raise questions about what it means and what it disrupts within university culture when (1) we reinvent pedagogy as inquiry, (2) we include, and sometimes privilege, practitioner inquiry as course and program content, and (3) we construct and attempt to assess inquiry as a legitimate outcome of teaching in courses, programs, and projects.

Inquiry as Pedagogy, Pedagogy as Inquiry

The central tenets of inquiry structure and inform every dimension of our work as university faculty, and nearly all of the courses, seminars, and institutes we are part of have in common posing—not just asking—questions, taking practice as a site for inquiry, interrogating one's own and others' practices and assumptions, and learning from and about practice by collecting and analyzing the data of daily work. Changing the form of our courses to intentionally and explicitly generate a sense of uncertainty disrupts university culture in that it violates some of the expectations of faculty and students about the purposes, processes, and outcomes of graduate school educational experiences. Rather than organize a course syllabus as a sequential study of topics via assigned readings and writing, reinventing pedagogy as inquiry means deliberately rethinking all of the primary assumptions about content and how it is best encountered.

Rather than examining and mastering a predetermined body of knowledge, the goal is for instructors and students to engage a range of texts in an exploratory, experiential pursuit of understandings that will by definition vary from student to student, instructor to instructor. Participants in these inquiries are assumed to bring distinctive histories/herstories, cultural and linguistic resources, and goals. There is considerable time allotted for surfacing and interrogating participants' assumptions and prior experiences with topics related to the inquiry, and assignments entail systematic and intentional ways of looking at data sources, including the data of participants' lives and writings.

Inquiry pedagogy contrasts sharply with the more impersonal and transmission-oriented pedagogy that is typical of many university courses. When pedagogy is inquiry-based, participants attempt to create respectful, intellectually challenging, and supportive relationships across race, ethnicity, gender, class, age, culture, sexual orientation, and other differences. In fact, often the intention is to mine these differences deliberately and constructively in order to yield new insights about teaching, learning, and schooling. Often, small inquiry communities within the larger class complement and extend the whole-class experience. Small groups bring to their collaborations not only oral and written responses to readings but data collected in field settings for careful description and analysis. A premise of inquiry-based courses is that rich, intellectually demanding inquiry grows out of the social practices the course helps to create.

With inquiry pedagogy, courses are structured to investigate and critique a set of overarching questions, initially established by course planners but continually renegotiated. With some courses we have taught over the years, we have included an additional layer of inquiry by working with teams of graduate students interested in studying the practice of teaching in higher education. In these instances, the course then becomes both a context for generating local knowledge and a site for revising the learning environments we create with others in courses, programs, institutes, and projects. Thus, inquiry-based pedagogy is an overarching approach to graduate education that aims to have significant impact on how practitioners envision and structure their own workplaces in the present and future.

In advanced doctoral courses with inquiry-based pedagogy, the goal is collaboratively constructing and elaborating all participants' theories about a subject. For example, one of us designed a course with the goal of expanding the notion of "theories of reading" beyond conventional definitions of reading and/or theory in academic settings. Participants in the course community read from their various locations as researchers, teachers, and graduate students and bring different perspectives related to gender, race, class, and sexual orientation. The course entails inquiry-based exploration of different kinds of texts and genres, including film, photographs, graphic and experimental novels, poetry, critical essays, academic articles and monographs, autobiographies, and digital media. It is structured so that participants read within and about various contexts, such as classrooms, schools, political and policy environments, universities, and communities, while also reading within and about a range of conversations in the field of reading.

With inquiry-based pedagogy, as with the course mentioned above, there are often common texts, but participants are also expected to conduct their own simultaneous inquiries by searching for other sources that relate to particular interests and to bring these to bear on the work of the class in ways that are integral, rather than peripheral, to the focal inquiry of the group. Rather than limit the inquiry to what is being studied in the relevant literature, participants are invited to engage the notion that knowledge can come from inquiry into the questions, issues, and contradictions arising from everyday life.

These ideas about inquiry-based pedagogy have been the bedrock of the teacher education, professional development, and other graduate programs we have been involved in creating over many years. Inquiry-based pedagogy is in many ways the antithesis of learning to teach or learning to do research by demonstrating mastery of the tools in some "certified" toolkit. Inquiry pedagogy intentionally disrupts the expert–novice expectation and challenges the assumption that the point of university courses is learning theory to be implemented in practice. Rather, a consistent theme of inquiry pedagogy is the reciprocity and interconnection of theory and practice, and the goal is to develop working theories of practice that blur the traditional distinctions. Eschewing the rhetoric of "best practices" and "what works" in teaching and research, with inquiry pedagogy, we pursue instead questions about what counts as working, where, and for whom.

The disruptions to university culture that are entailed in inquiry-based pedagogy are more or less obvious in what we have described above. However, it is essential to recognize that while this approach intentionally disrupts university culture in many ways, it also carries with it all the dangers of imposition attached to any other set of pedagogical premises. When inquiry is a primary pedagogy and a theme for graduate education programs, this perspective is in certain ways imposed as a particular way of seeing, interrogating, and approaching educational problems. There is a fine line between inviting teachers or prospective teacher educators to engage in inquiry and requiring them to do it in order to earn a degree or credit for course. There is also a fine line between collaboratively constructing an agenda within a course or inquiry community and predetermining the "syllabus" (i.e., the content, processes, and outcomes) within a framework to which one is deeply committed and which has actually been developed with a variety of groups over time, not with the particular group in a given course. The paradox here is that the inquiry-based pedagogy makes possible and informs the conversations that occur in a given course or program at the same time that it prefigures and delimits them.

Inquiry as Content

Over the years, we have integrated practitioner research into the content of the courses we teach and into the seminars and institutes we organize with others. What we assign or recommend in these contexts has changed dramatically as we have incorporated more and more published and unpublished work by practitioners from local as well as national and international settings. Treating practitioner research as content in university courses and seminars adds unique dimensions to what is known about major topics in the field of education. In the broad area of literacy, for example, we learn from practitioners' research about emergent literacy, multicultural literature, linguistic diversity, and the relationships among literacy teaching and learning and race, class, gender, and cultural differences. Incorporating a wide array of research written by practitioners across the professional life course and across institutional levels (K–12 schools, adult literacy programs, colleges, and universities) provides rich opportunities for all practitioners and those involved in educating practitioners, whether beginning or experienced, to construct and reconstruct their conceptions of practice as a social, political, and cultural act. Becoming familiar with this work is a powerful way, and perhaps the only way, to help people imagine research in a different key.

Because of the strong interest among our students, both of us have taught master's and doctoral level courses focused explicitly on practitioner research as content. These courses explore what it means for practitioners from a range of disciplines and interdisciplinary programs in education to take an inquiry stance as a framework for posing and investigating problems of practice in educational institutions such as schools and school districts, colleges and universities, public institutions of informal education, and government and community-based organizations. In paying particular attention to the frameworks practitioners bring to site-based educational inquiry, these courses provide the opportunity to study together participants' theories and knowledge of practice. The primary assignment in these courses is the design and enactment of a small-scale inquiry conducted across the semester in each individual's site of practice. By using the Internet for posting weekly writing documenting the inquiry process, the course makes explicit that each individual's research is essential content for all participants. In addition, reading each others' writing and working collaboratively to analyze each others' data sources are valued as much as reading the published literature in the field. Small groups use the documentary processes developed by Patricia Carini and her colleagues at the Prospect School to describe the data. The workings of the group also become a self-conscious site of inquiry, thus supporting the notion of collective responsibility for individual projects. The different viewpoints of participants are critical to making visible and sorting out the complex social and political relationships that are different from those of conventional research and are often conducted collaboratively with differently positioned colleagues and members of educational communities.

The literature of practitioner research is essentially a case literature made up of rich, elaborated examples of individual practitioners, groups of practitioners, and school- or site-based groups of practitioners and community members trying to understand a phenomenon, or change an existing practice, or instigate new practices. Instead of using predetermined cases generated by others to study change processes, participants in these courses have the opportunity to study where practitioners' questions come from, how they are tied to specific local contexts and cultures, and how they are taken up and to what ends. The intent of using cases as course content is not for practitioners to emulate the decisions of other practitioners (e.g., to get access to "best practices" in particular educational settings) but rather to uncover the complexity of local settings and to think *as* and *with* practitioners about how they understand and act on their investigations. In this way, local knowledge becomes public, open to scrutiny and reinvention, and the task of changing or improving practice is radically altered from the more common formulation of translating university-based theory into field-based practice. Learning to value this process within a university setting constructively disrupts university culture in that university teachers position themselves as learners, not simply teachers.

Treating practitioner research as content in teacher education and doctoral education also disrupts university culture by challenging the existence of a knowledge base for practice that has been constructed almost entirely by university-based researchers. Practitioner research legitimates practitioners' knowledge and emerging theoretical frameworks by interrogating and in many cases helping to dismantle the easy oppositions of science and craft, formal and practical, and theory and practice. Other useful tensions in this work come from disrupting the expectation that it is research conducted by university and other outside experts that certifies certain practices as evidence- or research-based practices. Focusing a course or program on uncertainties and doubts is more than simply rhetoric. It is intended to destabilize and question the "truths" that the power hierarchies of university research and policymaking institutions have promulgated without the involvement of practitioners who are the prime actors (and in some sense the local policymakers) in educational contexts.

Disrupting university culture is not the only consequence of treating practitioner research as content. There are often unintended consequences as well. Course and seminar participants who read the writing of practitioner researchers sometimes become articulate and impatient critics of university discourse and of the labored and rather inaccessible ways academics build arguments, cite each other extensively, and conclude long, expensive research studies with statements that seem obvious or self-evident. This positions university instructors in the admittedly awkward role of brokers, and sometimes apologists, for their own writing and the writing of their colleagues. An added irony is that even in courses or programs that depend heavily on practitioner research as content, some participants persist in equating whatever is enshrined in course reading lists as "theory" and thus as possibly irrelevant or inadequate for dealing with the real issues and challenges of practice. Even as university faculty who emphasize practitioner research as course content in part as a corrective to university hegemony, we also sometimes wonder whether or not we are including enough of what others would consider "the canon" of knowledge on particular topics or offering sufficient access to contrasting perspectives about critical issues in teaching, learning, leading, and schooling.

Inquiry as Outcome

Throughout this volume, there is a clear contrast between the meaning of inquiry, regarded as stance on teaching, learning, and schooling, and the much more common use of inquiry as a time- and place-bounded classroom or school research project completed within a teacher preparation or professional development program. As we have conceptualized it, inquiry stance is perspectival and conceptual—a worldview, a habit of mind, a dynamic and fluid way of knowing and being in the world of educational practice that carries across the course of the professional career—not a teacher training strategy, a sequence of steps for solving classroom or school problems, or a skill to be demonstrated by beginners to show competence.

However, we currently live in an age of accountability in which demonstrating that schools and teachers add value to students' learning by boosting annual achievement test scores has become the central driving force in K–12 education. To a lesser extent but also in a highly publicized and politicized way, accountability for educational outcomes is increasingly being emphasized at the higher education level. This is evident in a number of recent reports, most notably the report of Secretary of Education Margaret Spellings's Commission on the Future of Higher Education (U.S. Department of Education, 2006), which includes a highly controversial proposal to formalize and centralize efforts to monitor the learning outcomes of students at the nation's colleges and universities. As we suggested in Chapter 1, many aspects of the current accountability movement in K–12 schools, including its preoccupation with test-based outcomes, run counter to the premises and assumptions that are central to the practitioner research movement. What does it mean, then, to conceptualize inquiry as an outcome of university teaching in courses, programs, and projects? What aspects of university culture does this disrupt?

When inquiry is regarded as an outcome, then a goal of university teaching is producing uncertainty rather than certainty. From this perspective, teaching is intended—at least in part—to generate questions rather than answers, multiple possibilities rather than sure solutions, diverging perspectives rather than particular viewpoints. In a certain sense, of course, uncertainty and multiple questions are odd things to regard as outcomes of university teaching, especially in an age in which "what works" in educational practice is assumed to be "provable" (and, in many instances, already "proven"), and sure-fire strategies are assumed to be the ultimate goal of educational inquiry and the proper content of courses of study for educators. Constructing inquiry as an outcome runs counter to and disrupts many expectations in both K–12 schools and universities regarding the appropriate outcomes of teaching and learning.

In many school settings and collegiate teacher development or administrator programs, the competent practitioner is assumed to be self-sufficient, certain, and independent. Asking questions and being uncertain are considered inappropriate behaviors for all but the most inexperienced teachers, and once in schools, even they have only brief periods of grace during which they may ask limited numbers of questions. Practitioners are generally not encouraged to talk about classroom and school failures, ask critical questions, or openly express frustrations. Inquiring practitioners, on the other hand, are noted for their questions. They may indeed be self-sufficient, competent, and (sometimes) certain. But they also pose problems, identify discrepancies between their theories and their practices, challenge common routines, and attempt to make visible much of that which is taken for granted about teaching and learning. They often count on other practitioners and university colleagues for alternative perspectives on their work. They seek help not because they are failing but because they are learning. And they regard struggle and self-critical questioning as integral parts of their intellectual lives. Going public with questions, seeking help from colleagues, and opening up one's own practice to others go against the norms of appropriate practice in many places.

When inquiry is an outcome, it collides with many traditional aspects of university teaching. With inquiry, course assignments and summative assessments are often critical reflections, portfolios, and other formats that document students' intellectual journeys and their grappling with as well as generating new questions and issues that emerge within the context of courses that function as inquiry communities. This stands in sharp contrast to the more traditional outcomes of university teaching, such as course assignments, examinations, and research papers that demonstrate individual students' grasp of particular course material or their application of that material to particular problems or issues. With inquiry, supervision and mentoring of beginning education professionals are more likely to focus on posing questions and challenging assumptions within the context of nested inquiry groups of beginners and mentors—all of whom are regarded as learners—than they are to focus on evaluating the extent to which beginners have demonstrated "best practices" in schools and classrooms. With inquiry, program reviews and program evaluations, such as those required for state program approval or national accreditation, are likely to be organized to address authentic questions posed by people deeply involved in the day-to-day work and for which there are not *a priori* answers. This stands in marked contrast to the confirmatory approach often involved in accreditation reviews where the outcome is verification of compliance with external standards, and there is little room for asking genuine questions or exploring actual problems.

As these examples suggest, when the outcome of university teaching is conceptualized as inquiry, the emphasis is not simply the development of an open and questioning intellectual stance on teaching, learning, and schooling (although this is important), but, as importantly, working with and from that stance to approach all of the complex problems of this work. With inquiry as the outcome of university teaching, the point is not simply the development of a way to think, but the development of a way to be a professional in the world of educational practice. And finally, with inquiry as the outcome, the focus is not simply the individual student who satisfactorily completes a course by demonstrating that he or she has developed an inquiry stance. Rather, the emphasis is on the power of inquiry as the stance of practitioner communities and other groups that challenge many of the pillars of the current educational regime by radically rethinking and recasting the purposes of schooling, the meaning of accountability, and the roles of practitioners as agents in school and social change.

CONCLUSION:
PRACTITIONER RESEARCH AND UNIVERSITY CULTURE

In titling this chapter *Constructive Disruption*, we have intentionally coupled two words whose meanings are somewhat at odds—*constructive* calls to mind something carefully considered and meant to be helpful, while *disruption* connotes an unwelcome or unexpected break in a process or activity. When juxtaposed, the words convey tension and contradiction—an unwelcome interruption that is nonetheless helpful, a carefully considered but nonetheless unexpected disturbance or rupture. Of course, the appropriateness of any of these words (*interruption, rupture, disturbance, break*) and their modifiers (*unwelcome, helpful, carefully considered, unexpected*) for describing the roles and impact of practitioner research within the cultures of universities depends in the first place on one's viewpoint regarding existing knowledge hierarchies and power structures in universities and schools, the meanings of teaching and learning in university courses and programs, and the traditional values and reward structures of research universities. This also depends on where one stands on many of the most complex epistemological, methodological, and ethical issues of our time and on one's working theories of school reform and accountability.

To say that there are multiple viewpoints about these issues among those who work at research universities and in K–12 schools is at best an understatement. As this book went to press, we learned that the public schools in one major urban area had decided that teachers could not do research in their own classrooms as part of the process of getting a degree and that some area colleges and universities were falling into line with their own institutional review board (IRB) policies. At about the same time, we were told by a doctoral student that a faculty colleague had asserted that doing a dissertation based on case study or practitioner research would not only preclude the research having much value or relevance but also greatly diminish the student's chances of securing a faculty position at a research university. Along similar lines, we know that some students are routinely advised by their university instructors not to include in reviews of the literature practitioner inquiry or other research carried out in the context of the researcher's own course or classroom because it is too difficult to generalize the results and rigor is often questionable.

When these and other similar instances are considered alongside the 2 decades of experiences with practitioner inquiry at research universities that we have described in this chapter and the thriving worldwide practitioner research movement we detailed in Chapter 1, many questions emerge. Are recent prohibitions regarding practitioner research, like the ones mentioned above, isolated instances, or are they part of larger trends to circumscribe the roles of practitioners and narrow what counts as research in the larger educational community? Are our own efforts to "recount research" and "recast teaching" similar to those of others engaged in this work at research universities? How have others dealt with the inherent contradictions in the notion of constructively disrupting university culture? Why and how is this work constructive and/or disruptive across university contexts? Because so little has been written about practitioner research and university culture, cross-university comparisons are difficult, and potentially larger alliances among those with similar goals and objectives are limited. In addition, it is difficult to know who among those located at universities actually considers himself or herself a practitioner. Although the vast majority of university faculty members teach courses and are engaged in some way in the recruitment, curricular, or assessment work of various degree programs, very few university people (unless they are directly involved with practitioner research) think of themselves as practitioners, and many of the university faculty members we know are puzzled or caught off guard by the notion of university teachers "having a practice" or regarding their professional work as a potential site for inquiry.

As we noted in the section of this chapter on inquiry as outcome, the point of inquiry-centered university teaching is not simply for participants to develop an inquiry stance about teaching and schools but to develop an inquiry-centered way to operate as professionals in the world of educational practice. This same point applies to university-based scholars and practitioners as well. Constructively disrupting university culture ultimately depends on communities of university-based colleagues working in partnership with those in schools and other educational contexts to challenge the stranglehold of the current testing regime and radically rethink the purposes of schooling in a democratic society.

CHAPTER 5

Inquiry as Stance: Ways Forward

This chapter highlights "inquiry as stance" as a powerful and affirmative notion that recognizes the collective intellectual capacity of practitioners to work in alliance with others to transform teaching, learning, leading, and schooling in accordance with democratic principles and social justice goals. We theorized inquiry in the first two chapters of this book. In Chapter 1, we described practitioner inquiry as a highly variegated, but thriving worldwide movement that is represented in multiple ways. We suggested that, despite these trying times, there is strong evidence that many practitioners and other stakeholders in a wide array of contexts are engaged in the difficult struggle to democratize the knowledge and power arrangements of schooling in order to improve students' opportunities to learn and to enhance their life chances. In Chapter 2, we characterized practitioner inquiry as a research genre with multiple forms that have grown out of different historical and epistemological traditions but share a view of the practitioner as a knowledge generator and agent for change. We defined practitioner inquiry as a conceptual umbrella for the many versions, variations, hybrids, and genres of inquiry that have the following eight features in common: practitioners as researchers; assumed links among knowledge, knowers, and knowing; professional contexts as sites for study; emphasis on communities, networks, and other forms of collaboration as the central social structure that fosters and sustains inquiry; blurred boundaries between inquiry and practice; new conceptions of validity and generalizability; systematicity in terms of data collection and analysis; and efforts to make the work public and open to the critique of a larger community.

This chapter, which builds on and expands our descriptions of practitioner inquiry in the first two chapters, focuses explicitly on the book's title idea, "inquiry as stance," and on its meanings and use for the next generation. We first coined this phrase in the late 1990s. Since then, we (and others) have used it in discussions about many topics—the characteristics of teacher research and other forms of practitioner inquiry, preservice teacher education, professional development, knowledge–practice relationships, curriculum development and enactment, practitioner learning in inquiry communities, and school and social change (e.g., Cochran-Smith & Lytle, 1997, 1998, 1999a, 1999b, 2001, 2004, 2008; Dana, Silva, & Snow-Gerono, 2002; McLaughlin & Talbert, 2006; Snow-Gerono, 2005; Sperling & DiPardo, 2008; Weinbaum et al., 2004; Whitney et al., 2008). In this chapter, we extend our previous discussions about inquiry as stance by elaborating its affiliated perspectives on knowledge, practice, community, and the purposes of education in a democratic society. We conclude with a discussion of inquiry as stance as a framework for moving forward with the agenda to transform teaching, learning, leading, and schooling.

INQUIRY AS STANCE

We regard "inquiry as stance" as a grounded theory of action that positions the role of practitioners and practitioner knowledge as central to the goal of transforming teaching, learning, leading, and schooling. We see inquiry as stance as a positive thesis that goes beyond mere critique of the current educational regime and contributes to efforts to re-envision the work of practitioners in global societies. There are three sets of issues to unpack here: (1) what it means to conceptualize inquiry as stance, (2) what it means to conceptualize inquiry as stance as a theory of action grounded in the dialectic of knowing and acting, inquiry and practice, analyzing and doing, and (3) why it is critical to position practitioners and practitioner knowledge at the center of such a theory. We take up each of these issues in the sections that follow, paying relatively more attention to the first than the other two. In the next part of the chapter, we discuss specifically what it means to connect inquiry as stance to the goal of transforming teaching, learning, leading, and schooling for democratic purposes and social justice goals.

When we began to write about inquiry as stance more than a decade ago, we explained what we meant by "stance" as follows:

> The construct, inquiry as stance, is intended to offer a closer understanding of the knowledge generated in inquiry communities, how inquiry relates to practice, and what teachers learn from inquiry. In everyday language, "stance" is used to describe body postures, particularly with regard to the position of the feet, as in sports or dance, and also to describe political positions, particularly their consistency (or the lack thereof) over time. In the discourse of qualitative research, "stance" is used to make visible and problematic the various perspectives through which researchers frame their

questions, observations, and interpretations of data. In our work, we offer the term inquiry as stance to describe the positions teachers and others who work together in inquiry communities take toward knowledge and its relationships to practice. We use the metaphor of stance to suggest both orientational and positional ideas, to carry allusions to the physical placing of the body as well as to intellectual activities and perspectives over time. In this sense, the metaphor is intended to capture the ways we stand, the ways we see, and the lenses we see through. Teaching is a complex activity that occurs within webs of social, historical, cultural, and political significance. Across the life span, an inquiry stance provides a kind of grounding within the changing cultures of school reform and competing political agendas. (Cochran-Smith & Lytle, 1999b, pp. 288–289)

Although our current ideas about inquiry as stance are consistent with this statement, they are now more expansive and inclusive, and we put additional emphasis on inquiry as a collective, and not simply an individual, stance. We connect the idea of inquiry as stance to the work of a broad array of educational practitioners, and not just K–12 teachers, including school and district leaders, university- and college-based teachers and teacher educators, teaching mentors and coaches, and practitioners in community programs for adults and families. Likewise, we see the notion of inquiry as stance as pertinent to the work of practitioners in the full range of formal and informal educational settings, including schools and tertiary education, to be sure, but also including early childhood education settings, alternative teacher certification programs, museums, tutoring and family literacy projects, prison- or shelter-based educational programs, and many others.

As we noted in Chapter 4, our notion of inquiry as stance is perspectival and conceptual—a worldview, a critical habit of mind, a dynamic and fluid way of knowing and being in the world of educational practice that carries across professional careers and educational settings. Our focus on stance makes for a sharp contrast with two of the most common instantiations of inquiry in teacher development: inquiry as a time- and place-bounded classroom research project, usually completed as a requirement for a teacher preparation program and intended to demonstrate competence at "lifelong learning" or related professional skills; and inquiry as a sequence of steps or a method employed in the process of training experienced teachers to solve classroom or school problems, particularly translating test data into classroom practices intended to boost test scores. The first of these conveys the message that inquiry is something one turns off and on at given points in time and space with clearly demarcated lines between when and where one is teaching and when and where one is doing inquiry. The second positions the practitioner as a receiver of information with little or no space for questioning the ways problems are posed in the first place or for problematizing the terms and logic of the accountability frame. Neither of these conveys the idea of inquiry as a critical habit of mind that informs professional work in all its aspects.

On the other hand, our use of the language of "stance" and "perspective" should not be equated simply with being reflective or with developing an open and questioning intellectual viewpoint about practice; these are necessary, but not sufficient, aspects of an inquiry stance. When practitioners work from an inquiry stance, every site of professional practice becomes a potential site of inquiry—the elementary school reading group that meets on a daily basis, the team-teaching arrangement of a special education and a general education teacher, the middle school committee assigned to examine the curriculum in light of new state standards, the grade group and the IEP meeting, the secondary mathematics department directed to engage in more test preparation, the school committee charged with selecting new textbooks, the process of preparation for school or program accreditation, institutional deliberations about the selection and placement of students, the introduction of new and more challenging curriculum in a subject area, and the task force charged with enhancing relationships among parents, school, and community.

Fundamental to the notion of inquiry as stance is the idea that educational practice is not simply instrumental in the sense of figuring out how to get things done, but also and more importantly, it is social and political in the sense of deliberating about what to get done, why to get it done, who decides, and whose interests are served. Working from and with an inquiry stance, then, involves a continual process of making current arrangements problematic; questioning the ways knowledge and practice are constructed, evaluated, and used; and assuming that part of the work of practitioners individually and collectively is to participate in educational and social change.

The continual process of questioning and using the data of practice to investigate those questions critically and collaboratively, which is fundamental to the notion of inquiry as stance, is akin in some ways to a number of other initiatives related to inquiry-centered teacher learning that have emerged over the last decade. To mention just a few, in Gonzalez, Moll, and Amanti's (2005) seminal work on "funds of knowledge," they argued that when teachers were ethnographic researchers who investigated household knowledge and learned about their students' everyday lives, the teachers' understandings and their pedagogy were transformed. Along quite different lines, Morse and Davenport (2000) and Hammer and Schifter (2001) each described efforts to foster in teachers a "stance of inquiry" that positions teachers and students as sense makers, learners, and partners in new mathematics and science curricula. Weinbaum and colleagues (2004) suggested that collaborative inquiry turned classroom experience into teaching expertise by creating opportunities for teachers to "make sense of their experiences in the classroom, learn from those experiences, and draw upon the perspectives of colleagues to enhance their teaching and their students' learning" (p. 3).

Our notion of inquiry as stance is also consistent in a general way with action research's continual cycle of questioning, observing, and acting. According to Carr and Kemmis's (1986) now classic text, there are three conditions of action research:

> Firstly, a project takes as its subject-matter a social practice, regarding it as a form of strategic action susceptible of improvement; secondly, the project proceeds through a spiral of cycles of planning, acting, observing and reflecting, with each of these activities being systematically and self-critically implemented and interrelated; thirdly, the project involves those responsible for the practice in each of the moments of the activity, widening participation in the project gradually to include others affected by the practice, and maintaining collaborative control of the process. (pp. 165–166)

Carr and Kemmis (1986) made it clear that the essential aims of action research were the improvement of social practice and the involvement of those involved in the practice itself. As they noted, some of what "passed" for action research did not meet those criteria. This is all the more true today: The "cycle of action research" is often presented as a recipe or technique for instrumental problem solving that has little to do with what Carr and Kemmis (1986) called an "embodiment of democratic principles in research, allowing participants to influence, if not determine, the conditions of their own lives and work, and collaboratively to develop critiques of social conditions which sustain dependence, inequality or exploitation" (p. 164).

A THEORY OF ACTION GROUNDED
IN THE DIALECTIC OF KNOWING AND ACTING

This last point by Carr and Kemmis about research participants critiquing the conditions of their own lives and work is related to what we mean when we suggest that inquiry as stance can be thought of as a theory of action grounded in the dialectic of inquiry and practice. Argyris and Schön (1978) first used the phrase, "theory of action," to refer to the operating assumptions about how things work in organizations that are implicit in particular interventions intended to change things and are assumed to have the capacity to do so effectively. In many of his writings about educational change, Michael Fullan (1993, 1994, 2001) built on this idea, suggesting that successful educational change required both a "high quality" theory of action, which he explained as a theory of change that accounted for local contexts and the conditions under which the desired change occurred, as well as a "high quality" theory of learning, which he referred to as a theory of pedagogy based on assumptions about teaching, learning, and performance (Fullan, 2001, p. 187).

Along related lines, Knapp, Copland, and Swinnerton (2007) pointed out that although theories of action were not necessarily shared by all of those affected by particular educational changes, it was nearly always possible to identify and represent them as the "logic that connects the leaders' initial 'framing' of the problem, subsequent leadership actions, consequences for teaching and learning, . . . and the learning that participants do based on the results" (p. 83). In discussions about educational change, it is now fairly commonplace for the phrase "theory of action" to be used in this general sense to refer to either the assumed logic behind educational leaders' and policymakers' intended changes, or the flow of processes assumed to function as the mechanisms and levers by which particular educational changes are enacted in context, or both.

Our suggestion that inquiry as stance can be thought of as a theory of action grounded in dialectical relationships is informed by the above ideas about theories of action, but it is also different. Inquiry as stance is not a theory of action based on the logic of how leaders frame educational problems and their strategies for implementing solutions to those problems. Rather, inquiry as stance is grounded in the problems and contexts of practice in the first place and in the ways practitioners collaboratively theorize, study, and act on those problems in the best interests of the learning and life chances of students and their communities. As we discussed in Chapter 4, the assumption behind inquiry as stance is that the dialectical relationships of research (or theory) and practice, researcher and practitioner, knowing and doing, analyzing and acting, and conceptual and empirical research make for generative and productive tensions rather than dichotomies. In this same way, inquiry as stance redefines leaders as learners and thus blurs the boundaries between leaders and followers, between those framing the problems and those implementing the changes in response to those problems. In this sense, inquiry as stance conjoins theories of how to change things with theories of what needs to change and indeed assumes that these are inseparable. This means that inquiry as stance is neither a top-down nor a bottom-up theory of action, but an organic and democratic one that positions practitioners' knowledge, practitioners, and their interactions with students and other stakeholders at the center of educational transformation.

Repositioning the Collective Intellectual Capacity of Practitioners

As we suggest in previous chapters, it is now widely assumed that practitioners are the central determining factor in educational success and are the linchpin of reform. The result is that there are many reforms intended to improve the schools by improving the quality of practitioners. Unfortunately, although there are a number of promising alternatives, the primary mechanism for this has been controlling the work of practitioners through a system of close monitoring and tight public accountability along with highly qualified teacher provision that assumes that altering certification requirements (both tightening and creating easier access to credentials) will improve quality. When it comes to positioning practitioners in educational change, then, the current theory of action is a kind of palimpsest, created when new assumptions about the powerful influence of practitioners were written on top of longheld and still very discernible deficit perspectives about teachers as low-status workers and widespread scorn for the idea of teaching as a profession. This approach hinges on what we called in our earlier book an "outside–inside" perspective that locates knowledge and expertise regarding practice outside of the contexts of practice in which that knowledge is to be used. From this perspective, practitioners are positioned as important in educational reform, to be sure, but they are important by virtue of their faithful implementation and application of outside expertise, skills, and techniques.

We have already suggested that inquiry as stance is a counterhegemonic notion in the sense that it clashes with many prevailing ideas about teaching, learning, learners, diversity, knowledge, practice, expertise, evidence, school organization, and educational purposes. But inquiry as stance is not simply a strong counteractive notion that engenders critiques and arguments against the system. More importantly, inquiry as stance is a powerful, constructive notion that coincides with other initiatives and theories that recognize the collective intellectual capacity of practitioners and joins with other arguments in favor of repositioning practitioners and practitioners' collective knowledge at the center of educational transformation. The key assumption is that a core part of the knowledge and expertise necessary for transforming practice and enhancing students' learning resides in the questions, theories, and strategies generated collectively by practitioners themselves and in their joint interrogations of the knowledge, practices, and theories of others.

Our emphasis on the collective intellectual capacity of practitioner researchers stands in sharp contrast to the assumption that, given the generally weak quality of the teaching force, knowledge to improve the schools must be built into the tools and technologies practitioners are trained to use in the forms of best practices, scripted curricula, teacher-proof materials, and techniques certified by scientifically based research (Whitehurst, 2002). This approach is reminiscent of Braverman's (1974) influential argument that 20th-century progress in technological societies was being achieved by taking decision making out of the hands of workers and thus taking knowledge and skill off the shop room floor. Although Braverman's analysis was widely critiqued on many grounds (e.g., Meiksins, 1994), his larger point about the problems that come from de-skilling workers is related in a general way to our viewpoint here.

We want to argue loudly and clearly that practitioners who are deeply engaged in the work of teaching and learning know something about that work and, collectively with one another and with others, including parents and community groups, have the capacity to generate and critique knowledge, figure out how to use (or not use) knowledge generated by others, improve practice, and enhance students' life chances. The notion that those engaged in practice know something about that practice is not unrelated to the approach of those in "effective" organizations, as J. Lytle (2008) pointed out. He contrasted schools that were focused only on reaching AYP goals with corporations like Toyota that have a deep understanding of knowledge and how it is generated. Quoting Takeuchi, Osono, and Shimizu (2008), Lytle agreed that Toyota "views employees not just as pairs of hands but as knowledge workers who accumulate *chie*—the wisdom of experience—on the company's front lines. Toyota therefore invests heavily in people and organizational capabilities, and it garners ideas from everywhere: the shop floor, the office, the field" (Takeuchi, Osono, & Shimizu, 2008, p. 98). Central to the concept of inquiry as stance is the presumed potential power of collective practitioner knowledge and agency, or as Goswami and Stillman (1987) titled their book that helped launch the current iteration of the North American teacher research movement "reclaiming the classroom [by conceptualizing] teacher research as an agency for change."

CRITICAL DIMENSIONS OF INQUIRY AS STANCE

Throughout this book, we characterize inquiry as stance as a way of knowing and a grounded theory of action for educational transformation. We position inquiry as stance as both a counterhegemonic notion that challenges prevailing assumptions about practice and as an affirmative, transformative notion grounded in alternative—and, with regard to the collective capacity of practitioners, radical—viewpoints about teaching, learning, leading, and schooling. The concept of inquiry as stance permits closer understanding of knowledge–practice relationships, how inquiry produces knowledge, and what practitioners learn from inquiry within communities.

There are four central dimensions of the construct of inquiry as stance, which Figure 5.1 represents: (1) a perspective on knowledge that rejects the formal knowledge–practical knowledge dualism and instead puts forward a conception of local knowledge in global contexts; (2) an expanded view of practice as the interplay of teaching, learning, and leading, as well as an expanded view of who counts as a practitioner; (3) an understanding of practitioner communities as the primary medium or mechanism for enacting inquiry as stance as a theory of action; and (4) the position that the overarching

Figure 5.1. Inquiry as Stance.

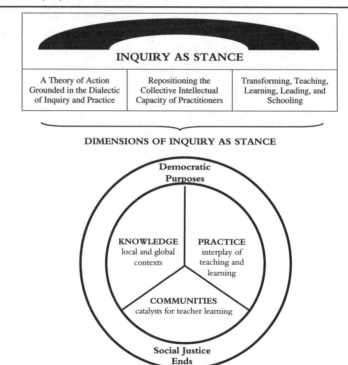

purpose of practitioner inquiry is to provide education for a more just and democratic society. We regard this fourth dimension, democratic purposes and social justice ends, as an encompassing idea that surrounds and is mutually constitutive of the others. For the sake of organizational clarity, however, we deal with each dimension one at a time.

Knowledge: Local and Global Contexts

As we have said, inquiry as stance is both a way of knowing and being in the world of educational practice and a theory of action for transforming teaching, learning, leading, and schooling. In this section on knowledge, we make clear that both of these senses of inquiry as stance are grounded in our belief in the central position of practitioners as knowers and in the transformative power of local knowledge in justice-related efforts to improve students' learning and enhance their life chances. This conception of knowledge, which intentionally turns on its head the usual knowledge hierarchy that privileges academic over local knowledge, has the potential to redefine power relationships between outside researchers and practitioners. From the perspective of local knowledge, research is an entitlement and a responsibility of practitioners who are confronted on an ongoing basis with local, but globally influenced, problems for which solutions do not already exist and questions for which answers are not already known. Although all practice is local at its heart, we argue below that local knowledge is interactive with larger, global influences and is often useful publicly beyond the local context.

The Knowledge Question. Reflecting on developments in the practitioner inquiry movement from the mid-1980s to the mid-1990s, we have argued that the most persistent issue was "the knowledge question," which involves the complex interrelationships of inquiry and knowledge for and about teaching (Cochran-Smith & Lytle, 1998). We located the knowledge question within general debates about the research enterprise writ large, debates which were prompted by emerging alternative paradigms, by postmodern/poststructuralist critiques, and, from a different perspective, by considerable dissatisfaction from those who sought to use research to chart improved policy and practice more or less directly.

The knowledge question takes two forms: Is practitioner inquiry research? and, Is what is generated by practitioner researchers knowledge? Taking up certain aspects of the first question, Hammer and Schifter (2001) pointed out that new, ambitious kinds of curriculum, particularly in mathematics and science, require new roles for practitioners that are more similar to the roles of researchers, resulting in a growing community of teachers and researchers who work "near the border between research and teaching" (p. 441). Although Hammer and Schifter clearly valued practitioners' inquiries, they concluded that practitioner inquiry was not research:

> We acknowledge that the border . . . is blurry. It is important to reiterate, moreover, that we do not suggest that teachers should not participate in research, if they are so inclined, any more than we would suggest women should not work out of the home. At the same time, we contend it is ultimately counterproductive not to acknowledge that the border between the two activities remains. (p. 475)

Over the years, many of those who have taken up the question of whether practitioner inquiry really counts as research have focused on: practitioners' adherence with the conventions of research, their "biased" perspectives inside practice, and their inability or lack of desire to abstract more general and generalizable theories and findings from their inquiries. The conclusion of these lines of reasoning is either that practitioner inquiry is not research or that practitioners cannot do research well.

The second set of questions has to do with whether practitioner inquiry generates knowledge and, if so, what kind of knowledge it is. Hiebert, Gallimore, and Stigler (2002) explored the possibility of converting practitioners' craft and case knowledge into a "trustworthy knowledge base to be shared and accessed widely" (p. 4). They contrasted practitioners' knowledge, which was detailed, concrete, specific, and in the form of examples not connected to larger theories, with professional knowledge, which was public, sharable, cumulative, and, because it was more abstract, more applicable to a variety of problems. To convert the former into the latter, Hiebert and colleagues argued that local hypotheses would need to be developed into larger theories through contact with outside expertise and controlled testing to insure that practitioners' knowledge was accurate, verifiable, continually improving, and able to be indexed by others. Here the idea is that practitioners' knowledge has the potential to be what we once called "knowledge with a capital 'K'" (Cochran-Smith & Lytle, 1990) only if it is transformed through scientific methods into something more generalizable and treated as "public object to be stored and accumulated" (Hiebert, Gallimore, & Stigler, p. 7).

A number of years before Hiebert and colleagues, Fenstermacher (1994) cautioned against coupling "teacher research" with "knowledge" as follows:

> If the exquisite complexities of knowledge claiming and justifying in the domain of TK/P [teacher knowledge/practical] are not fully appreciated

by the advocates of this genre of teacher research, an unfortunate permissiveness arises about what teachers may or may not know. (p. 41)

Despite the fact that many advocates, including ourselves (e.g., Anderson & Herr, 1999; Clandinin & Connolly, 1995; Schön, 1995), were calling for "new epistemologies" to better serve the knowledge needs of practitioners, Fenstermacher and others imposed on these new conceptions the conventions of the old, insisting that if practitioners' knowledge were to be considered *real* knowledge, then its epistemic claims needed to be "analogous to the science that yields formal knowledge" (Fenstermacher, 1994, p. 48).

Rejecting the Formal Knowledge–Practical Knowledge Distinction. Underlying both questions we have been discussing here—Is practitioner inquiry research? and, Does practitioner inquiry generate knowledge?—is the widely held assumption that there are two kinds of knowledge, formal and practical, which account for the universe of knowledge types for understanding teaching. According to Fenstermacher (1994), practical knowledge is "bounded by the situation or context in which it arises and it may or may not be capable of immediate expression in speech or writing . . . [and is] generally related to how to do things, the right place and time to do them, or how to see and interpret events related to one's actions" (p. 12). On the other hand, he said that formal knowledge is justified true belief—"gained from studies of teaching that use conventional scientific methods, quantitative and qualitative; these methods and their accompanying designs are intended to yield a commonly accepted degree of significance, validity, generalizability, and intersubjectivity" (p. 8).

Fenstermacher's characterization of the differences between formal and practical knowledge is similar to Hiebert and colleagues' distinction between professional and practitioner knowledge, on one hand, and Hammer and Schifter's distinction between research and inquiry, on the other. Many current reforms reflect these same distinctions, even if different language is used. The goal of evidence-based education (Trinder & Reynolds, 2000), for example, is to build a knowledge base of replicable interventions that have been "proven effective" through scientific methods (Coalition for Evidence Based Policy, 2002, p. 2). Although evidence-based practice is narrower than the idea of formal knowledge, both are grounded in the assumption that it is possible to generate a replicable, cumulative knowledge base to replace practitioners' knowledge, which is sometimes described pejoratively as lore, anecdote, fad, or intuition.

Knowledge and Power. In their discussion of "funds of knowledge," Gonzalez, Moll, and Amanti (2005) suggested that the "ultimate border is the border between knowledge and power" (p. 42). It is our position that the formal knowledge–practical knowledge distinction is a border that maintains the hegemony of university-generated knowledge and carries with it the same power and status differentials associated with the disconnect of basic and applied research and theory and practice. By implication, then, it is often assumed that practitioners' knowledge is low-status knowledge—bounded by the everyday, local, and particular (perhaps excessively so)—and possibly trivial. These assumptions reify divisions that keep practitioners "in their place," especially in instances when those who work from dominant epistemological and methodological paradigms use established terms, conventions, and standards to evaluate and dismiss alternative ones.

These divisions are related to what Foucault (1980) called "subjugated knowledges," that is, knowledges that are "disqualified as inadequate to their task or insufficiently elaborated" and "located low down on the hierarchy, beneath the required level of cognition of scientificity" (p. 82). Semali and Kincheloe (1999) used similar concepts to discuss issues related to indigenous knowledge and knowledge produced in the academy. In describing the relationship of the two, Semali and Kincheloe argued, "Despite their overt valorization of indigenous knowledge, western scientific archivists refuse to accept the worthiness of 'raw' indigenous knowledge. . . . [They] insist on testing its validity via western scientific testing" (p. 21).

This argument parallels almost exactly our point about the perspectives many university-based researchers take toward practitioner research and knowledge, even those who have great respect for teachers' knowledge. Although practitioner inquiry is often regarded as desirable for professional development or curriculum implementation, it is usually argued that to be worthwhile on a larger scale, "practitioner knowledge" must be transformed into "professional knowledge" through scientific methods (Hiebert, Gallimore, & Stigler, 2002) or the additional "layer of work" connecting practice to "larger issues" must be done by researchers, not practitioners (Hammer & Schifter, 2001), or that insiders' narratives must be placed "in relation to other actors and the world of ideas" by researchers who stand outside those contexts (Lampert, 2000).

In contrast to these gate-keeping statements, Appadurai (2006) used the term "the right to research" to characterize research as a special kind of entitlement connected to the "capacity to aspire—the social and cultural capacity to plan, hope, desire and achieve socially valuable goals" (p. 176). He suggested that, as globalization makes it more difficult for people with strictly local knowledge to improve their circumstances, research needs to be understood as part of what is essential for democratic citizenship.

Local Knowledge in Global Contexts. Borrowing Geertz's (1983) notion of "local knowledge" as the lens through which locals see and understand their world, we use "local knowledge of practice" to describe the knowledge practitioners generate through inquiry. With this language, we both signal a break with the formal–practical knowledge distinction, and we characterize what practitioners and communities come to know when they build knowledge collaboratively. We also assert, however, that local knowledge is often relevant and useful more publicly. Our local–public conception does not posit two kinds of knowledge analogous in any way to the distinction made between practical and formal knowledge. Rather, it is assumed that the knowledge practitioners need to practice well is generated when they treat both their own practice as the site for intentional investigation and the knowledge and theory produced by others as generative material for interrogation and interpretation. In this sense, practitioners learn when they generate local knowledge by working in inquiry communities to theorize and construct their work and to connect it to larger social, cultural, and political issues.

With the notion of local knowledge we are forwarding here, both knowledge generation and knowledge use are regarded as inherently problematic. That is, basic questions about what it means to generate knowledge, who generates it, what counts as knowledge and to whom, and how knowledge is used and evaluated in particular contexts are always open to question. However, we want to be absolutely clear that we are not suggesting that the knowledge generated by university-based researchers is of no use to practitioners. Nor are we suggesting that practitioners use roughly the same strategies as university-based researchers to add to "the knowledge base" a new body of generalizations based on their perspectives inside schools and classrooms. In other words, our assumption is *not* that what we need to solve the problems of education is a whole cadre of expert practitioners who will generate a new or supplementary kind of formal knowledge about expert practices. Rather, the idea is that through inquiry, practitioners across the professional life span make their own knowledge and practice problematic and also make problematic the knowledge generated by others. Thus they stand in a different relationship to knowledge than do those whose intention is to produce knowledge that is generalizable across all contexts.

Using the phrase local knowledge foregrounds the processes (not the products) of knowledge construction as they are expressed and integrated with daily life in schools and other educational contexts and emphasizes the link of knower to that which is known and the context in which it is known. In this sense, constructing local knowledge is understood to be a process of building, interrogating, elaborating, and critiquing conceptual frameworks that link action and problem-posing to immediate contexts. But local knowledge is always also connected to larger social, cultural, and political issues. Geertz (1979) aptly described the effort to get at local knowledge as "a continuous dialectical tacking between the most local of local detail and the most global of global structure in such a way as to bring both into view simultaneously" (p. 239).

We want to avoid exaggerating the power of local knowledge by recognizing its location in today's globalized society, where new markets, patterns of migration, and media forms have created unprecedented challenges and new conditions of cultural and social life (Appadurai, 2006; Luke, 2004). Brandt and Clinton's (2002) provocatively titled article, "Limits of the Local," is instructive here. They suggested that in rejecting autonomous models of literacy, social practice models gave too much credit to local contexts and under-theorized the material dimensions of literacy and, following Latour (1993, 1996), its "transcontextualizing" potential (p. 337). They pointed out that Latour replaced the dichotomy of local and global by acknowledging that everything was local but also asserting that local events had globalizing "tendencies and effects" (p. 6). Along these lines, Brandt and Clinton (2002) argued that literate practices were not invented or independently selected by practitioners and that literacy was not simply an outcome of local practices but a participant in them. They asserted that the new literacies paradigm had become something of an orthodoxy itself in that it "maintains its own tacit great divide—one that assumes separations between the local and the global, agency and social structure, and literacy and its technology" (p. 338).

In theorizing inquiry as stance, we want to connect, not divide, local knowledge and global contexts by recognizing that local knowledge generated by practitioners in inquiry communities is often constructed in response to national, international, and global demands that originate elsewhere and that local knowledge is often imbued with ideas, practices, and technologies created in other contexts. As it relates here to inquiry as stance, local knowledge of practice is thus both transcontextualized through the impact of outside pressures, media, and technologies, but it is also *transcontextual* in that it is often borrowed, interpreted, and reinterpreted in other local contexts. In examining the local knowledge generated by local communities, then, it is important to consider what is localizing and what is globalizing.

Practice as the Interplay of Teaching, Learning, and Leading

The second dimension of the concept of inquiry as stance is an expanded and transformative view of practice as the interplay of teaching and learning, the synergies of learning and leading, the synthesis of theorizing and acting, and the continuous reinvention of ways of connecting to and allying with colleagues, parents, and communities. From this perspective, practice is not limited to what a practitioner does or says. Rather practice encompasses students' learning as well as students', teachers', and leaders' ongoing investigations into the social, cultural, intellectual, relational, and political aspects of knowledge construction. This includes questions about what counts as learning, what learning counts, and to whom. This view of practice is more akin to the idea of praxis, in which educational practice always involves a synthesis of critical reflection and action, than it is to the technical transmission model of practice that has come to dominate both educational policy and the public imagination.

This perspective on practice is related to our previous discussion of the relationship of knowledge and practice (Cochran-Smith & Lytle, 1999). We have argued that knowledge *of* practice (as distinct from knowledge *for* practice and knowledge in practice) specifies that knowledge-generation and -use are inherently problematic and that knowledge-making is understood as a pedagogic act that is constructed in the context of use, intimately connected to the knower, and, although relevant to immediate situations, inevitably a process of theorizing. Teachers (and other practitioners) across the professional life span play a central and critical role in generating knowledge of practice by making their classrooms and school sites for inquiry, by connecting their work in schools to larger issues, and by taking a critical perspective on the theory and research of others.

The view of practice we are articulating here as a dimension of inquiry as stance is intended to be a credible, accessible, and complex alternative to the prevailing view. It is consistent with the experiences of vast numbers of practitioners and practitioner researchers whose work simply does not resonate with the linear and reductionist image ensconced in current education policy. The view of practice we are forwarding here includes the idea that pedagogies and strategies for transformative change are invented, reinvented, and continuously negotiated with learners, colleagues, and families in classrooms, schools, communities, and other educational settings. It also includes an expanded view of practitioners not only as teachers who work primarily in dialogue with learners as well as with colleagues and school leaders, but also as school leaders themselves and university-based educators who engage in dialogue about these fundamental issues with K–12 teachers, graduate students, and other faculty and staff.

Theories of Practice. In discussions of schooling, the term practice has typically been used to refer to doing, acting, carrying out, and/or performing the work of the profession. Often this term is juxtaposed with the terms theory and research to suggest both relationships and disconnections—as in the common phrases "putting theory into practice," "translating research for practice," and in the complaints that something is "too theoretical," "not practical enough," or, to the contrary, simply "practical" and even "anti-intellectual." These phrases seem to equate practice with that which is practical or useful, immediate, functional, and concerned with the everyday. From the perspective of inquiry as stance, however, neither the work of practice nor inquiry about practice is captured by the idea that practice is simply (or even mostly) practical.

Rather, practice (and thus practitioners' learning) are understood, at their center, to be about inventing and reinventing frameworks for imagining, enacting, and assessing daily work in educational settings. This notion of practice includes the ways practitioners co-construct curriculum with students by investigating experiences, drawing on cultural and linguistic resources, and integrating textual and other knowledge sources. Here, what practitioners choose to do at any given moment is understood to be informed by their more comprehensive and nuanced sense-making about a whole host of things—learners, languages, culture, race, class, gender, literacies, disciplinary content, social issues, power, institutions, neighborhoods, histories, communities, materials, texts, technologies, and pedagogies. Thus in all educational settings, practice, which is deeply contextual, relational, and interdisciplinary, is also and always theoretical and interpretive.

The inevitability of practitioners theorizing what they do is well explicated in the writing of McEwen (1991), who in turn drew on Carr's (1987) analysis of educational practice:

> Past efforts to understand the concept of practice within the field of education have tended to follow the natural sciences model in which theorizing is regarded as something distinct from the phenomena studied. In this view, practice is held to be, in itself, an atheoretical object—something theories are about rather than something that is inherently theoretical. The aim of theorizing according to the natural sciences model is to gain greater technical control over the phenomenal world. Thus, the concept of practice has become fixed in our minds as inhabiting the phenomenal world rather than the theoretical world. But to make such a division between theory and practice is to misunderstand the nature of practice. . . . By making the twin assumptions that all theory is non-practical and all practice is non-theoretical, this approach always underestimates the extent to which those engaged in educational practices have to reflect upon, and hence theorize, what, in general, they are trying to do. (pp. 13–14)

McEwen's commentary makes it clear that it is limiting to regard practice as primarily practical. As we noted, a more generative conception is the idea of "praxis," which involves a dialectical relationship between critical theorizing and action (Freire, 1970). The key idea here is that practitioners theorize all the time, negotiating between the immediacy of daily decisions and particular events and larger questions of equity and social change. Britzman (2003) described as a "lived relationship" the process of theorizing and the experience of teaching (and we would add leading), suggesting that theorizing one's own experience was "tentative and potentially transformative" (p. 65).

Our notion of "working the dialectic of inquiry and practice," which we discussed in some length in the previous chapter, is consistent with both McEwen's and Britzman's ideas about practitioners' theories of practice. As we suggested, practitioner inquiry turns on their head presumed dichotomies between inquiry and practice and between being a practitioner and being a researcher, and instead regards these as being related to one another in terms of productive and generative tensions. Along somewhat similar lines, Comber (2005) examined what it meant for teachers to work with and on theory to "disrupt and ultimately improve everyday educational practice" (p. 43). Intentionally avoiding the usual dichotomies, she pointed out that teachers' primary work was not to translate theory into practice but to "engage in assembling and working on repertoires of theories, and inventing and re-inventing continuously reflexive practices in non-linear ways" (p. 51). These ideas about the relationships between theory and practice apply not only to the work of K–12 teaching, but also to educational leaders, whether in schools, school districts, or universities.

An Expanded View of Practice. When practitioners take an inquiry stance, this transforms and expands traditional views of what counts as practice in the first place and thus what it means to be accountable for one's practice. When practitioners are regarded as activists and generators of knowledge, practice entails expanded responsibilities to students and families, transformed relationships with colleagues and other professionals in school and university settings, as well as deeper and altered connections to communities, community organizations, and school–university partnerships. Working from this expanded view means that practitioners see themselves as leaders (in and out of classrooms, schools, and universities) and as makers of knowledge. From this expanded view of practice, the walls of classrooms, schools, and other professional work sites no longer delimit practitioners' commitments nor define their responsibilities as educators. Applied particularly to teachers, this is not to suggest that an expanded view of practice results from adding teachers' activity outside classrooms to what they do inside, but rather that what goes on inside and outside of classrooms is profoundly altered when teachers redefine their work.

An expanded view of practice is compatible with a heightened sense of the possibilities of teacher leadership and of leaders' ethical responsibilities to students and their families and communities. Gill Maimon (2004), a 1st-grade teacher in Philadelphia, kept a 400-page journal to inquire into her own practice over a year's time. In the following excerpt, she wrote about her observations of children's test-taking strategies and the collision of her theories of practice as a teacher, on one hand, and the assumptions of the test-makers, on the other. This excerpt illustrates how, from an expanded view of practice, a teacher must engage in close observation and assessment of common activities like test-taking while also maintaining a lucid focus on what and how students learn:

> It is not hard to come to a conclusion that, on a test like this, the fact that the children know so much sometimes makes them appear not to know enough. A great example of a question that disadvantages good writers is this one, which asks students to complete a sentence by writing a word or words in a blank space: "My turtle_____to be alone." It seems clear that the test takers anticipate answers like, "wants" or "likes" or "hates" or even "does not want" or "does not like." From the miniscule size of the space, I can tell that they do not expect an answer like Ernest's—"My turtle *must go into the street* to be alone." In attempting to fit this entire idea into a too-small space, Ernest spells the words flawlessly, but so cramps them together that they are barely intelligible to me, one who is very familiar with his work. To a person not fluent in Ernest, I suspect that the correctness of his answer will not be recognized. Perhaps Ernest should have been more savvy and kept his answer clear and simple. If so, then I have done him a disservice, because I am teaching him to write, not to fill in blanks efficiently. (p. 270)

This example points both to the inherently uncertain nature of practice and the necessity for teachers, in these times, to maintain a stance of critical inquiry and advocacy in their work.

Maimon kept a journal to explore what it meant to live a deeper, more intellectual, and passionate life as a teacher, in part by struggling actively within and against the system. She was just as intellectually grounded in her daily interactions with her students as she was in her written accounts, perpetually thinking about what "the system" was assuming and expecting about how children learned and calibrating her own actions to mediate between those expectations and the individual needs of the children for whom she was responsible. Her ongoing questioning was her way of attending to what she wanted for her students, of having clear yet always-evolving curriculum goals for each of them, and of redesigning on a daily basis the contours of the classroom community based on what she was learning from and about the students who were actually there in front of her, rather than from some generic template for "urban first graders."

Like Maimon, many other practitioner researchers conceive of practice with full regard for all of its daunting specificity and its "unforgiving complexity" (Lamott, 1994). This produces powerful counter-narratives about practice as praxis that challenge the discourse of practitioner as technician, consumer, receiver, transmitter, and implementer of other people's knowledge. In Part II of this book, the chapters by Maimon, Harper, McPhail, Simon, and Campano also offer counter-narratives of praxis. Investigating students' linguistic and cultural resources, positionalities, strengths, and vulnerabilities, these authors ponder openly what it takes to structure appropriate learning opportunities for their students. In their accounts of the challenges in daily work, these authors provide rich, detailed analyses of the dynamics of attending to specificity and complexity in practice.

The significance of attending to complexity and specificity in practice is not unique to education. Atul Gawande (2007) has written persuasively about his life as a surgeon and public health consultant informed by the experiences of his everyday practice and his forays into the work of others in the medical profession (Lytle, 2008). In a book entitled *Better: A Surgeon's Notes on Performance*, Gawande puts forward a set of ideas about how to improve medical practice from the inside. He recounts stories of what he calls "positive deviance—the idea of building in the capability people already had rather than telling them they had to change" (p. 25). Using examples from his practice and the practice of other medical professionals from around the world, he shows what it means to believe and enact the concept that local understandings, observations, and insights can accumulate knowledge of critical importance to the challenges and problems at hand. Gawande confronts the notion of standardization of practice, pointing out that most medical researchers believe that the profession advances solely through "evidence-based medicine." From his perspective, Gawande sees that much improvement occurs by local efforts to pay attention to results and how to make them better, by generating new knowledge from the practice of medicine itself. He urges his colleagues to be more "transparent" about what they are doing, illustrating his argument with examples of deep collaborative work and medical practitioners' openness to the immediate and local parameters of the problem at hand. Similar to the conceptions of knowledge and practice that inform Mainon's work in a 1st-grade classroom, Gawande argues that medical practitioners can improve performance by using their own resources and ingenuity, laced with dedication and caring, attention to the data of everyday life, and buttressed by belief in the power of local practitioners to inquire by posing the right questions and seeking solutions in context.

As we noted, part of our expanded notion of practice is an expanded notion of practitioners. Classroom teachers, preservice teachers, school leaders, superintendents, teacher educators, professional development leaders, members of school boards, literacy program tutors, fieldwork mentors, community college, college, and university faculty and administrators, and many other educational practitioners all have "a practice," and thus can conceivably work from an inquiry stance on that practice. In his chapter in Part II, for example, Dinkins worked in his role as an assistant principal to create conversational spaces to learn from and with high school teachers about how race and racism structured and delimited equitable learning opportunities for African American students in the school. Documenting and analyzing this experience enabled Dinkins to reinterpret his roles as a leader and an advocate for students in the school community.

Relationships of Practice to Research and Policy. Just as conventional understandings of the relationships of theory and practice typically fail to capture the expanded notion of practice we are forwarding here, some current efforts to align practice with research fall short of recognizing the complexity of practice and the potential of practitioners collectively to contribute to larger understandings of teaching and learning. We contrast two discussions by educational researchers to sort out these issues and clarify our perspective on the relationship of practice to research and policy.

In recent publications intended for wide distribution in the educational community, Deborah Stipek, the Dean of the Stanford Graduate School of Education, argued that the educational community needed different strategies for "bridging the research–practice gap" (Stipek, 2007, p. 19) and revised understandings of "scientifically based practice" (Stipek, 2005, p. 33). She called for research focused on problems of practice and collaboration between researchers and practitioners. Stipek's view of practice, however, is very different from ours. Discussing the need to foster an "appetite" for research findings, Stipek (2005) wrote:

> Practitioners' decisions are based primarily on their own intuitions and experience and occasionally on advice from colleagues, principals or workshop leaders. The idea of basing decisions on research findings or even data collected at the local level is not part of the culture of teaching. (pp. 33, 44)

Although Stipek pointed out that some current initiatives focused on data-based decision-making and evidence-based practice were beginning to alter this circumstance, she argued that a change was needed in teachers' "desire to consult research and the skills to interpret it in the teaching community" (p. 33). From this standpoint, the changes needed in the organization of teachers' work had to do with time, training, and support for implementing scientific findings.

Contrary to Stipek's version of what is needed to move research into practice, we are arguing that practice-based research by practitioners has a greater likelihood of improving practice and increasing practitioners' interest in learning from research on practice done by university-based researchers. From the perspective of inquiry as stance, classroom- and school-based practitioners are regarded as researchers with important emic perspectives and highly relevant and consequential ideas about what needs to happen in particular schools and classrooms to enhance students' education. This represents a more complex interpretation of "evidence-based practice" that radically democratizes research.

A more promising perspective on practice is implicit in Huberman's (1999) examination of the influence of "sustained interactivity" between practitioners and educational researchers. He concluded that sustained encounters prompted researchers to refine and even recast their "conceptual frameworks, their methodologies, their teaching, and their modes of exchange with nonspecialists" (p. 316). He also suggested that the possibilities for powerful insights engendered by sustained interactions between researchers and practitioners might actually surpass in importance insights arising from conversations among peers in their own discourse communities. This might develop new ideas "better suited to understanding life in schools" (p. 317) and motivate desires to disseminate research in fresh ways that would lead to "the achievement of actual symmetry of power and influence between researchers and teachers" (p. 317).

Rethinking and realigning relationships of power and knowledge between practitioners and university-based researchers is part and parcel of the view of practice that underlies inquiry as stance. The potential for transforming teaching, learning, and research comes not only from achieving symmetry in power and knowledge relationships, but also from recognizing that many researchers are themselves practitioners. Many participants in the larger practitioner research movement have for many years been involved in initiatives that renegotiate the nature of collaborations and dramatically shift common assumptions about the nature of practice within and beyond schools and universities.

Communities: Catalysts for Practitioner Learning

The third dimension of our concept of inquiry as stance is community, and in particular practitioner inquiry communities as the primary medium or mechanism for enacting the theory of action we are proposing. Inquiry as stance is a theory of action not just about individuals, but rather about collectivities—pairs, groups within or across schools, face-to-face or virtual networks, graduate classes, teacher education cohorts, school–community partnership groups, and many other varieties of educational collaboratives in which practitioners work together and/or with other colleagues and stakeholders to improve the cultures of practice, enhance students' learning and life chances, and ultimately to help bring about educational and social change. The essential purposes and functions of inquiry communities are to provide rich and challenging contexts for practitioner learning over the professional life span as well as making available productive locations for linking communities of educators with larger change efforts, both nationally and internationally.

What Learning from Inquiry Means. In positing practitioner learning in communities as a central dimension of the concept of inquiry as stance, we are conscious that the last decade or so has brought considerable attention to teachers as professionals and schools as critical sites of learning for teachers as well as students. In fact, the concept of learning communities has become so common that one might well wonder what there is left to say that has not already been articulated many times over. However, what we want to suggest is that the popularity of professional learning communities has led not only to important new opportunities for some practitioners, but also to the proliferation of a new brand of highly directive, top-down initiatives that affix themselves to some concept of professional community. We are not alone in this observation. Hargreaves (2007) has made a similar point about the growing number of teacher groups studying test data at mandatory afterschool meetings. Although nearly all practitioner communities appear to be (and, indeed, intend to be) supportive of professionals' learning in certain ways, those that limit the focus and tasks of communities to what fits within a narrow accountability frame may actually contribute to the de-skilling of practitioners and may constrain participants from contributing to more encompassing educational transformation. Rather than assume that simply coming together as a group to collaborate is a good thing, we have tried to make it clear that even when described with seemingly similar language, there are many different iterations of communities. What is needed, then, is to continue a critical discourse about this work across contexts and levels of education.

The practitioner inquiry communities that are central to our concept of inquiry as stance are not convened primarily to examine assessment data from standardized tests. In the event that inquiry communities did use test data as one source of evidence, the communities that we envision here would approach the task with a very different valence. In short, we are suggesting that practitioner inquiry communities embrace a much wider, deeper, and more critical agenda than test scores or "what works." Rather, they work together to uncover, articulate, and question their own assumptions about teaching, learning, and schooling. In the process, practitioners pose problems of practice that require studying their own students, classrooms, schools, programs, colleges, universities, and communities. They collect intentionally and examine systematically a wide range of data sources including but not limited to student work. They also work collaboratively to construct and reconstruct subject matter and curriculum, to examine critically content standards and the assessments and rubrics that accompany them, to act as critically conscious readers and consumers of materials and programs, and to develop ecologically valid approaches to identifying and interpreting a range of significant educational outcomes. Contrary to the charge that advocates of practitioner research deny or disregard the value of "outsider" perspectives, most inquiry communities utilize a wide variety of resources, including but not limited to a great deal of published theory and research by academics.

When practitioners work from an inquiry stance, they often challenge practices that are fundamental to schooling, such as tracking, teacher assignment, promotion and retention policies, expectations for mentor–mentee relationships, testing and assessment, textbook selection, school–family–community relationships, leadership roles, personnel decisions, grading policies, school safety, students' participation in decision making, and relationships among student teachers, teacher education programs, and schools while also raising questions about what counts as meaningful teaching and learning in classrooms at the primary, secondary, and tertiary levels. They investigate, critique, and seek to alter cultures of collegiality; ways that school or program structures promote or undermine collaboration; norms of teacher evaluation; relationships among student teachers, teachers, and their university colleagues; and the power exercised in teacher to teacher, teacher to administrator, mentor to teacher, graduate student to faculty relationships in advising, teaching, and mentoring, not to mention the complicated dynamics of school–university partnerships.

Inquiry communities of the sort we propose here support practitioners—individually and collectively—in engaging their day-to-day work as much more than routine performance and in seeking opportunities for leadership and activism within and beyond their immediate sites of practice. Seriously taking on complex and often highly charged issues of equity and access does not occur incidentally, but rather necessitates that practitioners observe and gather data about the practices and policies of their own institutions and their consequences for children, youth, and adults. Constructing and interpreting different kinds of evidence are in themselves distributed practices, as Spillane and Miele (2007) point out, and depend on how participants are "making sense" of their local (and we would add more global) contexts. This built-in diversity in the processes and practices of practitioner communities is echoed in Westheimer's (1999) analysis of how variation reflects differences in schools' missions, underlying beliefs, and the ways these beliefs inform teachers' practice.

Purposes and Dynamics of Inquiry Communities. Over the past 2 decades or so, many school- and university-based teachers and researchers have created and sustained practitioner inquiry communities or looked closely at what goes on inside them, or both (see Cochran-Smith & Lytle, 1999b, 2004, for detailed lists of citations). These communities often involve joint participation by teachers, researchers, school leaders, and others who are differently positioned from one another and who bring distinctive kinds of knowledge and experience to bear on the collective enterprise. The key, however, is that all participants in these groups—whether beginning teachers, experienced teachers, teacher educators, facilitators, or parents—function as fellow learners and researchers. Consultants and outside speakers, as well as theory and research written from multiple perspectives, are almost always among the resources used in these groups. However, the underlying intent departs radically from simply extracting strategies from policy documents, the academic literature, or published instructional materials.

In these kinds of inquiry communities, participants learn by identifying and critiquing their own experiences, assumptions, and beliefs. Practice, in the expanded sense described above, is the primary site for inquiry. Engaging in systematic and intentional inquiry into practice entails collaboratively reconsidering what is taken for granted; challenging school, classroom, and other institutional structures; deliberating about what it means to know and what is regarded as expert knowledge; rethinking educational categories; constructing and reconstructing interpretive frameworks for making sense of information; revising and creating curricula and syllabi; and attempting to uncover the values and interests served, and not served, by the current arrangements of schooling and educating. Whether called research, inquiry, action research, or teacher research, the goal is not to produce findings, nor is it simply to analyze the results of standardized tests to identify areas for reteaching. Rather, the goal is to create access for all learners to equitable and stimulating learning opportunities; to identify levers for needed change in people, institutions, and systems; and to act in ways that respect and honor the participation of various constituencies whose lives are implicated in the educational practices and policies under consideration.

There have been a series of studies that look closely at what actually goes on inside practitioner groups, each of which provides a window on their complex dynamics. Watanabe (2006), for example, showed how unpacking the meanings of common terms such as tracking and detracking created a space for teachers to struggle with ideas about ability and intelligence that had a great deal to do with the content and consequences of their teaching. Fairbanks and LaGrone (2006) looked closely at the patterns of discourse that contributed to different iterations of collaborative knowledge construction. Little (2002, 2003, 2007) has argued that in order to theorize the importance of professional community, we need careful analyses of how these communities achieve their intended (and unintended) effects. Constructing images of classroom events through talk and the structured use of artifacts are fundamental to the work of many teacher groups. Analysis of the complexities of group interactions, as the work of Little and others reveals, is an important way to make visible how practitioner talk in communities can both foster and frustrate learning and how different structures for facilitation, participation, and organization yield different processes and outcomes.

Informed by this work, an essential part of our perspective on communities is that there are many variations across communities and many complex issues associated with what practitioners learn in these settings. When guided by facilitators' use of protocols (Little & Curry, 2008), for example, the social participation structures of inquiry communities present opportunities as well as problems. These may contribute to communities becoming what Wood (2007) referred to as "catalysts for change," on one hand, or, on the other hand, "a new infrastructure for the status quo" (p. 699). Lieberman and Miller (2008) also pointed to the challenges associated with negotiating between the contrasting cultures of schools and professional communities, as well as threats to the autonomy of groups when external expectations impinge on the community's agenda. Stokes's (2001) portrayal of the complex impacts of multiple forms of teacher inquiry over 5 years in one elementary school—embarked upon to interrupt race-based patterns of achievement—serves as a provocative reminder that the social dynamics of inquiry communities reflect competing interests and power struggles endemic to collaboration around crucial issues of practice. Finally, Blackburn, Clark, Kenney, and Smith's *Acting Out: Teachers Combating Homophobia and Becoming an Activist Community* (in press) reflects the remarkable power of teacher groups to take on critical issues they may be uniquely positioned to address.

These strong portrayals of what goes on inside communities often disclose the depth of practitioners' passionately enacted responsibility for students' learning and life chances as well as their efforts to transform policies and structures that limit access to equitable and democratic education. Dinkins's chapter and Simon's chapter in Part II of this volume each depict teacher communities grappling with elusive but significant issues of practice. Simon's chapter looks closely at the ways preservice English teachers critically interrogate the social and political contexts in which they work by grounding their own theories and concepts in the discourse of the group and the lived experiences of urban classrooms. Campano's chapter in Part II explores what happens when teachers, administrators, and researches organize in a more systematic and intentional way to enact a vision of education justice by re-imagining a curriculum that builds on the students' heritage and literacy traditions and by creating a space for writing where students can make their texts accessible to larger audiences.

Altering the Expert–Novice Framework. In practitioner inquiry communities, as we are conceptualizing them here, new collaborative relationships replace older expert–novice models of proficiency, and new multifaceted goals replace the singular pursuit of best practice. The idea of beginning and experienced teachers, school- and university-based researchers, parents and students, all working together in inquiry communities "talks back" to the current emphasis on practitioner "expertise," which implies certainty and fealty of implementation of state-of-the-art practice. The expert–novice distinction is prevalent in many professional development efforts, where it is assumed that the expert is one who knows how to implement the formal knowledge base for teaching, which has been generated by experts outside schools, while the novice is one who learns effective practices by imitating the strategies of his or her more competent colleagues or expert trainers and coaches.

The image of all practitioners as lifelong learners, on the other hand, implies tentativeness and considerations of alternatives in practice that have been finely tuned to particular and local histories, cultures, and communities. An across-the-life-course perspective on practitioner learning calls attention to the essential role of communities over time and disputes the individual, in-the-head model of practitioner learning that maintains hierarchies based on privilege and individual differences. To undertake the complicated work of creating the educational contexts needed for all students to learn, the lifelong learner model privileges intellectual, social, cultural, and intergenerational diversity among those participating in various communities. This in turn makes it possible for participants to access and value multiple perspectives and knowledges as rich resources for deliberating about problems of practice. The chapters by Mehta and Waff in Part II explore what it means to learn as a teacher through one's involvement in a range of inquiry communities across the professional life course. Mehta traces her personal, professional, and political journey, rooted in her South Asian immigrant narrative, using the concept of cultural hybridity as a lens as she recounts her experiences as a teacher and teacher researcher across time and geographic regions. Waff writes from her perspective as an African American educator who has worked as a teacher, teacher leader, and district and school leader and administrator committed to urban school reform over more than 20 years. In her chapter she creates vivid portraits of the ways inquiry communities have played a highly significant role in every aspect of her learning, teaching, and leading as a professional.

When practitioner learning is regarded as a lifelong project, there are ongoing opportunities to question and reframe even the most enduring assumptions about the relationships of teacher learning and student learning. One prominent aspect of these relationships is the complex, ongoing ways students and teachers mutually shape each others' learning and participation in educational situations. Erickson (2007) made a related point in his discussion of "proximal formative assessment" as a site where teachers perform this process interactively with their students:

> In any classroom, proximal formative assessment is continually being done from beneath as well as from above—while teachers are assessing students within the real-time, ongoing course of instruction, those students are assessing the teacher. The judgments made of the teacher—as "fair," as "caring," or as "capable"—influence the ways in which students interact with the teacher, and those interactions in turn influence how the students come to be seen through the eyes of the teacher. (p. 193)

Similar dynamics characterize the interactions of faculty and graduate students, administrators and school board members, and teacher educators and preservice teachers. Participants in inquiry communities can unpack these dynamics together and thereby learn about the contingent relationships, for example, between their own learning and students' learning, or between the meanings intended and the meanings constructed in dissertation advising conferences at the university, or the significance of talk and silence in school board meetings. When educators (and other stakeholders) come together in intentional inquiry communities or decide to inquire into their practices as members of educational groups, there is much to be gained by not reverting to traditional hierarchies of knowledge and expertise, which can shut down rather than open up possibilities for diverse perspectives on posing or solving educational problems.

Democratic Purposes and Social Justice Ends

As we noted, the fourth dimension of inquiry as stance—democratic purposes and social justice ends—surrounds and encompasses the previous three dimensions of knowledge, practice, and communities. This means

there are important ideas about the purposes and ends of practitioners working from an inquiry stance already woven into and around our discussions in
the previous sections of this chapter and in nearly all of the chapters in Parts
I and II of this book. In this section, however, we explicitly take up these
issues. We take the position that the larger purpose of drawing on the collective intellectual capacity of practitioners is that this is a necessary condition
for creating a more just and democratic society. This perspective on purposes
and ends overturns the common assumption that learning communities are
means toward the end of practitioners having better tools for producing the
nation's labor force and thus preserving its place in the global economy. But
we also reject the idea that the larger purpose of inquiry stance as a theory
of action is to elevate the role of practitioners in educational change efforts
and to solidify their status once and for all as professionals within the existing
larger educational system. Behind the framework of inquiry as stance is a new
idea of professionalism and new notion of what it means for practitioners to
work as professionals in these new times when the challenges they confront
require knowledge and skills that do not yet exist, but must be invented in
the course of working on the problem itself.

When practitioner researchers work from an inquiry stance, they are
working both within and against the system—an ongoing process, from the
inside, of problematizing fundamental assumptions about the purposes of the
existing education system and raising difficult questions about educational
resources, processes, and outcomes. Collectively, practitioners working from
an inquiry stance call into question the effect of existing curriculum, instruction, and assessment practices and policies and consider how the arrangements of teaching and school leadership challenge or sustain the deep
inequities inscribed in the status quo. As we see it, then, the ultimate purpose
of inquiry as stance—always and in every context—is enhancing students'
learning and life chances for participation in and contribution to a diverse
and democratic society.

Transforming What It Means to Educate. We connect the notion of inquiry as stance to the goal of transforming teaching, learning, leading, and
schooling, rather than to something that could more simply be called "educational improvement" or "educational change." "Improvement" implies both
that current educational goals and directions are appropriate and that what
is needed is to do better (more effectively, more efficiently, more inexpen-
sively) at what we are already doing—or to do what we are already doing for
some portion of the student population for a larger and more inclusive segment of that population. "Change," on the other hand, is somewhat vague

about directionality of movement and rationale. The valence of the term "transforming," however, at least as we are using it here, connects inquiry as stance to a questioning, critical edge and aims for something much larger—a profound change, a paradigm shift, a different direction in terms of purposes and aims, with the ultimate goal of enhancing students' learning and their life chances.

As the chapters written by practitioners in Part II of this book and many other practitioner researcher writings make clear, teaching and learning from an inquiry stance are reciprocally and synergistically related: Inquiry pedagogy engenders inquiry learning. Teachers who work from an inquiry stance that involves continual and critical questioning foster the development of students who do the same. Teachers who see themselves as knowers ask questions and pose problems, and so do their students. School leaders who take an inquiry stance encourage joint problem-posing among faculty and staff as a community norm. In turn, faculty and staff are attentive to and encouraging of students' questions and to learning from and with school leadership. It is important to note, however, that the conceptions of learning and knowledge assumed here are quite different from the conceptions of many policymakers and others who argue that the major goal of schooling is to produce students with basic knowledge and skills so they are well-prepared to enter the labor force. When practitioners work from an inquiry stance, the goal is that their students will have basic knowledge and skills, to be sure, but also that they will raise questions about knowledge sources and uses and develop the skills of critique, deliberation, and analysis.

Along these lines, Michelli (2005) suggests that, contrary to what some critics have argued is the case (see Cochran-Smith, Barnatt, Lahann, Shakman, & Terrell, 2008, for a review of critiques), practitioners who are committed to social justice agree with the prevailing belief that the fundamental purpose of schooling is to provide access to knowledge. However, as Michelli (2005) points out, immediately beneath the surface of that agreement are deep cleavages in viewpoints: Access to which knowledge? Assessed in what ways? For what purposes? Access to the same knowledge for all students? Higher order knowledge and critical thinking about knowledge itself or rote facts and information? Castenell and Pinar (1993) suggest other questions of the same order as Michelli's, including: Who decides what knowledge counts in school? Whose interests are served (and not served)? Whose perspectives are represented or omitted?

From the perspective of inquiry, then, promoting students' learning may well include teaching much of what is traditionally considered to be part of the canon of school knowledge, but it also includes teaching students to critique that knowledge, to challenge the universality of the traditional knowledge base in the first place, and to consider this in relation to the knowledge traditions and the epistemologies of marginalized groups that have been omitted from the "official" knowledge base (King, 2008). The assumption here is that attention to social and knowledge critiques is not a diversion from the goal of student learning, but a central part of it, and a part that motivates students and stimulates knowledge acquisition and agency.

The role of an inquiry stance in transforming teaching, learning, and leading into pursuits that go beyond the basics is important to our discussion of larger educational goals and purposes. It is closely related to Gutman's (1987/1999; Gutman & Thompson, 1996) argument that "deliberation" must be considered a basic skill and a fundamental outcome of teaching and learning in a democratic society. She argues this persuasively:

> Why should deliberation be considered primary even for public education when the opportunity for most citizens to live a good life today requires many more basic skills and virtues, such as numeracy, literacy and nonviolence? Deliberation is not a single skill or virtue. It calls upon skills of literacy, numeracy, and critical thinking, as well as contextual knowledge, understanding and appreciation of other people's perspectives. The virtues that deliberation encompasses include veracity, nonviolence, practical judgment, civic integrity, and magnanimity. By cultivating these and other deliberative skills and virtues, a democratic society helps secure both the basic opportunity of individuals and its collective capacity to pursue justice. (Gutman, 1987/1999, p. xiii)

Gutman goes on to suggest that justice is more likely to be pursued by participants in a democratic society who "reason together" about the decisions that affect them than it is by people who are "uninterested in politics" or interested, but only in terms of their own power (p. xiii).

In educational settings where teachers, students, and other stakeholders are engaged in inquiry and mutual deliberations, common assumptions about the roles and outcomes of teaching, learning, and schooling are debated and transformed. So too are ideas about teachers as leaders. For example, in arguing that teacher leadership has generally been under-conceptualized, Fullan (1994) offered a "more comprehensive" conceptualization toward "wholesale transformation" of the teaching profession. He suggested that all practitioners had to be leaders, not just a chosen few, and that leaders needed knowledge of teaching and learning, collegiality, educational contexts, continuous learning, the change process, and the moral purposes of education. Reconceiving the role of teachers as leaders and learners, in and out of classrooms, is considered both a goal and an outcome of the theory of inquiry as stance.

As we discussed in Chapter 4, many university-based faculty have worked with school-based and other educational colleagues to re-imagine relationships of inquiry, knowledge, and practice. In a sense, these initiatives and innovative projects have as a goal disrupting or transforming aspects of university culture and thus interrupting traditional assumptions about teaching, learning, and knowing. In exploring the notion of "recasting teaching," for example, we described inquiry-based pedagogy as a transformation of the more typical transmission-oriented teaching characteristic of universities. Parallel to critical inquiry-based pedagogies in K–12 schools, inquiry in universities can be both method and outcome, intentionally framed to foster uncertainty. University-based practitioners may see their purpose as promoting questioning, problem-posing, and challenging common routines and the status quo. When the goal or outcome of university teacher education is conceptualized as an inquiry stance, the point is not simply intellectual openness. The purpose of this transformed perspective on teaching and learning is to offer university students images of what it means to work with and from that stance in order to engage critically the complex problems of the educational world.

Inquiry for Justice and Change. In Chapter 1, we pointed out that a major trend in the practitioner inquiry movement worldwide is that more and more practitioners are involved in inquiry about equity, educational access, and agency in educational settings. Likewise, in the eight chapters in Part II of this book, eight very differently positioned practitioners take up eight very different questions, but each of these has something to do with the conditions that support and constrain students' learning opportunities as well as the ways these opportunities are shaped by the dynamic interplay of gender, race, class, identity, culture, language background, and immigrant status in interaction with the social processes of classrooms and the structures of schools and educational systems.

It is important to point out that in none of these instances were practitioners engaged in inquiry simply for accountability's sake, at least in the narrow, test-based sense that this term has come to convey in today's educational parlance. None of these practitioners was studying practice to find better ways to boost students' test scores. However, it is also very clear these practitioners were not engaged in inquiry simply for inquiry's sake. That is, they were not inquiring into equity and access because they wanted to create a documentary record of parities and disparities in the resources and outcomes of particular groups or individuals. And they were not in the business of simply noting that the knowledge traditions and lived experiences of marginalized groups are rarely represented in the curriculum or pedagogies of K–12 schooling or higher education (King, 2008). Rather, practitioners engage in inquiry of the kind we are describing here because they are committed to taking action to improve the day-to-day school lives and futures of the students and families with whom they work. In short, the larger purpose—the bottom line—of inquiry as stance is education for social change and social justice.

In contemporary political philosophy, two paradigms of social justice are debated (Fraser, 2003).[1] The distributive paradigm of justice, where *in*justice is defined as inequalities rooted in the socioeconomic structure of society (Rawls, 1971), dominated theories of justice for the latter half of the last century (Fraser, 2003). From this perspective, the remedy for injustice was redistribution of material and other goods, including opportunity, power, and access, with the goal of establishing a society based on fairness and equality. However, an understanding of justice in terms of the "politics of difference," which emerged from the social movements of the 1960s and 1970s (Young, 1990), has now taken center stage. From this perspective, which challenges liberalism's notions of neutrality and the common good, failure to recognize and respect social groups is a central dimension of *in*justice, and thus the goal of recognition is central to justice theories (Honneth, 2003).

Many political philosophers now agree that the central question in theorizing social justice is how to conceptualize the relationship between liberalism's notion of distributive justice and the politics of identity and difference. A number of theorists and philosophers have framed these issues for education, including Howe (1997) and Reich (2002), both of whom acknowledged the tension in schooling between respect for cultural diversity and the need for civic unity, and King (2008), who challenged the hegemony of ideologically based knowledge in school and called for the incorporation of the knowledge traditions of marginalized groups. Applying these concepts to the problems of practice in the day-to-day world of classrooms, schools, and other educational settings, however, is difficult. In the work of practice, there are ongoing and on-the-ground tensions between, for example, the idea of a knowledge and skills base that all students should know and be able to demonstrate on high-stakes measures of achievement, on one hand, and acknowledgment, on the other hand, that school knowledge and curricula privilege some cultural and racial groups and dismiss the knowledge traditions of other groups. Along these lines, Gewirtz and Cribb (2002) have argued that most contemporary theorizing about social justice in education has glossed over these inherent tensions at a relatively high level of abstraction rather than examining how these play out concretely in actual practice.

Practitioners who participate in inquiry as we conceptualize it in this book—as stance and as grounded theory of action for the transformation of teaching, learning, and leading—are working from inside the lived world of real problems of practice. As the examples in this book indicate, they are engaged in the complex dialectic of inquiry and action while working toward the dual social justice goals of equity and recognition, even though these are inherently in tension with one another. Unlike those researchers who study practice from the outside and those philosophers who theorize social justice at a highly abstract level, practitioner researchers have to work simultaneously within and against larger accountability systems by taking responsibility for their students' learning at the same time that they challenge narrow means of measuring that learning. They have to be astute observers of individual learners with the ability to pose questions that transcend cultural attribution, institutional habit, and the alleged certainty of outside experts while simultaneously building on the linguistic and cultural resources and the knowledge traditions that students and families bring to school. They have to see beyond and through the conventional labels and practices that sustain the status quo by raising difficult, sometimes unanswerable, questions about their own assumptions and practices and the assumptions and practices of their colleagues. They have to wrestle with their own doubts, fend off the fatigue of reform, and depend on the strength of their individual and collective convictions that their work ultimately makes a difference in the fabric of social responsibility. Perhaps most importantly, practitioners who work from an inquiry stance have to continuously form and reform the interpretive frameworks that guide their moment to moment actions as well as their deliberate and more considered long-term decisions in the interest of educating for a more just and democratic society.

INQUIRY AS STANCE, WAYS FORWARD

Just days before the final pieces of this book went to press, Barack Obama was elected the 44th President of the United States. There is widespread agreement that his historic election was the accomplishment of a broad-based and unprecedented coalition of supporters who had different agendas, backgrounds, and politics, but who shared a common sense of hope about the possibilities for transforming the nation. We are among the many who resonated strongly with these sentiments and reveled in the triumph of a campaign based on a spirit of efficacy and the ability to both imagine and articulate a different future for the diverse peoples of our nation.

Although it remains to be seen what kind of educational policies the new administration will enact, in the concluding section of this chapter, we draw from the new sense of hope that has galvanized so many Americans and their allies worldwide and write with optimism (cautious and measured optimism, perhaps, but optimism nonetheless) about the possibilities for transforming teaching, learning, and leadership in the nation's educational institutions by drawing on the collective intellectual capacity of practitioners working in alliances with others to create the kind of schooling that can sustain a just and democratic society.

As we have noted throughout this book, there is now widespread agreement among researchers, policymakers, politicians, and reformers of all stripes and with widely differing political and professional agendas that teachers are among the most important factors, if not the single most important factor, in educational change. Likewise, it is now widely believed that any educational reform that does not account for the role of teachers and school leaders cannot be successful in either the short or the long run. Although a long time coming, this acknowledgment of the essential role of practitioners in educational change represents the right ideas about practice and practitioners, and such acknowledgment is, in fact, vital to the kind of transformation we are imagining and advocating throughout this book.

Unfortunately, however, prevailing federal and state educational policies have taken the right idea about the central role of practitioners in educational change and gotten it all wrong. They have relied on close external monitoring of practitioners' work, heavy investments in technologies and materials that supposedly have the needed knowledge and skills built into them and thus do not require the professional judgment of practitioners, and severe penalties for failing to meet requirements for annual gains on high-stakes tests.

This book is an attempt to get it right. Throughout the book, we have conceptualized inquiry as stance as a theory of both how to change things and what needs to change. We think this kind of theory about the roles of practitioners and local knowledge in school reform is a critical part of what is needed in these new times, when words like hope and transformation are on the lips and in the hearts of more of the people who care about public education and when many of the problems that will confront tomorrow's educators have not yet been posed, let alone resolved.

We want to make a point of noting that we do not claim or presume to speak for the practitioner inquiry movement writ large in this book. Nor do we attempt to propose a recipe or a list of dos and don'ts about how to engage in practitioner research or build practitioner inquiry communities more effectively. Either of these would be antithetical to our own perspectives and to what makes practitioner inquiry a movement that draws its strength from deep local work and differently positioned actors and communities that are unified around central ideas regarding knowledge, practice, and the purposes of education.

What we do claim to do here is to speak for ourselves as long-time participants in, and advocates for, the practitioner inquiry movement from our location as university-based practitioners and researchers. In concluding this section of the book, we want to suggest that inquiry as stance can be a powerful and generative framework for moving toward the goal of transforming teaching, learning, leadership, and schooling in these new times.

Chapter 1 begins this book by describing key themes in the practitioner inquiry movement since 2000. We intend this description to update our previous overview of the movement, which we titled, "The Teacher Research Movement: A Decade Later" (Cochran-Smith & Lytle, 1999a), because it followed by just short of a decade our first overview of the movement, "Research on Teaching and Teacher Research: The Issues that Divide" (Cochran-Smith & Lytle, 1990). Like both of our previous descriptions, the description in Chapter 1 offers a necessarily partial account of the practitioner inquiry movement, constrained by space limitations, dependence on published accounts, and the challenges involved in trying to access and document a variegated, dispersed, and largely grassroots effort that resists documentation in many ways. Despite these limitations, it is clear to us that almost a decade after "a decade later," initiatives based on the idea of practitioners' generating knowledge and taking action collaboratively in local educational settings have immense appeal for a wide range of practitioners in schools, universities, and community-based organizations across the United States and around the world. The evidence suggests that the practitioner inquiry movement is flourishing but also continuously re-inventing itself, perhaps in part because it embraces, or at least contains within it, many competing visions of what practitioner research means and what its potential is for contributing to a more just and democratic society.

As we suggest throughout the first section of this book, "inquiry as stance" is a framework that repositions practitioners at the center of educational transformation by capitalizing on their collective intellectual capacity when working in collaboration with many other stakeholders in the educational process. To conclude this chapter in a spirit we hope is congruent with both the healthy but sprawling practitioner inquiry movement, and with an inquiry stance itself, we highlight four ways forward for the next generation that build on many efforts that are already occurring nationwide and globally, but we also call for new alliances and bridges. As Figure 5.2 suggests, these four ways forward for inquiry as stance include: (1) deepening the local

Figure 5.2. Inquiry as Stance: Ways Forward

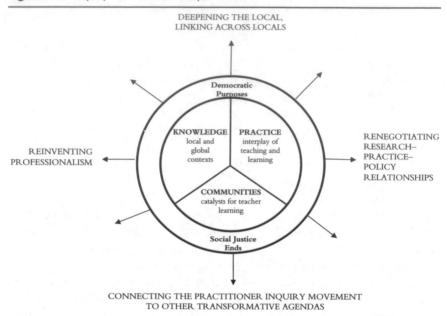

CONNECTING THE PRACTITIONER INQUIRY MOVEMENT
TO OTHER TRANSFORMATIVE AGENDAS

work of practitioner inquiry communities and linking across multiple local communities; (2) reinventing the notion of professionalism and reconsidering what it means to call for the professionalization of practice; (3) renegotiating the relationships of research, practice, and policy and, concurrently, rethinking the relationships of researchers, practitioners, and policymakers; and (4) connecting the practitioner inquiry movement to other transformative agendas and larger movements for school and social change.

Deepening Local Work/Linking Across Local Communities

At the level of schools and school districts, there is much we have learned about what it means to create and sustain the conditions for critical inquiry communities within and across settings. An absolutely crucial condition is that we make inviolable the necessary time for substantive collaboration, time that is protected from absorption into the rituals of school life. Another relates to school or district culture wherein practitioner deliberations about teaching and learning become widely valued as vital sources of knowledge and action on behalf of democratic and just education. Institutions and organizations that recognize their dependence on accessing the knowledge of practitioners who in turn access the knowledge of students and their communities can work to create trusting, responsive, and supportive workplaces.

We know that schools characterized by sufficient time for meaningful collective work are more likely to attract and keep committed teachers. Educational leaders at all levels are aware that high teacher turnover interferes with student learning and does not foster collaborative communities. Strong, stable teaching staffs and sufficient opportunities for meaningful dialogue are fundamental to creating rich learning contexts for students. When leadership is shared in a school community, teachers and others can make remarkable things happen just by beginning to focus on: deep questions and problems, rather than technical solutions; students' cultural and linguistic resources as assets, rather than deficits; and creating contexts where current assumptions about teaching, learning, and schooling are always open to critique and reformulation.

We are inspired here by Campano's chapter in Part II of this volume, wherein he describes practitioner research as a "collective struggle for humanization," reminding us of the "many localized pedagogical revolutions where communities of educators are theorizing from practice and creating educational arrangements 'from the ground up' that are more conducive to the fuller human potentials of their students." There are countless, though widely distributed, grassroots practitioner groups that meet regularly to construct practices congruent with their theories and experiences and that resist the dominant discourse and mandates that constrain what they can accomplish (Edelsky, 2006). Many of these groups engage in forms of systematic and intentional inquiry into their own pedagogies. Some of them support teachers and other practitioners in reading professional literature and in writing and publishing about their work for immediate and distal audiences. Portraits of deep, vulnerable teaching like those provided by the authors in Part II of this book and by many teachers and other practitioners who are doing this work (and sometimes writing on the web or in books or journals) are a testament to the power and importance of building on and supporting local work.

At the very least practitioners' counter-narratives complicate the technicist images of educational practice that dominate the public landscape and the popular discourse about schools and teaching. These narratives illuminate the complexity of the work of teaching, learning, and leading, as well as the intellectual projects of practitioners who work inside educational systems. As insiders to the system who are also compensated for their work, practitioners are often required to comply with expectations they do not believe provide access to the education their students need and deserve. We are alluding here to what someone once called "the theft of our profession"—that is, the regulations that make it difficult for educators to exercise fully their desires for ongoing learning about practice and their professional judgments about pedagogy, curriculum, and assessment.

We are, however, struck by an obvious but startling realization. In spite of the current context and legislation against individual and collective initiative, many practitioners are nevertheless unwilling to allow outsiders to dictate what goes on in their classrooms and schools. We are not talking simply about what was long ago dubbed "teaching as a subversive activity" or about outright refusal to comply with regulations or oversight. Deepening the local entails living with contradictions: affirming the prerogatives of professional judgment to critique and reject those policies and practices that are not in the best interest of students' growth and learning, while at the same time choosing to work within the system when policies and practices do serve students well. That practitioners across the country continue to raise and organize around pertinent (and impertinent) questions—questions of curiosity, critique, and passion for their students' access to meaningful learning experiences—testifies to their individual and collective commitment to *living* an inquiry stance on practice, buttressed by supportive relationships and collectivities that may or may not be institutionally sanctioned.

Deepening the local work of practitioner inquiry means sustaining and intentionally proliferating and connecting intellectually and socially engaged communities and networks of various kinds. It means encouraging new teachers to stay in the profession by bringing them into existing communities and networks to learn from them about their questions and experiences in schools and classrooms. Deepening the local work and linking across local communities also means acknowledging that practitioner researchers and their communities are sometimes at risk. In some instances, educators are being strongly discouraged from taking an inquiry stance, being transferred or fired for asking too many or the wrong questions, for disrupting tests, and for failing to be on the right page at the right time. These acts of resistance can invite new forms of solidarity grounded in increasingly complex analyses of the politics of teaching and learning in these times. We are referring here to what has been called "a movement for education rights" guided by an adequate analysis of current problems and policies, a galvanizing issue (such as high-stakes testing), and images of education that depict justice and civic responsibility (Edelsky, 2006).

We know that many, if not most, practitioners experience acute pressure to get on board with the new orthodoxies of test-based accountability, and some are isolated on the borders in their own schools. There are countless new teachers who cannot remember a time without mandated curricula and high-stakes tests and have never had access to the conversations of colleagues who see themselves as working for positive change both within and against the system. Cultures of intimidation can, as we know, sometimes effectively stifle opposition. However, strengthening connections across local communities and national networks enables strategic advocacy and activism on behalf of students and families. Practitioners and practitioner groups need to continue to identify a range of differently situated allies as well as create collaborative structures that foster reciprocity, co-learning, and activism with universities and community organizations working in support of equity and justice in education.

Reinventing Professionalism/ Reconsidering the Professionalization of Practice

Throughout this chapter, we elaborate the idea of inquiry as stance by describing: the nature of educational practice as both theoretical and practical, the knowledge that is needed to practice well as local knowledge influenced by global conditions, the central locus of practitioners' work as both local and extended inquiry communities, and the ultimate goals of practitioner research as social justice and social change. Implicitly underlying all of these descriptions—and explicitly stated in some of them—is the assumption that educational practitioners are professionals who are knowledge generators, decision makers, and deliberative collaborators. This contrasts dramatically with the idea of practitioners simply as users of received knowledge, faithful implementers of curricula and instruction worked out and certified by others, or employees whose main job is to comply with the decisions of administrators and other overseers.

During the last several decades, there have been many highly publicized and politicized debates about whether teaching is or is not a profession and whether teachers and other practitioners can or cannot legitimately be considered professionals. The frequent occurrence in this contentious discourse of phrases describing teaching that hook prefixes like "quasi-," "not quite," "minor," and "pseudo-" with the word, "profession," provides some sense of its overall tone. As has been pointed out by many scholars, most of the debates about teaching as a profession revolve around issues related to autonomy, expertise dependent upon specialized knowledge and skill, accountability and responsibility, shared sense of purpose, and norms for professional behavior that are common to and reinforced by those within the professional group. Other debates about teaching as a profession hinge on whether or not teacher unions in and of themselves disqualify teaching as a profession and instead relegate it into the same category as other organized labor occupations.

To understand these debates, it is important to note that there are many different definitions for "profession," none of which are givens, some of which are contradictory, and many of which have emerged at particular historical moments in connection with specific political, strategic, and other agendas. In addition, the various definitions for "professional" and "professionalism" are complex and nuanced, depending to a great extent on their underlying definitions regarding the relationships of teaching, learning, and educational leadership, as well as on the contexts in which those definitions are enacted. Along these lines, for example, Edelsky (2006) has pointed out that increased responsibility is one of the common dictionary definitions for "professional." However, as she notes, many of today's teachers and other practitioners have enormous (and increasing) clerical and management responsibilities for their students' test outcomes and for providing instruction that will presumably boost overall test scores at the same time that they have decreased autonomy regarding decisions about curriculum, content, and the social organization of schools and classrooms. As this juxtaposition makes clear, it is not just a matter of responsibility and accountability that defines a profession, then, but a question of responsibility and accountability for what and in relation to what larger contexts and goals.

It is not our intention here to wade into the long and complex debate about what a professional is (or should/could be) or whether and how teachers and other practitioners measure up to expectations. Rather, we depend here on the fact that, despite scholars' and lexicographers' disagreements about how to define these terms, most of us have understandings of professions and professionals with enough in common to make some basic points and communicate with one another.

As we show in our discussion of the four critical dimensions of inquiry as stance, in order for the practitioner inquiry movement to move forward for the next generation, our position is that we need a reinvented notion of professional practice in education and a reconsidered approach to practitioners as professionals. From our perspective, teachers and other educational practitioners *are* already professionals—whether outsiders believe that they should be considered as such or not and even if they are employed in oppressive working conditions. They are professionals in that they are engaged in daily work that is relational and uncertain and that takes place under constantly changing conditions. They are professionals in that they must deal not simply with what Heifitz (1994) called "technical" problems, which although sometimes complicated, can be solved by knowledge and capacity that already exist. They must also deal with what he refers to as "adaptive" challenges, which require creating the knowledge and the tools to solve problems in the act of working on them. They are professionals in that their work depends on making deliberative decisions about how to understand and act on who their students are and what they bring to school, how to respond to mandates from school and district overseers, and how to connect curricular knowledge with the knowledge perspectives of students and their communities.

We are not suggesting, then, that the practitioner inquiry movement can move forward into the next generation by clinging to the same notions of professionalism that have been emphasized previously—notions that revolve around teachers and other practitioners who have broader and deeper knowledge of subject matter, enhanced knowledge of pedagogy, and more savvy about schools as organizations and the politics of education more broadly. These things are important, to be sure, but in today's society, new patterns of migration, new media forms, and new globalized markets have created new patterns of social life as well as new epistemologies (Appadurai, 2006; Luke, 2004). As Luke suggests, teachers and other practitioners now need to be prepared for "new forms of work, new formations of youth, and difficult economic conditions" (p. 2). We see as a critical part of a new professionalism acknowledgment of the fact that although practitioners' knowledge has previously been "subjugated knowledge" (Foucault, 1980, p. 82), it now must be recognized that professional practitioners have the collective intellectual capacity to help pose the new adaptive challenges of practice and also create the knowledge and tools to address those problems by working together in inquiry communities.

Renegotiating Research, Practice, and Policy Relationships

The current educational regime in the United States is based on the assumption that policy is (and should be) the driver of reform in schools and classrooms. The major policy levers—standards and accountability—are based on the further assumption that goals must be clear and consistent, information about school outcomes must be publicly available, and stakes for teachers, students, and schools must be high. When all of these conditions are in place, students are presumably motivated to perform at the highest levels, and practitioners are likewise motivated to try harder, work more effectively, and continuously figure out how to alter classroom techniques and organizational structures in line with data. The most important focus of the policy community currently is research, specifically: using research to establish empirically certified generalizations about "what works" in schools and classrooms, ensuring that research findings are produced and disseminated in ways that are easily translated and utilized in practice, and training practitioners to be more effective consumers and implementers of such research.

As we note throughout this chapter and in several previous chapters, this approach is based on the assumption that the relationships among research, policy, and practice are straightforward and more or less linear. Likewise the roles of researchers, policymakers, and practitioners are assumed to be distinct and separate with the boundaries between researchers and practitioners clear and well-defined. However, as Willinsky (2001) points out, a "translational" model of the relationships of research, policy, and practice takes as a premise that the question of what is needed to improve schooling through research already has a definitive answer—training practitioners to be better consumers of research information (p. 5). This model completely ignores questions about how practitioners and others might generate knowledge of practice from practice and reflect on, be informed by, challenge, and talk back to research knowledge in the interest of greater public engagement about issues of education in a democratic society. Along similar lines, Moss and Piety (2007) suggest that the current research focus of the policy community gives little attention to how various social structures and patterns of interaction shape the complex ways educators understand and use research information in particular local contexts.

As we argue throughout Part I of this book, inquiry as intellectual stance and as theory of action about educational transformation disrupts the dominant approach to educational inquiry. By definition, practitioner inquiry blurs the roles of researchers and practitioners and complicates considerably dominant assumptions about translating, implementing, and mobilizing research knowledge for practice. Rather than making practitioners better consumers of research knowledge or more skillful implementers of curricular and other policies based on scientific research, the concept of inquiry as stance highlights the notion of practitioners as knowledge generators, as collaborators with university-based and other researchers engaged in exploring practice-based issues, and as deliberators who use but also challenge and talk back to, research and policy that appears not to serve the best interests of their students.

A recent address by the newly named President of the Carnegie Foundation for the Advancement of Teaching, Tony Bryk, is instructive here. Bryk (2008) spoke directly about the relationships of research and practice toward the twin objectives of advancing "ambitious learning goals" for all students and making systems of schooling more efficient by using an innovative "educational engineering" orientation (pp. 6, 7). He discussed four guiding themes for this endeavor, the first of which involved aiming for a "science of performance improvement in teaching," which he characterized as follows:

> You take the day to day work of educators and you put that at the center of inquiry. What are the basic day to day problems of practice that people

are confronting? And those become the central problems in defining the inquiry agenda. So the problems of practice improvement are at the center. (pp. 12, 14)

Bryk argued that multiple core activities and outcomes involved in innovations should be measured with the goal of figuring out how innovations work in the hands of different individuals working within different contexts and circumstances.

To do this, Bryk called for new methods and methodologies that are different from conventional forms of naturalistic inquiry (which he said had no strategy for accumulating evidence) and also different from formalized field trials (which he said produced precise information about average treatment effects but were limited in their capacity to guide what actually happens with use at a larger scale). Instead Bryk called for "systematic forms of naturalistic inquiry," which accumulate evidence about innovations over time that can lead to greater reliability in how practices can be enacted (p. 18). Bryk's second theme was building a generative capacity for practitioners' continuous improvement based on clear understanding of the actual work of practice as organized complexity. This, according to Bryk, depends on the intersection of knowing students, having a goal-related theory of development and curriculum, and having a repertoire of strategies, tools, materials, and pedagogies. All of this work would be anchored on actually trying to take up some set of specific problems of practice as they are understood "on the job floor of classrooms, schools, colleges and universities" and studying the collaborative efforts of researchers and practitioners to solve these problems (p. 40).

Bryk's idea that in order to improve schools and schooling, we must begin with problems of practice identified by those who are engaged in the day-to-day work is very much in keeping with the ideas about the relationships of research, practice, and policy that underlie the whole notion of inquiry as stance. Putting practice at the center and drawing on the collective intellectual capacity of practitioners collaborating with others, such as university-based researchers and practitioners, are the crux of the grounded theory of educational transformation that exemplifies inquiry as stance.

We should also note, however, that what we are saying in this book about the relationships of research, practice, and policy is not completely aligned with Bryk's ideas about research and practice. In fact, some people might conclude that our take on practitioner inquiry falls into Bryk's characterization of naturalistic inquiry without a strategy for accumulation. However, as we point out in our discussion of deepening the local work in inquiry communities at the same time that we redouble efforts to link across locals, inquiry as stance carries with it a notion of extension, power, and use that is different from the traditional idea of accumulation. In the last section below, we also suggest that the practitioner inquiry movement and the organizing framework of inquiry as stance are aligned with other social movements for educational transformation in important ways. Here again the relevant notion is not so much "accumulation," but collective action.

Connecting Practitioner Inquiry to Transformative Agendas

In this final section, we discuss briefly the implications of practitioner research as a kind of social movement in and of itself. By virtue of its diverse roots and shared center of gravity in re-framing the participation and roles of practitioners, the movement is positioned to evolve so that it makes a substantial contribution to education transformation in the coming years. This will not happen, however, without a concerted effort to identify and construct significant relationships with other groups and movements dedicated to similar outcomes.

The critique of the status quo that we refer to throughout the book has been theorized and articulated by many others who take as their starting points the political, social, cultural, and economic systems that have historically structured inequality in American education and led to the era of NCLB and other policies that have contributed to reinforcing glaring disparities in our educational institutions. Many challenge the current educational regime for the same reasons we do so here, but have developed their own distinctive approaches to organizing and seeking change in ways that are instructive.

Most of these researcher activists have also drawn their insights from deep, local work. Pauline Lipman, for example, in *High Stakes Education* (2003), offers previously untold narratives about how the hegemonic educational agenda has negatively affected teachers and public schools and neighborhoods in Chicago. She sees organized resistance and educational change as growing out of broad social movements, such as the school reform efforts since the 1950s that have been orchestrated for an equity and justice agenda. Along related lines, Jean Anyon in *Radical Possibilities* (2005) examines the features of social movements for social justice, pointing to how schools can play critical roles in challenging inequities. She shows how education and educators—in collaboration or parallel with other movements and institutions—can contribute to this struggle by nurturing activist identities through participation in organizing and solidarity with community adults and youth.

The work of Ernest Morrell in *Critical Literacy and Urban Youth* (2007) provides rich images of pedagogies in classrooms, neighborhoods, and other institutions that contribute to advocacy work for social change and to the activist identities of both teachers and students. King (2008) argues that "if justice is our objective" in education, then we must recognize and account for the ways "ideologically distorted knowledge sustains societal *in*justice, particularly academic and school knowledge about black history and culture" (p. 337). King (2008) asserts that there is a "crisis of knowledge" in teacher education research and in practice caused by the absence of the epistemologies of African Americans and other marginalized groups as a foundation for teacher learning and instruction (p. 1095).

In a process that resonates with the vision of inquiry and the practitioner research movement we have been focusing on in this book, Oakes, Rogers, and Lipton (2006) describe "social design experiments as simultaneously research and intervention" in which knowledge creation and action function synergistically to foster ongoing inquiry (p. 41). In their book *Learning Power*, the authors make clear that the kind of learning that results from this situated social inquiry does not come from the "received ideologies of radical leadership" (Oakes, Rogers, & Lipton, 2006, p. 165). Rather, this learning comes from the strenuous process by which participants come to understand their own experience, the influences of history and historical contexts on their lives, and the ways to take action so that their own perspectives and voices can have a determining effect on their futures. In calling for common cause, including an "engaged university" where faculty work with community organizers, Oakes, Rogers, and Lipton (2006) offer a challenge to teachers, teacher educators, university researchers, community members, parents, and others to build new alliances and further develop the alliances already created (p. 169). They document what it has meant to work as a part of IDEA (the Institute for Democracy, Education and Access) at UCLA in order to create grassroots public activism deeply rooted in and informed by Deweyian social inquiry. Ultimately, their thesis is straightforward and resonates with our underlying premises about inquiry as stance: Education is a vehicle for social change. As Oakes, Rogers, and Lipton argue, change can occur when activist youth, teachers, parents, and community organizations work together to "learn about power," "explore the power of learning," and "learn to be powerful." Their conclusion, which is wholly consistent with a central point of our book, is that the creation of a healthy public sphere and civic engagement can be achieved through participatory social inquiry and inquiry-based organizing.

***

We do not believe that our vision of practitioner research for the next generation deepening and expanding and linking with other groups and movements is too far-fetched. Given the systemic pressure for educators, families, and communities to conform to some very problematic policies, we can envision the practitioner research movement forging new alliances that contribute to a proactive public discourse on educational transformation. We are not suggesting that all teachers who are engaged in practitioner research to improve student learning must become social activists beyond their own schools or networks. Yet it is clear that the importance of collective work and of organizing cannot be over-emphasized at this time. Countless participants in the practitioner research movement have been working on that assumption for years. The more grassroots support and meaningful co-laboring there is, the more likely it is for practitioners to articulate questions and to act in ways that impact on local discourses and local solutions, which, in turn, contribute to a wider public discourse about educational transformation.

There are some immediate routes for moving in these directions, as we suggest throughout this volume. Participants in the practitioner research movement can read and disseminate the critical work of teachers whose students are doing their own social action research projects on issues of the environment, democratic participation and social justice in the community, as we discussed in Chapter 1. The proliferation of practitioner websites about practice and their participation in web-based social networking around professional issues provide rich new resources for distal inquiry and distance organizing. University- and school-based researchers can do something as straightforward as feature on course syllabi and conference programs the important and often provocative work of practitioner researchers and inquiry communities, as described in Chapter 4. Those who publish practitioner research or write about it can make the work more visible by means of lateral citations and by creating new web-based alternatives for digital publication among practitioners in schools and universities. All of us who are engaged in the practitioner inquiry movement can make it a priority to identify common cause in the agendas of the practitioner inquiry movement and other organizations, including those progressive teacher unions negotiating for improving teachers' working conditions and activist organizations advocating politically for practitioners.

Perhaps we can even envision a kind of Move-On.org for the practitioner inquiry movement, an online nexus that links groups and networks with one another and finds innovative ways for practitioner researchers to be in solidarity with kindred social movements. Practitioners can use open source websites to share and discuss inquiry-based curricula and other local initiatives. We can follow the lead of innovative, community-based and participatory networks that already use the web and face-to-face meetings to link educators with people concerned with health care, social services, and local or national activism. We can also take up the challenge of dealing with issues of quality in practitioner research in ways that are respectful of divergence and help the work realize its goals of justice and educational transformation.

Our final thoughts here about "ways forward" range from the very immediate to the larger need for conceptual shifts and projects that will take more thought and time. Some of these are already happening and need more support and attention. Other new directions need to be invented. We have intentionally crafted Figure 5.2 (shown earlier) to be open-ended, suggesting by its many arrows that there are multiple directions that participants in and supporters of the practitioner inquiry movement have already taken up or will see as important in the coming years. In the next sections of this book, practitioners explore many of the issues we have raised in the previous chapters. They also theorize practitioner research from their own perspectives and explore how important themes that they identify play out in the contexts of actual sites of practice. In the work that follows, we see thought-provoking visions of the practitioner movement going forward into the next generation. Grounded in inquiry as stance, the practitioners whose work is featured in Parts II and III of this book provide encouraging images of what happens when communities (in classrooms and beyond) form around investigations of practice and their inquiry becomes central to re-imagining and re-inventing how and what adults, youth, and children teach and learn in educational institutions and beyond.

NOTE

1. See Cochran-Smith (in press) for a more elaborated discussion of contemporary theories of justice and their uses and implications for teacher education.

Part I References

Aaron, J., Bauer, E. B., Commeyras, M., Cox, S. D., Daniell, B., Elrick, E., Fecho, B., Hermann-Wilmarth, J., Hogan, E., Pintaone-Hernandez, A., Roulston, K., Siegel, A., & Vaughn, H. (2006). *"No deposit, no return": Enriching literacy teaching and learning through critical inquiry pedagogy.* Newark, DE: International Reading Association.

Abu El-Haj, T. (2003). Practicing for equity from the standpoint of the particular: Exploring the work of one urban teacher network. *Teachers College Record, 105*(5), 817–845.

Achinstein, B. (2002). Conflict amid community: The micropolitics of teacher collaboration. *Teachers College Record, 104*(3), 421–455.

Achinstein, B., & Ogawa, R. (2006). (In)fidelity: What the resistance of new teachers reveals about professional principles and prescriptive educational policies. *Harvard Educational Review, 76*(1), 30–63.

Acker, S. (1996). Gender and teachers work. In M. Apple (Ed.), *Review of research* (Vol. 21, pp. 99–162). Washington, DC: American Educational Research Association.

Allington, R. L., & Johnston, P. H. (2001). What do we know about exemplary fourth-grade teachers and their classrooms? In C. Roller (Ed.), *Learning to teach reading: Setting the research agenda* (pp. 150–165). Newark, DE: International Reading Association.

Allwright, D. (2005). Developing principles for practitioner research: The case of exploratory practice. *The Modern Language Journal, 89*(3), 353–366.

American Board for Certification of Teacher Excellence. (2006). Retrieved on November 1, 2006, from: http://www.abcte.org

Anderson, G. L. (2002). Reflecting on research for doctoral students in education. *Educational Researcher, 31*(7), 22–25.

Anderson, G. L., & Herr, K. (1999). The new paradigm wars: Is there room for rigorous practitioner knowledge in schools and universities? *Educational Researcher, 28*(5), 12–21.

Anderson, G. L., Herr, K., & Nihlen, A. (1994). *Studying your own school: An educator's guide to qualitative practitioner research.* Thousand Oaks, CA: Corwin.

Anderson, G. L., Herr, K., & Nihlen, A. S. (2007). *Studying your own school: An educator's guide to practitioner action research,* (2nd ed.). Thousand Oaks, CA: Corwin.

Anyon, J. (2005). *Radical possibilities: Public policy, urban education, and a new social movement.* New York: Routledge.

Appadurai, A. (2006). The right to research. *Globalisation, Societies and Education, 4*(2), 167–177.

Apple, M. (1987). The de-skilling of teachers. In F. Bolin & J. M. Falk (Eds.), *Teacher renewal: Professional issues, personal choices* (pp. 59–75). New York: Teachers College Press.

Apple, M. (2006). *Educating the "right" way: Market, standards, God, and inequality.* New York: Routledge.

Argyris, C., & Schön, D. (1978). *Organizational learning: A theory of action perspective.* Reading, MA: Addison-Wesley.

Atwell, N. (1987). *In the middle: Writing, reading, and learning with adolescents.* Upper Montclair, NJ: Boynton/Cook.

Ballenger, C. (1998). *Teaching other people's children: Literacy and learning in a bilingual classroom.* New York: Teachers College Press.

Ballenger, C. (Ed.). (2004). *Regarding children's words: Teacher research on language and literacy.* New York: Teachers College Press.

Barnatt, J., Cochran-Smith, M., Friedman, A., Pine, G., & Baroz, R. (2007, April). *Inquiry on inquiry: practitioner research and pupils' learning.* Paper presented at the annual meeting of the American Educational Research Association, Chicago.

Benson, C., & Christian, S. (Eds.). (2002). *Writing to make a difference: Classroom projects for community change.* New York: Teachers College Press.

Berdan, K., Boulton, I., Eidman-Aadahl, E., Fleming, J., Gardner, L., Rogers, I., & Solomon, A. (Eds.). (2006). *Writing for a change: Boosting literacy and learning through social action.* San Francisco: Jossey-Bass.

Berliner, D. (2006). Our impoverished view of educational research. *Teachers College Record, 108*(6), 949–995.

Bertfield, J., & Merrill, M. (2008). The challenge of adoption in implementing comprehensive data-driven, decision-making solutions. In E. Mandinach & M. Honey (Eds.), *Data-driven school improvement: Linking data and learning* (pp. 191–208). New York: Teachers College Press.

Berthoff, A. (1987). The teacher as researcher. In D. Goswami & P. R. Stillman (Eds.), *Reclaiming the classroom: Teacher research as an agency for change* (pp. 28–48). Upper Montclair, NJ: Boynton/Cook.

Beyer, L. (1988). *Knowing and acting: Inquiry ideology and educational studies.* London: Falmer.

Bissex, G., & Bullock, R. (1987). *Seeing for ourselves: Case study research by teachers of writing.* Portsmouth, NH: Heinemann.

Blackburn, M. V. (2005). Agency in borderland discourses: Examining language use in a community center with Black queer youth. *Teachers College Record, 107*(1), 89–113.

Blackburn, M. V., Clark, C. T., Kenney, L. M., & Smith, J. M. (in press). *Acting out: Teachers combating homophobia and becoming an activist community.* New York: Teachers College Press.

Blankstein, A., Houston, P., & Cole, R. (2008). *Sustaining professional learning communities.* Thousand Oaks, CA: Corwin.

Bolam, R., McMahon, A., Stoll, L., Thomas, S., Wallace, M., Greenwood, A., et al. (2005). *Creating and sustaining effective professional learning communities* (Research Report 637). London: DES and University of Bristol.

Borg, S. (2006). *Teacher cognition and language education*. London: Continuum.

Boudett, K. P., City, E. A., & Murnane, R. J. (Eds.). (2005). *Data wise: A step-by-step guide to using assessment results to improve teaching and learning*. Cambridge MA: Harvard University Press.

Boudett, K., & Steele, J. (2007). *Data wise in action: Stories of schools using data to improve teaching and learning*. Cambridge, MA: Harvard Education Press.

Boyer, E. L. (1990). *Scholarship reconsidered*. San Francisco: Carnegie Foundation for Advancement of Teaching.

Bracey, G. (2003). April foolishness: The 20th anniversary of *A Nation at Risk*. Retrieved February 22, 2004, from http://www.pekintl.org/kappan/k0304bra.htm

Bracey, G. (2004). *Setting the record straight: Responses to misconceptions about public education in the U.S.* Portsmouth, NH: Heinemann.

Brandt, D., & Clinton, K. (2002). Limits of the local: Expanding perspectives on literacy as a social practice. *Journal of Literacy Research, 34*(3), 337–356.

Branscombe, N. A., Goswami, D., & Schwartz, J. (1992). *Students teaching, teachers learning*. Portsmouth, NH: Boynton/Cook.

Braverman, H. (1974). *Labor and monopoly capital: The degradation of work in the 20th century*. New York: Monthly Review Press.

Brennan, M., Day, C., Meyer, J., Munn-Giddings, C., Somekh, B., Walker, M., & Zeichner, K. (Eds). (2005). [Special Issue]. *Educational Action Research,13*(3).

Britzman, D. P. (1991). *Practice makes practice: A critical study of learning to teach*. Albany: State University of New York Press.

Britzman, D. P. (2003). *Practice makes practice: A critical study of learning to teach. (Revised Edition)*. Albany: State University of New York Press.

Brydon-Miller, M., McGuire, P., & McIntyre, A. (Eds.). (2004). *Traveling companions: Feminism, teaching, and action research*. Westport, CT: Praeger.

Bryk, A. (2008). The future of education research, an address by Anthony S. Bryk. Washington, DC: American Enterprise Institute.

Bryk, A., Camburn, E., & Louis, K. S. (1999). Professional community in Chicago elementary schools: Facilitating factors and organizational consequences. *Educational Administration Quarterly, 35*(Supplement), 751–781.

Bullough, R. V., & Pinnegar, S. (2001). Guidelines for quality in autobiographical forms of self-study research. *Educational Researcher, 30*(3), 13–21.

Burnaford, G., Fischer, J., & Hobson, D. (Eds.). (2001). *Teachers doing research: The power of action through inquiry*. Mahwah, NJ: Erlbaum.

Bush, G. (2002, September 4). Press release: President higlights progress made on education reform. The East Room, the White House, Office of the Press Secretary. Retrieved May 1, 2006, from *https://www.whitehouse.gov.news/releases/2002/09/20020904_6.html*

Calliari, M., Rentsch, J., & Weaver, M. (2005). *The Saginaw teacher study group movement: From pilot to districtwide study groups in four years*. Berkeley, CA: National Writing Project.

Cammarota, J., & Fine, M. (Eds.). (2008). *Revolutionizing education: Youth participatory action research in motion*. New York: Routledge.

Campano, G. (2007). *Immigrant students and literacy: Reading, writing and remembering*. New York: Teachers College Press.

Campbell, A., & Groundwater-Smith, S. (Eds.). (2007). *An ethical approach to practitioner research*. New York: Routledge.

Carini, P. F. (2001). *Starting strong: A different look at children, schools and standards*. New York: Teachers College Press.

Carini, P. F., & Himley, M. (1991). The study of works: A phenomenological approach to understanding children as thinkers and learners. In M. Himley (Ed.), *Shared territory: Understanding children's writing as works* (pp. 17–72). New York: Oxford University Press.

Caro-Bruce, C., Flessner, R., Klehr, M., & Zeichner, K. (Eds.). (2007). *Creating equitable classrooms through action research*. Thousand Oaks, CA: Corwin.

Carr, W. (1987). What is educational practice? *Journal of Philosophy of Education, 21*, 163–175.

Carr, W., & Kemmis, S. (1986). *Becoming critical: Education, knowledge, and action research*. London: Falmer.

Castanell, L., & Pinar, W. (Eds.) (1993). *Understanding curriculum as racial text: Representations of identity and difference in education*. Albany: State University of New York Press.

Center on Education Policy. (2006). *From the capital to the classroom: Year 4 of the No Child Left Behind Act*. Washington, DC: Author.

Chiseri-Strater, E., & Sunstein, B. S. (2006). *What works? A practical guide for teacher research*. Portsmouth, NH: Heinemann.

Christensen, L. (2000). *Reading, writing, and rising up: Teaching about social justice and the power of the written word*. Milwaukee, WI: Rethinking Schools.

Clandinin, D. J., & Connelly, F. M. (1990). Stories of experience and narrative inquiry. *Educational Researcher, 19*(5), 2–14.

Clandinin, D. J., & Connelly, F. M. (Eds.). (1995). *Teachers' professional knowledge landscapes* (Vol. 15). New York: Teachers College Press.

Clarke, A., & Erickson, G. (Eds.). (2003). *Teacher inquiry: Living the research in everyday practice*. London: Routledge Falmer.

Clifford, G., & Guthrie, J. (1988). *Ed school, a brief for professional education*. Chicago: University of Chicago Press.

Coalition for Evidence-Based Policy. (2002). *Bringing evidence-driven progress to education: A recommended strategy for the U.S. Department of Education*. Washington, DC: Council for Excellence in Government.

Cobb, P., McClain, K., de Silva Lamberg, T., & Dean, C. (2003). Situating teachers' instructional practices in the institutional setting of the school and district. *Educational Researcher, 32*(6), 13–24.

Cochran-Smith, M. (1991). Learning to teach against the grain. *Harvard Educational Review, 51*(3), 279–310.

Cochran-Smith, M. (2003a). Learning and unlearning: The education of teacher educators. *Teaching and Teacher Education, 19*(1), 5–28.

Cochran-Smith, M. (2003b). Inquiry and outcomes: Learning to teach in an age of accountability. *Teacher Education and Practice, 15*(4), 12–34.

Cochran-Smith, M. (2005). The new teacher education: For better or for worse? *Educational Researcher, 34*(6), 3–17.

Cochran-Smith, M. (in press). Toward a theory of teacher education for social justice. In M. Fullan, A. Hargreaves, D. Hopkins & A. Lieberman (Eds.), *The international handbook of educational change* (2nd edition). New York: Springer.

Cochran-Smith, M., Barnatt, J., Lahann, R., Shakman, K., & Terrell, D. (2008). Teacher education for social justice: Critiquing the critiques. In W. Ayers, T. Quinn, & D. Stovall (Eds.), *The handbook of social justice in education* (pp. 625–639). Philadelphia: Taylor and Francis.

Cochran-Smith, M., & Fries, K. (2005). Researching teacher education in changing times: Paradigms and politics. In M. Cochran-Smith & K. Zeichner (Eds.), *Studying teacher education: The report of the AERA panel on research and teacher education* (pp. 69–110). Mahwah, NJ: Erlbaum.

Cochran-Smith, M., & Lytle, S. L. (1990). Research on teaching and teacher research: The issues that divide. *Educational Researcher, 19*(2), 2–11.

Cochran-Smith, M., & Lytle, S. L. (1993). *Inside/outside: Teacher research and knowledge*. New York: Teachers College Press.

Cochran-Smith, M., & Lytle, S. L. (1997). *Teacher inquiry and the epistemology of teaching*. Paper presented at the Annual Meeting of the American Educational Research Association, Chicago, Illinois, April, 1997.

Cochran-Smith, M., & Lytle, S. L. (1998). Teacher research: The question that persists. *International Journal of Leadership in Education, 1*(1), 19–36.

Cochran-Smith, M., & Lytle, S. L. (1999a). The teacher research movement: A decade later. *Educational Researcher, 28*(7), 15–25.

Cochran-Smith, M., & Lytle, S. L. (1999b). Relationship of knowledge and practice: Teacher learning in communities. In A. Iran-Nejad & C. Pearson (Eds.), *Review of research in education* (Vol. 24, pp. 249–306). Washington, DC: American Educational Research Association.

Cochran-Smith, M., & Lytle, S. L. (2001). Beyond certainty: Taking an inquiry stance on practice. In A. Lieberman & L. Miller (Eds.), *Teachers caught in the action: Professional development in practice* (pp. 45–60). New York: Teachers College Press.

Cochran-Smith, M., & Lytle, S. L. (2004). Practitioner inquiry, knowledge, and university culture. In J. Loughran, M. L. Hamilton, V. LaBoskey, & T. Russell (Eds.), *International handbook of research of self-study of teaching and teacher education practices* (pp. 601–649). Amsterdam: Kluwer.

Cochran-Smith, M., & Lytle, S. L. (2006). Troubling images of teaching in NCLB. *Harvard Educational Review, 76*(4), 668–697.

Cochran-Smith, M., & Lytle, S. L. (2008). Teacher research as stance. In B. Somekh & S. Noffke (Eds.), *Handbook of educational action research* (pp. 30–38). Thousand Oaks, CA: Sage.

Cohen, D. (1995). What is the system in systemic reform? *Educational Researcher, 24*(9), 11–17, 31.

Cole, A. L., & Knowles, J. G. (1995). A life history approach to self-study: Methods and issues. In R. Russell & F. Korthagen (Eds.), *Teachers who teach teachers: Reflections on teacher education.* London: Falmer.

Cole, A. L., & Knowles, J. G. (1998). The self-study of teacher education practices and the reform of teacher education. In M. L. Hamilton (Ed.), *Reconceptualizing teaching practice: Self-study in teacher education* (pp. 224–234). London: Falmer.

Comber, B. (2005). Making use of theories about literacy and justice: teachers researching practice. *Educational Action Research, 13(1),* 43–55.

Comber, B., & Kamler, B. (Eds.). (2005). *Turn-around pedagogies: Literacy interventions for at-risk students.* Newtown, NSW, Australia: Primary English Teaching Association.

Comber, B., Nixon, H., & Reid, J. (Eds.). (2007). *Literacies in place: Teaching environmental communications.* Newtown, NSW, Australia: Primary English Teaching Association.

Compton-Lilly, C. (2003). *Reading families: The literate lives of urban children.* New York: Teachers College Press.

Compton-Lilly, C. (2007). *Rereading families: The literate lives of urban children four years later.* New York: Teachers College Press.

Crocco, M., Bayard, F., & Schwartz, S. (2003). Inquiring minds want to know: Action research at a New York City professional development school. *Journal of Teacher Education, 54*(1), 19–30.

Crosby, W., George, A., Hatch, A., Robinson, R., & Thomas, T. (2006). *Writing to be heard: Building respectful communities.* Philadelphia: Research for Action.

Cunningham, G. (2008). *University of North Carolina education schools: Helping or hindering potential teachers?* Raleigh, NC: John William Pope Center for Higher Education Policy.

Cunningham, J. B. (1983). Gathering data in a changing organization. *Human Relations, 36*(5), 403–420.

Cunningham Florez, M. (2001, May). *Reflective teaching practice in adult ESL settings.* Retrieved September 19, 2008, from www.cal.org/caela/esl_resources/digests/reflect.html

Dana, N., Silva, D., & Snow-Gerono, J. (2002). Building a culture of inquiry in a professional development school. *Teacher Education and Practice, 15*(4), 71–89.

Darling-Hammond, L. (2004). From "separate but equal" to "No Child Left Behind": The collision of new standards and old inequalities. In D. Meier & G. Wood (Eds.), *Many children left behind: How the No Child Left Behind Act is damaging our children and our schools* (pp. 3–32). Boston: Beacon.

Darling-Hammond, L., & Sclan, E. (1996). Who teaches and why. In J. Sikula (Ed.), *Handbook of research on teacher education* (pp. 67–101). New York: Simon & Schuster/Macmillan.

Decker, P., Mayer, D., & Glazerman, S. (2004). *The effects of Teach for America on students: Findings from a national evaluation* (No. MPR Ref. No.: 8792-750). Princeton, NJ: Mathematica Policy Research.

Donnelly, A., Morgan, D. N., DeFord, D. E., Files, J., Long, S., Mills, H., Stephens, D., & Styslinger, M. (2005). Transformative professional development: Negotiating knowledge with an inquiry stance. *Language Arts, 82*(5), 336–346.

Dudley-Marling, C. (1997). *Living with uncertainty: The messy reality of classroom practice*. Portsmouth, NH: Heinemann.

DuFour, R., & Eaker, R. (1998). *Professional learning communities at work: Best practices for enhancing student achievement*. Alexandria, VA: Association of Supervision and Curriculum Development.

DuFour, R., Eaker, R., & DuFour, R. (2005). *On common ground: The power of professional learning communities*. Bloomington, IN: Solution Tree.

Duncan-Andrade, J., & Morrell, E. (2008). *The art of critical pedagogy: The possibilities of moving from theory to practice in urban schools*. New York: Peter Lang.

Edelsky, C. (2005). What's resisted, who's resisting, and other questions. *Practitioner inquiry day at the Ethnography in Education Forum*. Philadelphia: University of Pennsylvania Press.

Edelsky, C. (2006). *With literacy and justice for all: Rethinking the social in language and education*. Mahwah, NJ: Erlbaum.

Elliot, J. (1985). Facilitating action research in schools: Some dilemmas. In R. Burgess (Ed.), *Field methods in the study of education* (pp. 263–269). London: Falmer.

Elliott, J. (2005). Becoming critical: The failure to connect. *Educational Action Research, 13*(3), 359–373.

Erickson, F. (2005). Arts, humanities and sciences in educational research and social engineering in federal education policy. *Teachers College Record, 107*(1), 4–9.

Erickson, F. (2007). Some thoughts on "proximal" formative assessment of student learning. In P. A. Moss (Ed.), *Evidence and decision making* (186–216). Malden, MA: NSSE/Blackwell Publishing.

Fairbanks, C. M., & LaGrone, D. (2006). Learning together: Constructing knowledge in a teacher research group. *Teacher Education Quarterly, 33*(3), 7–25.

Falk, B., & Blumenreich, M. (2005). *The power of questions: A guide to teacher and student research*. Portsmouth, NH: Heinemann.

Fecho, B. (2003). Yeki bood/yeki na bood: Writing and publishing as a teacher researcher. *Research in the Teaching of English, 37*(3), 282–294.

Fecho, B. (2004). *"Is this English?": Race, language, and culture in the classroom*. New York: Teachers College Press.

Fecho, B., & Allen, J. (2002). Teacher inquiry into literacy, social justice, and power. In J. Flood, D. Lapp, J. Jensen, & J. Squire (Eds.), *The handbook of research on teaching the English language arts* (2nd Ed., pp. 232–246). Mahwah, NJ: Erlbaum.

Fecho, B., Allen, J., Mazaros, C., & Inyega, H. (2006). Teacher research in writing classrooms. In P. Smagorinsky (Ed.), *Research on composition: Multiple perspectives on two decades of change* (pp. 108–140). New York: Teachers College Press.

Feldman, A., Konold, C., & Coulter, B. (2000). *Network science a decade later: The Internet and classroom learning*. Mahwah, NJ: Erlbaum.

Fenstermacher, G. (1994). The knower and the known: The nature of knowledge in research on teaching. In L. Darling-Hammond (Ed.), *Review of research in education* (Vol. 20, pp. 3–56). Washington, DC: American Educational Research Association.

Fishman, S. M., & McCarthy, L. (1998). *John Dewey and the challenge of classroom practice*. New York: Teachers College Press.

Fishman, S. M., & McCarthy, L. (2000). *Unplayed tapes: A personal history of collaborative teacher research.* Urbana, IL: National Council of Teachers of English.

Fishman, S. M., & McCarthy, L. (2002). *Whose goals? Whose aspirations? Learning to teach underprepared writers across the curriculum.* Logan: Utah State University Press.

Fishman, S. M., & McCarthy, L. (2007). *John Dewey and the philosophy and practice of hope.* Urbana: University of Illinois Press.

Fleischer, C. (2000). *Teachers organizing for change: Making literacy learning everybody's business.* Urbana, IL: National Council of Teachers of English.

Flood, J., Heath, S. B., & Lapp, D. (Eds). (2008). *Handbook of research on teaching literacy through the communicative and visual arts* (Vol. II). Mahwah, NJ: Erlbaum.

Florio-Ruane, S. (2001). *Teacher education and the cultural imagination: Autobiography, conversation, and narrative.* Mahwah, NJ: Erlbaum.

Foucault, M. (1980). *Power/knowledge: Selected interviews and other writings, 1972–1977.* New York: Pantheon.

Fox, M., Martin, P., & Green, G. (2007). *Doing practitioner research.* London: Sage.

Franke, D. (1995). Writing into unmapped territory: The practice of lateral citations. In L. W. Phelps & J. Emig (Eds.), *Feminine principles and women's experiences in American composition and rhetoric* (pp. 375–384). Pittsburgh: University of Pittsburgh Press.

Fraser, N. (2003). Social justice in an age of identity politics: Redistribution, recognition and participation. In N. Fraser & A. Honneth (Eds.), *Redistribution or recognition: A political-philosophical debate* (pp. 7–109). London: Verso.

Freese, A. (2006). Reframing one's teaching: Discovering our teacher selves through reflection and inquiry. *Teaching and Teacher Education, 22,* 100–119.

Freire, P. (1970). *Pedagogy of the oppressed* (translated by M. B. Ramos). New York: Seabury.

Friedrich, L., Tateishi, C., Malarkey, T., Simons, E. R., & Williams, M. (Eds.). (2005). *Working toward equity: Writings and resources from the Teacher Research Collaborative.* Berkeley, CA: National Writing Project.

Fries, K., & Cochran-Smith, M. (2005). Teacher research and classroom management: What questions do teachers ask? In C. Evertson & C. Weinstein (Eds.), *The handbook of research on classroom management* (pp. 945–981). Mahwah, NJ: Erlbaum.

Fuhrman, S., & Lazerson, M. (Eds.). (2005). *The public schools.* Oxford UK: Oxford University Press.

Fullan, M. (1993). *Change forces: Probing the depths of educational reform.* London: Falmer.

Fullan, M. (1994). Teacher leadership: A failure to conceptualize. In D. R. Walling (Ed.), *Teachers as leaders: Perspectives on the professional development of teachers* (pp. 241–253). Bloomington, IN: Phi Delta Kappa Educational Foundation.

Fullan, M. (2001). *The new meaning of educational change* (3rd edition). New York: Teachers College Press.

Gallas, K. (2003). *Imagination and literacy: A teacher's search for the heart of learning.* New York: Teachers College Press.

Gawande, A. (2007). *Better: A surgeon's notes on performance.* New York: Metropolitan.

Geertz, C. (1983). *Local knowledge: Further essays in interpretive anthropology*. New York: Basic Books.

Geertz, C. Geertz, H., & Rosen, L. (1979). *Meaning and order in Moroccan society*. New York: Cambridge University Press.

Gewirtz, S., & Cribb, A. (2002). Plural conceptions of social justice: Implications for policy sociology. *Journal of Education Policy, 17*(5), 499–509.

Ginsberg, A. E., Shapiro, J. P., & Brown, S. P. (2004). *Gender in urban education: Strategies for student achievement*. Portsmouth, NH: Heinemann.

Giroux, H. (1988). *Teachers as intellectuals: Toward a critical pedagogy of learning*. Westport, CT: Bergin & Harvey.

Gold, E., Rhodes, A., Brown, S., Lytle, S., & Waff, D. (2001). *Clients, consumers, or collaborators? Parents and their roles in school reform during Children Achieving, 1995–2005*. Philadelphia: Consortium for Policy Research in Education.

Gonzalez, N. E., Moll, L. C., & Amanti, C. (Eds.). (2005). *Funds of knowledge: Theorizing practices in households, communities, and classrooms*. Mahwah, NJ: Erlbaum.

Goswami, D., Lewis, C., Rutherford, M., & Waff, D. (2009). *On teacher inquiry: Approaches to language and literacy research*. New York: Teachers College Press.

Goswami, D., & Stillman, P. R. (Eds.). (1987). *Reclaiming the classroom: Teacher research as an agency for change*. Upper Montclair, NJ: Boynton/Cook.

Greene, M. (2008, March). *From bare fact to intellectual possibility: The leap of imagination*. Paper presented at the annual meeting of the American Educational Research Association, New York.

Greenwood, D., & Levin, M. (2007). *Introduction to action research: Social research for social change* (2nd ed.). Thousand Oaks, CA: Sage.

Gregory, G. H., & Kuzmich, L. (2007). *Teacher teams that get results: 61 strategies for sustaining and renewing professional learning communities*. Thousand Oaks, CA: Corwin Press.

Gutman, A. (1987/1999). *Democratic education*. Princeton: Princeton University Press.

Gutman, A., & Thompson, D. (1996). *Democracy and disagreement*. Cambridge, MA: Belknap.

Hamilton, M. L. (Ed.). (1998). *Reconceptualizing teaching practice: Self-study in teacher education*. London: Falmer.

Hammack, F. (1997). Ethical issues in teacher research. *Teachers College Record 99*(2), 247–265.

Hammer, D., & Schifter, D. (2001). Practices of inquiry in teaching and research. *Cognition and Instruction, 19*(4), 441–78.

Hammersley, M. (2000). Evidence-based practice and the contribution of educational research. In L. Trinder & S. Reynolds (Eds.), *Evidence-based practice, a critical appraisal* (pp. 163–183). London: Blackwell Science.

Hankins, K. H. (2003). *Teaching through the storm: A journal of hope*. New York: Teachers College Press.

Hargreaves, A. (2003). *Teaching in the knowledge society: Education in the age of insecurity*. Maidenhead, UK: Open University Press.

Hargreaves, A. (2007). Sustainable professional learning communities. In L. Stoll & K. S. Louis (Eds.), *Professional learning communities: Divergence, depth and dilemmas* (pp. 181–195). Berkshire, England: Open University Press.

Hargreaves, A. (2008). Leading professional learning communities: Moral choices amid murky realities. In A. Blankstein, P. Houston, & R. Cole (Eds.), *Sustaining professional learning communities* (pp. 175–197). Thousand Oaks, CA: Corwin.

Harvard Educational Review. (2005). Interview: U.S. Secretary of Education Margaret Spellings. *75*(4), 364–382.

Hatch, T. (2006). Improving schools in turbulent times. *The New Educator, 2,* 267–276.

Hatch, T., Ahmed, D., Lieberman, A., Faigenbaum, D., White, M. E., & Mace, D. H. P. (Eds.). (2005). *Going public with our teaching: An anthology of practice.* New York: Teachers College Press.

Hatch, T., & Shulman, L. S. (2005). *Into the classroom: Developing the scholarship of teaching and learning.* San Francisco: Jossey-Bass.

Heath, S. (1983). *Ways with words: Language, life, and work in communities and classrooms.* Cambridge, MA: Harvard University Press.

Heifitz, R. (1994). *Leadership without easy answers.* Cambridge, MA: Harvard University Press.

Herr, K., & Anderson, G. L. (2005). *The action research dissertation: A guide for students and faculty.* Thousand Oaks, CA: Sage.

Hiebert, J., Gallimore, R., & Stigler, J. (2002). A knowledge base for the teaching profession: What would it look like and how can we get one? *Educational Researcher, 31*(5), 3–15.

Himley, M., & Carini, P. (2000). *From another angle: children's strengths and school standards.* New York: Teachers College Press.

Himley, M., & Carini, P. (in press). *Jenny's story: Prospect's philosophy in action.* New York: Teachers College Press.

Hollingsworth, S., & Sockett, H. (Eds.). (1994). *Teacher research and educational reform: Yearbook of the NSSE.* Chicago: University of Chicago Press.

Honneth, A. (2003). Redistribution as recognition: A response to Nancy Fraser. In N. Fraser & A. Honneth (Eds.), *Redistribution or recognition: A political-philosophical debate* (pp. 110–197). London: Verso.

Hord, S. (2004). Professional learning communities: An overview. In S. Hord (Ed.), *Learning together, leading together: Changing schools through professional learning communities* (pp. 5–14). New York: Teachers College Press.

Hord, S., & Hirsh, S. (2008). Making the promise a reality. In A. Blankstein, P. Houston, & R. Cole (Eds.), *Sustaining professional learning communities* (pp. 23–40). Thousand Oaks, CA: Corwin.

Howe, K. (1997). *Understanding equal educational opportunity: Social justice, democracy, and schooling.* New York: Teachers College Press.

Huberman, M. (1996). Focus on research moving mainstream: Taking a closer look at teacher research. *Language Arts, 73*(2), 124–140.

Huberman, M. (1999). The mind is its own place: The influence of sustained interactivity with practitioners on educational researchers. *Harvard Educational Review, 69*(3), 289–319.

Hursh, D. (2006). The crisis in urban education: Resisting neoliberal policies and forging democratic possibilities. *Educational Researcher, 35*(4), 19–25.

Hutchings, P. (Ed.). (2000). *Opening lines: Approaches to the scholarship of teaching and learning*. Menlo Park, CA: Carnegie Foundation for the Advancement of Teaching.

Hutchings, P. (Ed.). (2002). *Ethics of inquiry, Issues in the scholarship of teaching and learning*. Menlo Park, CA: Carnegie Foundation for the Advancement of Teaching.

Hyland, N., & Noffke, S. (2005). Understanding diversity through social and community inquiry. *Journal of Teacher Education, 56*(4), 367–381.

Ingersoll, R. (2003). *Who controls teachers' work?* Cambridge, MA: Harvard University Press.

Jackson, D., & Temperley, J. (2007). From professional learning community to networked learning community. In L. Stoll & K. S. Louis (Eds.), *Professional learning communities: Divergence, depth and dilemmas* (pp. 51–62). Berkshire, UK: Open University Press.

Judge, H. (1982). *American graduate schools of education: A view from abroad*. New York: Ford Foundation.

Kemmis, S., & McTaggart, R. (1988). *The action research planner*. Geelong, New Zealand: Deakin University Press.

Kemmis, S., & McTaggart, R. (2005). Participatory action research: Communicative action and the public sphere. In N. K. Denzin & Y. S. Lincoln (Eds.), *The SAGE handbook of qualitative research* (3rd ed., pp. 559–603). Thousand Oaks, CA: Sage.

Kincheloe, J. L. (1991). *Teachers as researchers: Qualitative inquiry as a path to empowerment*. London: Falmer.

King, J. (2008). Critical and qualitative research in teacher education: A blues epistemology, a reason for knowing for cultural well-being. In M. Cochran-Smith, S. Feiman Nemser, & J. McIntyre (Eds.), *Handbook of research on teacher education: Enduring issues in changing contexts* (pp. 1094–1135). Mahwah, NJ: Lawrence Erlbaum.

Knapp, M., Copland, M., & Swinnerton, J. (2007). Understanding the promise and dynamics of data-informed leadership. In P. Moss (Ed.), *Evidence and decision making: The 106th yearbook of the national society for the study of education, Part I* (pp. 74–104). Chicago: National Society for the Study of Education.

Kruse, S. D., Louis, K. S., & Bryk, A. (1995). An emerging framework for analyzing school-based professional community. In K. S. Louis, S. Kruse et al. (Eds.), *Professionalism and community: Perspectives on reforming urban schools* (pp. 23–44). Long Oaks, CA: Corwin.

Labaree, D. F. (2003). The peculiar problems of preparing educational researchers. *Educational Researcher, 32*(4), 13–22.

Lagemann, E. (2000). *An elusive science: The troubling history of education research*. Chicago: University of Chicago Press.

Lamott, A. (1994). *Bird by bird, some instructions on writing and life*. New York: Anchor.

Lampert, M. (1990). When the problem is not the question and the solution is not the answer: Mathematical knowing and teaching. *American Educational Research Journal, 27*(1), 29–63.

Lampert, M. (2000). Knowing teaching: The intersection of research on teaching and research. *Harvard Educational Review, 70*(1), 86–99.

Lampert, M. (2001). *Teaching problems and the problems of teaching.* New Haven, CT: Yale University Press.

Lampert, M., & Ball, D. (1998). *Teaching, multimedia, and mathematics: Investigations of real practice.* New York: Teachers College Press.

Langrall, C. W. (2006). *Teachers engaged in research: Inquiry into mathematics classrooms, grades 3–5.* Greenwich, CT: Information Age Publishing.

Lankshear, C., & Knobel, M. (Eds.). (2004). *A handbook for teacher research: From design to implementation.* Berkshire, UK: Open University Press.

Lather, P. (1986). Research as praxis. *Harvard Educational Review, 56*(3), 257–277.

Lather, P. (2004). This is your father's paradigm: Government intrusion and the case of qualitative research in education. *Qualitative Inquiry, 10*(1), 15–34.

Latour, B. (1993). *We have never been modern.* Cambridge, MA: Harvard University Press.

Latour, B. (1996, Summer). On interobjectivity: Symposium on "the lessons of simian society". *Mind, Culture and Activity, 3*(3).

Lee, V. E., & Smith, J. (1996). Collective responsibility for learning and its effects on gains in achievement for early secondary students. *American Journal of Education, 104*(2), 103–147.

Levin, B., & Rock, C. (2003). The effects of collaborative action research on pre-service and experienced teacher partners in professional development schools. *Journal of Teacher Education, 54*(2), 135–150.

Lewis, C., Guerrero, M., Makikana, L., & Armstrong, M. (2002, Spring). Exploring language, identity, and the power of narrative. *Bread Loaf Teacher Network Magazine,* pp. 8–10.

Lieberman, A., & Miller, L. (Eds.). (2008). *Teachers in professional communities: Improving teaching and learning.* New York: Teachers College Press.

Lincoln, Y., & Guba, E. (1990). *Naturalistic inquiry.* Beverly Hills, CA: Sage.

Linn, R. (2003). Accountability: Responsibility and reasonable expectations. *Educational Researcher, 32,* 3–13.

Lipman, P. (2003). *High stakes education: Inequality, globalization and urban school reform.* New York: Falmer.

Little, J. W. (2002). Locating learning in teachers' communities of practice: Opening up problems of analysis in records of everyday work. *Teaching and Teacher Education, 18*(8), 917–946.

Little, J. W. (2003). Inside teacher community: Representations of classroom practice. *Teachers College Record, 105*(6), 913–945.

Little, J. W. (2007). Teachers' accounts of classroom experience as a resource for professional learning and instructional decision making. In P. A. Moss (Ed.), *Evidence and decision making* (pp. 217–240). Malden, MA: NSSE/Blackwell.

Little, J. W., & Curry, M. W. (2008). Structuring talk about teaching and learning: The use of evidence in protocal-based conversation. In L. M. Earl & H. Timperley (Eds.), *Professional learning conversations: Challenges in using evidence for improvement* (pp. 29–42). New York: Springer.

Loughran, J., Hamilton, M. L., LaBoskey, V., & Russell, T. (Eds.). (2004). *International handbook of research of self study of teaching and teacher education practices.* Amsterdam: Kluwer.

Loughran, J., & Northfield, J. (1998). A framework for the development of self-study practice. In M. L. Hamilton (Ed.), *Reconceptualizing teaching practice: Self-study in teacher education* (pp. 7–18). London: Falmer.

Louis, K. S. (2008). Creating and sustaining professional communities. In A. Blankstein, P. Houston, & R. Cole (Eds.), *Sustaining professional learning communities* (pp. 41–57). Thousand Oaks, CA: Corwin.

Louis, K., & Kruse, S. (1995). *Professionalism and community: Perspectives on reforming urban schools.* Thousand Oaks, CA: Corwin.

Luke, A. (2004). Teaching after the market: From commodity to cosmopolitan. *Teachers College Record, 106*(7), 1422–1443.

Lyons, N., & LaBoskey, V. K. (Eds.). (2002). *Narrative inquiry in practice: Advancing the knowledge of teaching.* New York: Teachers College Press.

Lytle, J. (2008). Personal communication. October 15, 2008.

Lytle, S. L. (1993). Risky business. *The Quarterly of the National Writing Project and the Center for the Study of Writing and Literacy. 15*(1), 20–23.

Lytle, S. (2000). Teacher research in the contact zone. In M. L. Kamil, P. B. Mosenthal, P. D. Pearson, & R. Barr (Eds.), *Handbook of reading research* (Vol. III, 691–718). Mahwah, NJ: Erlbaum.

Lytle, S. (2006). The literacies of teaching urban adolescents in these times. In D. Alvermann, K. Hinchman, D. Moore, S. Phelps, & D. Waff (Eds.), *Reconceptualizing the literacies in adolescents' lives* (pp. 257–277.). Mahwah, NJ: Erlbaum.

Lytle, S. (2008). Personal communication.

Lytle, S. L., & Cantafio, E. J. (2007, March). *Practitioner inquiry and the pedagogies of dissertation writing.* Paper presented at the Annual Meeting of the American Educational Research Association, Chicago.

Lytle, S. L., Portnoy, D., Waff, D., & Buckley, M. (2009). Teacher research in urban Philadelphia: Twenty years working within, against, and beyond the system. *Educational Action Research, 17*(1), 23–42).

Maimon, G. (Unpublished manuscript). *Journal, 2003–2004.* Philadelphia, PA.

Mandinach, E., & Honey, M. (2008). *Data-driven school improvement.* New York: Teachers College Press.

Mandinach, E., Honey, M., Light, D., & Brunner, C. (2008). A conceptual framework for data-driven decision making. In E. Mandinach & M. Honey (Eds.), *Data-driven school improvement* (pp. 13–31). New York: Teachers College Press.

Masingila, J. O. (2006). *Teachers engaged in research: Inquiry into mathematics classrooms, grades 6–8.* Greenwich, CT: Information Age Publishing.

McEwen, H. (April 1991). *Narrative understanding in the study of teaching.* Paper presented at the annual meeting of the American Educational Research Association, Chicago, IL.

McGuire, P. (2001). Uneven ground: Feminisms and action research. In P. Reason & H. Bradbury (Eds.), *Handbook of action research* (pp. 59–69). London: Sage.

McIntyre, A. (2008). *Participatory action research.* Thousand Oaks, CA: Sage.

McLaughlin, C., Black-Hawkins, K., Brindley, S., McIntyre, D., & Taber, K. S. (2006). *Researching schools: Stories from a schools-university partnership for educational research.* London: Routledge.

McLaughlin, M., & Talbert. J. (2002). Reforming districts. In A. Hightower, M. Knapp, J. Marsh, & M. McLaughlin. (Eds.), *School districts and instructional renewal.* New York: Teachers College Press.

McLaughlin, M., & Talbert, J. (2006). *Building school-based teacher learning communities: Professional strategies to improve student achievement.* New York: Teachers College Press.

McNiff, J. (2002). *Action research: Principles and practices.* London: Falmer.

Meier, D. R., & Henderson, B. (2007). *Learning from young children in the classroom: The art and science of teacher research.* New York: Teachers College Press.

Meier, M., & Wood, G. (Eds.). (2004). *Many children left behind: How the No Child Left Behind Act is damaging our children and our schools.* Boston: Beacon.

Meiskins, P. (1994). "Labor and monopoly capital" for the 1990s: A review and critique of the labor process debate. *Monthly Review, 6*(46), 45.

MetLife Fellows. (2008). *The missing link: Connecting teacher research, practice and policy to improve student learning* (E. Meyers, F. Rust, & P. Paul, Eds.) New York: Teachers Network.

Metz, M. H., & Page, R. N. (2002). The uses of practitioner research and status issues in educational research: Reply to Gary Anderson. *Educational Researcher, 31*(7), 26–27.

Meyers, E., & Rust, F. (Eds). (2003). *Taking action with teacher research.* Portsmouth, NH: Heinemann.

Meyers, E., Rust, F., & Paul, P. (n.d.) *The missing link: Connecting teacher research, practice and policy to improve student learning.* New York: Teachers Network.

Michelli, N. (2005). Education for democracy: What can it be? In N. Michelli & D. Keiser (Eds.), *Teacher education for social justice and democracy.* New York: Routledge.

Mishler, E. (1990). Validation in inquiry-guided research: The role of exemplars in narrative studies. *Harvard Educational Review, 60*(4), 415–442.

Mitchell, J. (1984). Typicality and the case study. In R. F. Ellen (Ed.), *Ethnographic research: A guide to conduct* (pp. 238–241). New York: Academic Press.

Mohr, M. M., Rogers, C., Sanford, B., Nocerino, M., MacLean, M. S., & Clawson, S. (2003). *Teacher research for better schools.* New York: Teachers College Press.

Mohr, M., & MacLean, M. (1987). *Working together: A guide for teacher-researchers.* Urbana, IL: National Council of Teachers of English.

Moore Johnson, S., & The Project on the Next Generation of Teachers. (2004). *Finders and keepers: Helping new teachers survive and thrive in our schools.* San Francisco: Jossey-Bass.

Morrell, E. (2007). *Critical literacy and urban youth: Pedagogies of access, dissent, and liberation.* New York: Routledge.

Morse, A., & Davenport, L. R. (2000). *Fostering a stance of inquiry among teachers: Professional development in mathematics education.* Newton, MA: Education Development Center.

Moss, P., & Piety, P. J. (2007). Introduction: Evidence and decision making. In P. Moss (Ed.), *Evidence and decision making, the 106th yearbook of the national society for the study of education* (pp. 1–14). Malden, MA: Blackwell Publishers.

Mule, L. (2006). Preservice teachers' inquiry in a professional development school context: Implications for the practicum. *Teaching and Teacher Education, 22*, 205–218.

Myers, M. (1985). *The teacher-researcher: How to study writing in the classroom.* Urbana, IL: National Council of Teachers of English.

National Commission on Excellence in Education. (1983). *A nation at risk: The imperative for educational reform.* Washington, DC: U.S. Government Printing Office.

National Research Council. (2000). *How people learn.* Washington, DC: National Academy Press.

Nieto, S. (1999). *The light in their eyes: Creating multicultural learning communities.* New York: Teachers College Press.

Nieto, S. (2003). *What keeps teachers going?* New York: Teachers College Press.

Nieto, S. (Ed.). (2005). *Why we teach.* New York: Teachers College Press.

Nirantar. (2007). *Exploring the everyday: Ethnographic approaches to literacy and numeracy.* New Delhi, India: Nirantar & ASPBAE.

Noffke, S. (1997). Professional, personal, and political dimensions of action research. In M. Apple (Ed.), *Review of research in education* (Vol. 22, pp. 305–343). Washington, DC: AERA.

Noffke, S. (2005). Are we critical yet? Some thoughts on reading, rereading and becoming critical. *Educational Action Research 13*(3), 321–327. Washington, DC: AERA.

Noffke, S. E., & Somekh, B. (in press). *The SAGE handbook of educational action research.* Thousand Oaks, CA: Sage.

Nolen, A. L., & Putten, J. V. (2007). Action research in education: Addressing gaps in ethical principals and practices. *Educational Researcher, 36*(7), 401–407.

Oakes, J. (2005). *Keeping track* (2nd ed.). New Haven, CT: Yale University Press.

Oakes, J., Lipton, M., Rogers, J., & Renee, M. (2006, July). *Research as a tool for democratizing education policymaking.* Paper presented at the International Invitational Symposium on Figuring and Re-configuring Research, Policy and Practice for the Knowledge Society, Dublin, Ireland.

Oakes, J., Rogers, J., & Lipton, M. (2006). *Learning power: Organizing for education and justice.* New York: Teachers College Press.

Olson, L. (2004, December 8). Taking root. *Education Week*, pp. S1, S3, S7.

Olyer, C. (2006). *Learning to teach inclusively: Student teachers' classroom inquiries.* Mahwah, NJ: Erlbaum.

Orfield, G., Losen, D., & Wald, J. (2004). *Losing our future: How minority youth are being left behind by the graduation rate crisis.* Cambridge, MA: The Civil Rights Project at Harvard University.

Paige, R. (2001, June 20). Remarks by the U.S. Secretary of education at the summit on the 21st century workforce. Retrieved February 23, 2009, from http://www.ed.gov/news/speeches/2001/06/010620.html

Paige, R. (2003, September 24). Annual back to school address. Retrieved February 23, 2009, from http://www.ed.gov/news/speeches/2003/09/09242003.html

Paige, R. (2004, September 24). Annual back to school address. Retrieved February 23, 2009, from http://www.ed.gov/news/speeches/2004/09/09242004.html

Pappas, C. C., & Zecker, L. B. (Eds.). (2001a). *Transforming literacy curriculum genres: Working with teacher researchers in urban classrooms.* Mahwah, NJ: Erlbaum.

Pappas, C. C., & Zecker, L. B. (Eds.). (2001b). *Teacher inquiries in literacy teaching–learning: Learning to collaborate in elementary urban classrooms.* Mahwah, NJ: Erlbaum.

Pear, R. (2004, February 24). Education chief calls union "terrorist," then recants. *New York Times*, p. A20.

Philadelphia Teachers Learning Cooperative. (1984). On becoming teacher experts: Buying time. *Language Arts, 6,* 731–735.

P.L. 107-110. (2002). No Child Left Behind Act: Reauthorization of the elementary and secondary act. Retrieved June 2002, from http://www.ed.gov

Poetter, T., Wegwert, J., & Haerr, C. (Eds.). (2006). *No Child Left Behind and the illusion of reform: Critical essays by educators.* Lanham, MD: University Press of America.

Popkewitz, T. (1991). *A political sociology of educational reform.* New York: Teachers College Press.

Pressley, M., Wharton-McDonald, R., Allington, R. L., Block, C. C., Morrow, L., Tracey, D., et al. (2001). The nature of effective first-grade literacy instruction. *Scientific studies in reading, 5,* 35–58.

Price, J. (2001). Action research, pedagogy, and change: The transformative potential of action research in pre-service teacher education. *Journal of Curriculum Studies, 33*(1), 43–74.

Price, J. N., & Valli, L. (2005). Preservice teachers becoming agents of change: Pedagogical implications for action research. *Journal of Teacher Education, 56*(1), 57–72.

Pritchard, I. A. (2002). Travelers and trolls: Practitioner research and institutional review boards. *Educational Researcher, 31,* 3–13.

Rawls, J. (1971). *A theory of justice.* Cambridge, MA: Belknap.

Reason, P., & Bradbury, H. (Eds.). (2001). *Handbook of action research: Participative inquiry and practice.* London: Sage.

Reason, P., & Bradbury, H. (Eds.). (2008). *Handbook of action research: Participative inquiry and practice.* London: Sage.

Reason, P., & Rowan, J. (1981). *Human inquiry: A sourcebook of new paradigm research.* New York: Wiley.

Reeves, D. (2007). *Ahead of the curve: The power of assessment to transform teaching and learning.* Bloomington, IN: Solution Tree.

Reich, R. (2002). *Bridging liberalism and multiculturalism in American education.* Chicago: Chicago University Press.

Richardson, V. (1996). The case for formal research and practical inquiry in teacher education. In F. Murray (Ed.), *The teacher educator's handbook* (pp. 715–737). San Francisco: Jossey-Bass.

Robbins, S., & Dyer, M. (Eds.). (2005). *Writing America: Classroom literacy and public engagement.* New York: Teachers College Press.

Rock, C., & Levin, B. (2002). Collaborative action research projects: Enhancing pre-service teacher development in professional development schools. *Teacher Education Quarterly, 29*(1), 7–21.

Rudduck, J. (1985). *Research as a basic for teaching: Readings from the work of Lawrence Stenhouse.* London: Heinemann.

Rust, F., & Meyers, E. (2006). The bright side: Teacher research in the context of educational reform and policy-making. *Teachers and Teaching: Theory and Practice, 12*(1), 69–86.

Rymes, B. (in press). *Classroom discourse analysis: A tool for critical reflection.* Cresskill, NJ: Hampton Press.

Sanders, W. (1998). Value-added assessment. *The School Administrator,* 24–27.

Sanders, W., & Horn, S. (1994). The Tennessee value-added assessment system (TVAAS): Mixed-model methodology in educational assessment. *Journal of Personnel Evaluation in Education, 8,* 299–311.

Schemo, D. (2002, October 24). States get federal warning on school standards. *New York Times,* p. 25.

Schön, D. (1995). The new scholarship requires a new epistemology. *Change, 27*(6), 26–34.

Schultz, R., & Mandzuk, D. (2005). Learning to teach, learning to inquire: A three-year study of teacher candidates' experiences. *Teaching and Teacher Education, 21*(3), 315–331.

Semali, L., & Kincheloe, J. (1999). *What is indigenous knowledge? Voices from the academy.* New York: Falmer Press.

Shen, J. (1999). *The school of education: Its mission, faculty, and reward structure.* New York: Peter Lang.

Sherman, F. T., & Torbert, W. R. (2000). *Transforming social inquiry, transforming social action: New paradigms for crossing the theory/practice divide in universities and communities.* Boston: Kluwer.

Shulman, L. (1999). Professional educational scholarship. In E. Lagemann (Ed.), *Philanthropic foundations: New scholarship, new possibilities* (pp. 159–165). Bloomington: Indiana University Press.

Shulman, L. (2000). From Minsk to Pinsk: Why a scholarship of teaching and learning? *The Journal of Scholarship of Teaching and Learning, 1*(1), 48–52.

Shulman, L., Lieberman, A., Hatch, T., & Lew, M. (1999). The Carnegie Foundation builds the scholarship of teaching with K–12 teachers and teacher educators. *Teaching and Teacher Education: Division K Newsletter, American Educational Research Association, 4,* 1–5.

Simon, K. (2005). Classroom deliberations. In S. Fuhrman & M. Lazerson (Eds.), *The public schools* (pp. 107–129). Oxford, UK: Oxford University Press.

Smith, S. Z., & Smith, M. E. (2006). *Teachers engaged in research: Inquiry in mathematics classrooms, Grades Pre-K–2.* Greenwich, CT: Information Age Publishing.

Smyth, J. (2001). *Critical politics of teachers' work: An Australian perspective.* New York: Peter Lang.

Snow-Gerono, J. (2005). Naming inquiry: PDS teachers' perceptions of teacher research and living an inquiry stance toward teaching. *Teacher Education Quarterly,* pp. 1–16.

Spellings, M. (2006a, April 27, 2006). Remarks at the No Child Left Behind summit: The path to 2014. Retrieved from http://www.ed.gov/news/press releases/2006/04/04272006.html.

Spellings, M. (2006b, March 2006). Testimony of Secretary Spellings on the role of educational global competitiveness before the House Committee on Science.

Sperling, M., & DiPardo, A. (2008). English education research and classroom practice: New directions for new times. *Review of Research in Education, 32*, 62–108.

Spillane, J. P., & Miele, D. B. (2007). Evidence in practice: A framing of the terrain. In P. A. Moss (Ed.), *Evidence and decision making* (pp. 217–240). Malden, MA: NSSE/Blackwell.

State group calls ESEA bills "seriously flawed". (2001) *Education Week, 21*, 31.

Stenhouse, L. (1975). *An introduction to curriculum research and development.* London: Heinemann.

Stenhouse, L. (1983). *Authority, education, and emancipation.* London: Heinemann.

Stenhouse, L. (1985). *Research as a basis for teaching.* London: Heinemann.

Stipek, D. (2005, March 23). "Scientifically based practice": It's about more than improving the quality of research. *Education Week, 33*, 44.

Stipek, D. (2007, November 14). Bridging the research–practice gap [advertisement]. *Education Week, 19*.

Stock, P. L. (2001). Toward a theory of genre in teacher research: Contributions from a reflective practitioner. *English Education, 33*(2), 100–114.

Stock, P. L. (2004, November). *Practicing the scholarship of teaching: What we do with the knowledge we make.* Address given at the NCTE ninety-fourth annual convention, Indianapolis, IN.

Stokes, L. (2001). Lessons from an inquiring school: Forms of inquiry and conditions for teacher learning. In A. Lieberman & L. Miller (Eds.), *Teachers caught in the action: Professional development that matters* (pp. 141–158). New York: Teachers College Press.

Stoll, L., Bolam, R., McMahon, A., Wallace, M., & Thomas, S. (2006). Professional learning communities: A review of the literature. *Journal of Educational Change, 7*(4), 221–258.

Stoll, L., & Louis, K. S. (2007). Professional learning communities: Elaborating new approaches. In L. Stoll & K. S. Louis (Eds.), *Professional learning communities: Divergence, depth and dilemmas* (pp. 1–13). Berkshire, UK: Open University Press.

Street, B., Rogers, A., & Baker, D. (2006). Adult teachers as researchers: Ethnographic approaches to numeracy and literacy as social practices in South Asia. *Convergence, 39*(1), 31–44.

Strieb, L. (in press). *Inviting families.* New York: Teachers College Press.

Tachibana, G. (2007, July). *TIC study group focuses on racism and homophobia.* Retrieved September 17, 2008, from http://www.nwp.org/cs/public/print/resource/2413

Takeuchi, H., Osono, E., & Shimizu, N. (June 2008). The contradictions that drive Toyota's success. *Harvard Business Review*, 96–104.

Temkin, J. (2005). Teachers become researchers. *Catalyst Chicago, 16*(8), 20–21.

Trinder, L., & Reynolds, S. (Eds.). (2000). *Evidence-based practice, a critical appraisal.* London, UK: Blackwell Science.

U.S. Department of Education. (2002). *Meeting the highly qualified teachers challenge: The secretary's annual report on teacher quality.* Washington, DC: Author.

U.S. Department of Education. (2003). *Identifying and implementing educational practices supported by rigorous evidence: A user friendly guide.* Washington, DC: U.S. Department of Education, Institute of Education Sciences, National Center for Education Evaluation and Regional Assistance.

U.S. Department of Education. (2004a). *No Child Left Behind: A toolkit for teachers.* Washington, DC: U.S. Department of Education, Office of the Deputy Secretary.

U.S. Department of Education. (2004b). *The secretary's third annual report on teacher quality.* Washington, DC: Author.

U.S. Department of Education. (2005). *The secretary's fourth annual report on teacher quality: A highly qualified teacher in every classroom.* Washington, DC: U.S. Department of Education, Office of Postsecondary Education.

U.S. Department of Education. (2006). *The secretary's fifth annual report on teacher quality: A highly qualified teacher in every classroom.* Washington, DC: U.S. Department of Education, Office of Postsecondary Education.

Valli, L. (1999). Connecting teacher development and school improvement: Ironic consequences of a pre-service action research course. *Teaching and Teacher Education, 16,* 715–730.

Valli, L., & Price, J. N. (2000). Deepening our understanding of praxis: Teacher educators' reflections on action research. *Teaching Education, 11*(3), 267–278.

Van Houten, L., Miyasaka, J., Agullard, K., & Zimmerman, J. (2006). *Developing an effective school plan.* San Francisco: WestEd.

Van Zee, E. H. (2005). Teaching science teaching through inquiry. In K. Appleton (Ed.), *Elementary science teacher education: International perspectives on contemporary issues and practice* (pp. 239–257). Mahwah, NJ: Erlbaum.

Van Zoest, L. R. (2006). *Teachers engaged in research: Inquiry into mathematics classrooms, grades 9–12.* Greenwich, CT: Information Age Publishing.

Vasquez, V. (2004). *Negotiating critical literacies with young children.* Mahwah, NJ: Erlbaum.

Watanabe, M. (2006). "Some people think this school is tracked and some people don't": Using inquiry groups to unpack teachers' perspectives on detracking. *Theory into Practice, 45*(1), 24–31.

Watkins, K. (1991, April). *Validity in action research.* Paper presented at the annual meeting of the American Educational Research Association, Chicago.

Weinbaum, A., Allen, D., Blythe, T., Simon, K., Seidel, S., & Rubin, C. (2004). *Teaching as inquiry: Asking hard questions to improve practice and student achievement.* New York: Teachers College Press.

Wells, G. (1986). *The meaning makers: Children learning language and using language to learn.* Portsmouth, NH: Heinemann.

Wells, G. (2001). *Action, talk and text: Learning and teaching through inquiry.* New York: Teachers College Press.

Wells, G. (2003). Language and education: Reconceptualizing education as dialogue. *Annual Review of Applied Linguistics, 19*, 135–155.

WestEd. (2006). *R&D alert: Focus on using data to drive reform.* Denver, CO: Author.

Westheimer, J. (1999). Communities and consequences: An inquiry into ideology and practice in teachers' professional work. *Educational Administration Quarterly, 35*(1), 71–105.

Whitehurst, G. (2002). *Scientifically based research on teacher quality: Research on teacher preparation and professional development.* Paper presented at the White House Conference on Preparing Tomorrow's Teachers, Washington, DC.

Whitney, A., Blua, S. , Bright, A., Cabe, R., Dewar, T., Levin, J., Macias, R., & Robers, P. (2008). Beyond strategies: Teacher practice, writing process, and the influence of inquiry. *English Education, 40*(3), 201–229.

Willinsky, J. (2001). The strategic educational research program and the public value of research. *Educational Researcher, 30*(1), 5–14.

Wilson, S. (2007). *"What about Rose?": Using teacher research to reverse school failure.* New York: Teachers College Press.

Wilson, S., Floden, R., & Ferrini-Mundy, J. (2001). *Teacher preparation research: Current knowledge, gaps, and recommendations.* Washington, DC: Center for the Study of Teaching and Policy.

Winter, D., & Robbins, S. (Eds.). (2005). *Writing our communities: Local learning and public culture.* Urbana, IL: National Council of Teachers of English.

Wisniewski, R. (2000). The averted gaze. *Anthropology and Education Quarterly, 31*(1), 5–23.

Wood, D. (2007). Teachers' learning communities: Catalyst for change or a new infrastructure for the status quo? *Teachers College Record, 109*(3), 699–739.

Wright, S., Horn, S., & Sanders, W. (1997). Teachers and classroom context effects on student achievement: Implications for teacher evaluation. *Journal of Personnel Evaluation in Education, 11*(1), 57–67.

Yasumoto, J. Y., Uekawa, K., & Bidwell, C. E. (2001). The collegial focus and high school students' achievement. *Sociology of Education, 74*(3), 181–209.

Young, I. M. (1990). *Justice and the politics of difference.* Princeton: Princeton University Press.

Young, L. A. (Ed.). (2006). *Hip deep: Opinion, vision, and essays by American teenagers.* Providence, RI: Next Generation Press.

Zeichner, K. M., & Noffke, S. E. (2001). Practitioner research. In V. Richardson (Ed.), *Handbook of research on teaching* (4th ed., pp. 298–330). New York: American Educational Research Association/Macmillan.

Zeni, J. (Ed.). (2001). *Ethical issues in practitioner research.* New York: Teachers College Press.

Part II

PRACTITIONERS ON TEACHING, LEARNING, AND SCHOOL LEADERSHIP

In *Inside/Outside* (1993) we argued that when teachers study and write about their work, they make their own distinctive ways of knowing about teaching and learning more visible to themselves and others. We tried to show, both with our own writing and with many examples of research by teachers, that the questions that prompt inquiry, the dimensions of classroom and school life that teachers consider evidence, and the interpretive or conceptual frameworks that teachers use to analyze and interpret their data can deeply alter what we know about teaching and learning and lend credence to the substantial value of the emic perspectives they are uniquely positioned to provide.

Part I of this volume has explored broadly what it means in the current educational arena to take a radically different view of the relationships of knowledge and practice and the role of practitioners in educational change. Parallel to the structure of our previous book, Part II offers provocative perspectives from differently positioned practitioners whose writing speaks to the meanings of an inquiry stance in relation to a range of educational practices in very different educational contexts. In keeping with our wider emphasis on practitioners' research, the writers include not only K–12 classroom teachers but also school/district administrators and university-based teacher educators who are or were engaged in practitioner research in K–12 schools or in programs in higher education. Contributors include urban and suburban, public and private, K–12 and university practitioner researchers, some of whom are publishing for the first time, while others have written and published their work over a number of years. All of the chapters were written expressly for this book, but many of them have roots in the work of cross-school, school–university, or other practitioner inquiry communities where inquiry is regarded as a central aspect of learning across the professional life course. Several are drawn from recently completed or in-progress practitioner research dissertations.

This section contains eight pieces, each taking up the concept of practitioner research in distinctive ways, but all intended to be accessible and meaningful to multiple audiences rather than specific groups. In each chapter, the author addresses explicitly, and sometimes implicitly, some of the distinguishing features of practitioner research (Lytle, 2000): the legacy of the work (where it comes from and what it's connected to), its location/ positionality (the researcher's identity and relationships to participants), the characteristic ways of knowing (assumptions about knowledge and practice implicit or explicit in the research), the orientation of the work (its content focus and purposes), ways of gathering data and sensemaking (what counts as data, analysis, and interpretation), its community (the social organization of the work), and, finally, its neighborhood (audiences for the research and their significance). For all of these chapters, the concept of "working the dialectic" we described in Part I is the mode of inquiry. Taken as a set, the chapters reflect the critical intersections of theory and practice, inquiry and action, as their authors blur and ultimately reconceive in ways unique to their setting and their purposes the so-called boundaries between being a researcher and being a practitioner. Each is grounded in the empirical documentation of the daily challenges and contradictions of practice, leading to new conceptual frameworks and understandings. Although their questions arise from situations in a particular context, they generate local knowledge of practice and thus offer both interpretive frameworks and theories of practice that shed new light on prominent problems of teaching, learning, and leading as well as perspectives and analyses that may be useful in other local contexts.

Each chapter makes a distinctive contribution, and each is written in a distinctive style and voice. There are, however, some common themes or threads across the set. Five of the chapters look closely at questions related to students' perspectives, students' work, and their development as learners and members of classroom communities. The chapter by Gary McPhail draws on his insights about the differential success of boys and girls in his 1st- and 2nd-grade Writer's Workshop over more than 10 years of teaching. Through his research, he learns from his students about how gendered literacy interests of boys and girls affect their engagement in classroom culture and their success in learning to write. Gillian Maimon's essay on practitioner inquiry provides a vivid portrait of how one 1st-grade teacher uses writing to make sense of the intricate life world of her classroom. Using entries from her yearlong journal, she explores the concepts of "mediated emotion," passion, and publication in relation to her generative struggles and sensemaking about children's learning and the classroom as a social environment. Kelly Harper locates her research in the frameworks of social justice, multicultural education, and critical pedagogical practice. By developing a reading curriculum that intentionally raises issues of race and diversity for her 6th-grade students in a predominantly White suburban community, she creates the context to explore systematically the range of ways children would read and write in response to these invitations and the various ways they construct meanings. Rob Simon writes about his research in his own graduate school classroom, where he has been teaching preservice secondary English teachers for a number of years. Encouraging his students to interrogate critically the social and political contexts in which they work, his chapter looks closely at his inquiry-based pedagogy that creates a space for new teachers to construct their theories of practice by using their teacher community to negotiate language as well as competing images and discourses of teaching. All of these chapters focus on one or several classrooms to explicate complicated questions of praxis that are dramatically different from seeking model methods or "best practices."

Several of the chapters included in Part II use a wider, more historical lens to look at what it means to take an inquiry stance over the course of a professional lifetime and are written in ways that foreground specific racial and ethnic identities. Gerald Campano draws on his work as a 5th-grade teacher in a large urban school district (where he reconnected with the Filipino side of his heritage) and as a university teacher educator in an urban school district. His work theorizes practitioner inquiry in terms of ethics and justice and their relationships to students' life chances, collectivities, and the lifeworld of the classroom. Using a documentary, a vignette of one student, and his work with one community of teachers, Campano offers considerations for practitioner researchers who construct their practice as what he calls a "collective struggle for humanization." Swati Mehta narrates her experience of teacher research from the personal, professional, and political perspectives of a South Asian Indian living in the United States. Invoking and unpacking the notion of cultural hybridity, Mehta examines her experiences over time as a teacher researcher working with young Indian women and immigrant students and as a graduate student critiquing the literature (and lack thereof) on Asian teachers to foreground ways identity, culture, and research may be both productively troubled and integrated into one's life as a practitioner. Diane Waff analyzes the narrative of her involvement as an African American female teacher/leader/administrator in three different inquiry communities where she examined what she calls the "constraints and possibilities" of urban school reform. Drawing also on experiences in her own classroom, her chapter emphasizes the power of collective inquiry to interrogate assumptions, surface hidden issues, and make public and accountable practices related to

race, subject matter (literacy and math), and student access to learning opportunities. Finally, in a chapter written from his perspective as a school
administrator, African American educator Delvin Dinkins documents and
analyzes the conversations of a secondary teacher group in a majority White
high-performing suburban district confronted with evidence of the Black
community's concerns about equity and access in the school culture and curriculum. Dinkins highlights the teachers' language and discourse to reveal
their lenses on the intersections of race, class, and achievement in the school
curriculum and the ways these discursive practices positioned students as well
as how students were perceived to position themselves.

We find these eight essays extraordinarily vivid and insightful, as they
create rich, intimate images of what it really means to do this work. Together, they offer ways to re-imagine the intentional blurring of the roles of
researcher and practitioner and the unique understandings that emerge from
deeply contextual investigation of issues that matter in a specific educational
context. In addition to the particular content and perspectives taken up in
the individual chapters, there are powerful ways the pieces resonate with and
talk to each other. For example, both Gerald Campano and Gill Maimon
describe the experience of bringing a new child into a school and classroom
culture. Their discussions here are deeply personal and heartfelt, yet they
are at the same time distant enough to theorize these situations. Their work
shows how the teacher's stance and sensitivity to individual children's backgrounds and current situations make these relationships extremely complex
and consequential, not routine or formulaic. Like Campano and Maimon,
Gary McPhail uses an extended case study of one child's situation, in this
case a young boy's response to a particular curriculum, to draw out in a moving way the more general issues about the implications of gendered identity
for school success. Swati Mehta and Gerald Campano both write from the
perspective of their own immigrant legacies, revealing the ways that location deeply informs and continuously transforms one's theory of practice as
a teacher. Simon, Campano, and Waff examine the dynamics and meanings
of collectivities in accomplishing the metatheoretical work of teaching and
learning to teach. Orienting their research around critical issues of race and
racism, Waff and Dinkins capture serious incidents and attitudes of school
professionals that function as obstacles and challenges for assuring access to
learning for diverse groups of children in primary and secondary schools.
Harper and Dinkins both uncover concerns about the ways race and social
justice are lived and understood in majority White suburban contexts, while
McPhail's examination of gender roles in writing workshop highlights how
schools may foster resistance to widespread curricular initiatives that are not

sufficiently attuned to particular aspects of student diversity. Harper and Simon pay particular attention to the nature and consequentiality of classroom discourse as it both reveals and affects the ways individual learners (and teachers) understand, embrace, and/or resist curricular goals. Campano's theorizing of practitioner research provides a lens for rereading and rethinking all of the previous chapters as expressions of what it means to different educators to take on the stance of practitioner researcher.

From these eight chapters, we learn—up close and in very rich, nuanced detail—what it means for practitioners to learn from their practice and what it means to work the dialectic of theory and practice, analyzing and acting, being in the day-to-day world of practice, but also being apart from it. These chapters show how practitioners question the assumptions that underlie curriculum and schooling; how they teach to understand the cultural and linguistic resources children, youth, and adults bring to learning; how they disrupt routines and procedures they deem problematic; and how they invent frameworks to make sense of their immediate practice and their larger stance on what it means to be a professional. Finally, these chapters reveal how practitioner researchers raise and pursue systematically, in ways ecologically valid in their local contexts, some of the most difficult, elusive, and important issues in education at this time and for the foreseeable future as well. While these essays paint vivid portraits of a set of individuals taking an inquiry stance, none of the authors has been working as a lone practitioner researcher. Their participation in various communities of inquiry is an aspect of their work that may be more or less visible in different chapters but is nonetheless absolutely central to the topics, analyses, and interpretations contained in these studies. In addition, all of these practitioners participated in the collaborative script for the readers' theatre production that forms Part III of this book.

REFERENCES

Cochran-Smith, M., & Lytle, S. L. (1993). *Inside/outside: Teacher research and knowledge.* New York: Teachers College Press.

Lytle, S. (2000). Teacher research in the contact zone. In M. L. Kamil, P. B. Mosenthal, P. D. Pearson, & R. Barr (Eds.), *Handbook of reading research* (Vol. III, pp. 691–718). Mahwah, NJ: Erlbaum.

Chapter Six

The "Bad Boy" and the Writing Curriculum

Gary McPhail

Gary McPhail currently teaches first and second grade at Shady Hill School in Cambridge, Massachusetts. He has taught in the primary grades for 11 years. In 2008, McPhail received his doctorate from Boston College. In an attempt to address the gendered achievement gap in writing that exists both nationally and internationally, McPhail conducted a yearlong teacher research dissertation focused on the gendered literacy interests of his 1st-grade students and how they responded to a writing curriculum he created that included genres intended to be of interest to both boys and girls. Based on his findings, McPhail is currently leading a group of teacher researchers featuring one teacher from every grade level at Shady Hill. This group is inquiring into their own practice and working to create a schoolwide writing curriculum that is of interest to a variety of young, budding writers. His publications include Faculty First: The Challenge of Infusing the Teacher Education Curriculum with Scholarship on English Language Learners *(co-authored with J. Costa, J. Smith, and M. E. Brisk).*

Learning to write is a complex social process that involves many aspects of student identity intersecting with specific requirements of each particular genre in the writing curriculum. Writer's Workshop is an approach to writing instruction, widely used in elementary schools across the country, which gives students the opportunity to reflect on their own lived experiences, write about them during class time, and share them with their peers. In many primary-grade classrooms, students spend the entire year writing personal narratives and honing the craft of writing by reflecting on their own experiences. The underlying idea is that students learn to become authors of their own stories while they simultaneously acquire age-appropriate writing skills. Writing is clearly integral to most other academic areas (such as math, reading, science, social studies, etc.), and in many elementary classrooms, including my own, children are given many varied opportunities to write in these subjects throughout the school day, but during Writer's Workshop, writing development and student authorship are the specific foci.

I have taught first and second grade for 11 years. Over these years, I have noticed that many girls seem to enjoy writing more and encounter greater success during Writer's Workshop than do many of the boys. As one of the few adult males working in an elementary school, this has always troubled me. Why don't boys perform as highly as girls in writing? Equally as important, why don't the boys like Writer's Workshop as much as the girls? In search of answers to these burning questions, I decided to pursue doctoral study with the intention of exploring young children's literacy development, especially the development of boys.

GENDER AND WRITING DEVELOPMENT

When I began to research the intersection of the two topics of gender and young children's writing development, I quickly realized that the phenomenon of girls outperforming boys in writing was occurring all over the nation, not just in my classroom. Since the 1969 inception of the National Assessment of Educational Progress (NAEP), a standardized exam given to 9-, 13-, and 17-year-olds across the country, girls at all grade levels have scored much higher than boys in writing skills. Newkirk (2002) points out that the gap between females and males in terms of NAEP writing scores is comparable to the "achievement gap" between Whites and other racial/ethnic groups that have long suffered systemic social and economic discrimination in this country. Furthermore, the gendered pattern of females outperforming males on NAEP scores is consistent across all racial/ethnic groups.

Much of the research on gender and writing suggests that boys and girls actually have differing literacy interests and prefer to write about very different topics. For example, Hunt (1985) found that boys in elementary school often wrote about sports, war, fighting, and catastrophes while their female counterparts wrote more frequently about themselves, their feelings, their families, and their friendships. Peterson (2001) found that the characters in girls' narrative writing demonstrated more emotion and pro-social behavior (sharing, helping, empathizing), while characters in boys' writing exhibited more aggressive behavior and engaged in more high-intensity, dangerous actions. It is important to note, of course, that generalizations about differing literacy interests based on gender do not apply to the writing of all boys and all girls. Some boys like writing, and some girls do not. Some boys are interested in writing about their feelings, and some girls are interested in writing about aggressive behavior and violence. However, a growing number of researchers (e.g., Dyson, 1997; Millard, 1997; Newkirk, 2002; Rose, 1989; Thomas, 1994) suggest that many schools gear writing curriculum and instruction to girls' learning and that boys are suffering because teachers do not acknowledge gendered differences in the writing preferences of their students. Along these lines, Newkirk (2002) argues that there is a hierarchy of genres in the writing curriculum across the country, with personal narrative and poetry at the top and the genres that many boys prefer (e.g., comic book writing, action-packed adventures, and nonrealistic fiction) near the bottom.

RETHINKING THE WRITING CURRICULUM

When I was preparing to be a teacher, I was instructed to teach writing using the Writer's Workshop model based on the work of Donald Graves and others (Calkins, 1986; Clay, 2001; Dorn & Soffos, 2001; Graves, 1983). I became a firm believer in this model as a way for students to develop the necessary writing skills while also exploring and sharing memories from their own lives. I learned that budding writers were the authors of their own personal experiences and that personal narrative gave children the chance to write about their own lives. This curricular emphasis on personal narrative gave the teacher the chance to know the children as social members of the class while they simultaneously grew as writers. In this way, their personal narratives could be viewed as a window into the self. The main idea here was that it was easier for young children to tackle the daunting task of writing a story when they were writing about their own experiences, mainly because these stories were their memories of things that had already happened. Literary components such as plot, characters, and setting were already in place, so young writers could simply focus on writing down their stories, casting themselves as the main characters. According to the traditional Writer's Workshop model, then, children would spend the school year writing about themselves, their feelings, and their own personal experiences. Looking back, I now realize that as a teacher candidate, I never questioned the idea that placing a large curricular emphasis on personal narrative might privilege some writers over others.

Since then, I have come to acknowledge that this writing instructional model biases certain literary interests over others. Many of the genres and styles to which many boys gravitate (e.g., comic books, adventure stories, silly fictitious stories, sports pages) are considered low-status by many teachers (and parents) and are not welcome in many classrooms during writing time because they are either "inappropriate" for school or deemed not worthy of instructional time (Newkirk, 2002). Thus, many boys come to realize that their interests are not worthy of being taught in the classroom and as a result come to view writing as more of a female activity than male. Newkirk (2002) argues that this problem—the construction of literacy as a "feminized" activity—cannot be countered if schools fail to be self-critical about what counts and does not count as valid literacy activity. In an attempt to reach more students, Newkirk (2002), Pollack (1998), and others urge teachers to look more critically at how writing is being taught in their classrooms and at whose interests are being privileged.

I decided that I owed it to my students to try something new and that I needed to follow Newkirk's advice. I created a writing curriculum that included some units that I believed would be generally more appealing to boys and some that would be generally more appealing to girls. I designed a revised Writer's Workshop curriculum with a focus on different genres of writing as follows:

September–October: Personal narratives
November–December: Letters
January–February: Comic books
March–April: Fiction
May–June: Poetry

I decided to engage in inquiry about this new curriculum and study my own practice as I made these curricular changes. I currently teach first and second grade at an independent coeducational day school in New England. The families that send their children to my school tend to have achieved a relatively high socioeconomic status and are very involved in their children's lives at school. The student body is nearly 30 percent African American, Asian American, Latino, or biracial. As a school, we have a reputation of being progressive in our integrated curricular approach and fostering strong critical thinking skills.

This chapter focuses on David, one child in my 1st-grade class, and his experiences with the revised writing curriculum. It is important to note that his experiences are only a segment of a larger study in which I closely examined the academic and social experiences of a group of boys in my class and also documented the experiences of the entire class, both boys and girls, during Writer's Workshop. For the larger study, I drew on a variety of data sources, including (1) all students' written work produced throughout the year, (2) whole-class and individual interviews within each of the five genres, (3) ongoing classroom observations, and (4) bi-weekly entries in a teacher research journal. Utilizing a three-dimensional analysis scheme, I systemically analyzed themes in student writing, gendered differences and preferences among genres, and the overall writing development of my students over time. Three different but complementary perspectives were integrated in the analysis: the teacher's perspective, the whole-class perspective, and the in-depth perspectives of six focal boys (McPhail, 2008).

In this chapter, I use David's experiences with the new curriculum to explore what happens when boys have the freedom and authority to write about their interests in class. In addition to documenting how David grew as a writer by connecting his own personal interests to the writing curriculum, I also show how important this connection was to David's social development. In fact, it was pivotal in his desire to transform his classroom reputation from a "bad boy" into an expressive and sensitive friend.

DAVID AS "BAD BOY"

As a social member of the class, David was somewhat of a live wire who enjoyed testing limits and manipulating situations. He enjoyed his status as resident "bad boy" and had a powerful presence in the classroom. Another teacher researcher, Karen Gallas (1998), wrote about the presence of "bad boys" in her primary classroom and how they craved attention in negative ways and strove to develop a rebellious identity that was counter to classroom culture:

> "Bad boys" is a term I first developed to describe particular boys and the effect they had on the classroom. I use it as a caricature for how these boys view themselves and are viewed both by other children and their teachers. In using the term, my intention is to highlight their behavior while also underscoring their intentions. Bad boys are "bad" in the sense of the street lingo that they so admire and try to use: they are bad meaning they push boundaries of all behavioral norms, and they are also bad, meaning attractive, risky, desirable, cool. The construction of their personae, however, is a performance that conceals many layers of social awareness, creative activity and ambivalence towards powerful others. (p. 33)

David is similar to the "bad boys" Gallas describes in that he craved attention from both his peers and teachers. He pushed boundaries in order to obtain his rebellious classroom reputation. Image was very important to David. In addition to wanting to be known as mischievous and cool, he also desperately wanted everyone in the class to realize that he was intelligent, which he was. David was loud and animated. He loved an audience and occupied more classroom time than any other student. He once told me that it would be the worst thing in the world if people thought of him as dull. David was also obsessed with violence, which was an intense interest of his. He talked about it extensively throughout the school day to get attention from anyone who would listen. He depicted violence in his play at recess and often mentioned it during class meetings. He frequently made up stories and used violence to exaggerate these stories in class. He admitted that he purposely exaggerated in class and enjoyed being inappropriate. As his teacher, it was truly a challenge to figure out how to channel David's energy in appropriate directions. Throughout the year, I often talked with David about how to be a positive community member. David and I had a close relationship. He was a rather verbose, animated student, and partly because I gave him the attention he desired, he trusted me and we engaged in many conversations about his social and emotional development. At the beginning of first grade, David was often mean and disrespectful of classmates, particularly those he did not consider friends. From my perspective as a teacher, I perceived David as a child with a keen understanding of power who enjoyed exerting it over anyone who would let him. I liked David. Despite his desire for a rebellious reputation, he was a very funny and curious boy who loved learning and cared deeply about his social reputation.

Compared to his peers, David's behavior was extreme. It is important to note, however, that there were "bad boys" like David in every class I have ever taught, and I suspect they are part of most primary classes across the country. Many primary-grade classes contain more than one bad boy; they are simply a part of the classroom population. They enjoy pushing boundaries and seeking out attention in negative ways. At an early age, they define themselves as rebels. As a result, they tend not to connect with the classroom culture or the curriculum in positive ways. They crave social acceptance but find pride in having a social identity that lies outside, or in direct opposition to, classroom expectations for appropriate behavior.

THE "BAD BOY" ABIDES BY "THE BOY CODE"

Early in the school year, David stood out to me as someone who struggled with embracing the personal nature of writing about himself. As a writer, he had strong skills and a solid working knowledge of how to sound out words. It was clear to me as a teacher that he was extremely bright, verbal, and articulate. It was also immediately obvious, however, that David did not like the subject matter of writing personal narratives. He did not like figuring prominently in his stories and being the main character. Below are David's own thoughts about writing personal narratives.

It's not completely boring, it's not exactly the same as that. I mean, don't get me wrong, sometimes it can get *really* boring . . . but mostly it's just kind of hard. Not the actual writing part, but the "figuring out what to write" part. Sometimes I get headaches because I have to focus so much and figure out what I want to tell everyone about myself. It just can get really tiring.

As a result, David was very hard to motivate during this unit. He spent the first several writing periods "thinking," which to me looked more like staring off into space or talking to other children.

When David finally decided on a personal memory to write about, he did everything in his power to diffuse his own personal emotions out of it and to not focus on how he actually experienced the memory. For his first personal narrative, David wrote a story about saying good-bye to his mother at the airport when she left for Denver the first time. David's mother was in medical school and was going to do her residency in Denver, which meant that she was spending the year away from her family. An excerpt from my teacher research journal on this personal narrative is as follows:

September 17
The cover of David's story shows an airplane ascending into the sky. The illustration is done completely in black crayon. The title of the story is "Sadness." The next step of writing a personal narrative [in our classroom] is to fill out a story web, in which students think about the following elements of their story: characters, main idea, setting, and story sequence (beginning, middle, and ending). Interestingly, after looking over the sheet, David wanted to fill out his story web alone. Toward the end of Writer's Workshop, David informed me that he was done, handed me his story web, and began to walk away. I called him back and told him that I needed to review his work with him. In the box marked "characters," David had drawn a picture of the airplane and explained that this was the central character of the story. I asked if there were any other characters in the story. He looked at me for several seconds with a strong gaze and then replied, "Yes, my mother is on that plane." I said, "OK, then you need to write 'Mom' in the character box." After he did this, I asked him if there were any other characters in this story. He said "no." Then I asked, "Your title is 'Sadness.' Who is the one feeling sadness in your story?" After a long pause he finally admitted, "Well . . . I'm

the one feeling sadness . . . (and then softly) obviously." I replied by saying that he should write his name in the character box as well. "But, I'm not focusing on me in this story, I'm focusing on my mother and the plane," he was quick to reply.

It struck me that David was trying desperately to diffuse the intensity of his sadness, the emotion that he chose to write about, by having his mom and the plane be the main characters instead of focusing on himself. He wanted his story to be told, he just didn't want to focus on his own feelings. I told him that next writing time we would work together to figure out how to do this but also on how to include his perspective into the story. "Because it is a personal narrative and writing about yourself is what 'personal' means," I said. His somber look showed me that he understood.

During the next few days, it became even more clear to me that David did not want to elaborate on how he actually felt about his mom being away beyond the poignant (and even powerful) title he gave his narrative— "Sadness." "Isn't it obvious?" he would say. I had to agree with him. It was, very. David wanted the creative freedom to tell the story his own way. He wanted to diffuse the intensity of his own sadness—remove it from his personal narrative. This story was important enough to David that he wanted to write about it, but he was very clear that he did not want to focus on his own sadness because doing so might tarnish his reputation as the resident bad boy. David was taking a risk in sharing this story with the class, and I was proud of him for choosing this personal event. I did not want this process to be more emotionally charged for him than it already was, so eventually I gave David permission to tell his story his way. His final version is as follows:

SADNIS[1]

ONSE MOM HAD TO GO LIVE IN DENVER. I COODINT GO
MY MOM ROD A JETPLAN TO DENVER
HER APARtMENT WAS SMALL
IT WAS COOl BECASe it had a MAIL Slot
SHE HAD A BALCONY. SHE SAID THE SIGHT WAS beautiful
BUT SOMETIMES IT WAS COLD.
THERE WAS A MAIL SLOT
THERE WAS A GARBAGE chute
THERE WAS VACUMING TO DOO!
Then it was time to go! No!

(*Sadness*

Once Mom had to go live in Denver. I couldn't go.
My mom rode on a jet plane to Denver.
Her apartment was small.
It was cool because it had a mail slot.
She had a balcony. She said the sight was beautiful.
But sometimes it was cold.
There was a mail slot.
There was a garbage chute.
There was vacuuming to do!
Then it was time to go! No!)

When reading David's story, complete with illustrations, I could feel David's sadness, but his actual writing did not tap into his own feelings about his mother living away from him. This was a deliberate decision on David's part. Although he wanted this story to be told, he was not comfortable expressing his sadness outright, especially since others would be reading this story. This connects with what Pollack (1998) says about boys not being comfortable talking about their lives and their true emotions. He states that many boys are in a gender straitjacket because they feel it is not OK to express emotions because they must present a strong, stoic front. Instead of revealing their true emotional side, they learn at an early age to abide by what Pollack calls "the boy code" and to hide behind a mask of masculinity. Boys who abide by the boy code, boys like David, "often are hiding not only a wide range of their feelings but also some of their creativity and originality, showing in effect only a handful of primary colors rather than a broad spectrum of colors and hues of the self" (Pollack, 1998, p. 7). Once David figured out how to diffuse the emotional intensity out of what was a very important experience to him, he wrote a strong piece. Protecting his emotional vulnerability, and saving face, he was still able to embrace the process of writing about a personal story and share it with the class in a way with which he felt comfortable.

My 1st-grade class wrote personal narratives for 2 months. Despite my constant prodding and talk of impending deadlines, David wrote only one story during this period. Despite his lack of motivation to write personal narratives, David's experience also validated that there were some benefits to including a personal narrative unit in a writing curriculum for the primary grades. David's personal narrative was indeed a window into the self. In fact, many of the students' stories, in one way or another, showed who these young writers were as people. I got a glimpse into their lives through the stories they wrote. It was important for me to realize that many of my students knew this as well. They knew they were telling others about themselves by writing personal narratives, and they were very deliberate about what they chose to reveal. For some boys, this personal exposure presented a struggle because they needed to decide which parts of themselves they wanted to reveal. In some cases, their classroom reputations were at stake. They struggled because they wanted their images to be different from their actual life experiences. In a sense, these 6-year-old boys were already conditioned to abide by the boy code, and they wanted to present themselves as cool, strong, or heroic while the writing curriculum required them to stick with their actual experiences, which might be just the opposite. As a teacher who paid close attention as they constructed their pieces, I not only got a glimpse into my students' actual lives through their personal narratives, I also got a glimpse into the images these boys wanted to construct for themselves and present to others.

Overall and for different reasons, most of the boys in my class did not find it particularly easy to write about their emotions, while many of the girls did. Most of the girls seemed motivated to write about their own feelings and readily wrote about their own experiences, such as losing a tooth, planning a birthday party, and having a favorite bracelet break. Meanwhile, many of the boys devised various avoidance strategies so they didn't have to write about their real emotions and experiences. It would have been a mistake, however, for me to think that these boys did not value writing or think it was interesting. They wanted to learn how to write. They simply did not want to write about and share themselves with a public audience.

DECONSTRUCTING THE "BAD BOY"

When the writing curriculum shifted from personal narratives to letter writing, David was more motivated to write. In this unit, writing became a meaningful form of social interaction for him. David wrote seven letters in 1 month, compared to one personal narrative in 2 months. This was similar to the experience of most boys in my class. They produced more during the letter-writing unit than they had during the personal narrative unit. Knowing that we were about to start writing letters but before I even taught the first mini-lesson to the whole class, David took the initiative during morning choice time and wrote the following letter to his friend Michael:

DERE MIKL–
SPY SUPLIS IS SO GRET!
I THINC THAT YOU ARE SO GRET!

WE WILL MEET AT THE BLOK AREA TOOMORO OK?
DOBLO-O AGENTS 005
SINSIRULY
DAVID
P.S. I LIK YOU!

(Dear Michael,
Spy Supplies is so great!
I think that you are so great!
We will meet at the Block Area tomorrow, OK?
Double 0 Agents, 005
Sincerely,
David
P.S. I like you!)

David was extremely attentive and excited throughout the unit on letter writing. He asked many questions and enjoyed sharing with the group what he knew about different aspects of a letter (such as the closing and the postscript) and when to use them. He liked that there was a very specific and private audience for his thoughts. Personal narratives were read by the class at large, but with letter writing David was in control of who would read his letters. He enjoyed having this level of control as a writer. The lines "I THINC YOU ARE SO GRET!" and "I LIK YOU!" really stood out to me. As a social member of our class, David had a very hard time giving compliments to other students. Instead of being nice, he often hurt other people's feelings. I continually worked with David about how to be a good friend. It struck me that one of the first times I saw David take the initiative to compliment someone was in the form of a private letter. There was an audience of one in letter writing, and David did not have to worry about his public image. David wrote this letter to Michael to tell him that he liked him as a friend and wanted to keep playing with him. Letter writing provided a safe, private forum for him to do just that. David used letter writing to strengthen relationships with chosen friends. Ironically, he revealed more about himself personally and felt more comfortable expressing his true emotions through writing during the letter writing unit than he did during the personal narrative unit mainly because he was in charge of his audience. He could maintain his "bad boy" reputation with the group at large while strengthening specific friendships and reaching out emotionally to those he held dear.

David's interest in writing peaked during the comic book and fiction units, primarily because these units allowed him to depict violent scenes in his writing, but within established parameters. He informed me that he liked incorporating violence because he thought it made his writing more exciting. From my perspective as his teacher, David was an emotionally needy boy who was constantly seeking attention and didn't seem to care if the attention he received was negative. Negative attention was better than no attention at all. Similar to how he exaggerated and enjoyed acting inappropriately in front of his peers and teachers, David seemed to include violence in his writing in order to make sure the social spotlight remained on him. He stated, "I do it because I don't want them to like, start telling everyone 'David's comic book is really boring. David's comic book isn't exciting at all. Don't read David's comic book.' I don't want them to think I'm dull so I get violent to get their attention."

Similar perhaps to the reasons David behaved aggressively on the playground, he created violent comic books so his classmates would not consider him dull. David also wanted to be known as smart. The following excerpt from my teacher research journal shows how David learned to portray himself as both intelligent and interesting by utilizing violence in his writing:

January 15

On day one of our comic book unit, David started illustrating a very violent scene. He was working on a comic strip that featured a crime-fighting character that battled bad guys. Every character in the opening illustration had multiple guns and knives. Some of the bad guy characters were drawn with cut marks on their bodies. David's first draft of this illustration was very grotesque and he looked forward to having people think it was either disgusting or inappropriate. Feeling very proud of his violent scene, he ran right over to James, a third grader who comes to the classroom to help during Writer's Workshop. James, who also enjoyed an occasional violent scene, told David that he liked the idea of this comic character but that there was a certain way to illustrate violence in comics and that it wasn't cool to show the goriest, grossest picture. As they were talking about this, I overheard James say to David, "As the author, you have to get creative. Remember, you have the power as the creator of the comic. Don't go overboard. Make the reader work for it a little. Give them a little bit, but leave a lot to the imagination for the reader. That's the sign of a good comic creator." This spoke volumes to David. It was very important for David to be portrayed as smart, and James, a big kid in David's eyes, was telling him how to be smart about depicting violence in his comics. What could be more important and more meaningful to David?

Using the old Batman comics as an example, I instructed James to explain how comic writers draw a cloud of smoke (possibly with a head or a foot sticking out around the perimeter) with the words like BANG or KAZOW written over the cloud. That way, you could include violence in the writing but you don't go overboard drawing it. David loved learning this strategy, especially since it came from a big kid that he respected. Halfway through Writer's Workshop, James had to return to his own class. After he left, I watched David turn to Hunter and explain how to depict violence in his comic. David recited verbatim what James had told him.

There was real power in David's realization that there was a smart way to depict violence in his comics. He understood that the authors of comic books and fiction stories have a lot of power and creative control. Power and control were extremely important to David. He stated many times that he found it "freeing" to write fiction and comic books and he liked that the subject matter wasn't directly personal.

As a teacher, I learned a great deal about David's personal development by observing him and paying close attention to what he wrote about during these units. David was obsessed with violence, and he was glad that this was not a taboo topic for Writer's Workshop during these genres. He depicted violent scenes in every comic book and fiction story he wrote. Even though violence was not an interest of mine, and one I hoped he would soon abandon, David connected this interest to the writing curriculum. He was fascinated by the guidelines (such as using the cloud and words like ZOWIE to disguise the gore) for incorporating violence into comic books. He abided by them, for the most part, because these strategies made him feel intelligent and creative as a writer.

Importantly, because violence was a personal interest of his and not considered a taboo topic for writing, David achieved personal growth by incorporating this interest into his writing and sharing his thoughts with his peers. Prior to this time, David had used violence to rebel, to shock, and to get attention. Once the topic of violence was included into the curriculum, David did not rebel or act out as much because his interests were connected to the curriculum. Importantly, I learned more about David by watching him while he wrote about topics of interest to him. By listening to what he had to say and observing his behavior when there was violence in his writing, I learned that David incorporated violence in his drawings and in his play when there was something emotionally upsetting in his life—his mother living in Denver, his best friend Ian moving to Brazil, his feelings of being excluded by some of his friends, his father working too much.

Throughout the year, David and I often engaged in talks about social issues that were important to him, and violence was a common theme that weaved together many of these conversations. I realized that there was usually a strong connection between David's depictions of violence in writing and his social life. The following excerpt from my teacher research journal explains the social ramifications of this very important point:

June 27

Many of the students in my class have expressed that it scared them when David talked about violence, wrote about it, or pretended to act out something violent. Even his close friends were beginning to think that his obsession with violence was inappropriate for school.

Ian is one of David's best friends. At the beginning of the year, Ian found it fascinating that David knew so much about violence, war, and catastrophe and sought out David's friendship. During the winter months, David became even more obsessed with violent movies and TV shows, and he gained popularity with Ian as a result. Talking about violence and including violence in his writing and play became a way for David to connect with Ian. During the spring, things began to change, however. Ian began to move away from David because of his violent tendencies. During the early spring months, it was noticeable that David was being increasingly rude to many of his friends and was drawing and writing more violent pictures of war and bombings. David also became more physical during games out on the playground like "Cops and Robbers." Ian began to pull away from David because he felt that David was spending too much time drawing, writing, and talking about violence and disasters. It scared him. When he began pulling away, Ian began to really feel David's wrath. David told Ian that he hated him and that he wasn't his friend anymore.

After talking with David and observing his behavior for a while, I realized that David was actually upset because Ian was moving away to Brazil for a year. And although Ian was coming back in third grade, missing someone for a year is like an eternity when you're in first grade. David had grown close to Ian and now he was moving away. David was acting out because he was upset, and he was channeling his anger in the only way he knew how to: by using violence in his play, writing and drawing to get attention. At that point, I realized that David's use of violence had become a social barometer I could use to know how he was feeling.

I asked David if he wanted to have "a private meeting" with Ian to discuss how he was feeling. In this meeting, David explained that he was feeling confused because he felt that earlier in the winter he had been drawing more violent pictures and talking about violence to strengthen his friendship with Ian. But now, Ian was pulling away because of the violence. It didn't make any sense to him. David expressed this to Ian, and in turn Ian acknowledged that he was indeed purposely pulling away from David. "I don't like it anymore when David gets obsessed with violence, and I don't want to go down a bad road myself and get in trouble. I don't want to be known as a bad boy like David," he explained. Ian expressed that he used to be more interested in violence but he felt that he had outgrown it. "People grow at different rates," Ian explained, "and sometimes people are just late-bloomers about some stuff. And maybe David is just a late-bloomer about outgrowing violence." Instead of being upset about this, or even insulted, David nodded and accepted this rationale. David then told Ian that he was going to miss him while he was away. This made Ian smile, and they spent the remainder of the recess devising a strategy to communicate with each other via their parents' emails using a secret code.

Similar to how I realized that my students' personal narratives could be considered windows into self, by using David's overall writing throughout the entire year as a window into self, I gained tremendous insight into his personal life. He used violence to communicate his emotions, and I believe he desperately hoped someone would pay attention. I realized I could use his depictions of violence as a social barometer to monitor how he was feeling emotionally without David having to state it outright. His actions spoke louder than his words.

In this way, David revealed a great deal more about his personal self during the letter-writing, comic book, fiction, and poetry units than he did when the curricular focus was on personal narratives. The real impact of David's social and emotional growth as a result of being able to connect personal interests (in this case, violence) with the writing curriculum was truly felt during our poetry unit at the end of the year.

DAVID ABANDONS THE "BAD BOY" STANCE

The following is a poem that David wrote the very next day after the conversation with Ian when he told Ian he hated him and that he was not his friend.

NO War　　　　　　　　　　　　　　　　　by DAVID
War is crazy, war is dumb. If war dozeNt stop I'LL eat MY
thumb. Gun's are dangerous and no fun, I'm out to make WaR say
GOODBYE. if I fail I'LL Pobably CRY.
　　HurrAY! I did it! YippY ME! Earth is pecefulk cause of me!

(*No War*　　　　　　　　　　　　　　　　by David
War is crazy, war is dumb. If war doesn't stop, I'll eat my
thumb. Guns are dangerous and no fun. I'm out to make war say
"Goodbye." If I fail, I'll probably cry.
　　Hurray! I did it! Yippy me! Earth is peaceful because of me!)

The picture that accompanied this poem depicted David and Ian, smiling
and holding hands, standing on top of the Earth with a big rainbow over-
head. When he was done, he walked around the class and shared the poem
with anyone who would listen. This was a social breakthrough for David.
Along these lines, Gallas (1998) said that "bad boys, like most children, are
not naturally mean spirited; they are experimental. They are small, social sci-
entists studying the effect of their behavior on others" (p. 44). David was one
such social scientist who experimented with violence throughout the year as
a way to communicate his emotional state to others.

In his poem "No War," David not only took an anti-war stance but also
publicly displayed affectionate feelings of friendship toward Ian. This was in
stark contrast to David's behavior at the beginning of the year when he was
consistently mean to the majority of his peers. By writing this happy anti-
war poem, David allowed himself to be vulnerable and showed his classmates
that he was kind and that he wanted to change his reputation as resident bad
boy. This social transformation took time, but by the end of the year, when
our poetry unit took place, David managed to break out of his emotional
straitjacket and abandon the boy code. Similar to his experiences during the
comic book and fiction units, I believe that David succeeded in our poetry
unit because he was in charge of the subject matter. Although I had taught
the children several formats for poems, which they were supposed to use
(e.g., acrostic poems, rhyming poems), they were in control of the content.
Once again, it seemed to me that with this genre, David could connect his
interests to the curriculum.

It is important to note that if the writing curriculum had not been able
to connect with David's interest in violence, he would not have been able
to write about this interest freely, which contributed to his desire to change
his social reputation. By being more inviting, the writing curriculum helped

David rebel less against the classroom culture and become more interested in Writer's Workshop.

THE BIGGER PICTURE

Throughout the year, I had whole-class conversations about every genre we worked on. During a conversation about poetry, Lisa said she liked the formats and structures for poems. She said she felt that she was free during this unit, and she likened the process of writing poetry to being on vacation where she could do whatever she wanted. During this same conversation, David stated that he felt stifled by the very same formats and structures that enabled Lisa to feel free. Interestingly, earlier in the year, David had used this same word, *free*, to describe his experiences with writing fiction, a genre that did not have an imposed structure or format to follow. David felt free during this genre because, in his own words, "you can just let your imagination run wild and do whatever you want." Lisa found freedom in structure while David found freedom in choice of content.

As I reflected on what each of the 23 children in my class needed in order to succeed as writers, I returned to this contrast again and again—and to the fact that although these two students were different with regard to their approach to learning, their social dispositions, and their genders, they both used exactly the same vocabulary and concept to describe their experiences with writing within their preferred genres: freedom. In a sense, the concept of freedom can be applied to the writing experiences of all my students. To experience success and enjoyment as writers, some students found freedom in the structure and formats that were provided during the poetry unit. Some found it freeing to realize that writing could be socially interactive, as it was during the letter-writing unit. Some found freedom in the creative control they experienced during the comic book and fiction units. Some found freedom in the reflective process of retelling their own personal memories. It is important to note that not all 23 students would have found their freedom as writers if they had been in a classroom that adopted a very traditional approach to Writer's Workshop model that focused on personal narratives.

David showed me that he had different literacy interests from those that are the focus of the traditional Writer's Workshop model. In fact, many boys in my class were similar to David in that they were not interested in writing personal narratives. When I opened the door and widened the circle of acceptable writing topics, most boys felt more connected to the writing curriculum and readily brought their literacy interests in. Their interests included fantastic intergalactic battles of good versus evil, imaginative stories about being a coach of an NBA Dream Team, gory poems about haunted houses, personal narratives about being kicked in the crotch, and letters to Rudolph the Red-Nosed Reindeer. These interests were not always appropriate and did not always focus on topics in which I was particularly interested. They were, however, of interest to these boys, and when they were allowed to pursue them, they wrote freely and willingly. I learned a great deal about these boys, both socially and as writers, when I paid close attention to them as they wrote within genres of interest to them. When discussing gender in any social context, it is important to talk about stereotypes and the risks involved with making judgments about students that appear to be based solely on their gender. When considering the concept of different gendered literacy interests and reflecting on the different experiences that boys and girls have as they learn to write in Writer's Workshop classrooms, there is real danger in oversimplifying. In my own classroom, for example, it was important for me to realize that there were not always clear-cut divisions regarding how the boys and girls experienced each genre. For example, not every boy hated and felt painfully restricted by the personal narrative unit. Not every girl hated the comic book or fiction units. In other words, there was variation within as well as between genders.

For the most part and with some exceptions, the boys and girls in my class seemed to have some differing literacy interests. What is most important about my study overall, however, is that both boys and the girls performed at higher levels when writing in genres that were of interest to them. Throughout the year, I assessed each piece of writing my students produced using *the Six Trait Assessment for Beginning Writing*, which was used throughout the primary grades as a schoolwide assessment. According to my students' rubric scores, most boys in my class, David included, obtained their highest scores when they were writing in genres that did not require them to write directly about their personal experiences and emotions. In order to take into account the developmental aspect of my students' writing as each boy and girl grew as writers throughout the year, I used a three-tiered structure, based on all my students' rubric scores, to determine how each student fared in each genre compared to their peers. This structure helped determine the genres in which each of my students succeeded and struggled the most throughout the year.

Overall, 10 out of the 12 boys in my class scored the lowest when writing personal narratives, and most boys achieved their highest scores when writing letters, comic books, or fiction. These are genres that are not traditionally taught in most primary-grade writing curricula. These boys might not have encountered success as writers with a more traditional writing curriculum that did not feature these genres. During the fiction and letter-writing units, most of my male students were interested in the subject matter and were motivated to write at a high level. Their high rubric scores revealed a direct connection between their interest level and their level of writing proficiency. Impressively, three-quarters of the boys performed at their highest level when writing fiction, the genre they stated they preferred overall. Comparatively, most girls stated they preferred to write personal narratives, and only 4 out of 10 girls achieved their highest scores during the fiction unit.

Boys and girls obtained similar scores during the fiction unit. The boys outscored the girls in letter writing and comic book writing. The girls outscored the boys in personal narratives and the poetry unit.

Learning to write is, in part, about both enacting identity, which includes one's gender, and expanding one's personal interests. If there are indeed differing gendered literacy interests among many young children, then would it not serve us well as educators to further investigate our approach to writing instruction? Perhaps we should offer a writing curriculum that includes a wide array of genres, including those that often tend to appeal more to boys or more to girls, especially if this shift will help many boys be more interested in writing. I wonder whether the bad boys in primary classrooms across the country, boys like David, might feel more connected to the classroom culture when the writing curriculum is connected to their own interests. I have known many boys who are not interested or able to readily process their emotions, reflect, or talk about their personal lives with great ease or willingness. Should this have to impact their writing development as well? By shifting the content of what we teach, and by diffusing the personal from the curriculum, I believe these boys can learn how to write and use this skill in a socially meaningful way that helps them connect writing to their own interests, as different as they may be.

ENDNOTES

1. I present and translate my students' writing exactly as they created it. The words I present are theirs. I have changed their names in order to protect my students' identities. The texts I present are exactly the same as the writing they produced, with exceptions for some key words that were changed to protect the anonymity of the child.

REFERENCES

Calkins, L. (1986). *The art of teaching writing.* Portsmouth, NH: Heinemann.

Clay, M. (2001). *Change over time in children's literacy development.* Portsmouth, NH: Heinemann.

Dorn, L., and Soffos, C. (2001). *Scaffolding young writers: A Writer's Workshop approach.* Portland, ME: Stenhouse.

Dyson, A. H. (1997). *Writing superheroes: Contemporary childhood, popular culture, and classroom literacy.* New York: Teachers College Press.

Gallas, K. (1998). *"Sometimes I can be anything": Power, gender and identity in a primary classroom.* New York: Teachers College Press.

Graves, D. (1983). *Writing: Teachers and children at work.* Portsmouth, NH: Heinemann.

Hunt, B. (1985). A leprechaun in King Arthur's court: Topic, theme, and mode in the writing of first graders using invented spelling. *Reading Research Quarterly, 10,* 74–75, 103–123.

McPhail, G. (2008). *Finding freedom as a writer: Genre, gender and identity in a first grade writers' workshop.* Unpublished doctoral dissertation. Boston College, Chestnut Hill, MA.

Millard, E. (1997). *Differently literate: Boys, girls and the schooling of literacy.* London: Falmer.

Newkirk, T. (2002). *Misreading masculinity.* Portsmouth, NH: Heinemann.

Peterson, S. (2001). Gender identities and self-expression in classroom narrative writing. *Language Arts, 78*(5), 451–457.

Pollack, W. (1998). *Real boys: Rescuing our sons from the myths of boyhood.* New York: Holt.

Rose, M. (1989). *Lives on the boundary: The struggles and achievements of America's underprepared.* New York: Free Press.

Thomas, P. (1994). Writing, reading and gender. *Gifted Education International, 9*(3), 154–158.

Chapter Seven

Practitioner Inquiry as Mediated Emotion

Gillian Maimon

Gillian Maimon has been a teacher in the Philadelphia public schools since 1996, where she has taught first, second, and third grades. A doctoral candidate at the University of Pennsylvania, Maimon is interested in exploring ways that particular stories from any classroom serve to interrupt the reductive impact of prescriptive curriculum. She writes regularly about her experiences with children, both to enrich her teaching and to inform others who work outside of classrooms. Since 2001, Maimon has taught preservice teachers at Penn, opening the doors of her elementary classroom as a site for fieldwork to all of her university students. She is an active member of the Philadelphia Teachers Learning cooperative, a practitioner inquiry group that has met every week since 1978.

I have never been certain whether I am a teacher who writes or a writer who teaches. To thrive as a writer or teacher, one must build. Composition, essentially, is construction. Classrooms, too, must be built anew every year. Over my 13 years in 1st-, 2nd-, and 3rd-grade classrooms in the school district of Philadelphia, writing and teaching have become richly and inextricably intertwined. I am always endeavoring to create meaning from the perpetual ambiguity that accompanies the work that I do in the world. It is for this reason that I have kept a teaching journal throughout my career.

WRITING IN PURSUIT OF THE UNKNOWABLE

Elizabeth Ellsworth (1997) describes teaching as an endeavor that is ultimately impossible. We can be certain that there is more to our students than we have the capacity to perceive, and we can be certain that their perception of us differs profoundly from who we think we are. One of the reasons I write about my classroom is to challenge the limits of the work, to keep trying to know more.

I intentionally observe and describe day-to-day life in my classroom in order to extend the boundaries of what I am able to perceive. Author and educator Patricia Carini (2001), whose descriptive processes help to frame the work I do as a teacher, writes that description "teaches me that the subject of my attention always exceeds what I can see" (p. 163). Writing about my classroom is a way of trying to know what can never truly be known.

The writing I do is an assertion of the inherently intellectual nature of teaching. It is a way that I keep learning. Cochran-Smith and Lytle (1999) contend that teachers learn from and about teaching by striving to "theorize and construct their work and to connect it to larger social, cultural, and po-litical issues" (p. 250). When I reflect in the pages of my teaching journal about what I've described of a day, I am trying to figure out how my class-room helps me understand the world and how the world helps me understand my classroom.

The gnawing inexactness of the work of teaching is not just the stuff of intellectual exhaustion; it elicits deep emotional response as well. Writing helps to make the inherent emotionality of the work generative rather than debilitating. I write on a regular basis about my classroom as much to help me to think more clearly as to mediate the often-intense emotional impact of the work I do with children.

FEELING MY WAY THROUGH MY WORK

In a chat following Back to School Night at the start of my 11th year in the classroom, the father of one of my 1st-grade students recounted an anecdote from a few weeks prior. Reporting to her father the vital facts of her first day at school, the little girl mused that Teacher Gill was "a lot more serious than I thought she would be." To say that I appreciated the story would be an understatement. In fact, the opening assessment of this 6-year-old made me aware of my own growth as a teacher in a way that far eclipsed my consider-able satisfaction at having endured another Back to School Night. The "seri-ousness" the girl identified was no mere withholding of smiles in a Pavlovian plot to assert authority in the first days of school, but rather stood as testament to a particular emotional demeanor that is as intentional on my part as it has been hard-won.

In the process of learning to feel my way through my work, I've sus-tained my fair share of psychological bumps and bruises. My memories of my first few years in the classroom are tinged in a wash of near mania. There were tears, of course, shed in abundance for the woeful circumstances of so many of my students, for my own ineptitude as a teacher, for the inhospitable nature of the school administration. Given how routinely crying obscured my vision behind the wheel, it is truly a mercy that I arrived home safely each day. As many days as not, the tears started long before I made it to the parking lot. How clearly I recall teetering on the brink of full loss of composure, surrounded by mutinous third graders. Crying in the car is one thing, but crying in front of the children is a true smash-up.

Miraculously interspersed amid these low lows of my first years of teaching were moments of near-ecstatic happiness. The Thanksgiving of my first year, when I told parents my plan to churn butter with the children and make a feast of several loaves of bread, they took it upon themselves to expand the menu considerably, whole turkey and all. It was a raucous, delicious, amazing time. As laughter-filled as this day was, it ended in a familiar way, driving and crying on the way home. These were different tears, though.

Now that I know they didn't kill me, I look back on my early years as a teacher with fondness. More than anything, though, I look back on this time with profound exhaustion. No doubt, I felt my work more deeply at this time period than at any other in my career, but I would not have been able to sustain this intensity of feeling for any significant length of time. And that's a big problem. The bottom line for me as a teacher is, and always has been, very simple: I need to be able to come back tomorrow. Feeling the work at the intense emotional pitch I experienced in the early years would have ultimately precluded doing the work. Hence, I needed to find a way to channel the emotions of teaching more productively.

Beyond the fundamental necessity of maintaining my psychological endurance for the work, the need to mediate the emotionality of teaching is key to creating a just community in the classroom. Aristotle's notion that "law is reason, free from passion" has always resonated for me. I interpret "passion" in this case as a particular reactive emotionality that I find as hazardous in classrooms as Aristotle would in courtrooms. I know of myself, arbiter of justice in my own pint-sized microcosm, that I am least fair when I am most emotional.

I had a very bad day a couple months ago. I had not slept well the night before. I was worried about an approaching deadline. I really needed a smooth day with the children. As I read aloud to the class, I saw out of the corner of my eye two of the boys poking each other playfully. These antics affronted me. I shoved the book aside and beseeched, "Why are you doing that to me?"

Such pathos in response to a little horseplay is, of course, ridiculous. The size of my reaction far eclipsed the minuteness of the breach. In a better state of mind, the incident would have merited no more than a "Stop!" But it wasn't just inflation that made me wrong. The grounds upon which I called the boys' actions into question—specifically, the impact those actions were having on me—personalized an infraction that would have been more productively and more fairly dealt with as a community issue.

In our classroom community, everyone has the right to be listened to. This is one of the most basic tenets of fairness that we live by. Given the nature of my job, I may do more of the talking, but no matter whose turn, the person who is speaking has a right to be heard. My emotional response to the boys obscured for them the reason they were wrong. It didn't just confuse for them their responsibility to the community but also served to amplify my own already unequal power. The boys' inattentiveness was a mistake, not because it hurt the feelings of an individual whose approval they wished to have, but because it infringed on rights that we all have as members of our classroom community.

Errors so clear in retrospect are not nearly as apparent when made in the heat of a moment. My scolding of the boys is just one of innumerable, often instantaneous, choices that I make every day as a teacher, many with far more serious consequence than what to do about a little roughhousing on the rug. It is very difficult to make just decisions on the fly. One way that I gird myself for a day's hard choices is through purposeful, ongoing reflection about my classroom.

Lest one think I am an advocate for numbness, let me clarify just how deep my feelings are for the work I do. Certainly I am mindful of ways emotion can cloud the judgments I make in my classroom, yet my emotional connection to the people with whom I spend my days is what makes the work matter. Teaching is no work for automatons. It is profoundly human work, with stakes higher than any other work I can imagine. To steel oneself so defensively as to lose the capacity to be touched and changed by it would be to miss the meaning of teaching.

My tightly controlled reading of Aristotelian passion as reactive emotionality has everything to do with the fact that, by other definitions, passion is what underlies my teaching. I believe in it. I mourn in it. I delight in it. I despair in it. I love in it. I rage in it. Make no mistake, my heart is in my work. But it would be neither wise nor sustainable for my heart to go it alone. Thus, I engage in purposeful, ongoing reflection about my classroom as a way to harness the emotion and hitch it to meaningful action. A key way I do this is through writing. The journals I keep about my classroom help me to fuse feeling and thought in order that I might act humanely and not emotionally.

When I write about my classroom, it is never difficult to know how I am going to start. I can always count on some unresolved incident to get me rolling. But once under way, I never know for sure which way I'm headed until I get there. And one way or another, I always get somewhere. I am a fool for narrative cohesiveness. I sit and puzzle over a piece of my day for hours just to get to the point that I can attach some semblance of retroactive meaning to it. In this way, writing sustains me. It helps me keep a grip on my sense of purpose in my work.

Writing also helps me to be a better teacher. In culling the stories from a day, I am able to relive them with the luxury of calm and of time. Like fashioning a pair of corrective lenses, I perceive situations anew, with the hope that some of this improved acuity might influence my sight in a permanent way. While no two crises in a classroom are ever exactly the same, odds are that there will be reason in the future to call upon some kernel of wisdom gleaned from today's misstep.

GOING PUBLIC: THE STORY OF TAESHAWN

While the process of writing is of great importance to me in my day-to-day work as a teacher, I also intend for my work to reach an audience larger than myself. I believe that the very particularity of the writing makes it both meaningful in a personal way and worthy of inclusion within the public discourse on education. It is for this reason that I write for publication. In the current climate of increased scripting of curriculum and reliance on high-stakes tests as mirrors of children's aptitudes, small stories from classrooms are emblems of resistance. Close accounts of the experience of teaching illuminate the specificity of the work in a way that belies the notion that standardization of the work is desirable, or even tenable.

While I publish my writing in order to help change reductive thinking about classrooms, my writing is itself changed by being made public. The transformative nature of publication was made especially apparent not long ago when I shared with a small group of colleagues some journal entries I had written about a former student named Taeshawn (pseudonym). While responses to the writing were as varied as the array of lenses that this particular group of readers brought to the text, I was taken by surprise by one person who commented that the tone of the journal made it seem that I was resigned to Taeshawn's eventual unfortunate fate. Having lived through the stories on the page and put them to paper, with tears as often as not, the idea of my own callousness seemed unfathomable.

And yet, knowing that the act of writing is so often what saves me from emotional paralysis, I had to consider that this particular reason for writing might produce a product emotionally different in pitch from the way the lived experience actually hit me. If the composition process helps soothe me when I am most unsettled, could it be that I am unintentionally leeching the feeling out of my descriptions? I want to go back to the story of Taeshawn. I want to reread what I've written. I want to try to work out for myself some sort of reconciliation between the respective experiences of writing and reading my practice.

Taeshawn did not come to me the usual way, in the mass of first graders as nervous as I was on the first day of school. Rather, he showed up unexpectedly toward the middle of the year, trailing an air of residual drama. Interestingly, as the journal entry below reveals, he showed up in my writing even before he became a physical presence in my classroom.

January 15
    The principal lets me know at lunchtime that a new student will be joining our classroom on Tuesday. The boy, Taeshawn, is, in fact, not new. I already know about him. He has spent the first part of the year in another 1st-grade classroom, where he has quickly acquired the reputation of being a troublemaker. It is not the typical itchy-first-grader type of trouble that he has gotten into, either. On more than one occasion, he has bothered female classmates in a way that was perceived to be sexually suggestive. In an incident that became the reason for his transfer to my room, he pushed another student up against a wall and rubbed up against her. Certainly his behavior sets off some alarm bells. When a 6-year-old is acting out in this sexualized way, one can assume that something may be happening in his life that should not be. So far we do not have evidence that anyone is touching Taeshawn inappropriately, though we continue to be alert. It could be that he is seeing some things that he is not supposed to. Whatever the origin, his behavior is cause for great concern, both for Taeshawn and for the children he comes into contact with.
    My first reaction to the news is not a generous one. I wonder why another teacher's problem student must disturb the harmony of my classroom. My next reaction is that I am going to have to think hard about how to prepare the children for the arrival of this troubled new classmate. I believe that our room could be an excellent place for Taeshawn to learn better ways to interact with his peers. My students could be wonderful teachers. But it is going to take some work by all of us to get ready for this new challenge. Tomorrow I will share the news with the children, and our work will begin.

How different it is to read this passage as a fixed piece of text than it was to compose it. The tone is jarring in more ways than one. As a reader, I am as thrown by the withering appraisal of my colleague and her "problem student" as I am by the naïve hopefulness at the end. As a writer, however, I was less concerned with how the piece would read than how the act of composition might equip me for challenges to come. The progression in tone from disdain to hope traces the path of a kind of personal truth and reconciliation process, subconsciously orienting myself toward the future, just as war-torn nations have done intentionally. Direct acknowledgment of strong feelings of fear and resentment helped to assuage inner strife and move me to a point of taking productive action.

And so I moved past the initial shock of learning of Taeshawn's impending arrival and began the work of preparing the children to meet him.

January 16

When we all gather together on the rug for the first time this morning, I tell the children the "great news" about Taeshawn joining our class. The boys are especially pleased that their ranks will be growing by one, because now we will have the same number of boys as girls in our classroom. Of course, I do not go into detail about his problems in his other classroom, but I do tell the children that he didn't always follow the rules. "He's a really good kid," I tell them. "But he isn't always sure what is the right thing to do." I haven't even met Taeshawn, but I talk about him to the children as if I know him. I tell them what I need them to believe about their new classmate and what I need to believe about him, too.

My desire to assert control over the classroom narrative is as apparent in the talk that I have with the children as it is in my subsequent recounting of the meeting. In my hopeful characterization of Taeshawn, I am writing the world as I wish it to be. It is as much for my own forward trajectory as it is for the children's that I need to frame Taeshawn in such a way. This is art intended for life to imitate.

Before I can feel too self-satisfied in my own mastery of the universe, an unexpected turn reminds me that, as often as not, days in a classroom unfold wholly independent of my attempts to shape them.

January 20

I am nervous about Taeshawn's introduction to our classroom but feel pretty confident that the plan for this morning is a good one. The only flaw in the day's plan is that it does not take into account the changeability of life. As it turns out, Taeshawn is sick today and will not be coming to school after all. The children are not pleased when I arrive at the door without Taeshawn. They do not like the idea that we will be working on our class mural about peacemakers without his assistance. When the mural artist comes, the first thing the children do is make him promise that we'll be able to leave a space for Taeshawn. The artist, who attentively listens to the children, both agrees that space should be left and compliments them on their desire to include children who are not able to participate in the work we are doing today. He tells them that, by considering the feelings of others who might feel left out, they are acting as peacemakers.

So often, my writing is actually an act of rewriting. The unpredictability of any classroom requires constant adjustment. Meaning is made and remade as the ground moves beneath us. Unsteady from the unexpectedness of this day, I find stability in the idea of peacemaking. Whether or not this is an idea that truly resonated for the children I cannot say. In text, peacemaking becomes an abiding theme. In fact, its meaning was for me.

A day later, Taeshawn's introduction to our classroom finally happens.

January 21

Taeshawn and I don't even make it upstairs to the classroom before it is clear to me that my new student's reputation precedes him to a much greater extent than I'd realized. As we turn from the first-floor hallway into the stairwell, we happen to pass a mother who is bringing her 4th-grade daughter to the office for a late slip. In a loud voice, the woman says to the girl, "Is that the little boy that's been bothering you?" I do not wait for the exchange to go any further. Pointedly, I say, "If your daughter is having a problem with another student, please tell somebody in the office." I do not make a friend of the woman with these words. She is probably justifiably concerned that another child is causing trouble for her daughter, but I cannot stand by silently as Taeshawn is convicted again before his second chance even reaches the second floor. I am beginning to see that Taeshawn's new beginning might be more challenging than I imagined.

I wonder if my advocacy on Taeshawn's behalf would have been nearly as vociferous had I not had the opportunity to believe in him in print before meeting him in the flesh. Encountering this obstacle to Taeshawn's fresh start mere minutes after officially meeting him, it must have been more the character that I put on a page that I was defending than the real, live puzzle that walked beside me.

Later that day, one of the children called me on a perceived inconsistency as I continued to try to shape the narrative of Taeshawn.

> With a few minor exceptions, the children are remarkably un-derstanding and accepting of Taeshawn. When Joseph responds in a prickly way to a silly comment by his new classmate, I remind him in private that we must be patient with Taeshawn. Joseph regards me seriously and says, "But you weren't patient with him when he was lying down on the rug." Joseph is right. I was decidedly im-patient when Taeshawn sprawled when he was meant to be sitting. As I see it, I must display for Taeshawn an abundance of kindness, but I also must make clear that I am the person in charge. For this reason, I have very purposefully told him "no" more than once to-day. I recognize that there are ways that I am expecting more from the children than I do from myself because I do not allow them to correct him. I am asking the children to be unwaveringly tolerant, while I have the power to determine which of Taeshawn's behav-iors are intolerable.

This passage strikes me as an interesting companion to the "truth and reconciliation" entry of a week earlier. On paper, I am owning up to an imbalance of power in a way that I do not (and would not) to Joseph. I am parlaying acknowledgment of an inequity into license to perpetuate it.

Though Taeshawn's first day with us unfolded fairly undramatically, I was never tempted to spin the events of the day into a tale of triumph. Over and over again, I have learned the hard way that progress seldom happens as sustained movement forward. To write as if we had reached a clear point of resolution at the end of one day would only have been setting myself up for heartbreak when my sense of mastery over my own narrative inevitably unraveled, as it did the very next morning.

> January 22
> The day gets off to a rough start with a sobbing Taeshawn sprawled on the floor of the hallway outside our classroom door. While I understand that the transition from his old classroom must be scary for him, prostrate hysteria is not a viable option for dealing

with fear in a public passage. I deal with the situation by scooping him off the floor and carrying him into the room. If the other children are shocked by the quasi-wrestling move I've placed on their new classmate, they give no indication. Taeshawn cries quietly in a corner for about 10 minutes, while the rest of us go about business as usual. When he is sufficiently cried out, he unpacks his bag, hangs up his jacket, and comes over to join us as if nothing out of the ordinary has occurred and he has only just arrived.

Taeshawn is not the first sobbing child I have dealt with, and he will not be the last. When things are going smoothly in a classroom, teachers can forget what bumps in the road feel like. Taeshawn reminds me that sometimes the day begins with my responsibilities walking through the door in an orderly fashion, and sometimes my day begins with my responsibilities being carried in, kicking and screaming. How many bankers and lawyers can make a similar claim?

How strange that the official record of what I know was a very trying morning reads like a funny little anecdote. Reading as a writer, I know full well that this was laughter to keep from crying, and yet the text that serves to document this time does not capture accurately the unsettling nature of the episode. I wonder if this is one of the pieces that misrepresents the deep emotional investment I had in Taeshawn.

As the weeks went on, despite a few bumps along the way—most notably music class, which I finally decided to hold him back from—Taeshawn made a smooth transition into our classroom community. In time, the degree to which I was directly involved in his socialization lessened as children took up some of the work for themselves. The net effect for me was more time to sit back and watch.

February 25

For days I have been noticing the close friendship building between Taeshawn and Taerem. After Taeshawn's breakdown in music class yesterday, I am trying to reassure myself that he has made progress in our classroom by watching his interactions with his new friend. Taeshawn really looks up to Taerem, and Taerem, in turn, acts the part of the patient older brother. At writing time this morning, the two boys work together on biographies of each other. First, Taerem interviews Taeshawn, and writes down the information that he gathered. Then Taeshawn asks the same questions to

Taerem, and with Taerem's help, writes down the data on his own page. At recess time, I watch from a distance as the two boys dig for worms under a tree. Taerem finds one and passes it back and forth with Taeshawn. At one point, Taeshawn seizes the worm and runs off with it. Taerem gives chase for a moment, then walks off in the opposite direction. Then Taeshawn switches course, too, walking back to Taerem, attempting to make amends for his flight. After a moment or two of talk from Taerem, the two boys are back under the tree looking together for worms once more. I am struck by the complexity of the interaction between the boys, by Taerem's wise leadership and Taeshawn's willingness to be his apprentice. In some ways, Taerem is a better teacher of Taeshawn than I, and I am grateful.

Perhaps because the nature of this passage is a close description of an intentional observation I made of the boys, I find that there is much less of a gulf between the experience of reading this text and my recollection of writing it. Much as describing the episode in writing allowed me an opportunity to see the two boys more clearly, they are again vivid for me as I read what I captured. Only at the end, where I muse on themes of leadership and apprenticeship, do I dip into the realm of analysis. It is here where myself the reader steps apart from myself the writer. I see, as I have so often before, purpose in the writing process, which was both personal and temporal: I have created a public statement of solidarity with Taerem, both to honor his efforts and to affirm for myself that I am not alone in the work.

While his social successes multiplied week by week, Taeshawn was making very slow academic progress in our classroom. Two months after his arrival, he and his classmates joined the number two pencil brigade. A week's worth of standardized testing proved particularly challenging for Taeshawn.

March 25
    Taeshawn, the one child truly overmatched by the assessment, has not complained for an instant that he is unable to read any of it. He has dutifully enough filled his share of little circles, betraying not a moment of displeasure until I happen to look over at him this morning and catch him rubbing away a silent tear. I walk over, kneel down, and whisper in his ear, "I know this is hard for you. I know you don't know how to do this yet, but you will. I am going to teach you." I want him to believe me and I want to believe myself, but I am having a hard time. The test has me focusing on all

that Taeshawn doesn't know, and I am overwhelmed by the magnitude of all that he needs to learn. This is a distorted vision of the boy, however, made so by the task at hand. I remind myself that he has made miles of progress already. He will make miles more. But it is hard for him and it is hard for me to see any hope when the only evidence the test provides is what he cannot do.

Shouldn't there be a better way to assess the growth of a little boy who, just weeks ago, was considered a danger to his classmates? Isn't there a better gauge of the progress of a child who, until recently, spent most of his time in his classroom throwing tantrums? This test is not a good measure of Taeshawn.

Perhaps that's not entirely true. I see in his stoic tolerance of this ordeal tremendous strength of character. Be that as it may, he should not have to endure that kind of test.

Which is the truer portrait of Taeshawn? The one I stumblingly cobbled together over the months that I knew him or the altogether different story told by his test scores? One of the most compelling reasons I have for writing is to confront and refute the mistellings that abound about children and classrooms. Rereading this passage long after putting it to paper, I experience anger of an intensity that feels fresh. This is emotion largely unmediated by the process of writing, and that is no accident. In this instance, I am not trying, as I so often do, to recast or diffuse deep feeling. The particular emotionality of this situation—profound indignation at injustice done to children in the name of quantifying their achievement—is one that drives my work as a teacher and my work as a writer.

Reductive measures notwithstanding, there was no obscuring the fact that Taeshawn's academic level was considerably lower than that of his classmates. As the end of the year approached, choices needed to be made as to classroom assignments for the following year. Clearly, Taeshwan was going to need another year in first grade. After stating my case for the advantages of maintaining consistency for this boy who struggled for so long to feel at home in a classroom, the principal agreed to assign him again to me the following year. After talking through this plan with Taeshawn, we decided to share our news with the other children.

May 28

Upon entering the room after lunch recess, Taeshawn solemnly walks over to one of our work tables, removes one of the chairs, carries it over to the rug area, and places it beside the wood seat that serves as a throne of sorts for children who have brought something to share. Taeshawn explains to his classmates that, because he and I have something that we want to share together today, we need two places to sit. I come over and fold myself into the little plastic chair that Taeshawn has set up for me, and preface our news with a few comments. What I say to the children is a version of what a now-retired colleague of mine said for many years at times when it became obvious to her students that some among them were progressing at a different rate. I tell the class that nearly everybody learns how to read. Some children learn very quickly, and some learn more slowly, but by the end of second grade, people's reading levels tend to be a lot closer together. Some people just need more time than others. This is true. What is also true that I do not tell them is that, when cities are trying to determine how many prison cells they will need in the future, they look at the percentage of children who are not reading by the end of second grade. I tell the class that Taeshawn is one of the children who needs more time. I try to banish from my mind thoughts of what it will mean if he still doesn't get it the second time around.

Taeshawn then takes questions and comments from the group. Taerem tells him that he is going to ask his grandmother if he can spend another year in our classroom, too. A few other children congratulate Taeshawn and others tell him that they will still be able to play together at recess time. All in all, it is a successful conversation. Taeshawn seems to be feeling good about the news that we have shared, and the other children are being very supportive. It will likely be another story when school begins again next fall. What sounds good in theory in the springtime can look quite different on the first day of school, when the child who is retained returns to his classroom and finds that his friends are no longer there. Taeshawn and I will weather that storm together when the time comes.

I read this piece as companion to the January one in which I first informed the children of Taeshawn's impending arrival. Back then, it was I wanting desperately to exert control over the narrative. On this day, I had a co-author. I savor this entry. It was a moment in time rife with unknowns, but it was one that Taeshawn and I together had willed into a sense of possibility. This is the one that I wish had come last, but it's not.

June 2

Innocuous events that set in motion calamities of grand proportion are seldom recognized for their auspiciousness at the moment they occur. When Mrs. O'Leary's cow kicked over the lantern, not a person exclaimed, "There goes Chicago!" Be that as it may, every once in a while, it is possible to foresee devastating conflagration from the smallest spark. When I go out to the yard this morning to retrieve the children after recess, three girls from Taeshawn's old classroom are waiting for me by the door. They report that, when they were playing together on the climbing equipment, Taeshawn rubbed up against them in a way that made them feel uncomfortable. Then he said that he was going to rape them. I thank them for the information and promise that I will take care of it, but this is no simple instance of horseplay and I know it. This is the commencement of Taeshawn's downfall.

There will be no dodging of consequences this time. Taeshawn is as good as gone. Just last Friday, Taeshawn and I shared big news about next year with his classmates. Now, all the progress and all the plans are kaput as a result of a single 15-minute recess. Trying not to betray my sense of panic and devastation, I walk the rest of the way from the door to my class's line. Without giving any reason, I send Raquel in search of the principal and lead the remaining children— including Taeshawn—back into the building. We are nearly to the door when one of the recess aides, a man who is especially fond of Taeshawn, calls for the boy. The aide is standing by Taeshawn's former teacher, and I can tell that they have both just heard from the same three girls who filled me in on Taeshawn's recess activities. As his former teacher glares down at Taeshawn, the recess aide announces his intention to have a conversation with the boy.

I do not think through what it is that I do next, I simply act on impulse. I tell the recess aide that I will not leave Taeshawn with him, that he must come with us to our classroom if he would like to have a conversation with the boy. It may be more reflective of my mounting sense of grief than any rational thought process, but I find myself holding others responsible for what has just taken place. Foremost, I am livid at the former teacher. She presides over a classroom in which children seem constantly to be at each other's throats. This is not just a quirk of bad chemistry in this particular group. Year after year, I am startled by the absence of a sense of community among her students. I find it significant that Taeshawn, despite his history with his former classmates, never once behaved inappropriately with any of the children in our room.

Much as blaming Taeshawn's old teacher serves as a convenient outlet for me, I cannot deny that something is terribly wrong with

Taeshawn. It is not normal for a child of his age to be acting out in such a sexualized way. The boy needs help. Unfortunately, the consequences for his misdeed as dictated by the system are ones that will likely do more harm than good. He will be taken out of our close-knit and responsive community and transferred to another school, where he will be a stranger. When the principal finally makes it up to the room, she confirms that this is what will happen. Because we are so close to the end of the school year, he will not be assigned to a new school until September, but in the meantime, he is to be suspended for the maximum allowable time—5 days. With only 9 days left until the end, Taeshawn may not even come back.

I may be in full protective mode, but I am not completely without objectivity on this issue. If I were the parent of a child who was approached by Taeshawn in such a threatening way, I would not want the boy to remain where he could cause further harm. Taeshawn's actions are likely reflective of the fact that he is in need of protection, but that does not mean that it is OK for him to victimize other children. Unfortunately, this seems to be a situation in which not everyone's needs can be served. To safeguard some, others must be abandoned.

Taeshawn has no idea of all that is about to happen to him. I don't tell him, and neither does the principal. We try a few times to reach his grandmother by telephone, then, when our attempts are unsuccessful, resort to a folded-up note in his bookbag explaining what has happened and what the consequences will be. As I see him out the door at the end of the day, I wonder: How do you say good-bye to a child who does not even know that he's leaving? Perhaps I will see him for 4 days at the end of the year, or perhaps I will not. Either way, this isn't how the story was supposed to go.

How was the story supposed to go? I'm reluctant to articulate the wish. No matter the thick callus of pragmatism I've built over years in this work, doesn't a part of me want this story to be of the *Stand and Deliver*, teacher-as-emancipator archetype? No doubt, the narrative that I make of my classroom is filtered consciously and unconsciously through this and myriad other representations of teachers and children. But what flavors this last entry more than any subconscious reading list is a profound loss of faith. In the end, I stop imagining that there is anything I can do for Taeshawn. Perhaps this is what my colleague meant when she commented that I seemed resigned to Taeshawn's fate.

My life and Taeshawn's intersected for a spell, and we had some good days. But I didn't save him and he didn't elevate me. That would have made for an elegant story arc, but, too often, that's not how this kind of work goes. The terrain that teachers inhabit is treacherous even on the best days. Stating publicly the perils of each step is what keeps me climbing. What is hardest to tell is how some passes are simply not navigable. If the tidiness of the telling leads anyone to believe that blood wasn't spilled, then I've told a lie.

Ultimately, the fundamental lie of the story is attributable to the fact that it is not, in fact, a story. This is a child's life, and this is my life. Putting narrative form to the days I spent with Taeshawn may have helped me to keep at least a tenuous grasp on the sense of purposefulness that is my oxygen in the classroom, but my authorship in no way confers upon me the ability to truly control meaning. It turns out that writing about teaching is as impossible as teaching itself. Meaning that I make of my work through writing is bounded by my capacity to perceive as well as my capacity to believe. My field of vision will always be eclipsed by my blind spots. But what gets captured on the page is not nothing. It is an artifact of the unremitting thinking and feeling that drive my work.

REFERENCES

Carini, P. (2001). *Starting strong: A different look at children, schools, and standards.* New York: Teachers College Press.

Cochran-Smith, M., & Lytle, S. (1999). Relationships of knowledge and practice: Teacher learning in communities. In A. Iran-Nejad & C.D. Pearson (Eds.), *Review of research in education* (Vol. 24, pp. 249–306). Washington, DC: American Educational Research Association.

Ellsworth, E. (1997). *Teaching positions: Difference, pedagogy, and the power of address.* New York: Teachers College Press.

Chapter Eight

Can We Read a Happy Book Next?: Using Children's Literature to Move Beyond Our White Space

Kelly A. Harper

Kelly A. Harper is an assistant professor of education in the Graduate Childhood Program in the School of Education and Human Services at Canisius College in Buffalo, New York. Harper's practitioner research in this chapter features her former role as a 6th-grade teacher in a school district outside of Boston, Massachusetts. Harper's scholarly interests include critical literacy, social justice, accessibility and universal design, teacher education, and professional development schools. She is the co-author of Teacher Planning for Accessibility: The Universal Design of Learning Environments, A Quest for Accessibility in Higher Education Institutions, *and* Inquiry in Teacher Education: Competing Agendas, *as well as other articles on effective teaching practices. Harper draws on her elementary and middle school teaching experiences as well as her year spent teaching abroad in Hiroshima, Japan, in her current work with preservice teachers and other practitioners committed to social justice and the inquiry stance.*

Although the nation as a whole has become incredibly diverse, there are many communities and schools that have been "resegregated" and are racially encapsulated. Many K–12 schools reflect an increasingly pluralistic society, yet some maintain predominantly White populations that Lewis (2001) defines as "White spaces." In communities that are almost entirely White and affluent, most schoolchildren live both racially segregated and privileged lives, alienated from the nation's diversity, which is absorbed elsewhere. Their sheltered White space supports the status quo, often at the expense of opportunities for them to learn to recognize and understand the powerful

impact of racism on all aspects of daily life. Furthermore, many school multicultural education initiatives tend to dissociate from social struggles and in
their place embrace celebratory experiences focusing on ethnic foods and
festivals (Sleeter & McLaren, 2000). Nieto (1999) suggests that this deficient
approach camouflages the massive failure of schools to improve education.

At the same time, however, as Lewis (2001) suggests, critical approaches
to multicultural education that confront societal issues and challenge the status quo are implemented mostly in urban settings, where such opportunities
exist locally. According to Wills (1996), "a multicultural history curriculum is extremely useful for White, suburban students, who often have little
contact with people of color in their everyday lives and are much more dependent upon cultural stereotypes and assumptions when trying to imagine
the situations of others in American society" (p. 385). For students living
in White spaces, the responsibility for exposure to "missing voices" in their
communities falls on the school as the primary source of racial information
that can challenge both previous attitudes and perceptions (Lewis, 2001).

These critical national issues and calls for increased critical pedagogical
practice resonated with my own teaching situation in the early 2000s. What
follows in this chapter is a partial account of a teacher research endeavor in my
"White space" that focused on literature as a medium through which issues of
social justice could be introduced and perhaps better understood. This study
examines what affluent White children learned when they read and talked
about books intentionally selected to confront issues of race and racism, injustice, and cultural differences. Although we have a fair amount of research on
how children make sense of fictional and historical literature, there is very little
research on how they—and their teachers—understand issues of race and racism
in books or how this literature affects their attitudes, beliefs, and dispositions.

The community in which I worked for many years, a town I call Orchard
Hills in this chapter, can be described as an affluent, predominantly White
(89 percent), aesthetically minded town incorporated in the late 1800s. Over
time, media attention to several race-related incidents preserved the town's
unfortunate historical reputation for racial insensitivity. In response to some
of these incidents, the school district initiated a writing tradition that invited
students to reflect on examples of social justice they had experienced or witnessed. On the surface, the assignment was apparently intended to be a progressive effort to restore tolerance and respect for differences and attend to a
need for greater critical awareness. However, systemic change requires much
more than this isolated learning experience as race-related issues prevail. In
hindsight, I believe that this writing assignment conveyed the message to
students and families that the community was progressing in terms of racial
tolerance and respect, but, in actuality, it may have further distanced us from

reality. While recognizing that individuals' growth is inspiring, I believe that talking about past and present injustices would have produced a more honest assessment of the racial climate of the school and the community and would have fostered less superficial attention to these issues.

In September 2003, graffiti scrawled on a bathroom wall in the high school claimed the school would burn and no more Blacks would attend. The incident surrounding this graffiti, which turned out to have been written by a Black student himself, subsequently sparked discussions about the role race played in this nearly all-White community. A columnist from a local newspaper, herself a resident and parent of Orchard Hills students, posed some thought-provoking inquiries regarding the graffiti incident at the high school. She questioned:

> What does it mean that the teenager who scrawled a threat on a bathroom wall to burn down Orchard Hills High so "there will be no Blacks in our schools" is Black himself? Why would a student, bussed from [the city] for 11 years to schools in this suburb, choose to vent his frustration or rage or pain by assuming the persona of a White racist? When is a troubled kid just a troubled kid? Did tensions in the overwhelmingly White school account for the racial nature of his threat? Did he push that button to wound a town trying to overcome a reputation for racial insensitivity? Or did an impulsive teen act heedlessly, with no thought to the implications of his words? (McNamara, 2003)

Reflecting on the situation, the school district superintendent commented, "Race is the American dilemma. If we haven't figured it out, why do we expect the kids have?"

Given how few students and staff members of color we had in our school, I believed that this incident was an outcome related to one of the community's biggest issues—challenging the structures of power and racial privilege maintained by the status quo. The school principal emailed the faculty:

> My hope for our school is that we can continue to find ways of pushing ourselves beyond our "comfort zones" and expand our knowledge and sensitivity about how culture and race impact our work as educators. (September 8, 2003)

Though we were encouraged to improve racial harmony and commit to self-examination as a collective body, very little happened outside of the annual writing initiative noted above; moreover, there was no established teacher research community or teacher network to provide a forum for sorting out and interrogating the issues.

In the school year previous to the one noted above, a teacher colleague had tutored a 4th-grade student in reading. Their discussions about African American issues that were central in the themes of the book *Roll of Thunder, Hear My Cry*[1] had made the parent uneasy. In an exasperated and caustic tone, the parent had challenged the curricular relevance of the novel to the White Orchard Hills community: "We never had to think about these issues until these books came along." In her angry words, I heard ignorance, concerns about risks, and overall racial insensitivity all wrapped into one. However, my long-standing observations of the students themselves, albeit privileged and sophisticated in some ways, revealed a genuine openness to learning about others whose lives did not mirror their own. As I thought back through my years of teaching, I admitted to myself that stereotypes were commonly heard in my classroom discourse, sometimes challenged, sometimes unquestioned as even I shied away from controversial topics at times. Perhaps some comments went unheard or unchallenged by me because students genuinely offered insight without malicious intent. As Fecho (2001) has argued, "When teachers shy away from controversy in the classroom, parents ask for changes in their children's curriculum, or students construct a new sense of their worldview, some aspect of their lives has come under some degree of threat" (p. 18). The teacher research inquiry that I describe in the remainder of this chapter placed me in a state of disequilibrium at times and challenged me to deal with competing commitments as well as my own uncertainty.

INQUIRING INTO MY PRACTICE

While aware of the resistant positions like that of the parent quoted above, I moved forward with questions I had and ideas I had long wondered about in my own teaching practice. Respect and responsibility for oneself and others were supposedly at the core of the school district's mission, while critical thinking was intended to be the foundation of students' experiences in general. And yet, in teaching in this community for over a decade, I had been witness many times to situations reflecting a provincial understanding of social class and race issues. With higher-order thinking skills so much a part of the learning culture in general, I questioned why I, myself, had stopped short of making race issues—the elephant in the classroom and the school district—problematic when I embraced challenges of all other kinds with my students. Mostly, I felt at a loss for tools to engage my students in discourse that would bring about a more socially just view of the world. Politically, I feared repercussions from the parent community by making highly sensitive race and class issues explicit within the walls of my classroom. As Lewis (2001) notes, working toward social justice needs to begin with creating an awareness among the members that societal issues are critical for *all* populations to face, in particular, those from White spaces.

The students I taught had been introduced to readers' response and had participated in literature circles since their early elementary years. But it was the systematic journaling and the dynamic discussions we experienced as a group that further nurtured my students' abilities to transact with text and construct personal meaning from their literary experiences with literary genres of all kinds. Perspectives based on critical literacy positioned us to view language as a social construct, and as a teacher I encouraged multiple viewpoints to unfold. This expectation of reading deeply, critically, and thoughtfully energized my students, and we produced a sophisticated reading culture that often astonished me. I believed that using the conflicts of stories to make connections with the social issues I feared would strengthen my instruction and commitment to social justice, while also supporting my students' explorations of their own beliefs and assumptions. Using the characters' voices would be a safer entry that would allow us to explore our own thoughts and actions regarding them. Reading with a reflective stance was a natural extension of the ways my students thought analytically in other areas of the curriculum. I believed that this would be the tool I could capitalize on to help my students consider how things might be changed. I wanted to bring my instruction this one step further.

I began this inquiry with great conviction, somewhat safeguarded by the seeming outward support of the school administration and in the context of renewed interest from the community at large to face difficult race issues with my students. Like Fullan (1993), I saw advocating for change and challenging the status quo as a moral imperative, and I began to examine the following questions:

> What happens when children of an affluent, almost all-White school community read children's literature that includes issues of race and diversity? What explanations do students use to describe their understanding of issues of social justice in the books? What do they ask questions about? What kinds of issues do the students and teacher gravitate toward and write about in their journals?

From the outset, it was clear that this kind of inquiry was sensitive and complex and could only be accomplished through examining my own practice as well as my students' learning. The teacher research tradition seemed most appropriate since it generated unique and important knowledge from an emic perspective. Informed by Cochran–Smith and Lytle's (2004) analysis of the characteristics of practitioner inquiry, I deliberately set out to investigate the salient issues related to race and culture within my own practice working with my 6th-grade language arts class of 22 White students. My hope was that inquiry would help me begin to transform my practice and generate a more democratic culture and movement toward building a more just society.

I used four different data sources, collected systematically and analyzed throughout the school year: my teacher research journal, classroom conversations, student response journals, and other relevant writing activities. Social issues books, a term used by many critical literacy practitioners, encompass contemporary issues or issues of the past that touch on a myriad of struggles that resonate with widely diversified populations. The literary texts I used were both fiction and nonfiction texts, each examining, directly or in subtle ways, issues of social justice. These may prompt the development of powerful sensitivities based on the readers' personal interpretations and transactions. While evoking inspiration and hope in some, however, these same issues can also awaken resistance and fear in others. I examined my students' independent reading choices to explore their overall interest in pursuing opportunities on their own to learn about unfamiliar worlds. My own reflections discussed many of the struggles I had with the students' varied reactions to the books and their many layers of complexity. The data suggested that social issues books provided exposure to the life experiences of other people and cultures, as well as opportunities for students to examine critically and more personally their own racial attitudes. In the discussion that follows, which draws on a much longer analysis, I focus on three time periods during the school year that illustrate an emerging critical literacy stance among students, a shift in students' receptivity levels toward social issues books, and my own ambivalence as a teacher about inviting students to "read against the grain" (Harper, 2005).

GETTING STARTED

The graffiti incident, which occurred near the beginning of the school year, helped quickly generate a classroom culture in which students shared their viewpoints openly and critically. My students held strong feelings about the incident, shaped by media interpretations and by family dinner conversations. Critical conversations around racial issues, which were so personal to this conservative community, felt foreign to me, especially with a new group of children I was just beginning to know. It was a jumpstart on my plans for the year—one I never expected. After all, the books were supposed to be the source, at least in the beginning, that would help me deal with the controversial and—at least in the culture of my school—previously untouchable topic of race and racism. Imagining the worst, I mentally prepared my rebuttal to parents who might object to my allowing political viewpoints to enter classroom discourse during the first week of school. For many educators, this may sound like an odd concern or even an extreme response, but for me, it illustrates both my own hypersensitivity about the issues and my deep knowledge of the very conservative culture of my school and school district. Nothing could have surprised me more than to see parental consent forms coming in from every family, granting permission for their children to be participants in a study of my own practice that would focus on discussions around social issues books. As the parents understood it, their children would read a variety of books considered to be high-quality children's literature that included characters from many different ethnic, cultural, and racial backgrounds, as part of our consideration of what it means to live in an increasingly diverse society. Which issues the students responded to within the books were of interest to me as their teacher. I wanted to know how they made sense of issues related to race and racism in connection to other themes in the curriculum and to their lives.

Every one of the books I chose highlighted issues, some of them deep and controversial, that were related to adolescence or race. Some had complexities that would be readily recognizable to the students, while others were quite different from their lived experiences. My plan was that we would ease into the books with "unfamiliar worlds" once we had examined social issues in novels that were more personally relevant—social issues I believed my sixth graders could resonate with. For example, *Crash*[2], our first core novel, brought up peer pressure, bullying, and exclusion.

Next, *The Great Gilly Hopkins*[3] served as a bridge that mirrored the lives of my students but also served as a window into the lives of others. *Gilly* allowed us to contemplate issues related to racism and socioeconomic status that concurrently eased us further into a critical stance when reading literature. The students reflected inwardly, connecting personally in their own way to the events unfolding in *Gilly* and often revealing their underlying stereotypes and misconceptions. This teacher journal entry illustrates examples of the sensitive and complex conclusions students drew from the story.

Teacher Journal Entry: Today we discussed Gilly's emotions as she faced leaving her foster home. A few people said that she would be undecided about leaving, broken-hearted, and sad as well. Regis commented that "the house was run down, and as Gilly learned, it doesn't always mean that it's not a good place to live, or that it's not a good home, just like if you're 'Black', it doesn't always mean that you're not a good person." Yesterday, Regis made another related comment: [Gilly's] . . . living with Trotter for even just the short amount of time she did was worthwhile. "Trotter, after all, got Gilly to like Black people."

Through this discussion students revealed a perspective that was widely shared and accepted among them: Black people were not to be automatically given the benefit of the doubt as far as character goes. They needed to work at showing they were good persons and at fitting into the mainstream, which came automatically if you were White. My students, in fact, were describing White privilege, although without the label. While students' inferences served as an impetus for teaching about White privilege, we focused on the story's theme of race in particular. Nora commented that Trotter could not afford to adopt Gilly. When I asked her why she thought that, she put her head down and didn't respond. I believed that Nora inferred that Trotter was poor and that socioeconomic status was tied to race and felt badly about it. The next excerpt, this one written by Albert, illustrates not only his awareness of Gilly's racist nature but also his own encounter with race and a seemingly uncomfortable experience. In his response journal he stated:

> *Albert:* Gilly is very shocked that an African American, Mr. Randolph, is eating dinner with them, which is very unusual for Gilly's lifestyle. Also, Gilly doesn't like how Mr. Randolph is old and blind. When my family hosted a METCO[4] student when I was in elementary school, we invited his whole family to dinner. They were African American, and it was the quietest dinner we ever had. The conversation just felt more difficult to keep going because we didn't have a lot in common.

Albert's assessment of his dining experience spoke volumes. I believed he saw that his privileged life was visibly apparent to the guests, and he found it difficult to find conversation that didn't flaunt it further. Albert grew to like social issues books increasingly throughout the year and often connected the stories' themes to personal experiences.

Like Albert, Nora enjoyed *Gilly* and showed interest in reading about "others" in her journal as well. Although she had an interest in reading books of many kinds, she was especially drawn to books that introduced complex topics that were realistic or historical in nature, ones she could wrestle with and contemplate. Nora remained interested in social issues books for the duration of our time together. One of the stories she read for her own enjoyment, *Homeless Bird*[5], prompted Nora to examine the character's struggle and journey.

> *Nora:* Sometimes it takes negative experiences to notice things in life. *Homeless Bird* captured my attention because it was about a struggling girl and what happened through the course of time that the book was in . . . it helped me learn about Indian culture and religion.

Nora often expressed her interest in different cultures and rejoiced that she was living in today's world versus a time when she felt social justice issues were more invisible in society.

Students' varying interpretations of the same books sometimes initially put me into a state of disbelief, though Rosenblatt's sage advice diminished it.

> Teachers need to constantly remind themselves that reading is always a particular event involving a particular reader at a particular time under particular circumstances. Hence, we may make different meanings when transacting with the same text at different times. And different readers may make defensible interpretations of the same text. (Rosenblatt, 1991, p. 445)

Although my students came from quite a homogeneous community in terms of race and class, they had different thresholds of awareness, different interests, and very different reactions to the books we shared.

While the class was immersed in *Gilly*, I searched for a new book to read aloud alongside it. Even though my students were in the sixth grade, read-aloud time was an integral part of my language arts program, with a time slot of its own that I cherished. When Nora requested that we read *The Devil's Arithmetic*[6], I thought it was just the book all the students would want to hear: a nice mixture of fantasy and historical fiction. For some, it was just right, but for other students, like Cassie, it was enjoyed with some reservation. Cassie's journal entry reveals both a curiosity and fascination with a book that more directly dealt with social issues founded on historical truth and an admittance of wanting a separation from books of this kind:

> *Cassie:* I had a lot of emotions when you read *Devil's Arithmetic*. Sometimes I was really happy for something Hannah did, but other times I was extremely sad. The way that Hannah stuck up for others, and put herself in danger for them, really touched my heart . . . the courage

Hannah had is extremely special. To put yourself in danger for people you barely know is amazing . . . I enjoyed this book, but I think that we should read a happy book now.

Cassie's concluding statement, however, was the earliest sign that she would eventually depart from her enthusiastic classmates and begin to grow resistant toward reading books that were just, according to her, "not happy." Cassie was Jewish and the storyline of *The Devil's Arithmetic*, which dealt with the Holocaust, may have caused her personal anguish. But by the middle part of the year, Cassie's enthusiasm for books emphasizing social issues had waned, and she became more vocal about wanting distance from the books she started the year off enjoying.

Overall, the first part of the school year was an exciting start to my project to expose my students to critical social and cultural issues using literature. On the whole, the students showed a real eagerness to join in complex discussions in which everyone in the class could engage. Talking about complexities was something my group embraced. Racial issues were, in the literal sense revealed by the incidents described earlier, in our own backyard and were there for us to discuss openly. But the books served as an opening and gave us impetus to consider many of the social issues and problems in our society. From September through late November, most of the students welcomed these discussions and the reading experiences we shared, although, even by then, I began to get a pulse on some of the resistance I saw later in December. In particular, my students had opposing views about whether racism was something that happened in the past or was something present and ongoing. This continued to be discussed by the students in the months to come, as did my own internal debates about my instructional decisions regarding when and how to confront misconceptions and stereotypes directly. In the next section of this chapter, I detail how the varying ways students experienced texts produced a shift for some students in their overall receptivity toward the social issues books they had once embraced. While many students maintained a strong interest, there was a small group who began to resist serious discussions. This influenced the choices I made about materials and instruction in ways I did not anticipate.

WINDOWS OPEN, WINDOWS CLOSE: DECEMBER THROUGH MARCH

During the winter months, noticeable changes surfaced in my students' receptivity to the social issues books presented to them. These books prompted different responses: some responded with increased curiosity, others maintained their initial high interest, and some began to display resistance. I struggled with the apparent divide among students. I use the metaphor "windows open, windows close" to represent the openness of some children in contrast to the resistance of others. Looking back, I realize that the resistance of a small group of students was actually another kind of opening—one that helped me understand what really mattered in the lives of my students and affirmed that my students existed on a kind of continuum of readiness for wanting to deal with difficult issues about race and racism.

In response to the slight resistance of a few of the students, I used a contemporary realistic story instead of a fantasy or historical fiction as a read-aloud so students might resonate with a plot more familiar to their worlds. Read-aloud was one of the ways the classroom community collaboratively processed and interactively wrestled with the intricacies of a story's plot and its themes. During the discourse of read-aloud time, some students shaped, co-constructed, and reconstructed their beliefs, while others held steadfast to their convictions based on deep connections and shared reflections on the common reading experience. *Ola Shakes It Up*[7] was a novel I anticipated would be familiar and would speak to us directly, since the setting and plot for the book, an African American girl entering an all-White school, greatly resembled our school's community. Although reading *Ola* aloud was not in my original plan, it combined what I perceived to be everything my students looked for in novels—personal relevance, a healthy dose of humor, conflict they could resonate with—and description of the racial issues that surfaced when a small number of African Americans attend school in a White community similar to theirs.

Ola in fact yielded a variety of reactions from students, which the following conversation excerpt reveals. *Ola* prompted reflection not only about White and Black racial issues in contemporary times but also about the September graffiti incident. Clearly, students had differing personal convictions about what had transpired:

> *Phyllis:* Mrs. Harper, when did this story take place?
> *Mrs. Harper:* I believe this could take place today.
> *Cassie:* This would never happen in our school.
> *Mrs. Harper:* What makes you think that? Let's see a few people respond here.
> *Albert:* Well, children today just aren't prejudiced and if they are, they get it from their parents.
> *Mrs. Harper:* What about the graffiti incident at the high school? Do you think that reflects a race problem in our community?

Wit: I don't think it was a race issue; I think he wanted to get kicked
  out.

Lilly: I disagree. I think he was trying to frame a White student. I think
  we have problems like Ola talked about in the book.

Mrs. Harper: Does anyone else think this could happen here in Orchard
  Hills?

Erin: Yeah, people here insult you if they feel you are a lower class than
  they are.

Mrs. Harper: Are you saying that you think African Americans, for example, may be mistreated here because they are a different class?

Erin: Sort of—they're all bussed in from Boston. They're not from here.
  I don't feel that way, though, but some people do.

Mrs. Harper: Does anyone think it would be more or less difficult if a
  White person moved to an all-Black community?

Nora: One time, my family and I visited the Bronx Zoo in New York,
  and we were the only Whites there. We felt so out of place, I wanted
  to leave. I felt richer than everyone, and I didn't like it.

Regis: Yeah, when I went to Mexico, I was called "rich boy," and I
  think the same could happen if I moved to an all-Black community,
  so I think it would be just as hard.

Cassie: I agree with what everyone said about the plot [not that exciting
  or realistic]. But today you don't really care anymore because stuff
  like that never happens.

Lilly: When you were reading it, I was kind of thinking that it was ste-
  reotypical because when somebody comes to our school from [the
  city], it's different. The book acted as though there wasn't anyone
  else in the school that was Black, or anyone cultured enough to accept them, and they were really stuck on themselves. Like, we would
  never go up to anybody who just transferred in from [an area of the
  city] and ask, "Are you a gangster?"

This conversation expanded our understanding of how powerfully race
impacts society. *Ola* was the impetus for students to share their ideas about
race and racism, such as the assumption that racism is generational and historical. There was a degree to which students' open responses represented
a release of feelings perhaps otherwise silenced. Their statements required
courage, and although some students felt the plot of *Ola* did not resonate with
our school culture, their acknowledgments indicated otherwise. I believed,
however, that the students were not ready to accept this story as a reflection
of their local community in some ways. *Ola* prompted several students to
draw personally on their own lived experiences with issues of social justice,

and the conversations that evolved illustrated both our growth in recognizing and confronting difficult societal issues, and the divergence of receptive responses from students toward social issues books.

A closer examination of Cassie's response to the books we were reading sheds new light on the issues several other students also encountered in the middle part of the year. Cassie's less receptive attitude mainly dealt with her perception that many of the books we were reading failed to relate to anything in life she had known or experienced. Cassie was constructing a completely different reaction toward the same issues and events that many students seemed to resonate with completely. Cassie resisted *Olive's Ocean*[8], a read-aloud book in which many other students in the class found intriguing and endless "what ifs" to talk about. In the following excerpt, Cassie describes her reaction—a resistant stance—to the story:

> *Cassie:* I think that *Olive's Ocean* doesn't really have a moral or lesson . . . I think we should read a funny book next. I think we should read:—a fantasy book—a happy book—whodunits—a ghost story, NOT:—historical fiction—depressing books. Good books: *Jade Green* [or] *The Last of the Really Great Wangdoodles*.

Although as a teacher I was troubled by this, I respected Cassie for not always saying what I wanted to hear. In her own words, books like *Olive's Ocean* and *So Far From the Bamboo Grove*[9] were books that were "hard to take." In a certain sense, I wondered what could be so wrong about the stories that had once seemed to interest her so, although by this point in the year, I had a pretty good sense of what Cassie and the other students in the small group who began to resist these books found uncomfortable—complex issues with no apparent, quick-fix solutions. Cassie began reading fantasy books more than all other genres, and four other students in the class seemed to share her sentiments. With resistance strengthening among this group of students, I felt that I needed to make some changes in the curriculum and demonstrate respect for their resistance and discomfort. It was a dilemma for me as a teacher, finding the right balance between wanting to persist and knowing what to do.

With wavering enthusiasm, I believed it was time to differentiate the reading material by offering students choices and facilitating small literature circle groups simultaneously. I cared deeply about my students, and it was difficult teaching them when they felt uncomfortable. I reasoned that small interest groups would restore comfort for those who experienced uneasiness with the social issues books. With some students who were rather quiet in the whole-class setting, I anticipated that literature circles would offer not only a more intimate setting but also an opportunity for them to read books that matched their interest levels more personally. Allowing for student selections gave me greater insight into their preferences, while also empowering them to challenge one another's imaginations in discussions about the very things they themselves felt were critical.

Every literature circle group, formed around the students' shared interests, chose its own novel. Student choices included books with different levels of complexities and crossed over several genres, including realistic fiction, fantasy, historical fiction, and autobiography. Most explicitly dealt with some issues related to social justice. Giving students more control allowed them a greater voice and the time to sort out the complex issues the books raised for them individually and with one another. For each of the literature circle groups, I offered an overall umbrella question to consider. The six students involved with the *The Giver*,[10] for example, were asked to reflect on whether or not they believed a community built around "sameness" and a lack of diversity was overall a worthwhile way to live. As implied in *The Giver*, this futuristic utopian community was founded on the principles of equality as sameness, where everyone presumably had equal advantages and rights within a colorless atmosphere. The students were intrigued and challenged to imagine the lifestyles of a community so very different from anything they had known. As Albert commented:

> *The Giver* is a very intriguing and strange book. I could not imagine such a lifestyle that everyone has to live: automatic apology phrases, sharing of feelings, and dreams, no lying! Their community is so much different than ours, I only began to adapt and understand it more than halfway through. I think Lowry wrote this book because she wants her readers to learn independence . . . to learn that to fight for your independence, it take risks to gain it. This is what Jonas does in *Giver*; he takes the risk of being caught and killed to gain independence and leave the dependent community. I think *Giver* is intriguing because it gets you excited to think about Jonas being able to escape.

Albert's impression paralleled everyone's in his group. Overall, the students in this group prized diversity over belonging to a society where differences were nonexistent. While a few of the students noted some advantages to living in a classless society or one based on "sameness," they believed that learning to live with differences was what made life complete. Several responses illustrated the group's overall sense that diversity was a worthwhile thing. Lilly responded:

I think sameness was bad because it made everything really boring, and without any feelings life would be really dull. I guess they don't know any other way, but the way that they know is in my opinion not the brightest. I guess that they're just trying to create a positive neighborhood for everybody who lives there and make nothing that people can disagree on. "Sameness" in my opinion is a bad thing. It's doing the opposite of respecting human differences. It also doesn't help because people need to learn to respect people of different cultures or ethnicities. It also seems that people don't move to this community because it's so locked in.

I saw an interesting parallel between Lilly's phrase "locked in" and our country's maintenance of White spaces, but the most powerful thing in her comments was her revelation that the ability to respect human differences was an important part of one's being. Without this integral ability to accept difference, she was pessimistic that people were capable of accepting people from different backgrounds. Her insights were mirrored in other students' responses. Candie reacted:

I think that some advantages of "sameness" would be that there would be a lot less bullies, since you'd all have the same clothes, the same stuff, the same money, and everyone would pretty much think the same. If everyone thought the same, there'd be no war and divorce, since there'd be nothing to disagree on. Also, many emotions would be erased. With sameness, there'd be no happiness or joy, no birthdays. Also, no moments where you feel like you're the center of attention, and everybody wants to know what you think. I think that differences are really good. Life is about discovering new things; I really don't think the loss of diversity is worthwhile. All throughout most of the book I felt powerless because the community that Jonas lived in didn't know how great life could be if they didn't have everything the same. I really wanted them to know or find out; if they did, though, the plot would be nothing, just like a repeat of daily life here.

Like Lilly, Candie commented on the importance differences played in our lives. Candie wanted to "step in" to the book and impart the notion that having some unique characteristics, and differences from others, offered people a chance to learn from people unlike themselves. Bart shared a similar sentiment in his reading journal:

I do not think that this community likes diversity at all because they seem to be exactly the same all of the time. I guess they don't know any other way of being, but if they knew about how people can live with differences, I think they would be much happier.

I believed Bart's message about how people could in fact live with differences was a little naive. Clearly people today do in fact live with differences, but not always peacefully and often in ways that are far from just. Bart believed racism was historical—a thing of the past—and I found his comment here to corroborate the line of thinking he had expressed earlier.

In another group, Cassie and some of her classmates chose to read *M.C. Higgins, The Great.*[11] They examined M.C.'s family's prejudice against the "witchy people" at the foot of the mountain. The students responded critically as they reacted to this excerpt from the story: "Those people aren't right," says M.C.'s father of the Killburn men who have six fingers on each hand. "Wash your hands, you let one of them touch you" (p. 195). The students considered M.C.'s struggle to decide whether or not to buy into his father's stereotypes. Nick and Cassie both reacted similarly to the quote above. Nick wrote:

> M.C. thinks that the Killburns are a very bad family because they do not have the same outside physical appearance. But after time goes on, M.C. starts to see that the Killburns are not bad people at all. He learned not to judge a person by their outside.

Cassie chose the same quote and reacted in a similar style.

> Jones thinks that anyone who isn't like him is weird. I think that he is very judgmental and he doesn't like the Killburns even though he doesn't know them that well. Also, the Killburns always treat the Higgins nicely and kindly, but the Higgins always treat the Killburns bad and inferior. After awhile, I think that M.C. thought better of it after he brought Loretta Outlaw to see the Killburn's house and saw how normal they are and how much their families are alike. He realized that Jones might have been wrong about them being "witchy."

The students noticed the nature of the prejudicial behavior against the Killburn family and acknowledged how M.C. grew to accept them despite their differences. Only Nick and Devon truly enjoyed this reading experience, however, as Cassie was disappointed once again. In her last journal entry with this book Cassie wrote:

> I think the author's plot was weak, and incomplete. Too many questions were left unanswered and there wasn't enough action. The author spent too much time focusing on the prejudices of M.C.'s family, and distracted the readers from the interesting part about whether or not M.C.'s family could be saved from the strip mining.

Cassie was turned off to this book, in part because, from her perspective, it overemphasized prejudice. Rosenblatt (1983) observes that: "The same text will have a very different meaning and value to us at different times or under different circumstances. Some state of mind, a worry, a temperamental bias, or a contemporary social crisis may make us either especially receptive or especially impervious to what the work offers" (p. 35). Cassie reacted much differently to *M.C. Higgins* than her two classmates. She showed a growing lack of interest in books that touched on social justice issues as well as books that she found either upsetting or sad. Cassie was also disappointed in herself for creating her own dissatisfaction, since she had chosen to read *M.C. Higgins* from among an array of other books. It just was not what she expected.

In the main, however, the literature circle groups fostered the social interactions necessary for the students to wrestle with difficult ideas, which were the very issues I had hoped they would find. Across all of the groups, students paid much attention to recognizing prejudice in particular. Taken together, these groups revealed a great deal about the responses and issues considered important by the class as a unit. The books provided my students with subtle issues, and their budding critical literacy stances helped them notice issues of various kinds pushing them to challenge things they felt were unjust.

Throughout the winter, I experienced many ups and downs as a teacher as I faced the reality that our once tightly knit classroom community, where everyone had embraced social issues books, was now experiencing a divide. I felt responsible and conflicted. In a certain sense, I wanted to protect my students from being uncomfortable and from facing the difficult truths of our world, yet I also wanted to expose them to the difficulties. I wanted them to become aware of reality and instill a desire to make the world more just. I believed that we had responsibilities as teachers and students to be proactive and that these complex books elicited powerful responses from the students that pushed their thinking to include looking for a means to justice. Students began noticing all kinds of issues across all of the books we read. At times, I felt very successful; at other times, I felt both overwhelmed and fearful. Students' increased reflectivity was evidenced through their open sharing of difficulties in comprehending the world of others, and I in turn also became more direct. Some students, including Cassie, referred to "depressing books" from time to time and talked about their lack of interest in reading them. Over time, I came to understand that for a small group of "resistant" students, depressing books came to be defined as those that dealt with difficult issues related to race, racism, and/or social justice and/or presented ideas and worlds that were foreign to them. In the same way, Cassie and a few others pushed the idea of reading "happy books," which I assumed were books with happy endings or light content. The expressed wishes of this small group informed my practice for the remainder of the year as much as did the responses of the majority of students.

WISDOM TO KNOW THE DIFFERENCE: MARCH THROUGH JUNE

Until this point in the year, although not using social issues books exclusively, I had prioritized them as tools to help students see and understand various social struggles. Out of respect for the five resistant students, however, I offered more choices to everyone. The following journal entry reveals some of the tensions I faced when students were given a choice for the selection of the next read aloud novel:

> *Teacher Journal Entry:* Today, I brought in three books as potential read-alouds; I thought there would be some interest in at least one of them. Or so I thought. I introduced *Loser*, and right away people shared that they had "already read it." I then announced *Cool as Ice* as another contemporary contender that featured a hockey player their age. With so many student athletes, I thought for sure this book had a fighting chance. I was wrong once again. Candie raised her hand and offered that she "had already read that book!" The next book, *Dangerous Skies*, set in the 1700s and featuring a White and Black friendship, met with Cassie's "Can we read a happy book next?" She seemed to be leading the entire pack with powerful persuasion. So, I asked for specific titles *they* wanted to read. The one we went with was *Séance*.[12] The children wanted to read a "scary book."

Although this book *Séance* did not necessarily fit my purpose as a teacher, its selection outwardly showed my students the respect I had for them as

learners. Moreover, I respected their right to resist talking about the social issues the books portrayed. This did not mean that I forfeited my larger project.
Rather, it shed new light on some students' definitions of a "happy book,"
which I apparently had all wrong up to this point. Initially, I believed Cassie's
notion of a "happy book" was one without sadness. By mid-year, I thought
she wanted a reprieve from historical fiction. But by May, I had come to the
conclusion that a "happy book" did not necessarily portray happy or light situations, but was a story that students could relate to in their own lives. These
books were valued for their familiar cultural links and personal frames of
reference. For students like Cassie, *Séance* was a much appreciated diversion,
and she claimed it was her favorite book out of the entire year. Most pleasing
to me as a teacher was the return of Cassie's positive contributions to class
discussions, which were fueled with enthusiasm once more. Interestingly, on
the other hand, *Séance* was the one book Nora felt was a waste of her time.

> *Nora:* I'm not really enjoying *The Séance* because it is confusing and not
> very interesting. . . . If we all want to read a "happy" book, then
> why are we reading a mystery about murders and death? P.S. Maybe
> *Séance* isn't that bad, but I don't LOVE it.

Nora questioned her peers' (and my own) "happy book theory" by pointing out the discrepancy between the term and the book selected, although
she never voiced this aloud in class.

Over the course of the year, I witnessed the growth of many students in
terms of their ability to think critically in all kinds of learning experiences.
With Cassie, however, I witnessed something more. Cassie remained very
clear—even headstrong—in her resistance to books she believed were not happy or were depressing. I came to understand that Cassie's discomfort with "sad"
events in stories was actually related to events that she claimed blasted the real
world in her face. Cassie unveiled a position she had never articulated before:

> *Cassie:* When you read a book that's nonfiction where somebody went
> through a really hard time I personally become really sad and I find
> it not depressing, but a blast from the real world, and I think that we
> all don't like it because we don't want to face the reality that these
> things really do happen.

Cassie's resistance was perhaps exacerbated by her discomfort with the
uncertain world we live in today. She consistently avoided books that referenced a reality she could not accept.

As the school year wound down, with my core curricula well covered, I turned to a different way to prompt my students to consider important issues related to race and racism. The idea of a media unit of study was born out of a conversation with my grade-level colleagues, who had noticed that their students' perceptions of all sorts of things were often shaped by media. Our goal was to look across media to examine ways our opinions were influenced by propaganda and help students connect it to how *they* might be influenced by others. Although literature was not the basis for this unit, it seemed to provide the foundation. Drawing on our experiences with *Gilly* and other novels we had read throughout the year, we returned our attention to stereotypes—but this time, ones we heard within the walls of our own school and community. When I asked the students to compile a list of stereotypes they had encountered in the school or larger community, Nick came to me with a concern:

> *Nick:* Mrs. Harper, is it bad that one of the stereotypes I wrote down is that all Blacks are dangerous?
>
> *Mrs. Harper:* No, of course not. Why would you think it was a bad thing to include?
>
> *Nick:* Well, I didn't want you to think that I believed it was true.
>
> *Mrs. Harper:* Oh, I see. Not at all, Nick. The assignment was to gather some ideas about things you have heard. Stereotypes like this one are upsetting, but they are important to discuss. I'm happy you included it on your list, and I understand that you do not believe it. Otherwise, you would not have mentioned it or recognized it as a stereotype.

Sensing other students had similar feelings, I assembled the class into a circular group meeting, as we often did to share important ideas.

> *Mrs. Harper:* We have another night to work on our list of stereotypes; how is the assignment going?
>
> *Jenna:* Good. I was able to create a long list pretty quickly.
>
> *Mrs. Harper:* Stereotypes are everywhere, as we will soon discover and discuss. . . . What I want to make clear is that the lists you will create will not necessarily reflect your own personal viewpoints . . .
>
> *Ronald:* I felt ashamed about the list I wrote. I don't really believe any of the stereotypes I mentioned, but I can't say that I haven't said some of them myself.
>
> *Mrs. Harper:* That's a very honest response. All of us have probably, at one time or another, said things we didn't necessarily mean, and it's

important to be aware of so that we can refrain the next time. Even better, we can challenge someone's offensive comments. Does anyone want to share an example they included?

Erin: One example I was afraid to write down was that METCO students in our school are not as smart as the kids who live in Orchard Hills.

Mrs. Harper: What made you afraid to include that?

Erin: Well, I wasn't sure if it was a stereotype or if it was true.

I connected this provocative and revealing comment back to the previous discussion about *Gilly*, when we had observed that it was never accurate to paint a group of people with the same brush. I shared with the students that this was a similar situation and that it would be unfair to judge all METCO students in that way.

> *Teacher Journal Entry:* I was anxious and surprised during this conversation when students brought up the METCO issue. While I did not know the origin of this student's reference, I did not want to be associated with validating it was perhaps reality to some degree. This was the kind of territory I felt most uncomfortable with. I navigated through territory that left me feeling uncomfortable and uncertain at times about whether I always said the right things. I felt like I opened up a can of worms without being prepared how to handle them.

It was an uncomfortable teaching moment, although I realized that all of the previous difficult discussions we had had about literature had helped to create this opportunity to be open, honest, and personal. This is where the real learning was. All along, we had worked from the outside in—looking first at characters' lives in literature before reflecting inward at ourselves. This contributed to the more personal way my students connected the curriculum to their own lived experiences. Looking back, I realize that directly teaching my students the concept of White privilege might have been useful in this situation and perhaps would have assisted them in understanding how their own assumptions and the stereotypes they listed fit into the bigger picture.

While some students wanted truth, others wanted protection from it. Some of the books we read dealt head-on with issues that even adults find confounding, such as racism, death, prejudice, and peer pressure. As a teacher, I could not pretend these issues weren't there. Author Katherine Paterson believes her job as a writer is to tell the truth (Elliot, 2007). Her hope is that children will read her (and others') stories long before they need them, since they can be a wonderful rehearsal for what may be needed later in life. A common thread across many of the books we read during the year was heavy content, like the themes of everlasting life, grace, and hope that are threaded through *Tuck Everlasting*[13]. For me, exposing children to themes like these, even if difficult and "not happy," is part of the responsibility I felt (and still do feel) as an educator. My job is to find ways to help children understand and cope honestly and proactively with issues not typically encountered in their everyday lives in White spaces.

FINAL THOUGHTS

I hope it is clear in what I have shared in this chapter that while some of the students in my 6th-grade class wanted books to mirror their worlds, others wanted windows into other worlds. It was fascinating to be part of this, and I was grateful that the students actualized their critical stance with such thoughtful reflection. Over the year, nearly all of the students read with a more critical literacy stance than when they began, and, more importantly, their awareness and acknowledgment of what was going on with some local issues sharpened. Ongoing inquiry into the dynamics of the class and into how individuals and groups of students were responding informed the choices I made, the changes I made in my practice, and my long-term plans in response to those dynamics. Using the particular books I had selected helped me orchestrate the kinds of discussions I felt it was important to have. The choices themselves were beyond general curricular consideration. They dealt more broadly with the context of my classroom, the culture of the community, and the obligation I felt to broaden students' understanding of worlds outside their own.

Throughout the year, my teacher research journal helped me sort things out, and I developed a critical sensitivity toward the kinds of books and reading experiences that met the needs and changed the interests of my students. Freire (1998) once stated, "If we escape conflict, we preserve status quo" (p. 45). While I downplayed the examination of social justice issues at certain points during the year in response to resistant students like Cassie, I remained committed to my goals and gave all students the opportunity to read rich and complex literature that dealt with difficult issues. Through building in choice, I accommodated those students who seemed to experience an attitudinal shift about books and reading as we pursued the social issues books. I was concerned about inadvertently creating an even stronger resistance and an increased disconnect between the resistant students and those they seemed to see as "others." Overall, engaging in teacher research about this prompted insights that allowed for more growth as an educator.

> *Teacher Journal Entry:* I realized it takes hard work to create a strong interest in issues my White students would not necessarily relate to in personal ways. I realized that literature made it possible for us to see the world where the world was not represented among ourselves. I realized that respecting the students' interests and locations with sensitive topics meant negotiating curriculum and differentiating instruction to advance growth and engagement. I realized that even in literature where we could pretend to imagine we were reading about the lives of others also meant that the stories were not always so distant from our own lives, and for some students, that would be difficult. I realized that being a teacher researcher myself often left me feeling vulnerable to the judgment of others reading about my experience and that no amount of years of teaching behind me would change that uncertainty I sometimes felt.

This entry evidences a commitment to teacher research and to the idea that growing from inquiry is as valuable in good times as in challenging ones. Through inquiry, I knew that I needed to offer more freedom and choice when stories pushed some students, like Cassie, beyond their comfort zones and their attitudes shifted negatively. For students like Albert and Nora, on the other hand, their critical stance prompted them to question and link their own life experiences with those of the story itself. Many students also came to see that issues of social justice were right in their own backyards. The purpose in reading social issues books was to help students discover the connections between familiar and unfamiliar worlds through opportunities to question assumptions and interrogate stereotypes. By employing a burgeoning critical literacy stance, many students read more inquisitively over the course of the year, connecting to texts and releasing deep questions that could only produce more inquiry.

Although my role is no longer that of 6th-grade teacher, the experiences I had teaching elementary school for more than a decade filter into my college classroom, where social justice remains an integral focus, every day. By promoting the importance of a critical literacy paradigm with the preservice teachers whom I teach, my hope is that the possibilities literature offers will be realized by the next generation of children when they are challenged to use their imaginations. As Maxine Greene (2001) said, "What you have to give kids is that 'not yet feeling,' of 'being on the way,' a question still not answered." This idea of uncertainty and openness captures the experiences we enjoyed and endured through a yearlong journey of reading against the grain.

NOTES

1. Taylor, M. (1976). *Roll of Thunder, Hear My Cry*. New York: Dial Books. During the Depression of the 1930s, an African American family residing in Mississippi face prejudice and discrimination. The family's children do not understand racism.

2. Spinelli, J. (1996). *Crash*. New York: Random House. This book deals with peer pressure and bullying in the seventh grade. Crash, the popular main character, must choose between doing what is popular and doing what is right.

3. Paterson, K. (1978). *The Great Gilly Hopkins*. New York: HarperCollins. Gilly, the main character, is a clever and largely uncontrollable foster child. This book describes the world of foster children and deals with issues of racism.

4. The METCO (Metropolitan Council for Educational Opportunity, Inc.) Program is a voluntary integration program funded by the Commonwealth of Massachusetts through the Racial Imbalance Act. It is designed to help isolated suburban children experience an integrated learning environment as well as to provide a quality public school education for children from a racially imbalanced urban school district. (http://www.arlington.k12.ma.us/METCO/facts.html)

5. Whelan, G. (2001). *Homeless Bird*. New York: HarperCollins. Koly, a teenager in India, is in an arranged marriage that is ill fated. She must choose whether to obey India's dictated tradition or find the courage to abandon it.

6. Yolen, J. (1998). *The Devil's Arithmetic*. New York: Viking/Penguin. Hannah dislikes and is bored with her Jewish heritage until she travels back in time to a Jewish village in Nazi-occupied Poland. This book explores racism and the Holocaust.

7. Hyppolite, J. (1998). *Ola Shakes It Up*. New York: Delacorte. An African American girl moves from an urban setting to a tightly planned all-White community. The book explores complex issues of community and race.

8. Henkes, K. (2003). *Olive's Ocean*. New York: HarperCollins. This novel involves the reflections of a 12-year-old girl on the death of a classmate, her plans to be a writer, her relationship with her grandmother, and her feelings for a boy during a summer spent with her grandmother.

9. Watkins, K. (1986). *So Far From the Bamboo Grove*. New York: Lothrop, Lee & Shephard. The novel is about an 11-year-old Japanese girl who flees the Korean Peninsula at the end of World War II. The journey is harrowing as the Korean people are hostile to their former Japanese occupiers.

10. Lowry, L. (1993). *The Giver*. New York: Bantam. In a utopian society with no conflict or pain, only the Giver holds knowledge of the true nature of life. Jonah, age 12, is assigned the role to be the next Giver and comes to understand what the society gives up for the sake of complete harmony. This book addresses socially complex issues including the trade-offs between individual choice and social stability.

11. Hamilton, V. (1974). *M.C. Higgins, The Great.* New York: Simon & Schuster. The grandson of an ex-slave, M.C. Higgins worries about the safety of his house, which lies downhill from the refuse of a strip-mined mountain. Two strangers come to town with the potential to change things in very different ways. This story deals with family, superstition, prejudice, and the environment.

12. Nixon, J. (1980). *Séance.* Orlando, FL: Harcourt Brace. Seventeen-year-old girls have a séance that leads to the murder of participants in a small Texas town. This is a suspenseful story in which the main character fears she will be next.

13. Babbitt, N. (1975). *Tuck Everlasting.* New York: Farrar, Straus & Giroux. The Tuck family gets eternal life after drinking from a magic spring. The gift is both a blessing and a burden. The novel explores many moral dilemmas and the meaning of life and death.

REFERENCES

Cochran-Smith, M., & Lytle, S. (2004). Practitioner inquiry, knowledge, and university culture. In J. Loughran, M. L. Hamilton, V. LaBoskey, & T. Russell (Eds.), *International handbook of research self-study of teaching and teacher education practices* (pp. 601–649). Manchester, NH: Kluwer Academic.

Elliot, D. (February 18, 2007). *'Terabithia' inspired by true events.* All Things Considered, national public radio. Retrieved February 23, 2009, from http://www.npr.org/templates/story/story.php?storyId=7387562

Fecho, B. (2001). "Why are you doing this?": Acknowledging and transcending threat in a critical inquiry classroom. *Reading Research Quarterly, 36*(1), 9–37.

Fullan, M. (1993). Why teachers must become change agents. *Educational Leadership, 50*(6), 12–17.

Greene, M. (2001). Flunking retirement: A chat with Maxine Greene. Teachers College, Columbia University. Retrieved February 22, 2005, from http://www.tc.edu/news/article.htm?id=2931

Harper, K. (2005). *Reading against the grain: Teaching for social justice.* Unpublished doctoral dissertation, Boston College.

Lewis, A. (2001). There is no "race" in the schoolyard: Color-blind ideology in an (almost) all-White school. *American Educational Research Journal, 38*(4), 781–811.

McNamara, E. (2003, October 15). Ugly scrawl hits home. *Boston Globe*, p. B1.

Nieto, S. (1999). *The light in their eyes: Creating multicultural learning communities.* New York: Teachers College Press.

Rosenblatt, L. (1983). *Literature as exploration* (4th ed.). New York: Modern Language Association.

Rosenblatt, L. (1991). Literature—S.O.S.! *Language Arts, 68*(6), 444–448.

Sleeter, C., & McLaren, P. (2000). The origins of multiculturalism. *Rethinking Schools, 15*(1), 12.

Wills, J. (1996). Who needs multicultural education? White students, U.S. history, and the construction of a usable past. *Anthropology and Education Quarterly, 27*, 365–389.

Chapter Nine

Teachers Talk About Race, Class, and Achievement

Delvin Dinkins

Delvin Dinkins is the Director of Electronic Learning for his school district. A former high school teacher, he has held positions as elementary school principal, high school assistant principal, dean of the high school academic program, and adjunct professor at the university level. In these roles, he has provided leadership in the areas of curriculum, instruction, assessment, and student services. His current research interests include teacher discourse, practitioner inquiry into problems of practice, and teacher learning in the school setting. His dissertation, Conversation as Intervention: How a Group of Teachers in a Suburban High School Talk About Low Achievement, *explored how teacher discourse with respect to race, class, and achievement surfaced ideologies and discursive practices in a particular high school setting. He has conducted dozens of workshops and given many talks covering a spectrum of subject matter. He also serves on several committees and advisory councils.*

This chapter presents research into race, class, and achievement in a suburban high school and sheds light on my complex role within the research. I begin with a brief discussion of the achievement gap, along with a description of my unusual positioning within the research setting. Following this is a presentation and discussion of inquiry into teachers' discussions of race and student achievement. I conclude with some reflections on the nature of this work.

The achievement gap and Black underachievement are complex challenges in historically high-performing suburban school districts, not just in urban areas or whole schools mired in poverty, academic failure, and severe resource constraints. A growing body of literature has begun to document the fault lines of achievement in suburban settings as well as the critical challenges educators face in making sense of them (see Ferguson, 2002; Gordon, 2002; Noguera, 2001; Viadero, 2002). Many higher-performing schools, some have observed, appear indifferent to the impact of racial differences in student achievement, often because the aggregate performance of their students looks just fine. These districts are often accused of remaining on the periphery of conversations about achievement or of turning a blind eye to performance differences among certain groups of students.

Few school reform initiatives emphasize the importance of practitioner inquiry conducted in professional learning communities, which is the focus of this chapter. Part of a larger study (Dinkins, 2005), this chapter focuses on the work of a group of teachers at top-performing suburban Clearfield High School (pseudonym), which has grappled with disparities in achievement between its primarily White, middle- and upper-middle-class students and its small population of Black, primarily working-class students. The teachers in the group represented a variety of content areas. Called the "Academic Achievement Group," it initially came together after I, in my role as Assistant Principal for Academics, gave a talk at a faculty meeting about what Black students and Black community members had shared with me about the state of Black achievement in the school. Black students felt that race figured prominently into their academic and social experiences at Clearfield. Black parents and community members knew that their students were underachieving and had concluded that academic preparation, racial and socioeconomic isolation, lack of self-motivation, lack of support, and lack of self-advocacy were factors.

For the study, I drew on traditions of qualitative research methods and, perhaps more importantly, my knowledge of the context, to report about as well as to try to understand the conversations that took place within the Academic Achievement Group. Studying how teachers talked about race, class, and achievement and how their language evolved and took shape was of critical importance to the school community and to the wider conversation about the achievement gap. Why the teachers? As key actors in the education process, teachers enjoy the greatest proximity to students. Possessing significant knowledge about and theories of schooling that often reflect personal and institutional ideology, teachers exert tremendous influence on school practices and school culture. I chose to focus on teachers because of my experience as an educator in the setting and because of the Black community's implication of teachers as critical factors in their children's underperformance.

Traditionally, research about teachers is undertaken by professional researchers and members of the academy who must negotiate their entry into a setting and gain the trust of the community in order to conduct their work (Cochran-Smith & Lytle, 1993). Conspicuous by their relative absence from this research are insiders, the practitioners. What happens when a practitioner takes on such work? What happens when a school leader makes his own complex backyard a subject of inquiry? How does he deal with a close, insider perspective and his own privilege vis-à-vis the research setting and subject matter? As a person of color and school leader within the research setting, what choices can/does he make in the research in light of racial politics and his intimate knowledge of and close proximity to the problem? How does he position himself ethnographically, racially, and thus politically? These questions are addressed in detail as part of a larger study (Dinkins, 2005) and cursorily here in this chapter.

Understanding how my role and my race are implicated in the research helps to illuminate the tensions and possibilities of school practitioner research. My role was inevitably complicated by my status as both an insider and an outsider in the research. As a school administrator and the only Black person in the group meetings most of the time, I was sometimes an outsider. At other times I was seen as an inside expert because of my position and race. I possessed some measure of direct authority over teachers in my legitimate role as an assistant principal. I was concerned, then, about inherent power dynamics. This was overcome by an "openness and authenticity [that] illustrated the difference between a community-based approach and a patriarchal, bureaucratic, controlling style of operation" (Stringer, 1999, p. 12). Still, because of my ascribed, institutionalized position of authority, at the outset of this project I opted for a purposely vague "shallow cover" (Fine & Sandstrom, 1988). I shared with people my interests in addressing student achievement at Clearfield. By specifically announcing that I was interested in the issue and that I would observe and participate in the discussions, I made my structural role explicit and maintained my credibility and that of the research (Fine & Sandstrom, 1988). Admittedly, teachers viewed me not as a researcher but as a "friend." My relationship with them had been cultivated in prior experiences as a teacher, coach, and fellow committee member.

As an African American, I was both a subject of (and reason for) inquiry and a source of knowledge. Consequently, I attended the meetings primarily as group member, observer, and neutral facilitator. I was involved as a group member, on the one hand, in order to hear others' perspectives and as an observer of the unfolding action, on the other hand, so as to remain unobtrusive. I participated on a personal level but not revealingly, nor did I function as a bona fide expert. While I did provide occasional interpretations of information for the sake of clarity, I did not wish to position myself as powerful. I did not want people to defer to me rather than construct their own reality through conversation. Therefore, I viewed myself more as a collector of stories and perspectives and less as an actor pushing a particular agenda. I involved myself in the action neutrally, not saying much but, of course, thinking a whole lot. There were times when teachers offered responses that made it difficult for me to remain on the periphery of discussion, but I did so for the sake of trying to understand their perspectives to the greatest possible extent. This had the unfortunate effect of sometimes allowing otherwise incorrect or insensitive comments to fly by without challenge or remark.

THE RESEARCH

The purpose of the larger qualitative study was to generate grounded, expert knowledge from the field in order to bring about change directed at improvement (Wolcott, 1992). A chief concern of this chapter is the important role that teachers and school leaders themselves play as questioners, theorists, and knowledge creators. As suggested earlier, the Academic Achievement Group was a provisional context for exploring the dimensions of academic achievement. The district had its share of ad hoc committees and professional development activities to address issues such as diversity and student achievement. The Academic Achievement Group was one such committee. Formed in response to remarks that I had made at a faculty meeting about the Black students' and parents' implication of teachers in their marginalization at Clearfield, this group met six times over a calendar year. The meetings ranged from 45 minutes to 2½ hours and were open to all faculty members. Because the number of teachers in attendance varied from 14 to 43, I focused my attention on a core group, that is, the 15 teachers who were present for at least five of the six meetings.

This section presents data from the first two meetings of the Academic Achievement Group. I have chosen to focus this essay on the first two meetings primarily for two reasons. The first is that I want to illustrate my role during the first two sessions as something of a biographer (Stake, 1995). I sought to map the beginning of the life of the group as well as distill vignettes that presented the teachers complexly. My charge was to stimulate people (Stringer, 1999) to discuss the circumstances of the community. Second, the first two meetings followed a series of critical events that highlighted racial and economic tension at Clearfield. There had been altercations and near-altercations between Black and White students. These incidents came on the heels of a student newspaper opinion piece/editorial arguing, in response to a proposed state bill about school funding, that it was futile to shift dollars away from wealthy districts to inner cities because the amorality of inner-city people would have deleterious effects on government money. Many in the school community, Black and White alike, found the article to be divisive. I have chosen to focus on these first two meetings because these events may have been on teachers' minds.

I use primarily transcripts of the conversations and quote teachers liber-
ally. However, stutters, false starts, and fillers have been edited out for clarity.
I also draw on teachers' written reflections, which were completed occasionally for meeting closure and particularly if someone felt more comfortable
expressing an idea in writing rather than orally. In the discussion, I identify a
range of discourses, which illuminate conceptions of underachievement and
reflect provocative elements of teachers' underlying thoughts, ideologies, and
epistemologies. I chunk the data thematically and then theorize discursive
complexities of race, class, and achievement.

TEACHER GROUP MEETINGS 1 AND 2

From the outset, teachers raised their general concerns about underachievement. One concern was the visible presence of Black students in the two
lower-level courses, Basic and College Prep, and their relative absence in
Honors and Advanced Placement (AP) courses. Many teachers recognized
that several factors, however, contributed to Blacks' presence in lower-level
courses and relative absence from higher-level courses. Among the factors
were teachers' labeling of and assumptions about students, and students' lack
of connection to school, lack of support from home, lack of preparation for
the rigor of higher-level courses, questionable commitment to school, negative peer-group influences, and antisocial behavior. These factors, which
are reflected in the achievement gap literature, were laced throughout the
discussions about Black student underachievement. The first two factors—
teachers' labeling of and assumptions about students and students' lack of
connection to school—seem to be transgressive in nature, or questioning
of school practices, while the remaining factors appear to be complicit with
existing power hierarchies (Fendler, 2003). I organize the data around two
themes: perceptions of students' oppositional behavior and the interruption
and maintenance of Black students' course of study.

STUDENTS' OPPOSITIONAL BEHAVIOR

Jan (a social sciences teacher in his late 20s and in his 5th year at Clearfield)
wanted to know what teachers felt were "the conditions attached to failure." Some teachers in the group felt that teachers held negative stereotypes
of students that affected students' experiences at Clearfield. Dana (a social
sciences teacher in her early 30s and in her 7th year at Clearfield) said, "I

hate that some students who are seen as behavioral problems are recommended for Basic classes. There is nothing wrong with these classes, but there are some students who could be taking College Prep or Honors." Nora (a natural sciences teacher in her late 40s and in her 20th year at Clearfield) elaborated, "It is unfair not to give students a try at another level if they are willing to put in the work." Others echoed similar sentiments. Lois (a humanities teacher in her early 50s and in her 4th year at Clearfield), for instance, wondered how many staff members had thought about their views of students. "I think we need to talk about how some of us teachers think about students," she said.

There were many other teachers, however, who believed that negative stereotypes attributed to Black students were justified because of their coarse behavior. Katrin (a humanities teacher in her late 40s and in her 8th year at Clearfield) remarked that she had noticed a decline in student respect, which she regarded as non-negotiable. "Some of these students are constantly wandering the halls, cutting classes, putting their heads down while in class, hanging out in the cafeteria," she lamented. Other teachers felt similarly:

> *Jan:* I don't know if it's the oppositional culture that students are a part of or what. They defy authority, are almost always negative and confrontational, and sometimes disrespectful. I don't know if it's the peer group or the glorified images they see on MTV.
>
> *Jim* (a social sciences teacher in his mid–20s and in his 3rd year at Clearfield): I feel like there is going to be some kind of confrontation whenever I ask them to take off their hats or do–rags. One time one of them told me that I was picking on him because of his race, and I told him that wasn't true. I said he was breaking the rules and needed to be respectful of the school like everybody else. He told me I was singling him out. This is why I won't ask him or probably most of his friends not to take off their hats any longer. I don't—no one wants—to have the race card played or be called a racist.

Along these same lines, Kent (a humanities teacher in his mid–30s and in his 7th year at Clearfield) told of a similar experience in which a student mentioned that wearing a hat or do–rag was part of his culture. Kent felt that the dress code should be revisited to ensure that sweatbands are "outlawed items." A number of teachers wanted to know whether the school should "allow culture of this sort."

There were several other occasions on which people expressed direct concern about the behavior of Black students. The following field note that I took during the research offers additional insight into the perception of Black students' behavior:

> A staff member just made the administration aware that there was a large group of African American students horse playing with each other and making *a lot of noise* and that this has happened *again and again*. The staff member said she had deep concerns that a lot of the African American students are not being disciplined.

During the first group meeting, Zeta (a humanities teacher in her late 20s and in her 4th year at Clearfield) suggested that there was an achievement gap between Blacks and most of the rest of the school not only academically but also socially:

> I don't know if it's the single-mother-raising-the-family issue or other issues, but many of them have a hard time accepting that they have done something wrong. There is always the race thing playing a part. I think we need to review punishment for cutting class. Repeated class cuts indicate a major issue, academic and/or social, with the student. A 10 percent and then 50 percent grade reduction doesn't benefit the student at this point in his academic career. Perhaps connect the punishment to some sort of mandatory study hall, counseling, mediation, or community service.

Others believed that many Black students were just angry and distrustful no matter what anyone tried to do to gain their trust. According to several teachers, the distrust was particularly true for Black males.

To combat this sense of mistrust, teachers focused on social relations, seemingly rooted in the notion that academically unsuccessful students feel detached from the school and need to feel attachment if they are to become successful (Lipman, 1998). Many teachers discussed the importance of relationships with students. Katrin argued that greater effort needed to be expended to connect teachers and students, both interpersonally and academically. She felt this could occur by diversifying the instructional levels to which teachers are assigned from year to year "so that teachers could have a mix of preps, from Basic all the way up to AP." Other teachers focused more directly on social relations:

> *Lela* (a humanities teacher in her 50s and in her 8th year at Clearfield): Some type of mentoring program providing personal connection with the individual—students and hopefully, active—and some type of liaison to parents.

Dean (a social sciences teacher in his late 50s and in his 33rd year at Clearfield): And we need to mentor at-risk students before problems begin.

Donna (a special areas faculty member in her late 50s and 2nd year at
Clearfield) suggested that the mentor be an advocate for students and be
someone not connected to the school. Jim concurred: "I like the idea of adding a support piece to flunking a course or even afterschool detention as a
way for teachers to connect to kids who are not as school-savvy as others."
Marge (a special areas teacher in her early 40s and in his 20th year at Clearfield) suggested that teachers use one of the planning periods for mentoring:

> I realize there might be a scheduling nightmare here, but if
> we're serious about this, wouldn't it be worth it to have group
> meetings once a month during period 8? No one leaves that day—
> meetings are mandatory. I would think a mentor group would be
> 20 kids and a mentor—all adults in the building used as mentors.
> From there students can schedule one-on-one appointments with a
> mentor as needed.

Ty (a social sciences teacher in his early 40s and in his 10th year at Clearfield) suggested that a tutoring program be extended to the community. In
doing so, he recalled a time when he was more connected to one of the Black
neighborhoods: "Years ago I used to go into the neighborhood, thinking
that I might do tutoring. I would wind up playing basketball instead [laugh].
But students knew I cared when they saw my car randomly pull up near the
playground." Marti (a social sciences teacher in her early 30s and in her 4th
year at Clearfield), however, expressed concern that mentoring would further burden teachers:

> While I like the idea of increasing the number of mentoring
> connecting between students and teachers, how many teachers can
> give extra time to do that? I, myself, would love to be able to de-
> velop some one-on-one relationships with students but can't find
> any time on top of what is already a 12- to 13-hour workday. How
> about making it an option for teachers during their duty period?
> The teachers would have to go through a few weeks of training
> first, and then spend time developing a few or several one-on-one
> relationships during that period.

Jan agreed and said that being a mentor should come with a stipend.

INTERRUPTING AND MAINTAINING
BLACK STUDENTS' COURSE OF STUDY

While many teachers believed that mentoring students might create a sense of belonging for some students, others advocated a more direct look at Black students' course-taking behavior.

> *Dana:* I am truly concerned that there aren't enough African Americans in my Honors classes. I have all White students and Asian Americans. I find it hard to believe that we're so disproportionate here.
>
> *Jan:* There definitely is a problem with this.
>
> *Ty:* We should be pushing students to challenge themselves.
>
> *Dana:* And for me this means some should be taking Honors and AP.
>
> *Jan:* Don't we have African Americans in Honors and AP?
>
> *Marge:* Some but not a lot.
>
> *Jan:* To be honest, I don't know if it's such a good idea to push so hard for more in Honors and AP.
>
> *Dana:* Why not?

Some teachers expressed concern about the increasing number of students trying to take Honors and AP. They believed that struggling students should not be permitted to take these courses. The demands of the higher-level courses would be far too great for struggling students. Besides, like Jim, some believed that "teachers would have to dumb-down the curriculum and lower expectations for them, which wouldn't do anyone any good." Some teachers argued that certain students should be kept at Basic or College Prep, where they could be successful and feel good about themselves until they developed the skills to do Honors and AP work.

Jan believed that Clearfield advertised its higher-level courses to a fault. He explained:

> The [school] profile that colleges receive hurts us and it hurts the kids, White and Black. Kids see Honors and AP courses and want to take them. We need to remove the rewards and acclaim accorded to AP. Lower-level courses need to be made more legitimate so that students can feel good about being in these courses and not feel that they had to take Honors, College Prep, and certainly not AP to have worth as a student.

Jan's remark about the profile, a concrete and visible document that acts as a thumbnail sketch of the school's academic program, sparked commentary about the meanings of upper-level courses in the school:

Dean: We teach students to believe that Honors and AP are the only things to live for. We teach them how to buy into that thinking. And the Black students I have mostly don't.

Denise (a social sciences teacher in her 40s and in her 5th year at Clearfield): There is such a tradition of academic excellence, and students think of this tradition only as Honors and AP. We need to talk about leveling in a very concrete and proactive way.

Jim: I believe that the conversation about different expectations at different levels is important.

Notwithstanding Clearfield's strong and explicit emphasis on academic achievement, Dana argued that the only kids who were celebrated were the academic stars. She, along with other teachers, agreed that Clearfield needed to de-emphasize AP and establish other examples of success so that different kinds of kids could be recognized.

Dana: We need to offer a broad array of ways to become successful. We have music, arts, academics. Many of the ones who get awards in these areas are the same ones. You know, many of our music kids are our top academic stars. Maybe we should be doing more to give recognition in other areas.

Jim: We put Basic-level students in College Prep and College Prep students in Honors and they fall short, especially the students in Basic level who really need to be there. We use the next level as the measuring stick.

Ray (a science teacher in his early 40s and in his 9th year at Clearfield): We need to make kids and parents see that achievement doesn't just mean Honors and AP.

A way to solve the problem of some students viewing achievement as purely Honors and AP, according to Zeta and many others, was to return to having an in-house vocational-technical program.

Zeta: The point of being in high school is to become prepared for the real world. A student involved in a vo-tech program will become more prepared for real-world interactions than if he or she remains in school as an academic failure. In addition to a vo-tech program, we can add options such as work-study programs for which students can get English, math, social studies, and science credits.

Ray: I agree. We should institute a tech program that will be viewed as an avenue to a viable career.

There was some agreement that the current arrangements for the vocational-technical program, which required students to be bused to a central location that drew students from several high schools, discouraged students who either did not want to leave Clearfield or did not want to be inconvenienced through special arrangements. Donna insisted that "it's a hassle for kids to go off-site and there is a stigma attached to doing so. Also, students are unwilling to go because of the additional step. We need to make it an easier option for those kids." Zeta said, in a half-joking voice, "We need to make sure the problem kids go to the tech program." Dean remembered when there had been a vocational-technical program at Clearfield:

> We had one right upstairs. There was a sizable shop, and the kids would do auto-body and everything. Then there was a feeling that we were not the type of school that should have that kind of program, so kids who were interested in the program had to take shop elsewhere.

Many agreed that a strong vocational-technical program would become a niche for many for students who were lost within the school's academic landscape. Marge also recalled that when she was in high school, there were work-study, technical, and business programs "for students who didn't fit in and needed something else," and "for your mainstream student," there were college preparatory classes. "I realize these ideas were replaced," she admitted. "But doesn't educational philosophy really always come back to old ideas—just new names?"

Teachers also felt that some students might be better served by exposure to options related to the military. (Military recruitment was not a popular option at Clearfield; every year, less than 1 percent of its graduating seniors enlisted.) Teachers felt there was not enough attention given to creating relationships between the military and Clearfield. Zeta lodged a critique of faint efforts:

> There is nothing in the Guidance Office about the military. How often do military personnel come here to talk with kids about the service? Do our counselors do their part to tell the military that we have kids they want? And are the kids encouraged or discouraged from being interested in the military?

Many teachers suggested that efforts to incorporate the military into the fabric of the school be improved.

Donna: Not enough students know about it, and think that college is the only option. There should be some community reeducation. The military is another option we should be telling students about.

Ray: The expectation is that most Clearfield students go to college. Parents need to be aware that a portion of these students do not succeed and may have been better directed in another direction— trades, armed forces, etc.

Ty: If students truly knew about the military as an option early enough, they could be taking the proper courses and not be so disrespectful, because they know the military doesn't tolerate that.

While there were many teachers who suggested that Clearfield had shifted its attention away from options such as vocational-technical training and the military, there were others, like Lela and Dana, who felt that the focus should be on the current educational program:

Lela: Shouldn't we be thinking about how best to teach students who end up in our classes, rather than thinking of programs outside the school? For instance, we probably should be doing a better job of teaching students in College Prep and not go about assuming that students should be in Basic.

Dana: The same is true for Honors and probably AP. The same thing is true for the tech school and the military. One thing I've noticed since I've been here these last few years is that we are quick to say kids should drop a class or don't belong because they are not doing well.

In a written reflection about the meeting, Lela wrote:

Parents should be more involved in course selection because this fosters a conversation among the parent, student, and guidance counselor so that the student is at a level that will help them achieve success, not just academic success. I think that too often students are put into classes without a great deal of thought. Often these classes don't meet them where they are or don't offer them outlets for their particular talents. We should revisit the curriculum to design ways students with various learning styles and abilities can be successful.

Dana also had strong feelings about working within the school context. She located the problem in the relationships among teacher expectations, school context, class, and achievement. In her reflection she wrote:

We need higher expectations, especially in the Basic and College Prep levels. Where I came from, there were students who were all over the spectrum. Some did well, some didn't. It was just a part of life that kids in a class might fail, and kids didn't really drop down. They either passed or didn't. One thing I see is that many of the Black students here are like many of the working-class and blue-collar people I went to high school with. They either pass or they don't. They did not always have what everybody else had, and they did not have all the supports. Things did not come easy for them. And I think it's tougher here because just about my whole high school was blue collar and so if you were blue collar, you were like everyone else. There weren't a lot of wealthy people. Here, you're in the minority if you are blue collar and this on top of being Black.

Marge also believed that many Black students did not have the same resources as other students and that teachers assumed they did, or simply did not care if they did not. She observed:

We work in an environment in which we assume students have all the materials they need in order to learn: computers, transportation, and other things. We think they have just as much as some other kids around here. As someone who grew up and did not have a lot, I can see it. I can see that there are many of us who expect kids to have everything in place and don't think twice about it. I was discouraged from becoming an English or music teacher and was geared towards health and physical education instead. I feel for these kids. I know what it is like to look around and have everyone have stuff you don't and for teachers to expect you to be able to get materials and resources at the drop of a hat and are not able to. It's hard, and I didn't even go to a wealthy school like this one.

Ty concurred. He believed that he too, with his working-class background, unlike many of the other teachers in the building, had "felt a subtle kinship with students who have less than the typical Clearfield student."

DISCUSSION

During the first two gatherings, teachers shared their knowledge and ideas about underachievement. They also tossed about solutions, deciding how their knowledge ought to be used. From the outset, it was clear that teachers' "ways of thinking and categories of understanding [had] been molded and disciplined by social practices and relations" (Fendler, 2003, p. 21).

Teachers shared a belief that ongoing time and support were needed to establish meaningful relationships with Black students or any students who felt marginalized within school. There was a feeling that demonstrating caring for students would be an effective way to increase motivation, connect students to school, and harness any unrecognized interests and abilities. Teachers felt that students' self-esteem and resiliency might be improved over time with support and attention from a mentor. In trying to demonstrate caring during these instances, a couple of teachers tried to relate to the experiences of Clearfield's Black students. They did this by drawing on stories of the past or of their own upbringing. These occasions reflected, as Grant (1991) argues, "the importance of acculturation and biography for influencing teacher behavior" (p. 249). Taking a subtle social justice stance, these teachers seemed to question school practices.

While virtually all teachers could articulate the important educational goals of intellectual, social, and cultural excellence and economic, political, and social empowerment of marginalized groups (Banks et al., 2001), their espoused beliefs and practices did not address the need to nurture or promote the agency of Black students. Most teachers framed the achievement question in terms of teachers' interests; their support was contingent upon the degree to which the problem and solution converged with their interests. Tensions among interpretations of the meanings of concepts like equality, equity, and excellence were evident, as some teachers seemed to resent students not buying into the ethos of Clearfield. Teachers simply were not pleased with students' obstinate behavior and refusal to act in accordance with school rules. They seemed to feel that if students were better behaved, their performance would improve.

Because they perceived Black students' behavior as divergent from the prevailing institutional ethos, teachers helped to maintain their marginality and differential access to positive status. For instance, not reprimanding Blacks for wearing hats inside the school for fear of the "race card" reflected teachers' discomfort with boundary encounters that could escalate to conflict if not handled properly. Rather than wrestle with their seeming discomfort with race and racialized situations, it seemed easier for teachers to accept the notion that wearing hats in school was part of Black culture. Cultural differences discourse sometimes allows people to accept things as they are, in the name of respect for "culture." An antidote to underachievement is to allow (or not) culture of this sort of to exist. "How cultural differences are defined by those with power is a means of maintaining that power. . . . [T]he imposition of the dominant group's language, behavioral norms, and values is a way of maintaining dominance" (Lipman, 1998, p. 27). In a sense, the real conflict was born out of teachers' assumption that students brought weaknesses that must be remediated, rather than strengths on which teachers could build and preferences for learning on which teachers could draw.

Teachers' unyielding ideas of race, class, and intelligence permeated the ways in which they discussed achievement as almost an immutable fact of life for some and an acute impossibility for others. Teachers viewed achievement as a largely stable, unitary, and linear attribute. Low achievement was regarded as an unfortunate reality for some students, many of whom were accorded negative attributes because they rejected the ethos of the school. Students' positionalities were "linked to discursive arrangements that advantage certain groups of people" (Estrada & McLaren, 1993, p. 29). In this way, students' positions and participation in the school were tightly controlled through patterns of interaction with others and by sociocultural identity. The discursive arrangements mediated the school experience for students, privileging some and restricting others.

These arrangements were evident as teachers articulated race and culture against several constructs: White, achievement, normal, and middle-class. They imposed a dominant ideological framework that Black underachievement was the obverse of White and Asian achievement, on the one hand, and was normal on its own terms, on the other hand. Because the high performers were generally White or Asian, teachers unconsciously constructed achievement as White and Asian. Since high performance was the norm and part of the institutional ethos at Clearfield, White was the norm, with Asians pejoratively viewed as honorary Whites. Underachievement, opposition, and defiance belonged to Blacks. Blacks constituted an explanation for matters wrong with the school: rule breaking, hat wearing, resistant behavior, disrespect, inconsistent discipline. Blacks were posited as counter to achievement. Black and achievement were often complementary contrasts, with Black students often positioned as deviant and thus in need of correction or remediation. The introduction of Basic, the lowest instructional level, into the discussion meant the introduction of Blacks and low achievers.

The near-absence of explicit references to White students during the meetings gave White students' school experiences greater authority as the mythical norm and further invalidated Black students' experiences as "other." "Whiteness," Keating (1995) observes, "has functioned as a pseudo-universal category that hides its specific values, epistemology, and other attributes under the guise of a nonracialized, supposedly colorless, 'human nature'" (p. 904). Given the predominantly White, middle- and upper-middle-class school context, it is hardly necessary to point out that "Whiteness is regarded as a positively valued, unspoken norm" (Brookfield, 2003 p. 499), while Blackness is intellectually, culturally, and politically alien. The tightly controlled focus on and positioning of Black students as "other" enabled teachers to avoid critical examination of race in which Whiteness, instead of being normative, was subjected to scrutiny.

In sum, the study examined discursive practices and how these practices positioned students and how students positioned themselves. The research reported in this chapter, which is based on the first two meetings of the Academic Achievement Group, indicated that teachers reflected and contributed to familiar institutional and historical patterns: long-held traditions of Black underachievement and low group status. The ways in which the teachers organized their insights about the problem of low achievement reflected personal experiences and organizational norms. As a result, the teacher group qualified and challenged, but mainly affirmed, individual and organizational ideologies and racialized practices that contributed to the positioning of Black students. Teachers resisted ownership of student failure. They generally located the problem of Black underachievement within students and, in the process, seemed to absolve themselves of responsibility.

At the remaining four meetings of the Academic Achievement Group, teachers continued to struggle to put forth a social justice agenda amid market influences within the school and succumbed to normalized, commonsense ways that people often think about race, class, and achievement. Their construction of low achievement was based primarily on race and class. With increasing expectations to accept Blacks' school experiences as valid as well as to accept responsibility for their academic success, the group's discourses became more self-affirming and protective and more resistant and blaming. In the end, by strongly implicating students (and their parents) in the construction of their own low achievement, the teachers acted in ways that preserved their sense of professional efficacy. Their knowledge and ways of knowing were constrained by social and institutional arrangements and the meanings that belie these arrangements. I did little to expose or interrupt the arrangements or the tacit understandings that support them.

NEGOTIATING ADVOCACY

By virtue of conducting this research, I saw myself as an advocate for and a sponsor of change. According to Sergiovanni (2001), an advocate is knowledgeable about the ways in which schools do business and uses social position to assist with the flow of information and to create opportunities for resources to accrue in support of a particular set of values or group of people. He works to ensure that the flows of information and resources are not compromised by the organizational context. The advocate, ultimately, facilitates change.

I likened my role in the research to what Meyerson and Scully (1995) refer to as a "tempered radical." Tempered radicals are individuals who "challenge the status quo, both through their intentional acts and also just by being who they are, people who do not fit perfectly" (p. 586). The decision to listen to Black stakeholders, the decision to share their thoughts and feelings with the faculty, the sponsorship of the Academic Achievement Group, and the methodological choices were examples of tempered radicalism. I tried to move people "closer to the problem they were trying to solve by getting them more intimately involved in understanding why students succeed or fail" (Newberg, 1991, p. 67). In this spirit, Meyerson and Scully (1995) suggest that tempered radicals are

> angered by the incongruities between their own values and beliefs about social justice and the values and beliefs they see enacted in their organizations. Temper can mean both "an outburst of rage" and "equanimity, composure," seemingly incongruous traits required by tempered radicals. (p. 586)

In order to navigate the incongruities they encounter and to effect significant changes in moderate ways, tempered radicals draw upon many approaches (Meyerson, 2001). Through their commitment to and productivity within the organization, tempered radicals are "vital sources of resistance, alternative ideas, and transformation" (Meyerson & Scully, 1995, p. 586). This chapter is an example of tempered radicalism with its "frank and unfettered reporting" (Becker, 1976, p. 86).

I was interested in engaging subjectivity and meaning. I tried to understand "people's subjective experience of their institutional situation and at the same time try to give some working accounts of the contexts in which meanings were constituted" (McTaggart, 1997, p. 36). I assumed shallow cover in which I asserted little voice in what occurred. I was intentionally neutral in disposition. As a member of the school community who had observed the factors that figured prominently in the racial politics of Clearfield, these methodological choices were difficult for me. Tension arose in the process as I allowed the needs of the research (to gather specific kinds of data) to supersede my need (to confront). By not affirming teachers' sometimes positive stance, on the one hand, and by not taking them to task for their sometimes insidious remarks and practices, on the other, I sometimes felt that I was inevitably in cahoots with them.

The teacher group was perhaps a disruption to teacher isolation and an invitation to reflect. The teachers decided to assume a stance of questioning and to engender a forum for questions to be generated and made problematic. Perhaps the teacher group supported Hargreaves's (2003) recognition that "teachers are not deliverers but developers of learning" (p. 202) who need to engage in social and moral questions.

To make sense of my experience and what I learned, I informally shared findings and reflections with different audiences during and after the research process. The audiences included administrative personnel at Clearfield, practitioner researchers, colleagues, and professionals in academia. Whether in the form of individual or group conversations with colleagues and administrative personnel or presentations at professional conferences, these audiences heard my recollection and sensemaking as well as examined my work and provided feedback to me. The sensemaking was in support of the reason for practitioner research, as Anderson, Herr, and Nihlen (1994) describe:

> Perhaps because practitioners do not necessarily find encouragement in their own school sites to see themselves as researchers, and perhaps because of the isolation many educators face in their day-to-day practice, the formation of wide-reaching groups outside of the school site for the support and feedback of reflective practitioners as researchers is highly appealing to many of us. (p. 70)

Practitioner research is a way of knowing, an attempt to peel back layers of knowledge and understandings in order to stimulate growth and generate new knowledge for use. The teacher group held potential for both enabling meaningful reflection and effecting change, for the teachers and for me. While some teachers took a social justice stance at various points during the life of the group, their construction of achievement on the whole did not take into serious consideration the complexity of class, culture, and race as social positions. In the final analysis, to preserve their own sense of professional efficacy, teachers generally believed that the burden of change was ultimately Blacks', since their host of ruinous values had caused them not to fare as well. Others, however, believed the remedy must be a joint effort. The different viewpoints satisfied particular beliefs and interests of individuals and groups by deflecting problems in such a way that no one was implicated.

So, in keeping with Stokes's (2001) findings, while shared interest created conditions in which the group could talk freely, and while common knowledge created a more focused context for inquiry, the teacher group as a lever for inquiry ultimately did not create the necessary conditions for teachers to explore latent ideologies. There was little interrogation of school and teacher norms, beliefs, and practices that perhaps contributed to Black student failure. There was little agency or commitment to change prevailing norms, only an interest in talking about why marginalized students fail. And that is why there remains that part of me that wonders what would have happened had I assumed a role of critical friend with a strong presence to ask questions, make observations, and push teachers' thinking. Assuming this role may have reconfigured the teacher group's stance as an empowered, knowledgeable community. Assuming the role as critical friend may have blown my shallow cover. Conversely, not doing so made me feel that I had violated, abandoned, or otherwise compromised some cardinal principle. This research was about the teachers and their knowledge and meanings, not mine. What right, then, had I as a researcher to disrupt their understandings or create new ones for them?

While I left my administrative position in the school to become principal of an elementary school within the same district shortly after the completion of this study, it is important to acknowledge that the group's inquiry was not without impact. In some respects, the meetings were a turning point in the life of the school. The teachers and administrative staff committed themselves to 3 years of self-study under the rubric of cultural competence. In the interest of understanding culture as it relates to teaching and learning, they developed an action plan that addressed issues of self-awareness, diversity, communication, and race. Even though I was not present to participate in the dialogue, I was satisfied to learn that the staff made this commitment and continued to work over time on understanding how race, culture, and class informed virtually every aspect of their teaching and learning—including interactions with students, traditions related to tracking and placement, assumptions about students' interests and abilities, and the intersections of their own autobiographies with those of the students.

REFERENCES

Anderson, G. L., Herr, K., & Nihlen, F. S. (1994). *Studying your own school: An educator's guide to qualitative practitioner research*. Thousand Oaks, CA: Corwin.

Banks, J. A., Cookson, P., Gay, G., Hawley, W. D., Irvine, J. J., Nieto, S., Schofield, J. W., & Stephan, W. G. (2001). Diversity within unity: Essential principles for teaching and learning in a multicultural society. *Phi Delta Kappa, 83*(3),196–203.

Becker, H. S. (1976). *Sociological work: Methods and substance*. New Brunswick, NJ: Transaction Books.

Brookfield, S. D. (2003). Racializing the discourse of adult education. *Harvard Educational Review, 73*(4), 497–523.

Cochran-Smith, M., & Lytle, S. L. (1993). *Inside/outside: Teacher research and knowledge.* New York: Teachers College Press.

Dinkins, D. (2005). *Conversation as intervention: How a group of teachers in a suburban school talk about low achievement.* Unpublished doctoral dissertation, University of Pennsylvania, Philadelphia.

Estrada, K., & McLaren, P. (1993). A dialogue on multiculturalism and democratic culture. *Educational Researcher, 22*(3), 27–33.

Fendler, L. (2003). Teacher reflection in a hall of mirrors: Historical influences and political reverberations. *Educational Researcher, 32*(3), 16–25.

Ferguson, R. F. (2002). What doesn't meet the eye: (Mis)understanding racial disparities in 15 suburban school districts. Tripod Project. Retrieved December 20, 2003, from http://www.ncrel.org/gap/takeon/intro.htm

Fine, A. F., & Sandstrom, K. L. (1988). *Knowing children: Participant observation with minors.* Thousand Oaks, CA: Sage.

Gordon, D. T. (2002). A return to segregated schools? *Harvard Education Letter, 7,* 28.

Grant, C. A. (1991). Culture and teaching: What do teachers need to know? In M. M. Kennedy (Ed.), *Teaching academic subjects to diverse learners* (pp. 237–256). New York: Teachers College Press.

Hargreaves, A. (2003). *Teaching in the knowledge society.* New York: Teachers College Press.

Keating, A. (1995). Interrogating "Whiteness," deconstructing "race." *College English, 57*(8), 901–918.

Lipman, P. (1998). *Race, class, and power in school restructuring.* Albany: State University of New York Press.

McTaggart, R. (1997). *Participatory action research: International contexts and consequences.* Albany: State University of New York Press.

Meyerson, D. E. (2001, October). Radical change, the quiet way. *Harvard Business Review,* pp. 92–100.

Meyerson, D. E., & Scully, M. A. (1995). Tempered radicalism and the politics of ambivalence and change. *Organization Science, 6*(5), 585–600.

Newberg, N. A. (1991). Bridging the gap: An organizational inquiry into an urban school system. In D. Schön (Ed.), *The reflective turn* (pp. 65–83). New York: Teachers College Press.

Noguera, P. (2001). Racial politics and the elusive quest for excellence and equity in education. *Education and Urban Society, 34*(1), 18–41.

Sergiovanni, T. J. (2001). *The principalship: A reflective practice perspective* (4th ed.). Boston: Allyn & Bacon.

Stake, R. E. (1995). *The art of case study research.* Thousand Oaks, CA: Sage.

Stokes, L. (2001). Lessons from an inquiring school: Forms of inquiry and conditions for teacher learning. In A. Lieberman & L. Miller (Eds.), *Teachers caught in the action: Professional development that matters* (pp. 141–158). New York: Teachers College Press.

Stringer, E. T. (1999). *Action research.* Thousand Oaks, CA: Sage.

Viadero, D. (2002). White students get enrichment; Black students more academic time. *Education Week, 22*(2), 6.

Wolcott, H. F. (1992). Posturing in qualitative inquiry. In M. D. LeCompte, W. L. Millroy, & J. Preissle (Eds.), The handbook of qualitative research in education (pp. 3–52). New York: Academic Press.

Chapter 10

Constructing a Language of Learning to Teach

Rob Simon

Rob Simon is currently a PhD candidate in Reading/Writing/Literacy in the Graduate School of Education at the University of Pennsylvania. Before coming to Penn, he worked with the Delancey Street Foundation, a residential, self-help rehabilitation center for former felons and addicts in San Francisco. Along with Delancey residents, he was a member of the Mayor's Juvenile Justice Implementation Team. As a part of this project, he helped to develop and run an Early Risk and Resiliency mentoring program, an afterschool program for middle school–aged youth (the Mission Safe Haven), and a high school (Life Learning Academy), where he taught for 5 years. His publications include a chapter about this work in Brian Street's (2005) Literacies Across Educational Contexts. Simon has taught the course he writes about for this volume for 6 years. His current research interests include completing a dissertation on the literacies of learning to teach.

Shaped by marketplace metaphors and models, and fueled by pressures to meet accountability requirements under the federal No Child Left Behind Act (NCLB), the school district of Philadelphia has advanced an aggressive reform agenda in recent years, including producing and disseminating mandated curricula closely calibrated to benchmark exams. As in other urban districts, Philadelphia's reform project has taken place in a district marked by poverty, underfunding, and racial segregation (Useem, 2005), amidst the turbulence of competing rhetorics about the need to attract, educate, and maintain "highly qualified teachers" and the concomitant debasing, de-skilling, and surveillance of urban teaching and teachers (Simon & Lytle, 2006). Within this context, I teach a middle and secondary English methods course at the University of Pennsylvania, in which I encourage student teachers to critically interrogate the social and political contexts in which they work, to consider the cultural and linguistic resources their students bring to class, and to view their classrooms—and our shared classroom—as sites of collaborative inquiry (Cochran-Smith & Lytle, 2001). For my students, learning to teach is about negotiating these, and other, competing images and discourses of teaching, and constructing their own theories and concepts. In this chapter, I explore one of these concepts—*transparency*, a term that came to have considerable epistemic significance for my students.

During a conversation in class about responding to student writing, Nicole, then several weeks into her student teaching, described feeling caught between wanting to allow students to do writing they find meaningful and having to ask them to do work that is mandated by the district's core curriculum. Her classmate Mona suggested a way to interrupt the deadlock:

> Have you tried transparency? Just telling them what you're going through and what you're experiencing? I'm very transparent with my students. I don't like assessment. I don't like grading. What are *we* going to do about this? How are *we* going to do this?

This was the first of many uses of the term transparency in our conversations. In the remainder of this chapter, I trace multiple uses of transparency in the discourse of one cohort of student English teachers and an inquiry group that Nicole, Mona, and I formed with other class members—a group that continues to write, publish online, and present together (e.g., Carlough et al., 2006; Zeiders et al., 2007). Looking at my students' uses of transparency in relationship to issues of authority, authenticity, vulnerability, and accountability, I argue that student teachers do not simply inherit and enact outside discourses of teaching, with their attendant recommended (or mandated) concepts and practices. Rather, concepts like transparency, developed socially and negotiated over time, provide a locus for their collaborative inquiries into teaching, shaping their individual learning and ontogeny as teachers. In a time of mounting pressures to standardize teaching, this work provides an example of how learning to teach is constructed, locally and socially, in the discourse of a particular community of student teachers.

THE PUBLIC LANDSCAPE OF TRANSPARENCY

Mona introduced the idea of transparency into our group discourse, but she didn't invent it. A term used in business and politics, transparency denotes ways in which persons, governments, or institutions make their practices visible, accessible, or understood. This sense of the term is illustrated by an example close to the context in which my students teach. The Philadelphia

Student Union (2008), a youth-led advocacy organization, recently under-took a campaign to pressure the school district's Reform Commission to be "transparent" about its budgeting and evaluation practices. In a meta-phor made manifest, Student Union advocates organized a protest involving washing the windows of the school district offices. For the Student Union, transparency is about equity and access as much as clarity. A photograph on a recent cover of the *Philadelphia Public School Notebook* (2008) shows newly appointed superintendent Arlene Ackerman talking with a Student Union member, holding a poster—a parody of the packaging for Tide detergent—that reads, "Now with Transparency: For a secrecy-free shine."

While the goal of transparency animates activist projects like the Student Union protest, the ideal of transparency is held in suspicion by those who work from poststructural perspectives, which emphasize the fluidity of identities and the perpetual slippages and elusiveness of meaning in language (Benton & Craib, 2001). From a poststructuralist perspective, language and discourse are by nature *not* transparent (Luke, 1997); the static-free commu-nication theorized by Habermas (1989) and others is idyllic and impossible. Poststructuralists would likely regard the desire for clarity that transparency implies as both unachievable and undesirable. There are no stable meanings to be transparently revealed: There are, rather, "nothing but interpretations" (Foucault, 1964/1990). By extension, poststructural theories of teaching consider clarity an impossible institutional demand (Aoki, 2000), forwarding pedagogies predicated on the unknowability of teaching, on its complexity and indeterminacy (Ellsworth, 1997).

TRANSPARENCY AND AUTHORITY

In her initial use of transparency, Mona drew on the public landscape of the term as well as her classroom experience. Mona's use of transparency seems to have affinity with the kind advocated by the Student Union: Transparency invites openness with the goal of fostering candid, productive, and, ostensibly, more equitable relationships with students. Mona defined transparency as "tell-ing [students] what you're going through and what you're experiencing"—in this case, telling them about her aversion to grading—and positioned herself and students in concert, asking, "What are we going to do about this?"

Subsequently, Mona's classmates, Nicole and Sylvia, pressed her to elabo-rate on what transparency looks like in her classroom:

Nicole: What do [your students] say?
Mona: What have they said? We're playing with it. We're writing about

it. We're going back and forth. They're giving me writing and reading and teaching goals, and I'm giving them reading and . . . we're
going to grade it on that. And of course, because of where we are, I
have to do quizzes and tests.

Sylvia: Have you actually gotten those goals from them?

Mona: We're working on them. I'm doing them in chunks of four
students.

Sylvia: So what are some examples of the goals?

Mona: I told them some of the things I want to do as a writer. I want to
be more prolific, so we've come up with I have to write 10 minutes in
the morning when I wake up, no matter what's going on in my life.
So I have my "10-minute journal." That's what I'm working on.

Sylvia: What about for them?

Mona: For them? Based on their journals they're giving to me, I'm giving critiques back. So some of them are very boring—antecedent–
pronoun connections—some of them are semicolons, some of them
are more descriptive voice.

By challenging Mona to describe more concretely what she meant by
transparency, Sylvia and Nicole asked for a kind of transparency from her.
What they received was less than "transparent." Their exchange demonstrates the complexity of surfacing ideas like these—and the indeterminacy
of teaching with them. Mona's explication is an example of what Elizabeth
Ellsworth (1997) has called a pedagogical "misfire," evincing the ways classroom discourse—and learning—is messy, unpredictable, and inconclusive,
belying the neat correlation between what is taught and what is learned that
institutions often assume.

Mona's "transparency" signaled her attempt to shift authority in her
classroom. Her claim that she is "very transparent" with students implies
that transparency is a fixed quality. In her elaboration, transparency appears
less determined, a "back and forth" conversation with students about work,
goals, and expectations, taking place against the backdrop of external requirements. Presumably to establish transparency, Mona portrayed herself as
a less-than-prolific writer to students and invited them to give her "assignments." This *quid pro quo* isn't equivalent: The difference between responding to "antecedent–pronoun connections" in students' writing and students
"requiring" their teacher to keep a daily writing journal inscribes rather than
ameliorates power differentials. That does not undercut the work Mona outlines here. Her attempt to be unambiguous with students about the specifics
of her expectations and assessments of them encouraged a kind of play at
inverting student–teacher positionalities. Transparency provided a literal and

discursive site for Mona to connect with students and revise some of the inherited mores of student–teacher interactions and authority.

Similarly, the use of concepts like transparency helped disperse authority to name and interpret promising teaching practices in our shared classroom. Mona was often recognized by others in her cohort as the originator of transparency and an authority on its meanings. In students' writing, this sometimes took the form of lateral citation (Franke, 1995; Lytle, 2000). In her course portfolio, Nora detailed her concern that the pace of the core curriculum, mandated by the school district of Philadelphia, allowed little time to explore her own and her students' interest in music, and she wondered if she should be "transparent" with students about the fact that while she values music in English class, "it's not the way everyone else involved in this process thinks they should learn." Nora credited Mona as the source of transparency. Her use of the in-text citation "Rowley, constantly in 2005" adopted and mocked an academic convention, challenging established notions of the style and appropriateness of citations.

Others assigned authorship of the term to the group. Jared referenced our inquiry group's first jointly authored conference presentation after his use of transparency in his program portfolio. His use of the citation "Carlough et al., 2006" suggests communal ownership of the term. In his portfolio essay, Jared wrote, "the call for developing 'realness' and authenticity with students [is] everywhere in the literature," and positioned transparency within that rubric. In support of his claim, he cited "Carlough et al." in the same paragraph as Shirley Brice Heath, Lisa Delpit, Marilyn Cochran-Smith, and Susan Lytle. As Hyland (1999) has noted, the social production of knowledge in academic communities is reflected in disciplinary citation conventions. By citing members of our community next to recognized authorities in the field, Jared placed them in conversation. In doing so, he repositioned authority for theorizing teaching locally.

Citing a peer defies expectations about who has the authority over the "big ideas" that animate learning to teach. For Jared, Nora, and others, citing transparency served to support an academic argument, but it was principally about emphasizing the connective aspects among their own and their peers' experiences and ideas (Franke, 1995). Their citations solidified their sense of discursive community.

TRANSPARENCY AND AUTHENTICITY

Transparency became nearly ubiquitous in our inquiry group conversations. We met weekly in the months leading up to our first presentation at the

University of Pennsylvania Ethnography in Education Forum; during that time, transparency became an ideational site around which our group co-alesced. As we searched for a conceptual frame for our presentation, Kelly commented, "If I were going to make a title for our group, I'd say something about 'balance' and 'transparency' because I think that everything that we've been saying fits under those two headings generally." Reading across notes and transcripts of our meetings corroborates Kelly's claim. Many of our conversations related directly or obliquely to transparency. A conversation about the pressures of teaching with mandated curricula provides an example of how transparency shaped our mutual inquiry.

Jared began by suggesting that the curriculum mandated by the school district presents teachers and students with "new problems—new ways to 'fake it' through the system," and asked, "What are the differences between learning and 'faking it'?" I responded that these "systems" increasingly ask teachers to create test-takers, which may invite "faking it" in the sense of requiring teachers and students to enact these roles, among others. Mona talked about the interrelationship between learning that "matters" and learning to play "the game" of school. In order to "play" successfully, the game needs to be made transparent for students. Sylvia, less comfortable with faking it as a part of her pedagogy, suggested that inquiry-based teaching (Cochran-Smith & Lytle, 2001) opposes faking it: "If we are *really* engaged in a process of inquiry with our kids, than I don't think we are really faking it." Inquiry, Sylvia suggested, involves transparency. Teaching with this framework means that we aren't "fake."

The ensuing discussion explored different meanings and uses of transparency:

> *Mona:* How does making things transparent solve a lot of problems? Or does it? Does *being* transparent, does *talking* transparently with students, make your teaching about anything better?
>
> *Kelly:* What do you mean about that?
>
> *Mona:* Better run, more engaging . . .
>
> *Sylvia:* [interjecting] More "real" . . .
>
> *Mona:* . . . make it a more real classroom, a classroom where more learning takes place, where more "authentic" learning takes place. When a teacher becomes *real*, and the students become real to the teacher, and they're both making meaning together transparently, how does that change the interactions?
>
> *Nora:* So what would be an example of that?
>
> *Sylvia:* [Saying,] "I don't know the answer to this . . ."

Mona: Yeah, I say that all the time: "I don't know the answer to this."
. . . I feel like transparency allows for flexibility. I really tell my students what I'm doing and why I'm doing it. I tell them why I'm in
a bad mood sometimes—they tell me why they are. . . . From really
mundane things, to the larger things: why we're studying what we're
studying.

Jared: I think making things transparent . . . reframes problems. . . .
Like today, rather than making [students] turn a paper in to me, I
created this alter ego—"the editor"—that they were turning it in
to, as a way to get them to extend their audience. But I'm making it
transparent: There are audiences for writing. . . . They are expecting
something else, and you are reframing the problem for them. And
that becomes a way for them to change their behavior, to change the
way they're going to look at it, to give them perspective.

In our conversations, meanings of transparency were negotiated and
constructed collaboratively. In their exchange, Mona did much of the ex-
plicating, but Sylvia's interjections provided the framework. Recalling poststructuralist pedagogies, Sylvia put forward the idea that being "real" with
students involves performing *not* knowing—a notion that runs counter to
the epistemic basis of mandated curricula and the image of teachers simply
teaching what they "know." Together, Mona and Sylvia suggested that a
pedagogy predicated on telling students "I don't know the answer" helped
them to construct other relationships to students and to knowledge in their
classrooms (Cochran-Smith & Lytle, 1999).

The use of "faking it" and "being transparent" in this conversation plays
out the productive instability of these ideas. These terms may be viewed as
ideational opposites, yet they bear similarities. Each is a response to systems
that students and teachers must navigate. Each implies that at some level
schooling is, as Mona and Jared claimed, a complex game with a set of power
codes, rules and requirements, determined both within and outside of the
classroom. Mona noted that the concepts are intimately related: "Faking it"
requires that "it" be made transparent. While school systems might be more
bearable, more navigable, when made transparent, the force of inherited
strictures encourages compliance. This invites "faking it."

As a site of shared inquiry, transparency never settled into a single
meaning. In this exchange, transparency was constructed as both stance and
method, something teachers do and a way of framing or making sense of
what teachers do. Jared and Mona talked about how transparency might be
taken up as a pedagogical strategy, a way to increase "flexibility" within

rigid systems, to "solve" or "reframe" problems in practice. Jared proposed that transparency could be a framework that students can adopt to interpret their work differently. Mona and Sylvia suggested a struggle to get at deeper levels of transparency, striving toward "real" or "authentic" relationships with students. They seemed to ask, how might mandates and teaching "authentically" coexist? Are there alternatives to "faking" our ways through the systems we work within and teaching students to do the same? How might "transparency" alter the relationships teachers and students encounter in institutions that demand and reward rote forms of participation?

TRANSPARENCY AND VULNERABILITY

The instability of *not knowing* that Sylvia and Mona explored paradoxically allowed Sylvia and others to *know* their students differently. For our group conference presentation (Carlough et al., 2006), Jared and Sylvia wrote about how transparency allowed them to develop closer relationships with students. In this excerpt, Sylvia described her attempts to be both teacher and advocate to a student, how transparency helped her to "break down the student–teacher divide" between them:

> It seems to me at this point that in being transparent—in telling him that I will not let him fail, emotionally or academically—I am putting myself in an absolutely vulnerable position, but somehow in these moments, I feel most like a teacher.

For Sylvia, transparency allowed for intimacy, advocacy, and productive vulnerability. She and Jared noted that this kind of teaching can be discomforting. The rewards, for them, outweighed the risks.

Others were less ready to destabilize relationships in their classrooms. In our inquiry group discussion about transparency and faking it, Kelly listened as others elaborated on how transparency might make their teaching "better." Later, she revealed feeling apprehensive about being transparent with her students:

> For me, with transparency, I hear what you're saying, and I admire it so much. I would love to do that. But I'm scared to death of doing it in my class. I feel like I'd be just flattened into a small bug.

In an entry entitled "Transparency" posted on the class Blackboard site (an online discussion board) several days later, Kelly elaborated, detailing her conflicted feelings about addressing issues of language and culture with students, and her questions about how transparency might, or might not, help:

> This weekend I feel awash in mistakes, misjudgments, and miscalculations. How can I find the time and silence needed to contemplate how to change the course of the class that I am teaching, now that I have possibly misguided it? . . . Right now my class is reading *Their Eyes Were Watching God*. . . . June Jordan [1985] expresses her shock and dismay that her students did not see the similarities between their spoken language and the written language of the book they were reading. This same scenario basically plays itself over and over in my classroom. . . . I have not mentioned to my students that they are judging Janie in the same way, and for the same reasons, that they know many in our society judge them. . . . It seems that I have sacrificed an opportunity for the class to look into this issue for the sake of maintaining my own comfort zone.
>
> On Friday some of us met to discuss the Ethnography Forum, and Mona brought up the idea of transparency in the classroom. I'm afraid, but upon reflection, this may be just what I need to do—approach my class and tell them up front about everything that I have just written and ask where they'd like to go from there.

In the article that Kelly cited, June Jordan (1985) recounts a similar incident following her students' readings of *The Color Purple*. Like Kelly, Jordan chose to "swallow [her] astonishment" that her African American students' "rejection [of the book] was aimed at the one irreducibly Black element of Walker's work: the language—Celie's Black English." Like Kelly, Jordan wanted to avoid making her students feel "self-conscious about their own spoken language . . . while they clearly felt it was 'wrong'" (p. 125). Jordan proceeded to write the first lines of Walker's book on the board, translating them into so-called Standard English with her students. Ultimately, at students' insistence, Jordan designed a university course on Black English.

Kelly's post was written from a moment of indecision. Her fear of harming students was counterpoint to the fear she expressed about students harming her. Though Kelly had taught before, she lacked Jordan's years of experience. Unlike Jordan, Kelly was a European American woman teaching predominantly African American students; she struggled with the tension between her and her students' different locations in relation to the issue of language use. The contemplative "silence" that Kelly desired is in contrast to the discomfort she expressed about her in-class silence. Her intended "comfort zone" became a source of unease. Kelly placed not speaking in contradistinction to transparency, which she characterized as revealing "everything." It proved to be a paralyzing dichotomy.

Mona responded to Kelly on Blackboard, in a post titled "Re: Transparency":

> Wow. That was a powerful and honest thread. . . . Before you reveal your entire hand, are there some activities you could structure around verbal pragmatics, code switching, power, access, and the media? Maybe your students would respond well to a "reading their world" activity where they considered how people code switch in advertising, banks, buses, parties, church, etc.? . . . You might be able to watch them come to their own conclusions about language and power?
>
> I know how you feel. In our adolescent development class, I was asking the professors whether or not telling students that life is unfair would some way harm them or lead them to become depressed? Both professors led me to [believe] that perhaps my students are all too aware that life is not fair, and what they need is a creative, supportive, and academic space to explore those issues? Yes, transparency looms large for me as well.

Mona interrupted the dichotomy between revelation and silence, qualifying that teaching with transparency might not mean uncovering all. Proposing a kind of critical language investigation not unlike Jordan's (1985), Mona suggested that risky topics might be made public through intentional activities rather than personal revelations. Mona shared Kelly's concern about "harming" students, suggesting that students might benefit from another kind of transparency—the chance to systematically inquire together into complex issues of race, language, and culture from their perspectives.

This is a different transparency from the kind Sylvia wrote about, though no less about vulnerability and risk. Sylvia talked about transparency as a way she makes herself vulnerable to students, inspired by her desire to advocate for a struggling student. For her, vulnerability represented risk but also intimacy. Kelly's sense of vulnerability was embedded in feelings of uncertainty and regret. The kind of transparency Mona recommended to Kelly is a pedagogical intervention intended to mitigate vulnerability rather than provoke it.

In her notes from an inquiry group meeting, Nora asked, "Can we be transparent without being vulnerable?" Sylvia's and Kelly's stories suggested the answer is no. They contended differently with what Britzman

(1999/2003) has called the "more private aspects of pedagogy: coping with competing definitions of success and failure, and one's own sense of vulnerability and credibility" (p. 28). While the systems they teach within promote certainties, for Kelly and Sylvia, learning to teach with transparency, instrumentally or relationally, involved confronting, mitigating, or marshaling feelings of vulnerability and uncertainty.

TRANSPARENCY AND ACCOUNTABILITY

As the above examples illustrate, my students' evocations of transparency expressed attempts to create alternatives to conventional student–teacher relationships. This entailed constructing other forms of accountability than those handed down from above (Campano, 2007). The kinds of accountability held in esteem by political and policy worlds intend to encourage learning by standardizing curricula and pedagogy, expecting teachers to perform roles authorized externally. Transparency represented these student teachers' attempts, discursively and practically, to revise inherited roles and to negotiate and author their own teaching—a self-determination fundamentally in tension with standardizing institutional directives.

My students often took on the idea that being a good teacher meant following a script or supervisor's checklist. Over time, they used the phrase *dog and pony show* to describe teaching that complies with or mimes systemic mandates. If transparency signified attempts to be differently accountable to students, *dog and pony show* referenced practices that are—or adopt the appearance of being—accountable to external expectations, within or against their intended purposes. In the following examples, Nora and Jared describe their struggles with dog and pony shows.

In a journal entry, Nora detailed a difficult professional development session in her school:

> The session began with an admonishment of teachers, "you know who you are," that are not meeting the Six Strategies for Success. . . . [The presentation], in all its chalk and talk behaviorism, reinforced that there is a group of people who listen while people with authority tell you what to do and why you do it. In this case, it's "Hey guys, play the dog and pony show! Move the desks around. Put up some posters. What? You don't have any. Well, use markers and poster board in your next lesson. Somehow! Oh, and don't forget to stay on pace with the curriculum. So,

don't take too long with those posters." In the meantime, I observe teachers passing notes, talking loudly over the presenters, dissenters laughing and mouthing off in the back, an all too familiar recreation of classrooms full of suspicious, angry students.

Colloquially, dog and pony shows are demonstrations manufactured for external approval. Nora's "playing the dog and pony show" echoed this sense of the phrase—a tragicomic performance of an administrator's checklist of "good" teaching: moving desks, using poster boards, "staying on pace" with authorized curricula. Nora juxtaposed the image of mock-compliance that dog and pony shows entail with the image of an audience of teachers mimicking "their own students' resistance." She described professional development as a form of public admonishment met by dissent and lack of interest. Teachers and administrators are portrayed oppositionally. Accountability is presented as a play, shaped by the call and response between administrators' injunctions and reprimands and teachers' compliance with or resistance to them.

The "play" of accountability is represented acutely in classroom supervisions. In a reflection written in advance of our second Ethnography Forum presentation, Jared described being observed in his classroom:

> [I knew] full well that I had given the administrator the type of language he wanted to see on the observation form, phrases like: collaborative group work, empowerment of student understandings, reciprocal teaching, extension of prior understandings, student-centered inquiry, etc. This wasn't a full-blown dog and pony show—my lesson really did employ these methods, or, at least, I could explain how I thought I was employing these techniques in my lesson—but the point is that I knew the lesson would travel well in part because of the language I used. As the lesson came to a close, the administrator said, "Good lesson, good group work," and I found myself wondering why this language, particularly the word *collaborative* was important to him, what it suggested about me as a practitioner, and to what extent this word actually had an impact on my students' learning.

Recalling his discussion of faking it, Jared described a command performance of *appearing* accountable. Employing terms and methods that he expects an administrator to respond positively to, Jared created the conditions for passing the dog and pony show of supervision with flying colors. Later,

Jared wrote, "I use collaborative groups because I was taught that way, and administrators look for collaborative work because research suggests that it works, which further reinforces my use of it in my practice." The suggestion here is that teacher educators, administrators, and teachers are complicit in perpetuating the dog and pony shows student teachers enact.

In their analysis of teachers' perceptions of supervision, Zepeda and Ponticell (1998) note that a majority of teachers they interviewed described supervision as a "dog and pony show." As in Nora's and Jared's accounts, these teachers portrayed supervision as "demonstrating all the 'right' steps or indicators on the supervisor's checklist" (p. 8). One teacher recounted the humiliation of showing her principal how she "really" taught and subsequently receiving a "poor" rating. Zepeda and Ponticell conclude that in these interactions, "Both teacher and supervisor were accomplices in meaningless compliance with a state-required system. Both discovered what was needed to toe the line successfully. Perhaps the dog and pony show was born on both sides out of the meaninglessness perceived in the supervision/evaluation process" (p. 15).

In my students' uses of the phrase, dog and pony show meant more than performing meaningless expectations. In Jared's reflection, the idea of the dog and pony show inspired an inquiry into his pedagogical decisions and their impact on students. He asked, "What effects does it have on my students? How to they perceive their work in the classroom as a result of my choices of strategies, and how does it change our positions in relation to the material we work with?" Rather than complying with them, Nora's description of doing a dog and pony show *mocked* the terms of accountability. Echoing the idea that a dog and pony show can be a mask or cover rather than an act of compliance, in a class conversation Jared described his perspective on teaching with mandated curriculum:

> I think a good teacher is going to take a look at [the core curriculum] and say this is a guide anyway. No matter what they say about mandates and all that. Oh yeah, I'll do the dog and pony, and pretend like I'm actually doing it, or do what I want, but retool it in language that fulfills whatever checkbox you need to fulfill.

This is not an instance of "meaningless compliance;" it is deliberate resistance. It complicates understandings of the relationship between mandates and their enaction. Doing a dog and pony show is described as masking teaching in the "drag" of compliance, while doing something completely other, "retooling" teaching to look like it fits checkboxes. There is a matter-of-fact tone to Jared's statement. But what does it say about the toxicity of the environments student teachers teach in that they require these kinds of performances?

The following week, Mona and Alex talked in class about what it means to teach in contexts that inspire dog and pony shows:

> *Alex:* I still think you can totally subvert [the core curriculum] . . . do-
> ing a few things, like writing the objective on the board before ev-
> ery class, you know.
> *Mona:* I'm good at that. I can do the dog and pony show. But how
> about not having one?

As Alex and others claimed, dog and pony shows can be subversive acts. Mona's response suggests two possible readings: What might happen if I re-fuse to perform dog and pony shows in contexts that require them? By con-trast, what might it mean to teach in schools where these performances are *not* needed? The implication of either is that dog and pony shows represented ways the accountability structures of schools hinder rather than support her teaching. The prior week, Mona had expressed her aggravation about the need for dog and pony shows:

> You're going to have to be in cahoots with your students when
> admin comes in and have a dog and pony show. . . . It's a very frus-
> trating place to be if you want to be a meaningful teacher in the
> Philadelphia school system with the core curriculum.

Mona suggested here that teachers need to marshal their students in a collective effort to execute this performance—in other words, dog and pony shows *require* transparency. The image of teachers and students collectively staging resistance in the form of a dog and pony show evokes the kind of civil protest undertaken by the Philadelphia Student Union. It recalls Bakhtin's (1984) notion of the carnivalesque: a performance that mobilizes subaltern resources against authoritarian discourses and practices. Unlike carnival, dog and pony shows are obligatory, not celebratory: They are collaborative dem-onstrations of compliance that knowingly satirize and subvert authority.

The relationship of dog and pony shows to transparency presents an im-age of a kind of "double consciousness" (DuBois, 1903/2007). As dog and pony shows require transparency, so teaching with transparency in a time of heightened accountability requires dog and pony shows of the kind Nora and Jared described. Because transparency helps to make teachers and students more *vulnerable* to each other in the sense of more near, dog and pony shows are a response to feeling vulnerable to, caught by, or susceptible to institutional demands. They are employed as a means to make student teachers *invulnerable* to external edicts, like supervisory checklists that parody "good" teaching. Making the inner workings of school systems a subject of critical scrutiny with students, to borrow further from DuBois (1903/2007), is akin to "lifting the veil" between the fragmented aspects of student teachers' experiences. In doing so, these teachers attempted to position themselves and their students on the same side of the accountability equation.

DISCOURSE AND AGENCY

In his articulation of the ideational and ontological significance of language in use, Gee (2005) has elaborated the idea of "large-D Discourses," which he describes as complex personal and professional identity kits. Discourses encompass ways of being and talking in particular communities. In Gee's terms, Discourses express themselves through individuals but are not constructed by them:

> It is sometimes helpful to think about social and political issues as if it is not just us humans who are talking and interacting with each other, but, rather, the Discourses we represent and enact for which we are "carriers." (p. 27)

My students' discourse suggests otherwise. Their uses of terms like *transparency* are socially constructed, intentional acts of signification and interpretation (Britzman, 1999/2003). As students of teaching, they are entering into a network of competing discourses (and Discourses) of teaching not simply as "carriers" of others' discourses, but as interrogators and interpreters of them, as agents, activists, and authors of their own practices.

Interrupting conventional distinctions between those who "theorize" from above and those who "do" below, Antonio Gramsci (1971/2005) argued for the development of what he called "organic intellectuals" from among subaltern groups, equipped with the task of understanding, articulating, and directing change from within. He asked:

> Is it better to take part in a conception of the world mechanically imposed by the external environment? . . . Or, on the other hand, is it better to work out consciously and critically one's own conception of the world and thus, in connection with the labours of ones own brain, choose one's sphere of activity, take an active part in the creation of the history of the world, be

one's own guide, refusing to accept passively and supinely from outside the moulding of one's personality? (pp. 323–324)

Gramsci wrote from a moment of unique political turmoil and struggle, as well as personal imprisonment. But as my students' descriptions of working in urban schools in a climate of heightened accounting and standardizing practices indicate, learning to teach in this context involves no small measure of struggle. It is deeply local, social, activist, and intellectual work. My students' negotiations of transparency suggest that to learn to teach "means to participate in dialogue: to ask questions, to heed, to respond, to agree," (Bakhtin, 1984, p. 293), as well as to disagree, to contest, to interpolate, to revise.

While the concept of transparency helped these student teachers to make sense of the complex project of learning to teach, it is not a virtuous paradigm. What rescues it from the realm of panaceas are its contested definitions—as the above examples show, the meanings of transparency are neither stable nor transparent—its connotations with humanness and fallibility, and its counter-hegemonic aspects. Transparency is not about clarifying regimes of truth but about complicating them, about unsettling traditional teaching and learning positionalities rather than reifying them.

My students' work has many implications for my own. I came to teaching teachers with my own theories of practice, constructed over years teaching at an alternative high school for mostly court-involved youth in San Francisco, Life Learning Academy (Simon, 2005). Teaching urban adolescents who had been institutionally constructed as *problems*, I learned the insufficiency and sometimes tragic implications of externally assigned categories like "at risk" or "illiterate." Life Learning students always proved to be—and be capable of—infinitely more than such a priori categories and theories claimed. Working with them necessitated learning *from* them, reinforcing that teaching is highly relational work that does not neatly fit imported frameworks. As a teacher educator, I continue to learn from my students' experiences of trying to understand *their* students, of teaching and learning with them in contexts marked by attempts to manage and standardize their work. I bring my own "certainties" to teaching student teachers, adding to the cacophony of perspectives they encounter. I continue my attempts to provide opportunities for them to interrogate my own and others' ideas about teaching, and to construct their own. My students' negotiations of concepts like transparency have reinforced my belief that learning to teach means entering into critical dialogue—with other teachers, with competing notions of expertise, with the individuals and politics that define and legislate teaching and learning, and most importantly with students. Helping my students to construct alternatives to accepting prefigured roles in the classroom has become central to my work. Teacher education has become a process of wondering with student teachers about what *is* and asking, as Mona asks with her students, "What are *we* going to do about this?"

REFERENCES

Aoki, D. S. (2000). The thing never speaks for itself: Lacan and the pedagogical politics of clarity. *Harvard Educational Review, 70*(3), 347–369.

Bakhtin, M. (1984). *Problems of Dostoevsky's poetics.* Minneapolis: University of Minnesota Press.

Benton, T., & Craib, I. (2001). *Philosophy of social science: The philosophical foundations of thought.* New York: Palgrave.

Britzman, D. P. (2003). *Practice makes practice: A critical study of learning to teach* (Rev. ed.). Albany: State University of New York Press. (Original work published 1999)

Campano, G. (2007). *Immigrant students and literacy: Reading, writing, and remembering.* New York: Teachers College Press.

Carlough, S., Greco, K., Kreft, J., McCartney, A., Neumeister, M., Rowley, M., Simon, R., Willard, E., & Zeiders, M. (2006, February). *From theory to life: Perspectives on student teaching in Philadelphia public schools.* Paper presented at the University of Pennsylvania Ethnography in Education Forum, Philadelphia.

Cochran-Smith, M., & Lytle, S. L. (1999). Relationships of knowledge and practice: Teacher learning on communities. In A. Iran-Nejad & P. D. Pearson (Eds.), *Review of research in education* (Vol. 24, pp. 249–306). Washington, DC: American Educational Research Association.

Cochran-Smith, M., & Lytle, S. L. (2001). Beyond certainty: Taking an inquiry stance on practice. In A. Leiberman & L. Miller (Eds.), *Teachers caught in the action: Professional development that matters* (pp. 45–58). New York: Teachers College Press.

DuBoise, W. E. B. (2007). *The souls of Black folk.* New York: Oxford University Press. (Original work published 1903)

Ellsworth, E. (1997). *Teaching positions: Difference, pedagogy, and the power of address.* New York: Teachers College Press.

Foucault, M. (1990). Nietzsche, Freud, Marx. In G. L. Ormiston & A. D. Schrift (Eds.) *Transforming the hermeneutic context: From Nietzsche to Nancy* (pp. 59–68). Albany: State University of New York Press. (Original work published 1964)

Franke, D. (1995). Writing in to unmapped territory: The practice of lateral citation. In L. W. Phelps & J. Emig (Eds.), *Feminine principles and women's experiences in American composition and rhetoric* (pp. 375–384). Pittsburgh: University of Pittsburgh Press.

Gee, J. P. (2005). *An introduction to discourse analysis: Theory and method* (2nd ed.). New York: Routledge.

Gramsci, A. (2005/1971). *Selections from the prison notebooks* (Q. Hoare & G. N. Smith, Eds. and Trans.). New York: International Publishers. (Original work published 1971)

Habermas, J. (1989). *The structural transformation of the public sphere* (Thomas Burger, Trans). Cambridge, MA: MIT Press.

Hyland, K. (1999). Academic attribution: Citation and the construction of disciplinary knowledge. *Applied Linguistics, 20*(3), 341–367.

Jordan, J. (1985). Nobody mean more to me than you and the future life of Willie Jordan. In *On call: Political essays* (pp. 123–139). Boston: South End Press.

Luke, A. (1997). Theory and practice in critical discourse analysis. In L. J. Saha (Ed.), *International encyclopedia of the sociology of education. Kidlington*, Oxford, UK: Elsevier Science.

Lytle, S. L. (2000). Teacher research in the contact zone. In M. Kamil, P. Mosenthal, D. Pearson, & R. Barr (Eds.), *Handbook of reading research* (Vol. III, pp. 691–718). Mahwah, NJ: Erlbaum.

Philadelphia Public School Notebook.(2008, Summer). Retrieved August 16, 2008, from http://www.thenotebook.org/editions/2008/summer/

Philadelphia Student Union. (2008). Retrieved June 17, 2008, from http://www.phillystudentunion.org/index.html#recent

Simon, R. (2005). Bridging life and learning through inquiry and improvisation: Literacy practices at a model high school. In B. V. Street (Ed.), *Literacies across educational contexts* (pp. 124–144). Philadelphia: Caslon.

Simon, R., & Lytle, S. L. (2006, April). *The literacies of teaching teachers: Troubling inquiry in a time of certainties.* Paper presented at the American Educational Research Association meeting, San Francisco.

Street, B. (Ed.). (2005). *Literacies across educational contexts.* Philadelphia: Caslon, Inc.

Useem, E. (2005). *Learning from Philadelphia's school reform: What do the research findings show so far?* Philadelphia: Sociology of Education Section of the American Sociological Association.

Zepeda, S. J., & Ponticell, J. A. (1998). At cross-purposes: What do teachers need, want, and get from supervision? *Journal of Curriculum and Supervision, 14*(1), 68–87.

Zeiders, M., Willard, E., Simon, R., Rowley, M., McCartney, A., Kreft, J., Greco, K., & Carlough, S. (2007, February). *Collaborative teacher inquiry in trying times.* Paper presented at the Ethnography in Education Research Forum, University of Pennsylvania, Philadelphia.

Chapter 11

Creating a Hybrid Space for Self, Teacher, and Researcher

Swati Mehta

Swati Mehta is a doctoral candidate in the Curriculum, Instruction, and Teacher Education program at the Lynch School of Education, Boston College, where she has also received a certificate in International Human Rights and Social Justice. Mehta is trained in elementary education and also holds a master's degree from Teachers College, Columbia University. She has been a teacher of youth (grades 5–12) and specifically focuses her efforts on immigrant youth. Mehta taught full-time in a combined 4th- and 5th-grade classroom in urban Chicago at a small immigrant student charter school. For the last 2 years, she has been collaborating and researching with an urban immigrant high school in Boston. Currently, in her work with preservice teachers at Boston College, Mehta draws on her experience of being a second-generation Indian immigrant who studies language and literacy through action research. Mehta's scholarly and teaching interests are found at the nexus of youth, language, and cultural studies.

A letter from my mother when I left for college:

> Betu [dear child], you can see culture and life like a lotus flower. The lotus flower blooms above the water and everything seems beautiful. Beneath the water where you cannot see, the lotus flower grows from roots in muddy and murky waters. The parts of culture that will be easy to keep will be the pretty parts that you can see. It is the vichara [thoughts] and prashna [questions] that cannot be seen and easily forgotten. Be pramanik [sincere] to the muddy waters of your future. You will know what it means to be a student and teacher.

   Why would I begin my story about teacher research with a letter from my mother? My mother's language reflects the tone of my story—a complex tale about teacher research told as a personal, professional, and political journey. My story is rooted in my own immigrant narrative. I am a Gujarati-speaking woman, raised in the predominantly White suburbs of Chicago. My parents, arrivals to the United States from Pune, India, worked hard at maintaining cultural ties to my home country. Rooted in my immigrant narrative, this chapter describes my journey as a teacher researcher.

I begin this chapter with a short discussion of the concept of cultural hybridity, which I employ as a lens to describe my personal narrative. In the first segment of the narrative, I describe growing up as a teacher. This section provides examples of my immigrant identity experiences, providing a context for my research. In the second segment of the narrative, on growing up as a researcher, I shift from the personal to the professional. Here, I describe three teacher research experiences conducted from three different subjectivities: as a developing practitioner, I engaged in action research with young Indian women in New York City; as a teacher, I led and participated in research with immigrant students in Chicago; and as a doctoral student in Boston, I critiqued the lack of research about Asian teachers in the literature. For each of these, I begin with what brought me into that particular professional location. Then, using excerpts from my researcher journals as a primary data source, I describe particular findings and implications as well as lessons about learning, teaching, and research.

CULTURAL HYBRIDITY

At the center of my immigrant story and subsequent journey into teacher research is the theoretical stance of cultural hybridity. Bhabha (1988, 1994) discusses cultural hybridity as a means of navigating between spaces, between differences, and between binaries of self and other. Simply put, an individual like myself cannot be put into one particular category of identity. Rather, cultural hybridity allows for a fluidity of my identities. As the child of an immigrant family, I am constantly making sense of my past, present, and future. As a teacher researcher, I am also committed to asking questions about immigrant culture. The idea of cultural hybridity is a tool I use to negotiate, represent, and assimilate various aspects of my work and myself.

In my journey as a teacher researcher, the concept of cultural hybridity also serves as a professional and political tool. I use this lens not only to share my own immigrant story but also to show the power of this framework within various teaching and learning contexts. Educators often downplay and undervalue the complicated issues of race, class, gender, and language by constantly ascribing labels to others. For example, they identify nondominant groups with labels such as "Asian Americans" or "Indian people." These labels come with assumptions attached to them. In much of my own work, I have tried to help young people "unpack" the labels used in their learning environments. But the idea of cultural hybridity does not allow me to deny the labels placed upon me. Rather, it calls for a constant critical stance of asking more complex identity questions. By understanding "cultures as fluid, dynamic, and negotiated at the intersections of race-class-gender-culture" (Asher, 2005, p. 1083), the notion of cultural hybridity helps situate the context and history of my experiences. I cannot generalize my narrative to other Gujarati-speaking women in the United States, since such generalizations are not possible. Rather, I use my own narrative to illustrate the dynamic nature of culture and its relationship to my evolving questions as a teacher and researcher.

GROWING UP AS A TEACHER

As a child of immigrant parents living in Chicago, I was constantly self-aware and observant about social contexts. Although I wanted to question various injustices and contradictions, I silently accepted the rules and expectations of a dominant culture. As a result, I became conditioned to forget the questions that affected me greatly. Today, as a teacher and doctoral student, I remember some questions I never asked. Why did I feel so embarrassed to speak in my first language at school but not at home? Why did my family not respond when someone in the neighborhood burned our garbage cans and threw eggs at our car? Why did I not ask my teachers why the history books equated India only with either Mahatma Gandhi's life or issues of poverty, when I had experienced many other stories during my visits? I realize now that many of the questions of my youth emerged at the cultural intersections of race, class, language, and gender. I begin my narrative about teacher research with snapshots of my cultural past.

Negotiating Indianness and Whiteness

Learning to speak my mother tongue, Gujarati, was at the center of my upbringing. As in many immigrant families, my parents deliberately worked to hold onto their home country's values through language (Suarez-Orozco & Suarez-Orozco, 2001). On weekends, our family gathered together with our Gujarati-speaking friends. We created an extended family, connected through language rather than shared blood. During these gatherings, I learned to negotiate gender, race, language, and power. While my mother and other elder women tended to domestic matters, I hovered at the door dividing the kitchen and the family room. To me, this door was the border that existed between men and women. On one side of the door—the kitchen—women conversed about recipes and children. On the other side of the door—the family room—men conversed about politics and work. Although I was attracted to the nurturing and creative environment in the kitchen, I was also attracted to the power and authority created by the discussion in the living room. In order to appropriate the best of both gendered positions, I created a classroom in the basements of these homes.

At the age of 9, I rounded up the younger children and taught them, assuming that my lessons could help them acculturate to their school environments. In this mock classroom, I was able to express authority. I felt more confident being with children who looked like me. Now, as I critically reflect on my first classroom, I see that even amidst my playmates, I chose to model my teaching style based upon my Indian White teachers. I appropriated their language—modeling their lessons, methods, and discourses. Interestingly, although I could have spoken Gujarati to my "students," I taught my lessons only in English. I see now that my construction of this classroom reflected the impact of the dominant school institution. As an example of cultural hybridity, my first role as a teacher in my first basement classroom embodied my perceptions of gender, race, language, and power.

A Product of Schooling—Acceptance and Rebellion

Being a member of a suburban middle-class community, my class background pushed me to accept a certain race status. Similar to other Indian professionals who came to America after the passage of the Immigration Act of 1965 (Maira, 2002), my family experienced economic success. As a result of growing up in a neighborhood and school where most of my peers were similar in class background, I appropriated certain norms and attempted to erase racial differences. In preschool, I asked my mother, "Why is my skin brown, not white?" As years went on, I seemed to equate accepting racial differences with merging into the dominant school culture. In elementary school, I asked my teacher to change her records so that my middle name was "Lynn" instead of "Arvind." While it is a common Indian practice for the middle name to be one's father's name, I thought I should change my name. My teacher was unable to provide any explanation about why the other girls did not have a father's middle name. During these moments, it seems that I had almost decided that it was my responsibility to establish a connection to my White peers at school, modeling their language and behavior.

As the years passed, I slowly began to express aspects of my Gujarati Indian culture in my school environment. I performed cultural dances in talent shows, ran twice for class president, and wrote papers and poetry with hybrid Gujarati/English language. At the peak of my high school years, my family moved to a small town outside Augusta, Georgia. In my new high school, I used my cultural isolation to experiment with various social identities. Through my outspoken convictions in my classes, my creation of a service organization (Service Over Self), and my refusal to enter the high school dating scene, I was in fact labeled "most likely to become a feminist" by my senior class. Drawn from my Indian heritage, many of these choices were misinterpreted by my peers. However, I began to care less about what others thought. I cradled my burning desire to teach and become an agent of change.

I decided to enter teaching through a program at the University of Georgia. My parents were hesitant about this decision. The majority of my immigrant Gujarati peers were entering medicine, engineering, and law. But I had been brought up with unwavering faith in and utmost respect for teachers, or "gurus," and the whole system of education. And so, with my mother's letter in my hand, I began my formal preparation in teacher education and teacher research.

GROWING UP AS A RESEARCHER

During my undergraduate years, I wrote my first teacher research journals. At this time, I began to ask questions about how teachers' race, language, and culture were represented. This was largely due to the constant labeling and isolation I experienced. I was one of only a few women of color in the school of education. I continued to reject cultural tags that failed to describe the complexity of culture. Although I was trained as a teacher in a formal teacher education program at the university, I did not feel ready to start teaching. It was only through research that I began to find spaces where I could "work the hyphens" (Fine, 1994) and embrace cultural hybridity. Instead of burying the question "Why did I not speak my home language at school?" I asked "What work can I do as a teacher to bring the languages of my students into the classroom?" as this journal entry indicates:

> I know I am supposed to go into teaching [right after graduation from my teacher education program], but I just can't! I have just begun to start probing some very important questions, and I just need more time to work through these questions. I want to be challenged with the theories that shape the job of a teacher. I want to discuss the culture of education rather

than gloss over education through methods. . . . And . . . I need to move to a place where I feel less like the token representative of all of India. If one more person at the University of Georgia asks me if I cook food like the Indian restaurant in downtown Athens, I think I might scream. I want to walk down a street where I might not be this visible minority . . . where some of those walls can break down! (Journal, summer 2000)

Queens, New York, 2000–2001

I was initiated into the research culture through the pursuit of a master's degree at Teachers College, Columbia University, during 2000–2001. During this time, I was given an important message: "Your development as a multicultural educator is synonymous with your development as a critical thinker and political activist in education." This message was communicated through critical dialogue. I often left class lectures uncomfortable yet motivated to ask deeper questions. Through these classroom communities in graduate school, I began to develop a professional definition of diversity, a definition that included a critical stance toward diversity initiatives in schools. As Nieto (1999) summarizes:

> The simple slogan "celebrating diversity" that is a part of many multicultural education initiatives, although it may be well-meaning, glosses over severe structural inequalities that are replicated in schools every day through the combination of uneven access, unfair practices, and harmful beliefs. No amount of cultural festivals or ethnic celebrations can turn this situation around. (p. 19)

Through this learning process within a context of peers and professors who shared similar immigrant narratives, I was nurtured into the academic culture.

During this time, I designed my first action research project, asking "How do high school immigrant Indian women in Queens articulate their identity narratives?" Over a 3-month period, I left the comfort of my Manhattan graduate student life and traveled to Queens, New York. At a large immigrant urban high school, I began to know three young "Indian American" women interested in sharing their identity narratives. In this initial attempt at qualitative research, I wrote observational notes, conducted interviews, and collected other data supporting the exploration of my research question.

As a developing teacher, I was determined to design spaces that gave agency to young people and promoted their voices (Sarroub, 2001). Based on my own understandings of critical multicultural education and youth studies, I posed the question "How do high school immigrant Indian women in Queens, New York, articulate their identity narratives?" Consequently, my research study focused on having spaces for shared dialogue with my participants. The young women wrote in journals, shared forms of art, invited me to family meals, and allowed me to observe other out-of-school activities. I also spent time in their high school. During this process, the young women were in constant dialogue with me, free to ask me questions about my life story, experiences, and intentions. In addition, these young women were also part of a recursive process of gathering and reporting data. I invited them to review, comment on, and make changes to my interpretations of their narratives. The paragraph that follows is part of what I wrote about my intentions at that time, which was later quoted in a book about teacher research written by my instructors:

> The purpose was to weave together the lives of these women through the lens of seeing them as multicultural, with multi-identities, and multi-realities. The purpose was not to place judgment, and thus data were not looked at for finding cultural contradictions within the lives of these women. Instead, I aimed to understand the multiple truths that these women created. As a result of the framework, typed-up notes and final narrative stories and analysis were shared with all three participants to establish a way to crosscheck the data that lead to their unique identity stories. (quoted in Falk & Blumenreich, 2005, p. 68)

In actually carrying out this approach, using a cultural hybridity lens was not an easy task. First, I had to build relationships with my participants. Second, I had to share the importance of my research and make myself vulnerable to their viewpoints. Finally, I had to be flexible with changing my agenda, negotiating power, and genuinely questioning whether and how this process was useful to the participants.

Through this teacher research study, a study based on the assumption that I could better teach adolescent youth in the future by researching with youth, I learned that complex research paradigms included complex research processes. Through this project, I learned that I had to be prepared for unpolished honesty. Immediately after I initiated the project, my three participants made it clear that I did not suddenly have the "inside" perspective on their lives because of our shared racial background. All three women pointed out our differences. As I sat with my researcher journal during my trips from Manhattan to Queens, I recall the shock of recognition that I was indeed different from these young women:

> These youth are honest, straight up, and cut to the chase. The girls pointed out we are not the same in significant ways. We look the same . . . two of the three young women speak the same first

language, Gujarati. But our school experiences are different in significant ways. I didn't live in a place that looked and felt like Queens, New York. I never experienced a social reality where I would wake up at 5:30 so I could catch a bus across town to attend the "good" high school (a high school surrounded by tall fences and metal detectors). This social reality did not bother these women, and I felt kind of odd. I have to admit my class privilege is a part of "cultural" identity that is not as visible. Although I was trying not to make generalizations about these girls . . . I was starting to. I am both on the inside and the outside of their lives. (Researcher journal, spring 2000)

These women's experiences were similar to my own in some ways in terms of the intersections of race, gender, and language. However, the specific intersections of hybrid spaces and hybrid identities could not be signified into a collective experience. Although we had obvious similarities, our cultural hybridity narratives did not mirror each other. As a result, a critical and telling moment for me as a novice teacher researcher was to step back rather than impose my researcher subjectivity upon my participants (Stevens, 2005). This meant listening, observing, and creating the process of data collection together.

One of the key findings from this project was the insistence of all three women that negative identity terms not be used in the telling of their narratives. Although these young women described moments of confusion and conflict, they each insisted on representing these conflicts on their own terms. In addition, they described how gender dynamics at home and racial dynamics at school were cultural tensions that they were constantly negotiating. However, they did not want these aspects of themselves to be juxtaposed against a standard accepted norm. These young women were determined not to be labeled as confused adolescent immigrants.

As a result of their insistence, all three women agreed they did not want the research data to be reported through narrative paraphrasing or paragraphs simplifying their lives. Instead, they agreed to report findings through statements that were less structured and without definitive conclusions. Although all participants chose similar themes in their narratives (e.g., mothers as symbols of strength), other aspects of their narratives were intentionally different. One young woman was an artist, another a dancer, and another a social activist. In their narratives, cultural hybridity was woven through dimensions of their lives. Even with respect to the syntax of their statements, each narrative line did not end with formal punctuation. This rhetorical move, co-

constructed through our dialogue together, reflected their stance as youth: "We are constantly negotiating who we are, and we do not want you to make us into conclusions."

Representing the complexity of their multicultural social realities, these young women had a great deal to say about culture, identity, and education. In my report about this teacher research, I talked about the implications for the larger educational community:

> As I look back to this first action research experience, I rec-
> ognize a hybrid space between self, teacher, and researcher. As a
> young woman with immigrant identification, I also recognize how
> I had to learn to listen more and impose less. As a teacher, I see the
> importance of extending our time together beyond the classroom
> and school walls. As a researcher, I recognize the construction of
> knowledge in action; research is the doing, thinking, reflecting,
> and representing of all learners involved. As someone constantly at-
> tempting to bridge theories behind critical multicultural education
> within the daily social contexts of youth, I also recognize teacher
> research as a tool to make this happen.

My first teacher research experience in New York City carved out a space for me to begin exploring questions that mattered to learning and teaching along with questions that mattered to me personally.

Chicago, 2002-2005

> I am right back to Chicago. But I can't do suburban life. No
> matter how much of a pay cut this job might be, I don't want to
> teach in the suburbs. I am moving forward with my commitment
> to work with immigrant students. I cannot wait to start my teach-
> ing job at Passages [Passages Charter School in urban Chicago].
> This is going to be my teaching home.
>
> Yikes! I already feel the pressure. I have so many decisions to
> make. How will I organize the tables and chairs? How will I teach
> five subjects? Where is space to have our weekly community meet-
> ings? How will I handle the numerous languages, histories, and lo-
> cations of my 4th- and 5th-grade students? How will my teaching
> philosophy come to life? Teacher research . . . with the pressure of
> state exams? Uh, we will see about that! Where will I have time?
> (Teacher journal, summer 2002)

I had mixed feelings of enthusiasm and fear as I took on my first role as a full-time classroom teacher. The charter school was focused on immigrant students, which was exciting; however, the school was just being founded during my first 3 years of teaching. Thus, I took on many roles during this time, including curriculum/literacy specialist, assistant to the principal in school initiatives, and organizer of school events. Although I was fortunate to have much freedom with regard to classroom curriculum, I was also working within a national and state culture with a heightened sense of accountability and standardized testing. My combined 4th- and 5th-grade classes meant preparing students for five Illinois state exams: reading, math, writing, social studies, and science. In addition, I had to learn to negotiate the tricky path of lesson planning and professional development within our school. Throughout this time, I was constantly trying to figure out who I was as a woman, teacher, and researcher within this intense environment.

During my second year at this school site, I began to focus on research and inquiry. I had two agendas. First, I wanted to engage my students in research. Second, I wanted to initiate a teacher research community as a type of professional development in our school. Using a model of teacher research that highlighted the inquiries of teachers (Cochran-Smith & Lytle, 1993), with the support of the leadership in the school, I started a teacher research group in the school.

During this time, my colleagues and I engaged in specific individual inquiries into our own classroom practice. But we shared power and leadership during our meetings. All of us had the freedom to share, critique, and discuss both our inquiries and our processes. Within this learning community, we raised specific questions. While we could not ignore the pressures of trying to survive as a public charter school, the teacher inquiry group gave us a positive intellectual community. During this process, I remember the distinct feeling of knowing my colleagues as intellectual partners, as I wrote in my journal:

> Wow, I never knew that the same people I've been working with every day have so many talents, interests, questions, and places they've been to, taught, and learned. I mean it makes sense that I'd get to know them, but I did not realize I would value the conversation this much. We are literally expressing theories for our classroom experiences. Together we are seeing whether we can make sense of what we notice. There is a dialogue happening here that does not happen in our staff meetings. I see us as public intellectuals *and* recess monitors. The realness, knowledge, and courage to

ask questions that don't have easy answers probes me. As demanding as this job is, this little group is giving me more energy. (Journal, fall 2003)

Meanwhile, my own childhood and immigrant stories led me to guide
my students to critique the immigrant language used in the social studies
curriculum. I wanted my students to find a voice in my classroom—a voice
that was missing in my own schooling experiences. When reading the Ellis
Island immigrant story, my students and I started critiquing the relevance
of this immigrant narrative for their own lives. Led by my own historical
struggles and the questions I had buried for too many years, I decided to
design a teacher action research plan around their burning question: What
is an immigrant? Through a systematic project done in small groups during the social studies and writing time blocks, my students learned, drafted,
wrote, and presented digital immigrant stories. Their stories, a combination
of written texts and images from popular media, described the complexity of immigration. Their stories ranged from humorous and imaginative to
deeply serious and even despondent. Through their narratives, they wove
sophisticated themes from social science education such as the impact of war,
economic disparity, capitalism, and globalization.

A salient finding from this experience was the importance of audience,
purpose, and utility when students and teachers do research (Falk & Blumenreich, 2005). I wanted to ensure that my students' work was given authority.
Consequently, we turned our classroom into a makeshift theatre where we
presented our digital stories to parents, students, teachers, and administrators
in what turned out to be quite a moving presentation. But the impact of their
narratives did not end there. The students' narratives led some of the individuals in power at the school to rethink what and how these students were
learning about being immigrants. After watching the presentation of these
narratives, the school staff had a discussion about how our mission statement
was vague in its description of immigrant education and subsequently revised
some of our school's "immigrant-focused" language. In addition, the school
decided not to adopt what we considered a poorly written standardized social
studies curriculum, a curriculum that had included a very superficial focus
on immigrant issues. It seemed that this action research project with students
as co-researchers had become a tool for social change.

Unexpectedly, the classroom-based research project went even further.
As a teacher researcher, I submitted our work to be shared at an education
conference at Harvard University. While only I attended the conference, the
students felt significant ownership and pride because their digital narratives

were presented. One student expressed the larger impact this project had on her future in a graduation letter to me:

> Mrs. Mehta, you taught me I could do anything even if it is hard. . . . You even took us to Harvard, and I'll never forget that I got to be a producer for our class stories! I mean I did not get to go with you, but I felt really proud of our immigrant project and that was one of my favorite moments in fifth grade. By the way, I thought we should have chartered a plane and taken our whole class, but thanks for the souvenir pencil anyways. Did you know I am going to go to Harvard to become a fashion designer and a lawyer one day? You can come visit me . . . (Letter excerpt from past student, June 2004)

Although this work proved to be important for individual students, as noted above, I also commented on the importance of this work for the larger school community during my presentation at the conference:

> My students and colleagues represent a microcosm of the diversity found in many of our urban schools. Their action research and insistence to ask tough questions about culture show their sincere efforts to claim authority, power, and voice to the meaning of diversity in the United States. These digital stories are not just samples of student work. . . . These narratives are examples of a community of students coming together to collectively state what they feel educators need to know. (Presentation, Harvard University, fall 2004)

Looking back on this second teacher research experience in urban Chicago, I noticed the various pressures associated with being a full-time teacher doing research versus a full-time researcher learning about teaching in New York. My research with the students in my own classroom was quite different from my research with high school students in Queens. Nonetheless, each project affirmed a commitment to using inquiry as a means to connect with the improvement of immigrant education. Teacher research had a great impact on me, both as an educator and as an advocate for social change. For me, as a developing scholar in education who was committed to the education of immigrant youth, teacher research was also a tool for creating a hybrid space where learning and teaching came together, no matter in which school context.

Boston, 2005–2008

A recent discussion of teacher burnout in my leadership course again pins me down as a generalization. The research says I fit the description of a teacher who teaches for 3 years and leaves. These teachers are described as tired and disenchanted and so they leave the classroom. But that's not me! I did not leave the classroom to become the researcher. I will not become a researcher who no longer describes herself as a teacher. . . . Can we get over this categorization of learner, teacher, researcher? . . . These identities live out within my cultural viewpoint and are part of my current and future narrative. . . . So, here again, I will find that space, make that space, for self, teacher, and researcher." (Journal, summer 2005)

I had more questions, and I needed more time to ask these questions. Becoming a teacher educator was important for the work I wanted to continue doing in the future. In 2005, I moved from Chicago to Boston to pursue doctoral studies in education. Once again, I was one of few nondominant students in a doctoral program in education. Through a rigorous exchange of ideas in my first course about research on teaching at Boston College, I was required to do an analysis of what the research on teaching had to say about a particular question of my own choice within the larger field. I initially considered this to be a completely academic and unfamiliar silent form of research, but later I came to think of it as an incredibly active form of teacher research. What was my burning academic question at this time? My students had asked the question "What is an immigrant story?" based on their reading and critiques of social science texts. Now, based on all the reading I was doing of research on teaching, I was asking, "Where are the 'Asian American' teachers in the research? Where are their voices?" I first began searching for research literature on Indian teachers, but I found absolutely nothing. Collecting and poring over any research I could find that had ever been published on Asian teachers meant being engaged in a much quieter form of teacher research. In the midst of long weekends and evenings spent in large libraries, sitting by myself among piles of journals, I described a feeling of being daunted:

This feels heavy, quiet, and lonely. From what I found, no one has ever done this review of research. I know many educators like myself, but they are not found in anything I've located. I wonder if I should accept this challenge and whether I am too personally impacted by what I find. I also wonder whether this process might describe findings important to teachers. Maybe one day someone will read what I found and feel validated that the question was even asked because the question mattered. Maybe making the question even matter begins by starting somewhere and that means starting here. . . . (Research journal, fall 2005)

Through this active yet subtle form of teacher research, I discovered that most of the literature on minority teachers' experiences focused on teachers who were labeled African American or Hispanic. By reading the research through the lens of cultural hybridity, I found that most research on minority educators reified simplistic cultural experiences. Although the research consistently called for increases in the number of minority teachers to parallel an increased population of diverse students in classrooms, very few studies recognized how teachers' experiences with race, class, gender, and language were based on their personal, contextual, and located experiences. In fact, nearly all of the studies asked questions that categorized the subjects of the research or the participants in the studies in terms of limited identity models.

While conducting this review of the literature, I was also struck by the strong connection between language and power. In order to critique the lack of complex discussions of minority teachers' experiences, I had to first appropriate society's powerful, though problematic, language. For example, although the term *Asian* was far too sweeping and generalized, I had to employ the term *Asian teachers* in order to search this area of research on teaching and teacher education. Although professionally and politically I wanted to take a research stance that did not appropriate "Asian teacher" language, I had to first assume the language of the field. From this inquiry about the research literature, one of my major findings was how language was at the center of reproducing culture, linking the undeniable connection of language, culture, and power. I realized as a result that in every moment as a future teacher researcher and teacher educator, I would have to consider how I was implicated in the language that I used, and how at the center of my work would be questions about the language used to describe immigrant youth. I summarized this in the conclusion of the literature review:

> The future of research on Asian teachers and teaching needs to move forward from the desperate calls for minority teachers and the analyses of how many Asian teachers are teaching. The perpetual question of why Asians choose not to teach overshad-

ows the actual Asian teachers who choose to teach. Often these teachers teach based on their beliefs of being social change agents. These Asian teachers can potentially share much insight into what they are experiencing in their classrooms each and every day. . . . Research can shift to include the unique nature, history, attitudes, beliefs, and experiences of specific Asian teacher experiences. Research studies thus far also fail to theorize the constructs that are used to describe issues around race, class, ethnicity, language, and gender. (Asian teacher paper, p. 25, fall 2005)

Since conducting this literature review, I have continued my process of gaining knowledge about teachers and teacher education. Now I can frame the problems and questions that I have through both the research of educators reporting their work in literature and teachers reporting their research out in the field. From this privileged position, I can now see the advantage of more than one type of knowledge construction. Inquiry as a stance was not simply a stage or step in my growing-up process as teacher and researcher. Instead, inquiry as a stance became the epistemological perspective through which I was able to make sense of the importance of my personal experiences, the richness of my learning and teaching experiences, and the necessity to see them serving each other in my work in education.

LOCATING CULTURE IN HYBRID SPACES: LOOKING TO THE FUTURE

I am satisfied by a summary of some of my "Indianness" taught through my spiritual upbringing, and now these merge with teaching and research. Three philosophical foundations: gnyan (knowledge), karma (action), and bhakti (selfless relationships) summarize my present understanding and work in teacher education. This philosophy, found in the roots and waters of my motherland, India, now orient me, ground me, and make sense in all of my social contexts, including the personal and professional.

Through teacher research, I have understood the importance of cultural hybridity as my own truth. Today, I find myself interrupting culture in my speech, in my writing, and in my teaching. My positionality as learner/teacher/researcher, a hybrid negotiation of the personal, professional, and political, gives me agency to perform the margins, and I won't apologize anymore. I am located in the muddy waters my mother described. . . . (Journal entry while traveling back home to India, summer 2007)

I have learned much about myself through the last 7 years of exploring the connections between self, teacher, and research and their relationships to culture. I have come to realize that it is potentially through the teacher research processes, paradigms, tools, conversations, and writing, as well as the building of relationships, that a more expansive and critical version of multicultural education can be explored. Today, I believe that cultural hybridity as a framework for making meaning of complex cultural lives is an important tool for the study of education. As our society becomes more diverse and less tolerant of vague or superficial identity markers, the role of critical multicultural educators will become even more vital. Although my story of teacher research cannot be generalized, it provides one example of the ability to describe pieces of the narrative in more complex ways and through a concept that brings together threads of culture, tying together some moments of explanation and leaving many questions still to be asked.

The muddy waters of my past, present, and future interactions with teacher research are precisely what bring together my mother's sage advice:

Betu [dear child], learning and education are not straightforward. Many of the lessons you uncover will be determined by your courage to dig deeper and ask complex questions. I'm not telling you this so that you do not become a teacher, I am telling you this so that you understand what teaching is—a muddy and complex journey.

After 7 years, a process that quite honestly is only a small beginning on the road to teacher research, I have come to a much deeper understanding of my mother's wisdom. Her letter, in itself, was a push for me to dive into a field with an insistence and commitment to go deeper, to get dirty and messy in the process, to actively play and learn with and through research, and to emerge, most importantly, a stronger and wiser woman committed to the education of all of my students searching for a hybrid space for self, teacher, and research.

REFERENCES

Asher, N. (2005). At the interstices: Engaging postcolonial and feminist perspectives for a multicultural education pedagogy in the South. *Teachers College Record, 107*(5), 1079–1106.

Bhabha, H. K. (1988). Cultural diversity and cultural differences. In B. Ashcroft, G. Griffiths, & H. Tiffin (Eds.), *The postcolonial studies reader* (pp. 155–158). New York: Routledge.

Bhabha, H. K. (1994). *The location of culture.* New York: Routledge.

Cochran-Smith, M., & Lytle, S. (1993). *Inside/outside: Teacher research and knowledge.* New York: Teachers College Press.

Falk, B., & Blumenreich, M. (2005). *The power of the questions: A guide to teacher and student research.* Portsmouth, NH: Heinemann.

Fine, M. (1994). Working the hyphens: Reinventing self and other in qualitative research. In N. K. Denzin & Y. S. Lincoln (Eds.), *Handbook of qualitative research* (pp. 70–82). Thousand Oaks, CA: Sage.

Maira, S. M. (2002). *Desis in the house: Indian-American youth culture in New York City.* Philadelphia: Temple University Press.

Nieto, S. (1999). *The light in their eyes: Creating multicultural learning communities.* New York: Teachers College Press.

Sarroub, L. (2001). The soujourner experience of Yemeni American high school students: An ethnographic portrait. *Harvard Educational Review, 71*(3), 390–414.

Stevens, L. P. (2005). Renaming "adolescence": Subjectivities in complex settings. In J. A. Vandeboncoeur & L. P. Stevens (Eds.), *Re/Constructing "the adolescent" sign, symbol, and body* (pp. 271–282). New York: Peter Lang.

Suarez-Orozco, C., & Suarez-Orozco, M. (2001). *Children of immigration.* Cambridge, MA: Harvard University Press.

Chapter 12

An Insider Voice:
Leading as a Teacher

Diane Waff

Diane Waff teaches at the University of Pennsylvania in the Graduate School of Education. Prior to joining the Penn faculty, Waff spent 3 years as a Senior Program Associate at WestEd in Oakland, California. She has extensive experience as a high school teacher, district and building administrator, K–12 teaching and learning coordinator, and teacher researcher. For over 2 decades, she has worked with teacher research communities as a convener and facilitator for the National Writing Project, the Bread Loaf Teacher Network, and Seeking Educational Equity and Diversity. She serves on the board of the Practitioner Inquiry Series for Teachers College Press and is the current Chair of the National Council of Teachers of English (NCTE) Secondary Section Steering Committee. Waff's active participation in local and national inquiry communities, such as the ones described in this chapter, allow her to continue to engage in research projects with school- and university-based colleagues.

My inquiry into the constraints and possibilities of school reform from my vantage point as an African American female teacher/leader/administrator working in the midst of school change initiatives centers on addressing the relationship among teacher knowledge, teacher practice, and how teachers learn (Cochran-Smith & Lytle, 1999). I explore how my work as a teacher researcher was influenced by participation in local teacher inquiry communities. These communities provided a safe space for the examination of familiar ways of thinking and the exploration of assumptions that have influenced my practice and my understanding of the social and cultural contexts that have shaped who I am, what I believe, and how I interact in the world both as a teacher and as a colleague. The changes that I identify in myself, as well as in my instructional practice, are linked to my participation in inquiry communities that have shaped and reshaped my knowledge as a professional. Access to these communities early in my career as a teacher influenced my perception of teachers as holders and producers of knowledge. This is politically significant because as my colleagues and I began to value what we as teachers know and do, we took responsibility for engaging in "systematic and intentional inquiry" (Cochran-Smith & Lytle, 1993, p. 7) with an eye to improving pedagogical effectiveness and school and classroom environments.

The narrative that forms the heart of this chapter was cultivated in three different inquiry communities—a cross-school teacher research community, a secondary community based on teacher leadership, and a school-based mathematics inquiry community. My story makes these communities visible and demonstrates the important role they can play in providing a safe place for teachers to share their practice and develop a sense of agency. It also describes the substantive, theoretical, and conceptual understandings arising from the inquiry and the importance they hold for advancing teacher practice and reform in schools and districts.

As I explore the educational landscape I traversed as an urban educator, I open up for reflection and examination the changes I made in myself and my pedagogy as I began to take into account the need to change curricula and methods to meet the needs of my students. As an African American educator, my own struggles to recover from the painful memories of childhood schooling experiences fueled my desire to interrogate and critique student underachievement by looking critically at my own classroom and how my actions influenced the lives of my students. My narrative illustrates how, as a teacher researcher, my sense of meaning about events experienced in schools changed as I constructed and reconstructed meaning in the company of colleagues from a range of backgrounds, teaching contexts, and experiences.

SETTING THE CONTEXT

When I think of my beginning experience as a teacher at Olney High School in Philadelphia, I recall a school steeped in traditions and practices that existed long before I arrived on the scene. Olney opened its doors in 1931. Despite changes in the student population and the world for which the students were being prepared, tracking was a tradition that continued. While the tracking that took place in the 1930s was in a largely homogeneous environment, in the 1990s race and class heavily influenced student ability placement at multicultural Olney. This was visible in the large numbers of African American and Latino students who swelled the rosters of general mathematics instead of advanced classes like geometry, algebra, and trigonometry. For several years, the significance of this tracking system remained invisible to me and many of my colleagues, although these inherited policies and practices marked our school experiences in particular ways on a day-to-day basis.

When I was hired to teach at Olney High School in 1985, I was elated because it was one of the city's largest, most culturally and linguistically diverse comprehensive high schools. Olney offered me the opportunity to work with students and faculty from a rich array of backgrounds and experiences. There were over 3,000 students at Olney, with approximately 225 teachers and school support staff. Unfortunately, there was little sense of community in this large, culturally rich school environment. Teachers had heavy teaching loads, and there was little opportunity for sharing or reflecting.

Any notions I had about meeting new colleagues, sharing ideas, collaborating, or just talking about students was not a part of the landscape. The rigid department structure, and the heavily tracked curriculum honed over the years, played a dominant role in creating and sustaining staff and student divides. "All are not created equal" was the message that these structures signaled to someone like me who was just beginning to learn the subtleties of the Olney context.

The content-area teachers, especially in English and mathematics, occupied the upper rungs of the academic ladder, along with Advanced Placement (AP) teachers and department chairs. They were the people who had been around for the longest period of time and who knew how things were supposed to work. They did a good job of maintaining the status quo and never entered into discussions that called any of the school's academic polices and practices into question. In fact, the only meetings that focused on teaching and learning issues were infrequently held department meetings. Teachers in these sessions talked to their content-area colleagues about what was best for the department and did not engage in discussion with colleagues from other disciplines. It was apparent that teachers did not have a schoolwide sense of responsibility for addressing teaching and learning issues outside of their discipline or department.

The special education teachers were randomly assigned to each department, so we never really had an official home. One experienced special education teacher whispered to me as we sat together in a mathematics department meeting, "The best way to survive is to keep your mouth shut and observe. If you say anything, you'll only be told that you teach 'special ed' so this discussion does not apply to you or your students." Over time, as I taught at Olney, I became increasingly dissatisfied with playing the role of the silent, invisible special education teacher. It became clear to me that, as a school, we needed to adopt a different vision of education for students, especially those who struggled academically.

THE PROMISE OF SCHOOL REFORM

In the late 1980s, a wave of high school reform swept across the city as a result of escalating attrition rates, academic underachievement, student discipline problems, and low staff morale. The school district of Philadelphia partnered with the Philadelphia Schools Collaborative to transform large comprehensive high schools like Olney into small learning communities. The traditional policies and structures that were failing poor and minority students in high schools across the city were scrutinized. Classroom teachers were invited to rethink what was happening in their classrooms, schools, and local communities as well as to think of themselves as agents of change. The grassroots, bottom-up nature of this initiative was unique because, for the first time, teachers were entering the conversation at the planning stage of a reform movement.

The Collaborative leadership decided that helping teachers to engage in critical inquiry would be a central part of transforming schools. The decision was made to invite the Philadelphia Writing Project, with the support of Susan Lytle and other university-based scholars and researchers from the University of Pennsylvania, to offer a seminar in teaching and learning. The seminar engaged teachers from three schools that served as pilot sites for the initial phase of reform. When the Olney principal presented the change plan to the staff, it really was not a hard idea to sell. With student–teacher ratios in classes often at 35:1, and teachers struggling to remember the names of the more than 165 students they saw daily, there was little resistance to a proposal that promised to reduce class size and give teachers an opportunity to get to know students. It also gave faculty an opportunity to build relationships with colleagues. As one teacher put it, "I have been teaching here for 20 years and I don't know the names of half of the people in this building. I think I would like to get to know the teachers I work with."

The flyer for the seminar promised "Cross-School Conversations, Collaborative Inquiry, and Teachers' Questions." The flyer really caught my attention. I was tired of attending staff development sessions where the district dispensed information and told teachers what to do without hearing our questions, our concerns, or our knowledge about the subject. This was an opportunity to be a thinking participant in something meaningful, not just a passive recipient of someone else's knowledge.

My journey as a learner in the seminar was anything but easy or automatic. Traveling this road was a new beginning, a chance to end the isolation from others and to take myself seriously. It was validating to hear teachers, especially special education teachers, engaged in critical dialogue about the social, emotional, and political dimensions of schools and schooling. My deficit-model teacher education program had not prepared me for this journey. I am indebted to the seminar community for encouraging me to question systems, to entertain multiple perspectives, and to rethink the very assumptions and processes that had become automatic for me as a special education teacher.

POLITICS OF LOCATION

During one of our early seminar sessions, we were asked to focus on our literacy histories. We were reminded by our facilitators of the importance of unearthing and understanding our own experiences to aid us in identifying possible supports and obstacles for our students' literacy development. To get us started on this journey of self-discovery, we were asked to share reflections on experiences with literacy at varied points in our lives. I recalled in a journal reflection what it was like going to school with little or no opportunity to see myself reflected in the curriculum and wondering, as a young Black girl, what people who looked like me had contributed to the world.

> I was an only child. I grew up in Philadelphia, attended Philadelphia public schools, and earned my undergraduate degree at the University of Pennsylvania. Although there were many positives in my early school experiences, there were many painful omissions in the curricula and discipline-based texts used in the schools during my formative years. The kind of knowledge seen as important did not include the writing of minorities, women, or members of society who were not politically well positioned. The perspectives that were taught reflected the cultural hegemony of the dominant group. The traditional canon did not allow for the integration of my voice as an African American female or the voices of my male counterparts into the classroom discourse. We were taught by culturally different instructors who privileged their knowledge by ignoring ours. While we were taught to read and write in the dominant discourse to gain the skills necessary to compete in American society, we were never encouraged to question what we read, to critically analyze the status quo, or to struggle with questions relating to the inequities we experienced in our everyday lives. Education was presented as the "Great Escape," not as the way to transform limiting real life conditions.

These painful memories made me think of my own students and the kinds of learning experiences I had been constructing for them. Adrienne Rich (1986) writes:

> When those who have the power to name and to socially construct reality choose not to see you or hear you . . . when someone with the authority of a teacher, say, describes the world and you are not in it, there is a moment of psychic disequilibrium, as if you looked in the mirror and saw nothing. It takes some strength of soul—and not just individual strength, but collective understanding—to resist this void, this non-being, into which you are thrust, and to stand up, demanding to be seen and heard. (p. 199)

The silences in my classroom about the realities of my students' lives positioned them as outsiders who were not able to use their stories and reflections to understand and make sense of the world. The highly structured classroom, the individualized folders, the constant reminders to stay on task and work independently were all used to separate the students from each other and inhibit social interaction. The social and personal dimensions of reading and writing together as a community were lost to my students because I was afraid to break away from old patterns of control and exclusion. What seemed to be missing in my classroom, which I found in the seminar, was an inclusive intellectual community that kept me attending seminar sessions year after year. Truly, the special world the seminar represented for me was not the world I had created in the classroom.

CO-PARTICIPATION AND CO-REFLECTION

One of the first things I learned about teaching at Olney was that there were few places to openly engage other teachers in conversations about issues we were struggling with in our teaching. Our time together in the seminar afforded us the opportunity of "breaking professional silence" (McDonald, 1992, p. 43), making our classrooms sites of critical reflection on issues of equality, justice, power, identity, and culture. As I gained new knowledge on critical pedagogy, I began to realize how my unvoiced personal beliefs were influencing my ability to apply this knowledge in my classroom practice. I shared the following journal entry with my journal response group:

> I grew up in the inner city, attended a predominantly Black high school, and lived in a neighborhood similar to that of my students. Yet I still feel a tremendous sense of separation from the students in my class. I do not understand how they can come to school without books, paper, or pencils. Their school performance is a sign that they do not give a damn about their education. Detentions, reprimands, and lectures are not able to reverse an "I don't care" attitude. My students just can't identify with my words, and I don't understand theirs.

Some White teachers couldn't understand how a Black teacher could have difficulty relating to students who shared racial co-membership. While many African American teachers understood my struggles, they questioned my decision to publicly share my tensions. One teacher said that if she didn't know me, she would question my right to call myself Black, because there was no place for class divisions within the Black community. It was inconceivable to some that achieving positive relationships with students and colleagues across difference both racial and otherwise was an ongoing challenge of reflective practice.

During the seminar we read Paulo Freire, Ira Shor, Bill Bigelow, Linda Christensen, Lisa Delpit, Joan Cone, Shirley Brown, and a host of other school- and university-based scholars and researchers. Their work inspired me to experiment with different methods of teaching. I was determined to move beyond the superficial worksheets that discouraged my students from making meaningful connections between their life experiences and course content. One vignette I shared at the end of my third year in the seminar illustrates the kind of transition I made as I crossed the boundary between teaching basic skills and taking myself and my students more seriously as learners and thinkers.

Gendered Perspectives: The Possibilities of Talk

It is Friday, and the Period 2 English class is about to begin. The students have just finished reading "Spilled Salt," a short story about the rape of a young woman by a man who offered her a ride home. The girls in the class, a mix of African American and Latina young women, begin pulling their chairs into a circle to begin our whole-group discussion of the text. The boys crowd in from the hallway, find seats, and fumble through their book bags for copies of the short story. Omar, a vocal student with a long white shirt and baggy pants, jumpstarts the discussion by stating, "Dress like a hooker, you get what you deserve." I pull up my seat, and ask, "Does the way you dress determine who you are or how you should be treated?" My question fuels lots of comments from male and female alike that begin to challenge sexism and demeaning stereotypes. Maritza, normally a quiet student, comments, "You should be able to wear what you want without fear of being groped or raped."

I constantly reiterate the norms for a text-based discussion such as talking one at a time, respecting each other, and using the text as a reference. The students engage in an impassioned discussion of what constitutes a "hooker" and what constitutes a "good girl," challenging the notion that a single woman without a man is sexually suspect or asking for trouble when she goes out alone. Brian, an African American male, questions, "Didn't her mother teach her not to get in a car with a stranger?" and is decisively answered by Tamika, a female student in the class, "Didn't his mother teach him not to rape people?" Omar, with some sheepish laughter, adds, "I guess you can't put it all on the woman either."

Another female student adds, "Yeah, why does the rapist's mother think she's responsible for her son's behavior? Why not put it on the abusive father?" At one point, Maritza quietly asserts, "It is the duty of fathers as well as mothers to teach their children." The discussion ends with a classroom of students labeled "special needs" beginning to question the universal perception that it is a female responsibility to teach moral behavior.

The students described in the vignette were engaged and were talking as much to each other as they were to me. Reading a story like "Spilled Salt" in a critical way was a departure from the decontextualized story excerpts found in most of my students' leveled readers. Date rape was a topic that had a real connection to their lives as young adults, and it certainly threw into sharp relief many of the gender issues faced by adolescents in Olney's special education program. As my colleagues and I discussed the lesson, I began to understand just how much I had used the special education label as an excuse for not nurturing intellectual curiosity and a desire for further learning. The discovery of my students' "incipient excellence" (Rose, 1989, p. 205) began a transformation in attitude, for me as well as my students, when I began to intellectually engage and challenge them.

As our dialogue proceeded, my vignette and others called attention to the way ability grouping and tracking reproduce societal social stratification patterns and inequalities. This was made painfully clear when Joan McCreary (1990), a math teacher at Olney, read her journal entry to the group:

> Why are African Americans so sparsely represented in elementary functions, algebra, and geometry [classes] in a school well over 60% African American? . . . It appears that a greater percentage of African American and Hispanic students are rostered to general math classes than any other groups. I would like to research this. I suspect the reasons this occurs fall into these four categories: Institutional racism, low teacher expectations, lack of proper counseling, and insufficient preliminary math preparation for the academic courses.

We listened to Joan dumbfounded. Why didn't we know Black and Latino students were being routinely routed to general math? Why hadn't we noticed the composition of the advanced math classes? What other kinds of tracking were taking place at the school? These kinds of questions really politicized the work of the seminar and caused all of the teachers to think critically about the need for continuous dialogue about teaching and learning across departments in our high school. As a staff, we were entering into new territory, raising questions, identifying pressing classroom- and school-based problems, and ending the isolation that had kept us in the dark and silent about many of the inequities in the educational program.

CAUGHT IN THE CROSSFIRE:
TEACHER LEADERSHIP AND DISTRICT POLITICS

After 6 years of working closely with colleagues at Olney to personalize student learning and build teacher collaboration by transforming our large comprehensive high school into small learning communities, the scene in the district changed dramatically. In 1994, when David Hornbeck became superintendent, he ushered in the second wave of reform, known as Children Achieving (CA), a systemic reorganization and standards-based reform agenda to restructure K–12 schools.

After CA had been under way for about 2 years, I decided to leave the classroom to join the professional development arm of the school district as a Teaching and Learning Network (TLN) Coordinator. I was given the responsibility of designing professional development and coordinating school-/ classroom-based support for approximately 700 teachers in nine schools in the northeast section of the city. I left the relational world of the school community where I had co-constructed knowledge with my students and colleagues to join the administrative ranks. I thought deeply about the inquiry community experiences that had led me to shift my stance toward collaboration and critical colleagueship. I wondered how I could draw upon what I had learned during my years at Olney in order to work with school staff from a totally different context, to build school and classroom environments that would have an impact on student achievement and teacher practice.

My work as an administrator in this new position was influenced by my participation in Project SOULL, a Study of Urban Learning and Leading, a monthly Philadelphia Writing Project inquiry community that met on Saturday mornings and focused on teacher leadership and school change. SOULL became the place where I discussed my experiences, questions, and struggles as I sought to build capacity and enable good practice in a school reform context complicated by issues of power, politics, race, and gender. After my first year in the TLN, I recognized the need to engage school staff in collaborative inquiry to raise critical awareness of diversity and its relationship to the beliefs, attitudes, and assumptions expressed by teachers toward children of color. I shared the following story during a SOULL session after writing about a dilemma in my practice.

Soon after I took the job as Teaching and Learning Coordinator in the northeast, a predominantly White working-class cluster, I was invited by a principal to discuss the schools' test scores and the district's accountability index. I stood in front of the elementary school faculty. The principal introduced me by saying that I would work with the staff to help them raise their test scores. The scores had been released to the paper, showing which schools in the cluster were below, at, or above proficiency levels in reading, math, and science. The principal was clearly upset that his school was outperformed in every category by other northeast cluster schools. The public documentation of scores put the staff on the defensive, and I was stunned by how quickly they were blaming the poor and minority students for the school's low performance. One teacher said, "How can we be held accountable for students who come from dysfunctional homes . . . students who come to school unable to read and write?" Another staff member said, "The neighborhood is changing and we will never be able to raise test scores with these students." And another particularly irritating comment from a recent college graduate: "They don't have any cultural capital. They already come to school with a distinct disadvantage."

As I listened, I was numbed by the statements I heard and saddened that many of the teachers truly believed that poor children could not learn. I, on the other hand, had my own doubts about the testing program. I thought about how disconnected the tests were from the students' lives and how strange the format was for many students. I also thought about how teachers who worked daily with students had been left out of the evaluation process. Yet I never doubted the students' capacity to learn. The politics of race and class reverberated in my head: the politics of who decides which students can learn, the politics of curriculum, the politics of what counts as cultural capital, the politics of [who "knowers" supposedly are] in the school system, and the politics of who tells whom what matters in the district. The inequities danced around in my head, but here I was charged with the responsibility to help the teachers at this school raise test scores.

I wondered how useful it would be to share the test scores of racially isolated schools in other parts of the city where poor and minority students are achieving (since they were ignoring the fact that other schools in the northeast with similar demographics were outperforming them—they dismissed this fact by saying the other schools were further north). Would it change the conversation?

Would the staff begin to question the goals they set for their students and the beliefs they hold about students they teach? Would giving this staff the opportunity to meet over time to engage in collaborative discussion, dialogue, and critique about their instructional program make a difference? Was I the right person to facilitate the conversation? Would I have the courage to raise the tough questions? The deficit rhetoric wore me down spiritually, and I left the meeting that day feeling defeated but still determined to find a way to work with teachers to develop strategies for change.

A colleague in my SOULL community asked, "Would anyone be right to facilitate in the face of such a set up?" Her question brought into immediate relief for me the issues of power and cultural dissonance embodied in my narrative. For many in the elementary school, I represented the poor, despised minority; for others, I was the district authority prescribing remedies and threatening sanctions. The discourse of deficit was powerfully illuminated in the use of the word *poor*. One SOULL colleague noted that she had heard two uses of the word *poor* in my narrative: one referring to class and the other describing minorities as "poor" things who can't learn. As a group, we wondered what it did to students of color to discover that in the eyes of many, they do not count as worthy, as already having cultural capital. The opportunity to write and share within SOULL helped me to begin to think in complex ways about my professional experiences from the multiple vantage points offered by other members of the inquiry community. Buoyed by the conversations in SOULL, I was able to return to the elementary school community determined to engage them in looking critically at school and classroom practices.

RETHINKING AND CHANGING PRACTICE

Cochran-Smith and Lytle (1993) argue that teacher inquiry is essential because the shifting demographics of U.S. schools make generic or behaviorist solutions to educational problems unworkable. In urban settings, students from diverse cultural and linguistic backgrounds fail in disproportionate numbers to meet academic expectations. Teachers commonly believe that most of these students lack the academic background or thinking skills needed to succeed in school. These negative perceptions all too often limit the teacher's ability to see and draw upon the considerable intellectual and social resources students of color bring to the classroom from their daily lives that could be leveraged for academic work. In my work with teachers in northeast Philadelphia, I learned the importance of making space in professional development sessions for personal reflection and writing/reading—as well as time to be in conversation with colleagues about their underlying beliefs and assumptions about race and cultural differences.

When I left Philadelphia to take a position as vice principal at a high school in Trenton, New Jersey, I discovered that when students did not meet subject-area teachers' expectations for performance on assignments, teachers often reduced their expectations and began to work around the texts in the classroom. As a result, students had less experience engaging academic tasks and their performance continued to decline. To arrest this cycle, I joined with the school leadership team to create a context for teachers in departments to engage in inquiry as a part of their ongoing teaching and to engage their colleagues in their inquiries.

FOCUS ON MATHEMATICS

I arranged for the mathematics teachers to meet on Saturdays to develop a new monitoring system to look closely at student performance in algebra. The leaders of the session included the math coach, the math point person, and a teacher who had attended the 2001 Leadership Institute in Reading Apprenticeship, a professional development experience that focused teachers on using literacy to support student learning in mathematics. At our third meeting, we were reviewing the results of the first assessment. The teachers were not happy with the results, so we looked closely at student performance item by item. We were surprised to find that some teachers were successful in teaching concepts like slope and others were not. What was it that made the students in Mr. C's class so successful and the students in the other classes struggle? The teachers invited Mr. C to teach a lesson. He was able to share with his colleagues how he was able to connect slope to popcorn, a horror movie, and spine-tingling scenes that directly influenced the rate of food consumption. He shared with his colleagues the thoughts that went into the planning of his lesson, why he made the choices he did, and how the students responded.

Looking back at my field notes, I noted my reluctance as a former English teacher to point out my difficulty in understanding a word problem. When several of the math teachers in the room voiced similar concerns, I felt affirmed. The experience deepened my understanding of how students feel when they are unable or afraid to voice a lack of comprehension. The teacher who developed the problem stood up and tried to give what he considered an easy way to find the solution, but I and a few others still did not understand. After hearing and interpreting our difficulties, the teacher reworded the problem, providing the group with a clearer understanding of the mathematics involved.

It became a routine in the group for the teacher who was presenting the lesson to continually step in and out of the instructional mode to talk to colleagues, hear diverse perspectives, talk about what he or she was doing in the lesson and why. Looking closely at our problem-solving processes helped us anticipate the difficulties students might encounter. These experiences began to have an effect on how teachers viewed the curriculum and the kinds of learning experiences they designed for students. A single lesson presented by one teacher often evolved into a series of lessons enacted in several classrooms.

As a community, they were beginning to feel comfortable questioning their own practices and that of their colleagues. They were teaching each other to teach while determining department-wide ways of interacting with students and communicating math content. The decision to teach a problem of the week, using strategies like "think aloud" and textbook annotation to help students who struggled to understand word problems, was unanimously reached. These teachers made a collective decision to implement change because they were a part of the culture of inquiry that drove the changes. The department members became much more reflective about their teaching and saw their inquiries as the starting point for instructional improvement efforts.

According to Lave and Wenger (1991), "learning involves the construction of identities" and becoming full participants in ongoing communities of practice (p. 53). The teachers in the math community were reinventing themselves as well as the department. As the words of this math teacher indicate, he was also beginning to identify with the larger institution in ways that he had not before. He wrote the following in a journal entry shared at a professional learning community (PLC) meeting:

> Walking through the halls early one preschool morning, I encountered a colleague with whom I have little or no interaction. As I was particularly "unencumbered," I offered the standard "Hello," and he responded in kind. Traveling together, I noticed he was carrying a program from an event that had taken place at one of our area's affluent high schools and inquired about it. This struck a chord with him, and he began to extol the wonderful experience he had at the school affair, as any proud parent would who had attended such an affair in which their children had taken part. Then

he added, "Now that's a real school." Somewhat mentally provoked by the comment, as we parted ways I heard myself say (good naturedly), "Well, fortunately, this is a *real* school, too" and continued down the corridor. (Journal reflection, 3/05)

He went on to share that he was troubled that his colleague did not seem to think that what was going on at Trenton High was worthy of being valued as "doing real school." As we discussed his reflection, we came to the realization that our thinking about the school as an institution changed as we began to see the institution reflected in the members of our community. We found that our definitions of "real teaching" and "real school" radically shifted as we took on more of the responsibility for what was going on in the school and within the district.

CONCLUSION

Educational researchers and scholars argue (Lipman, 1998; McIntosh & Style, 1994; Nieto, 1992) that standards implementation, decentralized decision making, schools within schools, flexible scheduling, and teacher teaming are not enough to enable urban students to succeed academically. It was the opportunity for sharing knowledge with colleagues in a community of inquiry that helped my colleagues and me to see systemically and take actions to create equitable classroom environments to support diverse learners. Cochran-Smith and Lytle (2006) argue "that there are critical relationships between teacher learning and student learning; that when teachers learn differently, students learn differently" (p. 689). From my experience, unless teachers experience something other than the banking model (Friere, 1971) of education in their own learning, they cannot create educational environments that foreground inquiry and exploration as key learning processes.

When I, as a teacher leader and later as an administrator, worked in collaboration with colleagues to change prevailing teaching practices in schools in Philadelphia and Trenton, we created safe organizational spaces where teachers felt comfortable tackling difficult pedagogical issues and exploring the social and cultural dimensions of teaching and learning. These experiences were often the starting place for teachers' inquiry into the debilitating factors that impacted student learning. The use of documentary processes (Carini, 1986), protocols, and other conventions for looking at practice were often painstaking, but they provided opportunities for teachers to hold ideas and interpretations out for scrutiny in a socially supportive environment.

I used my work in local inquiry communities as a resource to tackle challenging school problems and to bring diverse members of the school community together to problem-solve. Moving away from teaching as a private activity to one of collaboration and inquiry built a strong sense of professional identity among school staff and positively impacted staff and student learning. The critical examination of student work and instructional practice surfaced an awareness of what Nathan and Petrosino (2003) referred to as an "expert blind spot"—blindness to the developmental needs of learners. Gaining insight into what students needed to become more confident users and producers of knowledge in the disciplines prompted teachers to question their own practice and to accept being questioned about it.

Fundamental to school staff members beginning to learn differently in Philadelphia and Trenton was a willingness to learn about the blind spots, to engage in critical dialogue, and to develop new knowledge via interaction with others. Scholars have emphasized that systemic changes in education cannot have their intended effects without changes in "the core of educational practice—how teachers understand the nature of knowledge and the student's role in learning and how these ideas about knowledge and learning are manifested in teaching and classwork" (Elmore, 1996, p. 1). The establishment of teacher inquiry communities in schools focused on this core of educational practice brings teachers in relationship to the why, what, and how of education (Palmer, 1998) by addressing student needs, curricular factors, and the larger sociocultural dimensions that influence teaching and learning.

REFERENCES

Carini, P. (1986). *Prospect's documentary processes.* Bennington, VT: Prospect School Center.

Cochran-Smith, M., & Lytle, S. (1993). *Inside/outside: Teacher research and knowledge.* New York: Teachers College Press.

Cochran-Smith, M., & Lytle, S. (1999). Relationships of knowledge and practice: Teacher learning in communities. In A. Iran-Nejad & C. Pearson (Eds.), *Review of research in education* (Vol. 24, pp. 249–306). Washington, DC: American Educational Research Association.

Cochran-Smith, M., & Lytle, S. (2006). Troubling images of teaching in No Child Left Behind. *Harvard Educational Review, 76*(4), 668–697.

Elmore, R. F. (1996). Getting to scale with good educational practice. *Harvard Educational Review, 66*(1), 1–26.

Friere, P. (1971). *Pedagogy of the oppressed.* New York: Seabury.

Lave, J., & Wenger, E. (1991). *Situated learning: Legitimate peripheral participation.* Cambridge, UK: Cambridge University Press.

Lipman, P. (1998). *Race, class, and power in school restructuring.* Albany: State University of New York Press.

McCreary, J. (1990). *The miseducation of our children.* Unpublished manuscript.

McDonald, J. P. (1992). *Teaching: Making sense of an uncertain craft.* New York: Teachers College Press.

McIntosh, P., & Style, E. (1994). Faculty-centered faculty development. In P. Bassett & L. Crosier (Eds.), *Looking ahead: Independent school issues and answers.* Washington, DC: Avocus Publishing Inc. Retrieved March 1, 2005, from http://www.wcwonline.org/seed/development.html

Nathan, M. J., & Petrosino, A. (2003). Expert blind spot among pre-service teachers. *American Educational Research Journal, 40*(4), 905–928.

Nieto, S. (1992). *Affirming diversity.* New York: Longman.

Palmer, P. (1998). *The courage to teach: Exploring the inner landscape of a teacher's life.* San Francisco: Jossey-Bass.

Rich, A. (1986). *Blood, bread and poetry.* New York: Norton.

Rose, M. (1989). *Lives on the boundary.* New York: Penguin.

Chapter 13

Teacher Research as a Collective Struggle for Humanization

Gerald Campano

Gerald Campano was a full-time classroom teacher in Houston, Puerto Rico, and California's Central Valley and has worked with adult English language learners in North Philadelphia. He is currently an Assistant Professor at Indiana University, Bloomington. His research interests and publications address immigrant identities in the context of schooling, urban education, Filipina American studies, and teacher research. Throughout his work, Campano has been committed to creating opportunities for students to mobilize their identities and rich cultural resources in the literacy curriculum. Campano is a Carnegie Scholar and the author of Immigrant Students and Literacy: Reading, Writing, and Remembering. *He is currently participating in an inquiry community of urban teacher researchers in Gary, Indiana.[1]*

"Hey, there are people down here"—Ralph Ellison

Scholars have documented thoughtfully how the teacher research movement derives from its own contexts, intellectual lineages, and purposes for its work (Anderson & Herr, 1999; Cochran-Smith & Lytle, 1999a, 1999b). They have shown that although teacher research draws from a range of methodological approaches, it has an integrity of its own and should not strictly be expected to emulate more conventional or established research paradigms in education, whether ethnographic anthropology, discourse analysis, or the still-reigning quantitative positivism of the social sciences. In this chapter, I continue Cochran-Smith and Lytle's work of challenging the deeply held assumption that theory and practice occupy separate conceptual realms and of arguing for placing them in a more mutually generative dialectic. Specifically, I elaborate on two corollary propositions related to practitioner inquiry methodology that largely grew out of my own work as a teacher researcher and teacher educator. The first proposition is that teacher research involves a metatheoretical stance whose underlying ethical imperative is to respond to students in their full humanity and dignity and thus must be understood within the dynamism and life-world of the classroom. The second proposition is that when theorizing occurs in collectivities concerned with humanization, it becomes a form of practice that aims to create more just and equitable educational arrangements.

To illustrate the often fraught relationship between academics and community educators, I begin with a scene from Pierre Carle's (2001) documentary *Sociology Is a Martial Art*. Then, drawing from my experiences as a teacher researcher in a large, urban elementary school in California, I share a vignette that is meant to give a sense of the metatheoretical work of teaching: the ways in which the intellectual deliberations of practice are highly situational, improvisational, contradictory, and often uncertain. Next, I provide a brief account of my current work facilitating an inquiry community with urban teachers in northwest Indiana to suggest that what makes teacher research a unique and powerful form of inquiry is that it *moves* educational theory away from the spectatorial heads of individual academics or specialists and instead demonstrates how the process of theorizing can be the product of ongoing collaborative labor, often of school- and university-based educators working in solidarity to alter the material conditions of teaching and learning and liberate the fuller potentials of both students and teachers. I conclude by offering some initial methodological considerations for practitioner researchers who may see their work as a collective struggle for humanization.

SAID'S PROJECT: THEORY IS NOT GOD

Pierre Carles's (2001) documentary *Sociology Is a Martial Art*, about the acclaimed sociologist and public intellectual Pierre Bourdieu, provides an occasion to discuss the relationship between practice and theory. The penultimate scene of the film depicts Bourdieu and a panel of academics at a discussion and debate at a community center in a segregated and severely underresourced housing project in the suburbs of Paris. The topic is education and inequality, and the panel invites audience members to share their own stories. This appears to be an opportunity for the panel members to situate the community's experiences within a "larger" theoretical framework, including connections to global dynamics such as neoliberalism, migration, and the 1999 mobilizations against the World Trade Organization.

At the onset of the discussion, several residents convey their distrust of outside academics, researchers, and educators. Among them is an activist and teacher of 10 years, Said, who challenges Bourdieu to make his comments relevant to the community, to the actual people in the room. He questions the meaning of globalization protests in Seattle for local residents, asks who cares about the euro, and wants to know how things will change in the neighborhood once the evening's debate is over. Said goes on to poignantly recount inequalities and contradictions he has witnessed and experienced locally: the razing of green space, police brutality, racial profiling, constant surveillance, and the systematic underfunding of social services. Said expresses indignation that it is always those who are most vulnerable who have to make the concessions.

He provides testimony about individuals who have been victims of violence. Perhaps not surprisingly, his most pointed comments are reserved for the education system. He demands "real teachers," not individuals who are ready to leave the moment they enter the schools, doing their time in the projects so that they can be reassigned to more affluent districts. The young students sense this. Said explains that the ZEPs (zones of educational priority), a government label for areas in need of improved schooling, are more like zones of educational poverty. He closes his comments with the quip "Bourdieu n'est pas Dieu." Bourdieu is not God.

It becomes apparent that Said's critique is not an ad hominem argument against Bourdieu the individual. "Boudieu n'est pas Dieu" exposes and demystifies the aura of academic authority, which too often has been marshaled to legitimize oppressive social policies in the name of scholarship. The tension-filled scene captures what Susan Lytle (2000), borrowing a trope from Mary Louise Pratt (1991), has described as a "contact zone" between academics and community members, in this case educators who are from the neighborhood and have dedicated their lives to the neighborhood. Bourdieu does not respond defensively; rather, he engages Said in an intellectual dialogue. He agrees with much of Said's analysis and only takes issue with Said's pessimism that nothing can be done. He also encourages the crowd not to embrace anti-intellectualism by too readily forsaking the analytic tools academia may have to offer. During an informal conversation after the presentation, Said adopts a more conciliatory tone with Bourdieu. He mentions that he, too, is an aspiring sociologist, a "gutter sociologist." The film hints at a future collaboration.

I appreciate this film because it captures a productive exchange between a university researcher and a community educator. Bourdieu, emblematic of the high theorist, has stepped out of his university confines to participate in community organizing and activism. And Said, in his trenchant reading of the social conditions of life as an educator in one of the world's largest housing projects, both demonstrates and proposes the possibility of conducting inquiry from a location outside the academy, in particular one that has been historically the object of the academic gaze. The exchange, if not a synthesis of theory and practice, unsettles the distinction and puts them in more intimate proximity.

In this chapter I take as a point of departure an affirmation of Said's project that it is at once valuable and necessary to create the intellectual and structural conditions to support research and theory derived from marginalized communities and from practice. One of the most significant *interdisciplinary* contributions of the teacher research movement is its case for the epistemic status of agent inquiry. This has entailed a precise articulation of the relationships of "knowledge and practice" (Cochran-Smith & Lytle, 1999a) and a corollary redistribution of intellectual authority. Teacher research is produced primarily from a location that is distinct from, although often overlapping with, the academy—that is, the life-stream of the urban classroom that provides a potentially privileged emic vantage point from which to theorize the complexities of teaching and learning.

REVISITING THE COMPLEXITY OF TEACHING: VIRGIL'S JOURNEY

The following is an excerpt from my field notes as an urban 5th-grade teacher researcher:

> Today I was summoned to the office to meet a new student, Virgil. This was unusual. In our large and stressed district with its revolving mobility rates, I am usually not made aware of new students until they appear at my door, often somewhat lost with crumpled admissions slips. I knew there must be something unique about Virgil's situation. In the office Virgil stood with the principal, his brother, and his mother. I was introduced to the family. As they gathered their belongings in the hallway, I was informed that my class was Virgil's "last chance" in the district. He had already been expelled from several schools and was just "released" from a school where they put students who have trouble "adjusting" to "regular classrooms" and that he was still learning about the "consequences of his actions." It was acknowledged that my class was already overcrowded but reiterated that I could "trade out" another student to another teacher if I'd be willing to work with Virgil.

I share this vignette in order to unpack what is involved and at stake in such a moment. It was immediately clear to me that by the age of 11, Virgil had already developed a conflictual relationship to schooling. He came to my classroom with a bureaucratic trail of paperwork that documented his "at-risk" status. One would not need to have studied Foucaultian critical discourse analysis to realize Virgil was already enmeshed in an oppressive language that anticipated a criminalized identity. As many activists have pointed out, injustices are often rather obvious, especially to those who experience them daily. Graeber (2004) discusses an "inner-scream" that alerts us to oppression, and I remember my own inner-scream at the moment of meeting Virgil, thinking to myself "My God, why is this child already so marginalized by the educational system?" It is also important to understand this moment as contact between group histories as well as personal histories. Virgil claimed multiple heritages, including African American and Filipino. He was born into an educational system that has historically failed communities of color. At the same time, he was also part of family and community struggles to break down educational barriers and enlist schooling as a vehicle for personal and social empowerment. He would eventually draw on these legacies in his academic work.

While these larger critical and social issues informed my initial reading of the situation, as a teacher researcher there were more immediate concerns to be considered that had to do with the ethics of response, practice, and the organization of classroom life. These concerns went far beyond traditional preformulated research questions, such as "What reading approach works best for 'high-needs' student populations?" or even "What are the homologies between the social and discursive construction of the 'struggling student' and the 'juvenile delinquent'?" There are also the activist's questions, equally conceptual and compelling, that arise from the day-to-day and must be grappled with at least partially in the moment, even before the point of full articulation. In the back of my head, I was probably wondering something like the following: What combination of structure and openness will communicate to Virgil that he can trust me to take his education seriously? Why would he even trust me? How can I provide Virgil with the requisite attention he deserves as a new member of our classroom community without exhausting energy for my other 35 students? Who in our classroom community might take a leadership role in making Virgil feel at home? When and how do I productively take issue with the idea that students are "tradeable"? What types of direct and indirect actions can I take to ensure that our school does not target Virgil for expulsion? And I was also wondering how, at that very moment, my other students were doing with the somewhat mean-spirited adult sent to watch them while I was in the office.

Of course, there were also urgent curricular issues, which would ultimately boil down to the following: What educational pathways will be most conducive to Virgil's intellectual flourishing? It is worth a momentary diversion to point out that there is no shortage of ideas regarding this curricular question. Many university-based researchers and educational experts have spent large portions of their careers arguing for a certain abstract and grand idea, often in direct opposition to another abstract idea that another expert is certain of (e.g., child-centered vs. teacher-centered pedagogy, skills vs. holistic instruction, etc.). These ideas often spawn a host of bureaucratically sanctioned social types (e.g., the "at-risk student," "children of poverty," the "English language learner," the "gifted and talented student,") and concepts (e.g., "stereotype threat," "critical literacy"), which all have attendant pedagogical implications.

My research and teaching lens is informed by the tradition of philosophical realism, which suggests that even though our understandings of social phenomena are invariably theoretically mediated, they may yield more or less reliable epistemic access to a world that exists independent of our constructions. I believe that these categories and social types are neither absolute truth nor merely ideological mystifications. They must be argued for, tested, revised, and modified in the life-stream of empirical situations. A teacher who adopts an inquiry stance into practice is thus engaged in the infinitely complex and never-ending task of adjudicating between various categories and concepts, deciding which ones to provisionally accept (e.g., "stereotype threat" seems a useful and valid concept), which ones to resist as damaging social distortions (e.g., the notion of "at risk" pathologizes individuals), which ones to push up against (e.g., who decides what constitutes critical literacy?), and which ones to consider with a grain of salt (e.g., aren't we all English language learners?). Perhaps most importantly, these ideas are understood in relationship to the teacher's own ever-evolving conceptual understandings derived from classroom life, her or his singular relationships to students, and the local knowledge of the community. Finally, teachers take action based on their interpretations, which engender new experiences, which, in turn, shape the conceptual landscape. In many urban schools and communities, these deliberations occur within severe structural constraints (e.g., overcrowded classrooms, students without adequate health care), under conditions of unremitting pressure and duress (e.g., the punitive measures of No Child Left Behind and the high-stakes testing paradigm), while negotiating the realpolitik of school districts, and in the face of occasional forces that shake the school day (e.g., lockdowns, the death of students' family members from poverty-related causes, a teacher's own personal hardships and life tragedies). These conditions are all part of the intricate causal web of teaching and learning and are not isolatable or easily factored out in the interest of distilling monocausal explanations.

WE ARE ALL OUTLIERS:
INQUIRY AS A METATHEORETICAL STANCE

It is here that we can begin to see a less hierarchical and rigid distinction between theory and practice than is commonly assumed. Through a certain academic lens, Virgil would have been considered an outlier. The regular school arrangements, and the theories that undergird them, were not working for him. But, in another sense, theoretically speaking, are not we all outliers of theory? That is, our multifaceted existences are often not contained by the abstractions we use to explain them. Virgil could not easily be understood as "at-risk," with its attendant deficit ideology and remedial instructional implications. And there really was no one-to-one correspondence between codified academic abstractions, such as "scientifically based reading research" or "culturally appropriate curriculum," and Virgil's own living, breathing intellectual journey, during which he would continually take in a range of influences to cultivate his own critical perspective, discover different aspects of himself, and realize new potentials.

This proposition, however, isn't limited to Virgil or to any individual student who has been mislabeled. All students, even those deemed "mainstream" or "successful," are stymied with respect to certain capacities because of the compromises entailed in progressing through school. Echoing Sonia Nieto's (2006) recent indictment of labeling in education, we can say that there are limits to categorizing-based theories. Or, to invoke Ralph Ellison and the epigram at the beginning of this chapter, we can point out that there are "people" beneath our almost ubiquitous top-down theories and categories. Rather than employing academic theories to put students' experiences in boxes, to develop generalizable laws (the positivist ideal associated with many quantitative approaches), or to discover an underlying cultural logic of behavior (the ethnographic inclination), I believe that teacher researchers improvise on theories in the process of acting in order to create the conditions for new and varied types of student flourishing. This process is procreative rather than merely analytical.

Doing research from the location of practice is therefore not about using abstractions to explain student behavior. It is also not a matter of "putting theory into practice" and is much more than merely being reflective. Adopting an inquiry stance involves a larger, metatheoretical position where theory takes on a pluralistic quality and pragmatically exists in a dynamism with practice in order to unleash student (and teacher) potentials. Analogous to a jazz impulse, an inquiry stance involves experimenting with a variety of forms in the constant flux and flow of classroom life and culture in order to generate new possibilities. And as I have suggested elsewhere (Campano, 2007), teacher inquiry is partially speculative research because it is about a larger process of imagining alternatives for students who have been most vulnerable in our schools.

What alternatives were imaginable for Virgil? In retrospect, it became clear that Virgil's literacy curriculum began almost immediately after our initial meeting, during our walk back to the classroom. As I explained that our class was in the midst of learning about the poetry of William Blake, Virgil and I discovered a shared admiration for Maya Angelou's "I Rise." Later in the day, Virgil sent me a poignant note recounting some of his previous frustrations with schooling and asking me if I would trust him. Part of my inquiry stance involved valuing students' experiences as intellectual resources and honoring their "epistemic privilege," defined as a special vantage point from which to analyze inequality due to their social locations (Moya, 2001, p. 38). Epistemic privilege also acknowledges students' fundamental capacities to make rational sense of and theorize their own lives. I came to understand that Virgil had a very rational suspicion of institutional authority, including school authority. He initially had trouble even being in the same room with our 5th-grade D.A.R.E (Drug Abuse Resistance Education) officer. Virgil and I began to co-construct, through almost a consensus model, a literacy curriculum around his own experiences and emerging interests. He cultivated a passion for Glenn Gould, and while listening to his rendition of the *Goldberg Variations*, Virgil would remain in class long after the recess bell rang to pen his ideas on paper. I believe writing became for Virgil one cultural outlet for oppositional impulses and a vehicle to explore profound social and ethical issues. Virgil composed critical essays on the criminal justice system, wrote a fantasy about a corrupt political leader, and developed a piece of realistic fiction entitled "The Struggling Life of a Young Boy," which was very much in the naturalistic spirit of Richard Wright and which won him accolades in a school district author contest. Virgil continued to endure constant surveillance by people in our school who I believe were hoping to catch him "messing up" so he could be expelled. But there were a number of caring adults as well, including a literacy specialist born and raised in the neighborhood, who on several occasions tactically intervened on Virgil's behalf to make sure he would have a consistent education. There was also a professor from a local university who introduced Virgil to the African American literary canon. The year after he was in my class, in sixth grade, Virgil had an amazing teacher with high expectations, and his academic identity continued to flourish.

I am not sure how Virgil negotiated middle school, but it is important to note that the conceptual and material project of altering his educational

trajectory during his last 2 years of elementary was in part a collective endeavor. I had often experienced teaching as an individual struggle, both the
successes as well as a persistent questioning of my own insufficiencies. In
retrospect, I understand how Virgil's process of educational becoming could
not be plotted a priori by educational researchers. There were many conditions that may have contributed to or been sufficient cause for Virgil's turn.
I had begun to see my job as working in solidarity with Virgil, situating
his relationship to schooling within group histories of resistance as well as
my own teaching within a Filipino American family legacy of social justice
and a struggle for educational access. I also learned from my colleagues
who combined high expectations for children with alertness to how schools
can be racist, classist, and can scapegoat individuals. Other students in our
classroom provided a safe space for Virgil to display his intellectual and
academic curiosity. Finally, Virgil himself was the most important agent of
change, knowing how to recruit support but also when to push back against
a structure that had been dehumanizing. We were all developing conceptual
frameworks in order to negotiate constraints and see opportunities.

THE "INVISIBLE" POLITICAL WORK OF TEACHING

The collective work of advocating for Virgil hovered beneath the radar of
official school collaboration. It probably occurred in this clandestine manner
for several reasons. First, it was a transgressive pedagogy to the extent that
the alternative curriculum we built went against district mandates, which
were largely standardized, prescriptive, and remedial. Second, there was no
professional development infrastructure to support rich collaborative discussions about individual students. Finally, the educators who were interested in
supporting Virgil and creating different options with him, including myself,
were probably just too busy to organize. The vignette I shared about Virgil
was just one moment in a seemingly endless stream of issues, injustices, and
challenges that are part of the daily phenomenon of urban teaching. With
so many social justice issues to attend to and so little time in the teaching
day, advocating for students must become integrated into everything one
does in the classroom, rather than being thought of as merely an additional,
separate realm of activism. Teachers find colleagues who share a similar set
of principles, and when opportunities arise, they take action together. Sometimes these actions are more momentous, such as when teachers in my district
protested the dismantling of bilingual education. But more often than not,
they are inconspicuous, part of the everyday invisible political work of urban

teaching. It is commonplace for university-based teacher educators with a progressive orientation to lament that teachers are politically passive and do not take stands against dominant educational policies. This view has some merit. But I would suggest that many committed urban teachers engage in everyday acts of resistance that may not always be intelligible to those who are not immersed in what Maria Lugones (2003) might call the "world of sense" of urban schools and communities.

BEYOND CRITIQUE:
COLLECTIVE INQUIRY AND TRANSFORMATION

What happens when teachers, administrators, and researchers across institutional boundaries organize in a more systematic and intentional way to enact a vision of educational justice? There are many examples of university–school partnerships and inquiry communities where participants bring their varied perspectives and experiences together in order to grapple with some of the most challenging issues, such as tracking, teaching across cultural and linguistic boundaries, and finding rich curricular spaces outside prescriptive mandates. I am beginning to apprehend the potential of this type of collective endeavor through my participation with an inquiry community in a school in northwest Indiana. The school is a public all-boys academy that serves several of the most impoverished neighborhoods and housing projects in the state. The teacher researchers and administrators at the school decided to (re)imagine a literacy curriculum that honors the students' heritage and literary traditions. They recently decided to revamp an empty classroom and turn in into a Writers House, where the boys could create a range of texts as well as make them public to larger audiences.

What has been most edifying for me about the collaboration is that many of the teachers and administrators are themselves from the community. They are quite familiar with educational inequality and have recounted powerful personal narratives about overcoming low expectations as well as structural barriers such as segregation. These "salient herstories" (Lytle, 2006) shape their inquiry stances. For example, there is very little "deficitizing" of families, and no one ever suggests that the students are anything but absolutely capable of success if provided what one participant called the "freedom to learn." The teachers' experiences may be "raw," if raw implies close to the concrete realities of the neighborhood and community. But they certainly are not raw in the sense of being "prereflective," "naive," "ungeneralizable," "unconscious," "falsely conscious," "undertheorized," or whatever other esoteric barbs those of us in the academy sometimes throw down to mark our own territory. Quite the contrary, their experiences are always already theoretically imbued and are often a repository for accretive personal and collective wisdom. They enable the participants to read the subtle and not so subtle permutations of racism and classism in the students' lives and learning. But perhaps more importantly, their shared understandings create the conditions for action. They do not need to expend intellectual energy merely demystifying or debunking power dynamics. The prerogative is to go beyond critique, to do something.

At a ribbon-cutting ceremony to celebrate our university–school district partnership, an administrator introduced the opening of the Writers House at the boys academy by announcing that it would be a space where the students will be able to "display their creative genius." Soon after, the boys themselves took the audience through the writing process and then recited incredible verses about their neighborhoods, families, and legacies, inspired by George Ella Lyons's "Where I'm From," a poem made popular in schools by the teacher researcher and critical educator Linda Christensen (2000). The students' words, in a sense, spoke for themselves, defying stereotypes about urban boys' supposed reluctance to write, refusal to invest in education, or lack of interest in the humanities. Their creative genius was on display.

KNOWING ABOUT THE WORLD INVOLVES KNOWING HOW TO CHANGE IT

During a recent talk at Indiana University, Patti Lather reminded the audience that each kind of research methodology must be understood and evaluated within its own logic and politics. What are the logic and politics of teacher research? In this chapter, I have provided several initial examples to illustrate how teacher research involves an ineluctable twinning of theory and the activism of teaching. At the heart of this project is the insight, theorized eloquently by the literary critic Satya Mohanty (1997), that an important part of knowing about the world involves knowing how to change it. Teacher researchers throughout North America, sometimes individually but more often in inquiry communities, are generating knowledge of practice in their local contexts in order to change the world by "teaching better" (Lytle, 2008). Teaching better, as we have seen, involves much more than honing an instructional practice, although this certainly may be part of the work. As I hope my examples have suggested, teaching better involves constructing, mobilizing, and modifying theories in sites of practice in order to unleash the fuller potentials of students.

This is quintessentially political and transformative research. In many urban contexts, teacher researchers have to resist and undo the damage of certain educational research and policies that dehumanize youth. These include labeling practices that circumscribe students' educational experiences; accusations that "children in poverty" somehow think less abstractly and do not understand "cause and effect" or the consequences of their actions; and the appallingly inequitable distribution of educational resources—to name just a few. As many individuals who spend their lives in classrooms know, there certainly are people beneath these abstractions and generalizations. Some of the most poignant examples of teacher research are at heart accounts of how, as the activist and hip hop artist Michael Franti (2001) might say, to "Stay Human" in teaching conditions that emphasize numbers over people, ends over means, and control over possibilities. At best, teacher researchers go beyond critique to offer more humanistic alternatives, ones that provide students the freedom to participate in processes of educational self-determination and becoming. This emphasis on humanization places teacher research squarely within Freirian traditions. But many teachers see their work as heir to other legacies as well, such as the African American civil and human rights movements, a link that has been made explicitly by my teacher researcher colleagues in northwest Indiana and members of Philadelphia's project SOULL (Study of Urban Learning and Leading), a groundbreaking teacher inquiry community dedicated to advocating for urban adolescents (Lytle, 2006). I hope that teacher researchers also find common cause with the immigrant rights movement, because the idea that some populations are categorically "illegal" and should therefore be denied basic rights is an extreme form of objectification: a linguistic dehumanization of many who are already dehumanized by the economic system and exclusion from the civic community.

As an emerging intellectual and activist movement, teacher research entails some very different methodological considerations than more dominant research paradigms. I do not wish to be prescriptive or circumscribe the genre of teacher research. Given the location from which this scholarship is conducted and its particular logic and politics, I would like to offer several interrelated potential qualities of teacher research that may help define its relative autonomy from other forms of inquiry and thereby clarify its contributions to the field of education. My concern is that if we do not continue to make a case for what makes this form of emic inquiry unique, teacher research will be evaluated by criteria ill suited to its project of student self-determination.

1. *Teacher research as personal.* Both teachers and students invariably bring their identities into the classroom. Teachers cannot shed or transcend

their own social locations in pursuit of an unobtainable notion of neutrality. And they probably need to do more than simply "come clean" about their identity markers or political commitments in the beginning of their work. Instead, they may make visible how their culturally influenced perspectives and values are imprinted throughout their research. Cynthia Ballenger's (1999) groundbreaking *Teaching Other People's Children* offers a wonderful example of how a teacher uses research to unearth her own presuppositions in order to arrive at more nuanced understandings of the literate work of her Haitian preschool children.

2. *Teacher research as an ongoing process.* Ideally, adopting an inquiry stance is ongoing, or, as Susan L. Lytle has described, part of the "air teachers breathe" (personal communication). I believe this stems from the fact that teaching itself is humbling. A teacher who systematically and intentionally investigates her practice may develop a heightened sense of fallibility, which is at odds with the premium placed on certainty in the academy or "definitive findings." The progress of teacher researchers may be more Sisyphean than linear, marked less by conventional professional signposts than by a larger commitment to actual people and to change, whose fruits may not ripen in any foreseeable future. As long as students are disenfranchised because of their identities, the work of the teacher research movement should continue. I think, for example, of the teacher researcher Rebecca Akin, who has been investigating her practice for decades and writing lengthy accounts of this work, often in the absence of institutional support. Akin has been motivated by a sense of urgency to help improve the educational opportunities of her Oakland students.

3. *Teacher research as a process of intersubjective knowledge production.* What makes teacher research an intellectually robust form of inquiry is that it values multiperspectival understandings of teaching and learning and the local knowledge of teachers, students, and community members. Teacher researchers learn from their students, disrupting the traditional research dichotomy between those who know and those who are studied and foregrounding the epistemic significance of relationships. Representations of teacher research might capture this process of learning from others. For example, the teacher researcher Marsha Pincus (2005) describes how her inquiries develop from classroom "dissonances," which are often an intellectual challenge from a student that prompts her to rethink her practice. Elizabeth Cantafio (2002) refrains from framing the voices of her community

college students in terms of esoteric academic categories. Instead, she quotes her students in order to deepen her own understandings, affording their voices the same epistemic status as an academic citation.

4. *Teacher research methods as arising organically out of the interactive and relational context.* Since knowledge is generated in the process of shared action—not "discovered" or "extracted" from a static site—it makes sense that the methods for inquiry are part of the life-stream of the classroom. In my own work with immigrant, migrant, and refugee students in California, stories became our primary mode of inquiry. I employed the efficacy of narrative—rather than, say, more artificially imposing a series of structured or semistructured interviews or a survey—because, given the space, my students often shared very powerful stories about their experiences crossing cultural and political boundaries. These stories raised profound social and ethical issues that became part of our literacy curriculum. I also needed to piece together and critically reflect on aspects of my own family's migrant history, often passed down anecdotally, in order challenge some of my own presumptions and to better relate to my students. Narrative thus became a classroom practice, a research method, and a means of representing my scholarship.

5. *Teacher research as a form of prefigurative pedagogy.* Some of the most powerful teacher research does not merely analyze classrooms and students. It also aims to change education for the better. The faculty and students at the boys academy resisted the pervasive discourse of deprivation of urban youth and communities by embodying and enacting an alternative through the Writers House. In the process of critique, they prefigured a new educational world literally in the shell of the old. What I am calling prefigurative pedagogy is inspired by the activist term *prefigurative politics.* It suggests that pedagogy needs to go beyond critique to enact more liberatory educational arrangement more conducive to full student flourishing.

In the debate portrayed in the documentary I described at the opening of this chapter, Pierre Bourdieu commented that the "best hope" for change is to organize into a social movement. His call resonates with another, more recent documentary, *Granito de Arena* (Freidberg, 2005), or *Grain of Sand,* which tells the story of the grassroots struggle of educators in southern Mexico to resist the neoliberal privatization of the school system. The teachers in the region have a long history, rooted in indigenous rights, of advocating for poor and marginalized communities. One activist interviewed in the film comments that public mobilizations have been essential for the survival of the schools. But he also suggests that a pedagogical revolution is needed in addition to a social revolution. What good are the lofty human rights ideals professed on the streets if they are not mirrored in classroom practice? How can educators better meet the people's needs and their aspirations? How can teachers teach better and in a more relevant fashion?

North of Mexico's border, there still does not seem to be much of a social revolution. But in school districts across the United States, often in partnership with colleges and universities, there are many localized pedagogical revolutions where communities of educators are theorizing from practice and creating educational arrangements "from the ground up" that are more conducive to the fuller human potentials of their students. This collective work may be education's best hope.

NOTES

1. I would like to acknowledge the Center for Research and P-16 Collaboration at Indiana University for support of the Watson Teacher Research Inquiry Community. I would also like to thank Rob Simon and Gregory Wolmart for their thoughtful feedback to an earlier draft of this chapter.

REFERENCES

Anderson, G., & Herr, K. (1999). The new paradigm wars: Is there room for rigorous practitioner knowledge in schools and universities? *Educational Researcher, 28*(5), 12–21.

Ballenger, C. (1999). *Teaching other people's children: Literacy and learning in a bilingual classroom.* New York: Teachers College Press.

Campano, G. (2007). *Immigrant students and literacy: Reading, writing, and remembering.* New York: Teachers College Press.

Cantafio. E. J. (2002). *"What we would perish without": Response and responsibility in developmental education.* Unpublished doctoral dissertation. University of Pennsylvania, Philadelphia.

Carles, P. (Director). (2001). *La sociologie est un sport de combat* [Documentary]. New York: First Run/Icarus Films.

Christensen, L. (2002). *Reading, writing, and rising up: Teaching about social justice and the power of the written word.* Milwaukee, WI: Rethinking Schools.

Cochran-Smith, M., & Lytle, S. L. (1999a). Relationship of knowledge and practice: Teacher learning in communities. In A. Iran-Nejad & C. Pearson (Eds.), *Review of research in education* (Vol. 24, pp. 249–306). Washington, DC: American Educational Research Association.

Cochran-Smith, M., & Lytle, S. L. (1999b). The teacher research movement: A decade later. *Educational Researcher, 28*(7), 15–25.

Franti, M., & Spearhead. (2001). Stay human. On *Stay human* [Audio CD]. San Francisco: Six Degrees.

Freidberg, J. I. (2005). *Granito de arena* [Documentary]. Seattle: Corrugated Film.

Graeber, D. (2004). *Fragments of an anarchist anthropology.* Chicago: Prickly Paradigm Press.

Lugones, M. (2003). *Pilgrimages/peregrinajes: Theorizing coalition against multiple oppressions.* Lanhan, MD: Rowman & Littlefield.

Lytle, S.L. (2000). Teacher research in the contact zone. In M. Kamil, P. Mosenthal, P. D. Pearson, & R. Barr (Eds.), *Handbook of reading research* (Vol. 3, pp. 691–718). Mahwah, NJ: Erlbaum.

Lytle, S. L. (2006). The literacies of teaching urban adolescents in these times. In D. E. Alvermann (Ed.), *Reconceptualizing the literacies in adolescents' lives* (pp. 257–278). Mahwah, NJ: Erlbaum.

Lytle, S. L. (2008). At last: Practitioner inquiry and the practice of teaching: Some thoughts on *better. Journal for Research in the Teaching of English, 42*(3), 373–379.

Mohanty, S. (1997). *Literary theory and the claims of history: Postmodernism, objectivity, multicultural politics.* Ithaca, NY: Cornell University Press.

Moya, P. (2001). *Learning from experience: Minority identities, multicultural struggles.* Berkeley: University of California Press.

Nieto, S. (2006). The limitations of labels. *Language Arts, 84*(2), 171.

Pincus, M. (2005). Learning from Laramie: Urban high school students read, research, and reenact *The Laramie Project.* In T. Hatch, D. Ahmed, A. Lieberman, D. Faigenbaum, M. White, & D. Pointer Mace (Eds.), *Going public with our teaching* (pp. 147–165). New York: Teachers College Press.

Pratt, M. L. (1991). Arts of the contact zone. In P. Franklin (Ed.), *Profession 91* (pp. 33–40). New York: Modern Language Association.

Part III

PRACTITIONERS' VOICES

In 1993, in conjunction with the publication of *Inside/Outside: Teacher Research and Knowledge* (Teachers College Press), we organized the first performance of Practitioners' Voices, which was held at the Ethnography in Education Research Forum at the University of Pennsylvania. Participants were authors of the journals, oral inquiries, classroom and school studies, and essays that made up the second part of *Inside/Outside*. Subsequently, similar performances, with some additional participants, were given at the annual meeting of the American Educational Research Association (AERA), the annual meeting of the Holmes Group, and at the National Center for Restructuring Education, Schools, and Teaching (NCREST) at Teachers College, Columbia University. The new version of Practitioners' Voices that is included in this book was first performed at AERA in 2008[1]. Based on audience requests for the script and evident interest among audience members in mounting similar efforts in their own educational settings, we decided to publish it in this volume.

The script draws on excerpts from the work of 20 practitioners who work or worked in K–12 schools and colleges in Philadelphia, Boston, California, New Jersey, Tennessee, and New York. (Note: All of the chapters in Part II of this volume were written by practitioners who took part in this performance.) Each of the participants in the presentation contributed classroom snapshots, vignettes from practice, journal entries, excerpts from interactions with students, reflections, and commentaries, which were intended to invite listeners into the inquiries they had undertaken about their practices and their theories of practice. Many of the excerpts in the readers' theatre script emerged from the work of practitioner research groups or were developed initially for local publications, conferences, and graduate courses and programs. Several were written with no audience in mind other than the practitioner herself or himself. These individual voices and perspectives were braided together into a collaborative performance that evidences the range and variation and the generative potential of practitioner inquiry at all levels of practice, from K–12 teaching and administration, higher education, teacher education, and other educational work. The script juxtaposes related and contrasting perspectives on practitioner research and makes visible some of the many personal, professional, and political decisions and struggles practitioners face every day in their work in classrooms, schools, and other educational contexts.

★ ★ ★

We have listed below the participants in this performance. Following each participant's name is the position from which he or she wrote in the excerpts used in script. If the participant's current position and/or institutional affiliation is now different, it is listed in brackets. Rebecca Akin and Gerald Campano co-edited this script and wrote the Afterword, which follows the script.

Rebecca Akin (Script Co-Editor): 1st-grade teacher, Korematsu Discovery Academy, Oakland Unified School District. [Doctoral candidate, Stanford University.]

Alan Amtzis: Director, Master of Education Program in Educational Leadership: Instruction, The College of New Jersey.

Joan Barnatt: 7th-grade social studies teacher. [Professional Development Coordinator/Mentor Supervisor, Cape Cod Lighthouse Charter School; doctoral candidate, Boston College.]

Robert Baroz: English teacher, Champlain Valley Union High School, Hinesburg, Vermont. [District instructional coach, Boston Pilot Schools.]

Elizabeth J. Cantafio: Assistant professor of English, developmental education specialist, Community College of Philadelphia.

Gerald Campano (Script Co-Editor): 5th-grade teacher. [Assistant professor, Indiana University.]

Delvin Dinkins: Assistant principal for the academic program, high school. [School district Director of Electronic Learning.]

Miriam Fife: Co-instructor, 1st-grade English Language Learners. [Doctoral candidate, Reading/Writing/Literacy, University of Pennsylvania.]

Maria Paula Ghiso: Dual-language kindergarten teacher. [Doctoral candidate, Reading/Writing/Literacy, University of Pennsylvania.]

Kelly Harper: 6th-grade teacher, suburban school district near Boston, Massachussetts. [Assistant professor, Canisius College.]

Sarah Hobson: 7th-grade drama and writing teacher, Philadelphia charter school. [Doctoral candidate, Reading/Writing/Literacy, University of Pennsylvania.]

Gillian Maimon: 1st-grade teacher, Samuel Powel School, school district of Philadelphia. [Instructor and doctoral candidate, Reading/ Writing/Literacy, University of Pennsylvania.]

Gary McPhail: 1st-grade teacher, Shady Hill School, Cambridge, Massachusetts.

Swati Mehta: Teacher and graduate student. [Doctoral candidate, Boston College.]

Monica Rowley: Special education and high school English teacher, Secondary School for Journalism, New York City Department of Education.

Rob Simon: Instructor of middle and secondary English methods. [Doctoral candidate, Reading/Writing/Literacy, University of Pennsylvania.]

Andrea J. Stairs: University Teaching Fellow and Doctoral Student, Boston College. [Assistant professor, English education, University of Tennessee.]

Lynne Yermanock Strieb: 1st- and 2nd-grade teacher, school district of Philadelphia. [Retired teacher, currently writing a book about parent–teacher relationships.]

Diane Waff: Teacher and school administrator. [Practice professor, Reading/Writing/Literacy, Graduate School of Education, University of Pennsylvania.]

Sherri Wu: College writing instructor, Taiwan Community College. [Adjunct professor of reading and writing, community college.]

NOTES

1. The AERA 2008 script evolved from an earlier version developed for the 2007 Ethnography Forum with the leadership of Sarah Hobson and Miriam Fife.

Chapter 14

Practitioners' Voices in Trying Times: A Readers' Theatre Script

Rebecca Akin and Gerald Campano, Editors

Stage Directions: All readers are seated in a double semi-circle behind five microphones.
Stage Directions: Gill standing at microphone #1.

Gill Maimon: September 8, 2003. On this, the first day of school, I cannot help but hate the new students a little bit. I realize how harsh this sounds, harboring such negativity toward all of these eager-eyed children decked out in back-to-school clothing that will never again look quite so pristine, but I miss my previous life, when I knew all the people in the room and they all knew me. Judging by the death grips that the new kids lock on their former kindergarten teachers when they see them this morning, I am not the only one starving for a little familiarity. What I wouldn't give for just a bit of shared history.

While the first day is a trial, it is at least an anomalous trial. It is the only time in the year that the children and I will have no shared past. By the second day, we will at least be able to look back on what happened the day before. By the second day, we will have known each other across a span of time, which, though tiny, will be long enough to begin noticing things that are different than they were before. On the first day, I have nothing to go on. On the first day, I am gripped by the fear that the year will pass by and nobody in the room—not the children, not I—will change. By tomorrow, this fear will no longer be stark, because we will have already started to change.

On the first day, I have more trouble than I ever will again distinguishing individuals from the mass of students. I confuse Rain and Raquelle because their names start with the same letter. Deja and Lana are about the same size, so I have trouble remembering who is who. All morning I avoid calling on certain children because I am not sure who they are. I am feeling outnumbered, disoriented, and useless. I can't see the trees for the forest.

One of my friends has likened the cumulative sensation of a first day to being hit with a bat. At the end of this day, as I am reeling from the wallop, the principal comes to my room and informs me that, because there are more students on roll in my classroom than in the other first grades, that I will be losing two of my students. This is not news that I greet happily. All day long I have wanted nothing more than to cast off every one of the new students. Now that two of them are actually going, their departure is the last thing I desire. It seems only fair that, if I had to be resistant to them today, they should at least stick around long enough for me to like them.

Stage Directions: Gill sits down.

PART I: STUDENT PORTRAITS

Stage Directions: Rob stands at microphone #1. Alan stands at microphone #2. Elizabeth stands at microphone #3. Gary stands at microphone #4. Maria stands at microphone #5.

Maria Ghiso: Writing is a way to share from your life, I tell my students. With them I write about traveling home to Argentina and how my grandmother used to make me *café con leche* and say it tasted so special because she used *leche de vaca negra*—milk from a black cow. In class Daniela writes about a visit from the *ratoncito*, the large rodent that is the Latin American version of the tooth fairy. Lenny only writes about Pokémon. Alejandra writes about playing mom in the housekeeping corner, and the baby is always sick with fever. Bianca writes about visiting her dad in jail. Paul's dad worked at the World Trade Center and walked all the way to 109th Street to pick him up from class, showing up at 5 P.M. drunk and with scuffed feet. On September 13th, Paul draws tall buildings with stick figures standing at the open windows looking down or plummeting to the ground.

Gary McPhail: During our personal narrative unit, David wrote about the fact that his mother was living in Denver for the year while she completed her residency. It gave me pause to realize that David was doing everything in his power to not write about his own feelings and about how he was processing this very powerful personal experience. He wanted his story to be told in an indirect way, but he did not want to document on paper how he actually felt about his mother living away from him. The cover of David's story showed an airplane ascending into the sky. The illustration was done completely in black crayon. The title of the story was "Sadness." In the story web box marked "Characters," David had drawn a picture of the airplane and explained that, as opposed to himself or any person he knew, the airplane was the central character of the story. Pushing further, I asked David if there were any other characters in the story. He looked at me for several seconds with a strong gaze and then replied, "Yes, my mother is on that plane." I said, "OK, then you need to write 'Mom' in the character box of your story web. After much pause, he finally did this. Then I asked him if there were any other characters in his story. He said no. Finally I asked, "Your title is 'Sadness.' Who is the one feeling sadness in your story?" He continued by saying, "Well, I'm the one feeling sadness, (and then softly) obviously." I replied by saying that he should write his name in the character box as well. "But I'm not focusing on me in this story, I'm focusing on my mother and the plane," he was quick to reply.

It struck me that David was trying desperately to diffuse the intensity of his own sadness, the emotion that he chose to write about, by having his mom and the plane be the main characters instead of focusing on his own emotions. I told him that next writing time we would work together to figure out how to do this but also on how to include his perspective into the story. "Because it is a personal narrative and writing about yourself is what *personal* means," I said. His somber look showed me that he understood.

Looking back, I realized that it was much more difficult for David to write a personal narrative that required him to directly focus on his own emotions than it was to write fiction because he had to process and share his true emotions and experiences with his peers. He desperately wanted to diffuse the emotional component of his story by not casting himself as the main character and not deliberately focusing on his own emotions. Eventually, I gave David the freedom to do this and he wrote a very powerful piece.

Elizabeth J. Cantafio:

THIS IS A BLANK SHEET OF PAPER.

(I am the student in the back row. I am the student with her head down. I am the student wearing sunglasses. I am the student who doesn't speak. I am the student you will never know. I am the student who won't let you in. I am the student who is not *in* her papers. I am the student who is not. I don't want to talk to you. I don't want you to know me. I don't trust you. I don't like you. It's none of your business. Get out of my business. That's my business. Why are you always in everybody's business? Leave me alone. I want to sit alone. I want to work alone. I want to be alone. Go away. Get out of my face. I am the student who won't answer your questions. I am the student who never smiles. I am the student you refer to the principal's office or the counseling center or the learning lab or the school psychologist. I am the student being disruptive in the hall. I am the student who's always late. Don't ask me what's the matter. Don't ask me what's wrong. Don't ask me if I'm in trouble. Don't talk to me. Ignore me. Pretend you don't see me. Don't excuse me. Don't put up with me. Don't let me get away with it. Don't lower your standards for me. Don't take any time with me. I don't deserve it. I won't appreciate it. I'll never get it. I don't want it. I don't need it. I am the student you want out of your class. I am the student you hope stays home. I am the student you never look in the eye. You don't want me in your classroom. You don't want me in your office. You don't want me at your school. Give me away. Bump me off on someone else. Pass me around. Send me back. Test me. Diagnose me. Drug me. Restrain me. Punish me. Fail me. Reject me. Don't try to talk to me. Don't reach out to me. Don't try to understand me. Don't be patient with me. Don't accept me. I'm just getting over. I'm using you. I'm taking advantage of you. I'm playing with you. I'm laughing at you. I hate you. I'm all right. I'm cool. I'm hanging in there. I'm doing fine. I'm OK. I'm doing the best I can. I'm trying as hard as I can. You can't understand. You can't know. You don't get it. You just don't get it.)

Alan Amtzis: "Oh, I'm just not creative," Eleanor said, apologizing beforehand for her portfolio. Her comment made me both sad and angry. "How can you be a teacher and not believe that you are creative?" I thought, but didn't say. I hear this too often from teachers and wonder how they've been prevented from seeing themselves as creative.

The portfolio is an assignment that asks teachers to assemble images of themselves by exploring artifacts from their professional life. Most students submit a scrapbook-like document with artifacts encased between plastic protective layers, as they might for a job interview.

Eleanor, however, brought in a huge poster board with a cut-out construction-paper depiction of herself. Velcroed on top of that, like a paper dress-up doll, were layered outfits. She assembled dresses, skirt–blouse combinations, pants, and separates—a full array of professional attire. As she presented her portfolio, peeling away layers adorned with photos, lesson plans, journal pages, and other aspects of her teaching profile, Eleanor narrated each deepening layer with a story about classroom conflict or tensions. Often these concerned her own questions about teaching writing more creatively or organizing lessons more meaningfully.

Never had I seen a portfolio that so deeply and creatively seemed to embody the self-study spirit of the assignment so literally and metaphorically, simultaneously.

"You don't think you're creative?" one of the teachers shouted.

Rob Simon: I went into teaching and researching my English methods class in 2005 with some idea of wanting to research "with" my students—all student middle and secondary English teachers—and little idea of what that might look like. In October, at my invitation, eight student teachers and I formed an inquiry group with the goal of presenting at the University of Pennsylvania Ethnography in Education Forum. We continue to work together. I learned immeasurably—and still learn—from our conversations, but I sometimes struggle to simultaneously write *with* my students and *about* them.

Case in point: I wrote a dozen drafts of my two pages for that first group presentation. In what I believed to be my final version, emailed to the group for suggestions, my pronouns still vacillated between *they* and *you*. At a weekly group meeting, Nicole responded to what she perceived to be tentativeness in my writing. It might have had something to do with, among other things, my uncertain pronouns. Nicole challenged: "You shouldn't be afraid to write about us—we're *your* students." I thought, but didn't say: Can I be anything but? And I wonder as I write this now: How do I write about people I care about in the shadow of Adrienne Rich's cautionary words: "Everything we write / will be used against us / or against those we love"?

As in previous years, in this year's methods class we read Debra Britzman's analysis of the cultural myths of teaching. This reading I noticed for the first time that Britzman writes in the third person about someone called "the student teacher": *them*. I was struck by how naturalized this kind of representation is in academic prose, and I was again reminded of my persisting difficulties in trying to write with and about my students. How do *they* read an article written about *the student teacher*? As practitioner researchers, how might we write differently if we think about our students not as subjects but as our co-authors and audience?

Stage Directions: Rob, Alan, Elizabeth, Gary, and Maria sit down.
Stage Directions: Swati stands at microphone #2. Gerald stands at microphone #4.

Gerald Campano: I think of how easily, how naturally, my grandfather's migration sounds like a narrative of intergenerational upward mobility through hard work and sacrifice. I still have trouble letting go of this parable. It is challenging for me to see his life in its full complexity and contradiction, to hold in mind at once the sense of historical plausibility and idiosyncratic personal odyssey that was his story and is my story to (re)discover, to realize his life could have taken very different turns and to understand both what was gained and what was lost on that trip across the Pacific.

I believe it is also challenging to view the lives and learning of contemporary urban and immigrant students with equal complexity. Nevertheless, it may be the work that needs to be done if we are to transform their all-too-often-imposed secondary status in the educational system and create alternative communitarian spaces conducive to their capacities for survival, self-definition, and social empowerment. It may also be necessary for us to surpass our own boundaries and grow as educators.

Swati Mehta: We say the mission of our school is to focus on immigrants and to honor our students whom we label refugee, English language learner, coming from the South Side. Do we? There is not a single piece of literature in our school discussing immigrant stories not having to do with Ellis Island! What about my Indian parents and my students' families? Where do their stories live? How would my 5th-grade students define the concept of an immigrant story?

Gerald Campano: Leticia was a Filipino student in my 5th-grade class. In response to Langston Hughes's (1994) poem "Mother to Son," she wrote:

"Daughter to Mother"
Mom I know you work hard and you work to feed me
I remember that you told me that you have to walk on your knees and
    scrub the floor
Your boss would treat you like a slave
Your back hurts, your knees hurt, your hands hurt
And your heart hurts
I want to help you get an easy life
You emigrated from Mexico
When you were small you had no papers and no home in America
You worked in the fields in the hot sun
Sweat would come down your back
Then again your back, hands, knees, heart and your soul hurts
Dollars a day
I love you mom because you did the hardest thing that a child shouldn't do
I wouldn't be here if it weren't for you

Swati Mehta: There is a power in my question—how would 5th-grade students define immigrant stories?
Who can forget how these fifth graders wrote their versions of immigrant narratives with images, videos, and writing? They owned their research, while I helped them navigate the tricky path. They pointed out important themes, while I helped them see the depth. They shared their stories, while I made sure they had an audience. They made me the proudest teacher when their voices, images, and knowledge made it, and made it far; all the way to Boston, all the way to Harvard, all the way to a forum where they

shared their work among other Indian educators. The power of the question validated my own story.

Gerald Campano: Leticia's concern for her own family's experiences would eventually translate into a commitment to migrant families more generally. She researched the history of the United Farm Workers of America, specifically the life of Dolores Huerta. Leticia even attended a rally for more expansive health care sponsored by an interfaith community organization. The students' writings and interests often indicated alternative sources of value that privilege cooperation and collective well-being. Today, 7 years after writing this poem and now in high school, Leticia is a leader in the immigrant rights movement.

Stage Directions: Gerald and Swati sit down.
Stage Directions: Gill stands at microphone #2.

Gill Maimon: September 26, 2003. At choice time this afternoon, Danny and Taerem are building together when, all of the sudden, Danny is by my side looking very upset. I ask him what is the matter and he tells me, "Taerem said I'm Black." Of course, White and Black are generalization, each encompassing varying shades. On the White spectrum, Danny is one of the whitest children I have ever seen. His skin is so pale that, in certain lighting, the veins under his barely pigmented face cause him to appear slightly blue. With hair and eyelashes as light as his skin, only his deep green eyes, which are now brimming with tears, provide him any color contrast. Taerem is as dark as Danny is light. I am fearful of all of the potential implications of Taerem's comment: Was Taerem teasing Danny because he is White? Did Taerem call Danny Black because Taerem perceives his own race as a negative? Does Danny perceive "Black" as a negative?

In my head I am contemplating possibilities, but I force myself to tread lightly with this one. I must not jump to any conclusions. I ask Taerem, "What did you mean when you said Danny is Black?" Taerem looks surprised—and a bit worried that I am asking him about this. He explains to me that all people are Black, but some are just lighter than others. He says that all he meant to say was that he and Danny were the same in some ways.

Danny's upset takes Taerem by surprise. He cannot imagine what causes it, and I want to make sure I understand the cause. I ask, "Why did it make you feel bad when Taerem called you Black? Is it bad to be Black?" Danny looks at me like I'm crazy, tells me there's nothing wrong with being Black, puts his arm in front of my face, and says, "But I'm not." In some ways, my adult worries are projecting onto this incident much higher stakes than the boys experienced. Taerem was simply saying to Danny, "We are alike." Danny's upset simply signified, "But you're not seeing me." In fact, none of this is simple. The terrain we are trying to inhabit in a classroom, the space between "we are the same" and "we are different," is full of ambiguity.

Stage Directions: Gill sits down.

PART II: QUESTIONS

Stage Directions: Elizabeth stands at microphone #1. Andrea stands at microphone #2. Miriam stands at microphone #3. Monica stands at microphone #4.

Monica Rowley: Eight weeks into school, Kyle asked me, "What is Women's Studies?" I felt pretty small in that moment.

How had I managed to teach a high school elective for 8 weeks and not provide the students with a clear definition of what it was I was teaching them? Was I totally off the mark? Was I doing a disservice to my students by not having a clearer definition for them? I, who in conversations with friends and colleagues readily admitted that Women's Studies was not something I could easily define, was not comfortable without having a "right" answer for Kyle regarding what Women's Studies is. I felt that my answer to him—versus, say, responses to friends or acquaintances—needed to be something that I could later go back and test. How could I be a good teacher without a testable definition of the subject matter I was teaching? This disconnect between what I expect out of my conversations in "real life" compared with my expectations of conversations from "teacher life" still unsettles me. It also brings me back to my continual struggle with assessment: What are we asking our students to really do, know, and become?

Miriam Fife: Carlos, a student who has just moved here from Mexico, has begun to write stories in which his whole family is

present. He writes a primary sentence such as "I went to the movies" or "I went to the mall" and then he lists everyone's name in
his family, including his dog, in attendance. When he is done, he
walks around the room holding his paper and saying, with a somewhat skeptical look, "What does this say?" as if to test prospective
readers and check if he has really written what he was aiming to
write. He is elated when he hears what he's written read as he intended and often asks for a reread. Is he impressed that he has written something others can read in this new language, is it the sound
of familiar names that makes him smile, or is it the satisfaction of
hearing someone read the words he has worked so hard to write
that he enjoys?

Andrea Stairs: Before beginning my career as an urban teacher
educator, I taught high school English at what was considered by
many to be one of the best public high schools in the state of Colo-
rado, if not the best high school. But something was missing. I was
encouraged to observe master teachers in action with students and
emulate their practices. Every classroom was teacher-centered,
and, much like my college English classes, the teacher was telling
the students about the "right" interpretation of the classic texts we
were required to teach. As I kept plugging through *Macbeth* every
year, trying hard to conform to the culture that silenced the voices
of less experienced teachers and encouraged didactic instruction, I
began to wonder, "Whose knowledge counts?" The master teachers didn't encourage me to inquire into my practices; they expected
me to conform to their way of teaching, believing it was best for all
students. At this point early in my teaching career, I began to question whether teaching at the supposed "best" high school was right
for me, since it meant becoming a teacher I didn't want to be.

Monica Rowley: Upon returning from a class trip to the Brook-
lyn Public Library, Cathy—another student from this class—
remarks as soon as I walk in the room, "Ms. Rowley! We saw
Whistle for Willie at the library." Marissa, who has severe speech
impediments, excitedly tries to tell me about *The Snowy Day*. My
month's lessons plans with this class involved a study of Ezra Jack
Keats's work. We examined his art, characters, colors, and word
choice. We created art. Some students worked on developing their
own stories, while others worked on phonics lessons that were

taken from our texts. Still, I wonder, am I being too frivolous with my students' time? Do they need me to be more practical with their lessons? I hope not, but I wonder. My students' recognition and excitement in seeing the author they studied in a different context—outside of school—inspired me to believe that I was making the right choices for my students. Is the work I am giving them too "academic" and not tied to future realities of their lives? What exactly does it mean for a special education student to read his or her world?

Elizabeth J. Cantafio: From my perspective, taking an inquiry stance as a teacher and conducting research for social justice and educational change are intimately related. Questioning my assumptions means I am perpetually asking myself: What am I doing here? What am I doing it for? Who am I to be doing it? What am I paying attention to? What am I overlooking? What am I ignoring? Why? How? What does it mean? While these questions are descriptive of my pedagogy, they also provide a dynamic that enables me to work within the hegemonic structure of the school, a place of constant "unease" (Greene, 1988). As a framework for my teaching and research, these questions provide the possibility for the construction of what I consider an ethical practice, a practice characterized by ongoing inquiry and grounded in the struggle to assist my students in creating a literacy that, as Lankshear and McLaren (1993) describe, "makes possible a more adequate and accurate 'reading' of the world . . . in which people can enter into 'rewriting' the world into a formation in which their interests, identities, and legitimate aspirations are more fully present and are present more equally" (p. xviii).

Stage Directions: Elizabeth, Andrea, Miriam, and Monica sit down.
Stage Directions: Rob stands at microphone #2. Alan stands at microphone #4.

Alan Amtzis: "What are the questions you ask yourself on the car ride home from school when you are alone?" I want the teachers I work with in my master's program to speak the deepest level of question they have about their work, the questions that seldom get voiced. "Who are the students you sometimes wish were absent?" I ask and they nervously laugh with embarrassed recognition. "What are the issues underneath that?" Such questions have a central place in our classroom.

In class we journal about who our best and worst teachers were. I hear rich and moving stories about humiliating, scornful teachers or teachers who went out of their way to be nice and to appreciate individuality. No one ever writes, "Wow, could she differentiate!" but I do hear that a teacher cared and had a way of showing and enacting it. The stories highlight the interpersonal, interactive, and relational aspects of teaching.

"For which students are *you* not a good teacher?" I often ask as a follow-up. "Who might be likely to write about you in 20 years? What are the issues and attitudes toward teaching embedded in that relationship?"

The journaling we do, both in and out of class, offers a way of getting at our deepest images of ourselves as teachers, often leading to meaningful, workable, and provocative questions that generate and support further inquiry into our own teaching and classroom cultures.

Rob Simon: In my English methods class at the University of Pennsylvania, I continue to try to make my work more relational, more connected to students' questions about what is at stake for them in learning to teach in urban contexts. I teach about inquiry, encourage my students to consider inquiry as a stance on practice and an approach to pedagogy and curriculum and pursue my own inquiries into my teaching. But writing about my practice has, to say the least, been less than straightforward. Questions about goals, audience and representation in my work persist. Who I am writing with, and in what ways? Who I am writing about, to, and for? I worry them, maybe too much, as students sometimes remind me. This fall I teach this class again, transcribe the one last year, and recall Adrienne Rich: "These are the terms/Take them or leave them."

Stage Directions: Alan and Rob sit down.
Stage Directions: Gill Maimon stands at microphone #3.

Gill Maimon: March 17, 2004. At recess time, I happen upon one of my former students, a second grader, being consoled by her teacher in the hallway. I hover for a minute or two, unable to walk by without finding out more, and ascertain that the source of the upset is a snack that the child brought in to share with her class-mates. Today is St. Patrick's Day, and the snack in question is Irish potatoes, candy I recall fondly from my childhood but assiduously avoid along with all other sweets now that I'm grown. The second grader is upset because, once she and her classmates arrived outside with their snacks, a number of the children took one look at the confections in their hands, pronounced them "poisonous rocks," and tossed them in the garbage can. Wanting to console the child, I say, "Oh. I just love Irish potatoes." To which she responds, "I'll give you one." "Great," I say, as we walk down to her classroom, to retrieve the box of candy, plotting all the while that I will simply palm the treat and dispose of it back in my classroom. But when we reach the girl's room, she hands me the potato, then looks at me expectantly. I have no other choice than to take a bite. The girl is still watching, so I take another. For me—a person admittedly a bit irrational about sugar consumption—this is tantamount to taking a bullet.

Teachers commit fraud for the benefit of children all the time. My little falsehoods do not always have caloric implications. I feign fascination with a child's account of a cartoon show that, in truth, sounds both inane and incomprehensible. I react with surprise when another child tells me for the first time that his mother is expecting a baby, even though the mother shared the news with me weeks ago. I tell the class that the standardized test is a col-lection of interesting activities that we don't need to worry about even though I believe it is something altogether different. It is not insignificant that the second grader watches so closely what I do with the candy. She must have at least an inkling of my potential for false declarations. In one way, I suppose, I should celebrate this child's doubtfulness, as it seems to be evidence of a critical take on the world. But in other ways, it makes me sad to acknowledge that, even though my intentions aren't bad, I do not always deserve to be believed.

Stage Directions: Gill sits down.

PART III: GENDER AND RACE

Stage Directions: Delvin stands at microphone #2. Diane stands at micro-phone #4.

Diane Waff: Soon after I took the job as teaching and learning
coordinator in the school district of Philadelphia's northeast cluster,
I was invited by a principal to discuss his elementary school's test
scores and the district's accountability index. Once an exclusively
White enclave, Black, Asian, and Latino families were just beginning to purchase homes in northeast Philadelphia. According to
the Philadelphia City Planning Commission Census Tract data for
the year 2000, 75.1 percent of the Whites who lived in the city re-
sided in the northeast (Simon & Alnutt, 2007). Staff and students of
color in this section of the city were in the minority. In 1997, there
were only two Black administrators in the northeast cluster, a Black
principal and me, the teaching and learning coordinator. The principal introduced me by saying that I would work with the staff to
help them raise their test scores. He was clearly upset that his school
had been outperformed in every category by other northeast cluster
schools. The school's demographic data for the 1996–1997 school
year was 20.9 percent African American, 9.7 percent Asian, 8.4
percent Hispanic, 0.6 percent Native American, and 60.4 percent
White. The public documentation of scores put the staff on the
defensive, and I was stunned by how quickly they were blaming
the poor and minority students for the school's low performance.
One teacher said, "How can we be held accountable for students
who come from dysfunctional homes, students who come to school
unable to read and write?" Another staff member said, "The neighborhood is changing, and we will never be able to raise test scores
with these students." And another particularly irritating comment
from a recent college graduate: "They don't have any cultural capital. They already come to school with a distinct disadvantage."

Delvin Dinkins: As a classroom teacher at Clearfield, a predominantly White suburban school, I noticed that African American
students comprised 30 percent of the lowest-level course offerings
at the school. Upon returning to Clearfield as an assistant principal
after a leave of absence, I found the teachers had formed a group to
discuss the achievement gap between White and African American
students.

There were many teachers who believed that the negative
stereotypes attributed to Black students were justified because of
their coarse behavior. One teacher remarked that she had noticed

a decline in student respect, which she regarded as non-negotiable. "Some of these students are constantly wandering the halls, cutting classes, putting their heads down while in class, hanging out in the cafeteria," she lamented. Other teachers felt similarly. For example, Jan said, "I don't know if it's the oppositional culture that students are a part of or what. They defy authority, are almost always negative and confrontational, and sometimes disrespectful. I don't know if it's the peer group or the glorified images they see on MTV."

Another teacher, Jim, said: "I feel like there is going to be some kind of confrontation whenever I ask them to take off their hats or do-rags. One time one of them told me that I was picking on him because of his race, and I told him that wasn't true. I said he was breaking the rules and needed to be respectful of the school like everybody else. He told me I was singling him out. This is why I won't ask him or probably most of his friends not to take off their hats any longer. I don't—no one wants—to have the race card played or be called a racist."

Along these same lines, Kent told of a similar experience in which a student mentioned that wearing a hat or do-rag was part of his culture. Kent felt that the dress code should be revisited to ensure that sweatbands are "outlawed items." A number of teachers wanted to know whether the school should "allow culture of this sort."

However, another teacher believed that many Black students did not share the same resources as other students. She observed: "We work in an environment in which we assume students have all the materials they need in order to learn: computers, transportation, and other things. We think they have just as much as some other kids around here. As someone who grew up and did not have a lot, I can see it. I was discouraged from becoming an English or music teacher and was geared towards health and physical education instead. I feel for these kids. I know what it is like to look around and have everyone have stuff you don't and for teachers to expect you to be able to get materials and resources at the drop of a hat and are not able to."

Ty concurred. He believed that, he, too, with his working-class background, unlike many of the other teachers in the building, had "felt a subtle kinship with students who have less than the typical Clearfield student."

Diane Waff: As I listened, I was numbed by the statements I heard and saddened that many of the teachers truly believed that poor children could not learn. I wondered how useful it would be to share the test scores of racially isolated schools in other parts of the city where poor and minority students are achieving. Would it change the conversation? Would the staff begin to question the goals they set for their students and the beliefs they hold about students they teach? Would giving this staff the opportunity to meet over time to engage in collaborative discussion, dialogue, and critique about their instructional program make a difference? Was I the right person to facilitate the conversation? Would I have the courage to raise the tough questions? The deficit rhetoric wore me down spiritually, and I left the meeting that day feeling defeated but still determined to find a way to work with teachers to develop strategies for change.

Delvin Dinkins: The entrenched deficit perspective that was applied to Black students unfolded in significant ways. Even though teachers occasionally theorized about cultural, political, and structural realities that affected the lives of students, the discourses they took up followed from the widespread belief of teachers that Blacks are, in strong part, responsible for their academic failure.

Stage Directions: Delvin and Diane sit down.
Stage Directions: Kelly stands at microphone #1. Robert stands at microphone #2. Gary stands at microphone #3. Diane stands at microphone #4.

Kelly Harper: What happens when sixth graders in an affluent, almost all-White school community read children's literature specifically selected to address issues of race and diversity? At first, students were overwhelmingly positive. After reading *Cart and Cwidder*, for example, Cassie commented: "I think that the author is making a point about the world today, and I think it's sad that people are always living in fear. This is a great story, though, and I look forward to reading what happens next."

In the coming months, however, as our conversations got deeper, my students' receptivity levels shifted—growing enthusiasm for many, but emerging resistance for some. Cassie wrote in her reading journal: "I think that *Olive's Ocean* doesn't really have a moral or lesson. . . . I think we should read a funny book next. I think we should read:—a fantasy book—a happy book—whodunits—a ghost story. *Not:*—historical fiction—[*not*] depressing books. Good books: *Jade Green, Last of the Really Great Wangdoodles.*"

The social issues books we shared raised issues of many kinds that were both familiar and unfamiliar to the lives of my students. Among them, issues of race, socioeconomic status, and peer pressure helped bring in voices otherwise missing in the all-White community in which I taught. Resistance to the diversity of ideas expressed in the books we were reading didn't come from just within the walls of my classroom. While we were discussing one of Mildred Taylor's novels on African American issues, for example, one parent commented, "We never had to think about these issues until these books came along."

Robert Baroz: One year, via a fellowship through Middlebury College's Breadnet Teacher Network, an Arizona teacher and I used email to participate in a writing exchange with our 11th-grade high school classes. The students in Vermont and Arizona exchanged drafts of essays and responses to those drafts, and without our planning, a classroom inquiry arose from a spontaneous conversation in my class one day.

Looking at a draft of an essay by a student in Arizona, Hillary asked me, "Is Jerry a guy or girl, Mr. Baroz?" "It's a girl," Mary answered. "How do you know?" Hillary asked. "She spells her name with a *J*; that's the way girls spell it." Mary said. "No, girls spell it with a G, right, Mr. Baroz?" Hillary queried. "Well, when I was a kid, I remember the Mets had a catcher named Gerry Garote," I said. "He spelled his name with a G. But Jerry Seinfeld spells his name with a *J*. Does it matter if it is a boy or a girl?" "Yes, I think it does," Hillary said. "I'd like to know where they're coming from." At this point, another girl overheard our conversation and added, "Jerry's a boy. I remember reading his memoir, and he wrote about mountain biking. Girls don't mountain bike."

At this point, I had several questions swirling in my mind. What did Hillary mean by "know where they are coming from"? How are my students reading gender, and how does that matter in what we're trying to do?

Gary McPhail: As a male teacher in the primary grades, I have often been struck by the fact that my female students tend to both perform at a higher level with regard to writing proficiency and are far more interested in writing than my male students. Many genres and styles that boys gravitate toward (comic books, adventure stories, silly fictitious stories, sports pages, etc.) are considered to be of low status and are not welcome in many classrooms during writing time because they are either "inappropriate" for school or deemed not worthy of instructional time.

As a teacher researcher, I have become increasingly more interested in the role that a more open writing curriculum could play in closing the gender gap in writing. I have been curious to see what topics the boys would bring into the classroom if their interests were allowed to permeate the writing curriculum.

Diane Waff: It is Friday, and the period 2 English class is about to begin. The students have just finished reading "Spilled Salt," a short story about the rape of a young woman by a man who offered her a ride home. The girls in the class, a mix of African American and Latina young women, begin pulling their chairs into a circle to begin our whole-group discussion of the text. The boys crowd in from the hallway, find seats, and fumble through their book bags for copies of the short story. Omar, a vocal student with a long white shirt and baggy pants, jumpstarts the discussion by stating, "Dress like a hooker, you get what you deserve." I pull up my seat and ask, "Does the way you dress determine who you are or how you should be treated?" My question fuels lots of comments from male and female alike that begin to challenge sexism and demeaning stereotypes. Maritza, normally a quiet student, comments, "You should be able to wear what you want without fear of being groped or raped."

I constantly reiterate the norms for a text-based discussion, such as talking one at a time, respecting each other, and using the text as a reference. The students engage in an impassioned discussion of what constitutes a "hooker" and what constitutes a "good girl," challenging the notion that a single woman without a man is sexually suspect or asking for trouble when she goes out alone. Brian, an African American male, questions, "Didn't her mother teach her not to get in a car with a stranger?" and is decisively answered by Tamika, a female student in the class, "Didn't his mother teach him not to rape people?" Omar, with some sheepish laughter, adds, "I guess you can't put it all on the woman either." Another female student adds, "Yeah. Why does the rapist's mother think she's responsible for her son's behavior? Why not put it on the abusive father?" At one point, Maritza quietly asserts, "It is the duty of fathers as well as mothers to teach their children." The discussion ends with a classroom of students labeled "special needs" beginning to question the universal perception that it is a female responsibility to teach moral behavior.

Stage Directions: Kelly, Robert, Gary, and Diane sit down.
Stage Directions: Andrea stands at microphone #2. Swati stands at microphone #3. Sarah stands at microphone #4.

Swati Mehta: It cannot be. I must be missing something. Everyone has been talking about minority teachers for what feels like a really, really long time. Everyone has been talking about shifting the discourses and making a call for people of color. A lot of people have been talking about people of color defined through Black teachers and Latino teachers. Do Asian teachers not have much color?

And more than Asian, I guess South Asian teachers just don't exist. I found data and studies on Chinese American teachers, Japanese American teachers, Vietnamese American teachers, Cambodian American teachers, but this does not equal Asian or Asia. Asia is a continent, not a country, not one culture, and not one language. And part of Asia is the South Asian teachers—teachers whose history stems from Bangladesh, India, Pakistan. I talk to these Indian American teachers all the time, but I guess we have not talked enough. In order to actually make our voices heard, we need to talk to the field, not just to each other. Sure, we are a minority within a minority in the research literature, but the question of why there is such a paucity of research is daunting and marked by a weight of professional responsibility. I don't really know what to do with what I am finding.

Sarah Hobson: Mr. Smith, a counselor who had worked with young people in his north Philadelphia neighborhood, came to my 7th-grade drama and writing for social change class to share his narrative. They had loved and trusted him instantly, his football player size, his rapt attention on them, his transparency. I spent only 1 day a week with the seventh graders, helping them write a play I had suggested be titled "A Revolution of Respect." Many students were hesitant to believe they could make a positive impact in their communities. When I went in the next week, I asked the students what they remembered about their visitor and how many people's lives they thought he had impacted?

The students said 25, 50, but didn't go much higher. So I asked them: What impact did he make on you? We went around the room, one person at a time. "When I talked, he really listened." "He made mistakes, but he learned from them." "He was able to forgive himself." "He's big, but he's not scary." "He didn't have to, but he really cares." "He wanted to be here with us." "He spends time getting to know kids." "He was kind to us." "He believed in me." "My life, I've had to overcome some really tough things, and I like that he could overcome them." After 30-plus students had shared, I asked them again. How many people's lives do you think he has impacted for the better? The number had changed: 1,500! 2,000! 10,000!

That day was a turning point for the students and for me. I think throughout our first 7 months together, the majority of the students wanted to believe they could make a difference in their communities but had been skeptical. Once they met Mr. Smith, a man who had lived and experienced similar circumstances to them and had applied his life in service to youth like them, the momentum for their playwriting began. They had both experienced his love and belief in them and witnessed his impact on their peers. Now they wanted to take the lead in writing and staging their play on behalf of the rest of their school.

Andrea Stairs: Dave said, "It's time for Blacks to get over it. I'm tired of talking about race and inequality. Blacks were discriminated against a long time ago, and I had nothing to do with it, and I don't know why we keep talking about this in this class." Melinda, an African American woman who was the president of the Black student association at the college, patiently explained to Dave that discrimination and racism were still very much a part of life in America, while his other White classmates more directly told him he was wrong and even "ignorant" for making such a statement. The tension in the room was palpable, and as the instructor, I felt a bit helpless. Here I was trying to model a proper Socratic seminar for these preservice teachers in an urban teacher preparation experience, so I didn't interject my opinion, but I reminded students that we needed to trust each other and maintain a classroom environment where everyone could share their views without feeling like they were being judged. But the young man withdrew from the urban immersion experience the very next day. This was a salient moment for me as an instructor. I simply wasn't sure how to react. I felt vulnerable trying to model a student-centered, hands-off approach to class discussion that had moved in an unanticipated direction, and looking back, I'm not sure I handled the moment appropriately at all.

Stage Direction: Swati, Sarah, and Andrea sit down.
Stage Direction: Gill stands at microphone #4.

Gill Maimon: April 27, 2004. This morning after recess, we head off to a children's festival for the first of two visits this week. The event draws students from all over the metropolitan area, and we are lucky to be in walking distance from the university where it is being held. The university that is hosting the event also happens to be the one that Kelly, our student teacher, attends. The children are as eager to see her in her academic habitat as they are to take part in the activities that await them at the festival. Wanting to capitalize on their interest, Kelly and I have arranged a special opportunity for the children. Since January, Kelly has been a member of a dance team to which she has devoted many hours of practice. With considerable planning on her part, Kelly has arranged for the members of her team to mount a command performance this morning for an audience of us. The children are delighted to see Kelly in this context, and she seems equally glad to be able to show off our class to her fellow dancers. I sit back and congratulate myself for capitalizing on this opportunity.

I begin to get a whiff of what we are in for when I take a closer look at the dancers' costumes and notice that the colored strips of tape attached to the backs of a number of them are, in fact, crosses. I should have seen this coming. Kelly is so committed to her church work that it should not be surprising that her dancing has a religious element to it as well. Pleased with myself just a moment ago for arranging this performance, all I can do now is watch the scene unfold through half-closed eyes. The dancers are enthusiastic and well rehearsed. To a certain extent, the performance is no different from any contemporary dance presentation, but for the

up-tempo exhortations to Jesus that serve as musical accompani-
ment and the fact that supplication is the most frequently employed
dance move. There is absolutely nothing that I can do about it but
hope that it doesn't last much longer. I glance over at the children,
and they are completely enthralled by the exhibition. Next, I peek
at the parents who are here with us. By all appearances, nobody
seems excessively outraged. It is, no doubt, a mercy that the family members who accompanied us today all happen to be regular
churchgoers. Despite the inappropriateness of this presentation for a
public school group, it does appear that the performers are dancing
to the choir. If I am the only one traumatized by this unanticipated
unification of church and state, then I've gotten off easy.

Stage Directions: Gill sits down.

PART IV: PORTRAITS OF TEACHERS AND PEDAGOGY

Stage Directions: Robert stands at microphone #2. Joan stands at microphone
#4.

Joan Barnatt: "Slow learning," is characterized by reflection,
attention to nuance and detail, and a willingness to explore without knowing what you may be looking for. My first lesson as a 7th-
grade humanities teacher came when time seemed more precious to
me than ever before: as a National Board candidate. This conversation was recorded at the end of a video session for my portfolio. It
started an entirely new way of looking at my practice: through the
eyes of the students.

Sarah: Mrs. B, why do you keep videotaping us?
Mrs. B: It's part of a project that I'm doing that helps me look at how
   I teach and hopefully helps me to see what I do well and what I
   need to change. I'm supposed to reflect on my own practice.
Josh: Why do you want to do that? You've been teaching a long
   time.
Mrs. B: Sometimes doing things for a long time makes it harder to
   change. How do I know I'm doing the best that I can?
George: Can we look at the video? We can tell you what we're doing;
   give you ideas?

Stage Directions: Maria, Rob, Swati, and Elizabeth stand at their seats and read the parts below.

> *Robert Baroz:* Back in 1998, I did a teacher research study with two student researchers, funded by the Spencer Foundation, on how students talked in student-led discussions within small groups. We did our research in an 11th-grade American literature elective course. The student researchers helped to tape and transcribe the talk. This is the transcript of student talk the researchers brought to our first meeting to code, a discussion of Thoreau's *Walden* [participants read students' parts]:

> *Maria:* I wouldn't even think to write stuff like that.
>
> *Rob:* I know, I'm like ahhhh, nature. I love it.
>
> *Swati:* I'm like there's a chipmunk on the log next to me, that's about as deep as I get.
>
> *Rob:* I actually started thinking about Thoreau, sadly enough, when I was sitting there.
>
> *Swati:* I started thinking that it was cold.
>
> *Maria:* I thought about outward bound. I was thinking about how on my solo, I was sitting there, and I'm usually afraid of the dark, but on my outward bound it was awesome, on my solo.
>
> *Elizabeth:* I always thought that they just take you out to this island and just left you there.
>
> *Maria:* That's the sailing one, but I was in the middle of the woods. You know what else, all the girls had to go to the bathroom . . . and the girls have to pull down their pants, like when the guys are standing there.
>
> *Elizabeth:* That's what gets me, no toilet paper.
>
> *Maria:* No toilet paper, but you know what, though—we learned sticks, rocks, and pine cones are the best if you do it the right way.
>
> *Swati:* Rocks? Pine cones? What if you do it the wrong way!
>
> *Maria:* You don't want to use leaves, 'cause then you can get like poison ivy.
>
> *Rob:* Well, you look at what kind of leaf it is first.
>
> *Elizabeth:* Sticks and rocks!
>
> *Swati:* Imagine getting like spiky rocks!
>
> *Rob:* Pine cones, that can't be comfortable.
>
> *Maria:* The right way it is; if you do it the wrong way, then you're in trouble.

I looked up at this point into the smiling faces of my student researchers and they asked: How do you code crapping in the woods?

Stage Directions: Maria, Rob, Swati, and Elizabeth sit down.

Joan Barnatt: I invited my students into the process of reflection. I chose a brief segment of video, and my classes and I reviewed it. This is what I heard:

> *Sarah:* The boys are talking too much. At least some of them. Yup, they always have something to say.
> *Josh:* No, the boys don't talk most. Mrs. B does.

We counted and timed the exchanges: The boys talked more frequently; the girls talked longer. There were dominant figures among both sexes, but most girls participated, while only about half the boys were likely to offer a comment.

And I talked more than anyone.

This gave me the basis for critiquing my own work and changed, for all time, the way I took part in discussions, because I drew my students into the process of structuring, examining, and reacting to my teaching as I documented what we experienced in the classroom. Inquiry, like slow learning, demands listening, reflection, and collaboration—time to think, to question, to discuss, to act, to learn.

Stage Directions: Joan and Robert sit down.
Stage Directions: Sherri stands at microphone #1. Lynne stands at microphone #2. Maria stands at microphone #3.

Lynne Strieb: In 2000, I retired from teaching first and second grade in Philadelphia public schools after 31 years. Every day I miss being with children in the classroom. I've spent most of the past 6 years working on a book about parent–teacher relationships, based on my experiences as both an activist parent and a teacher. From the beginning, as I pulled entries on parents and families from my complete journal and newsletters to parents, I kept a separate chronological list of all the things parents did with—and for—the children and me. I have many wonderful stories connected to this list, but for me, even a portion of the much longer list of parents' both large and small contributions is itself a powerful record.

Parents helped organize the classroom: They unpacked and packed
at the beginning and end of the year; organized and maintained
the class library of about 7,000 books; sorted, organized, and filed
papers; organized my desk, with children's help.

Parents ran errands to home and store for things I forgot to bring.

Parents suggested and chaperoned many, many trips both on bus and
on foot.

Parents set up or fixed bulletin boards, an aquarium, computers,
broken bookcases.

Parents marked math papers, homework, workbooks, spelling tests.

Parents worked at home making books, typing children's stories,
marking papers, sewing costumes, helping their children with
homework.

Parents contributed food and decorations; set up, served, and cleaned
up for birthday and Halloween parties, Thanksgiving feasts, authors' breakfasts.

Maria Ghiso: Bulletin boards at my school were considered indicators of learning. They had to be eye-catching and vibrant, with a
process chart in the middle, student work surrounding it, a detailed
explanation of what we did, explicit links to the standards, and pictures of students at work, preferably with smiles on their faces, extra
points for racial diversity. I had been warned that I needed to change
each of my three bulletin boards every 2 weeks. The night before
an observation, weary from a day that began before dawn, 7 P.M.
and my steps the only ones in the dark hallway, I began the arduous
process of crafting appearances. In the pile of student work was Eduardo's, a self-portrait true to life, and I remembered how carefully he
had looked at the hand-held mirror before putting his pencil to the
paper. But that night I looked with different eyes, and I noticed with
panic that Eduardo's self-portrait was uncolored. The main objective
in this mandated science lesson was to use flesh-colored crayons in
various shades of pink and peach and brown to learn about "differences," and the stark absence of color could be read by others as an
absence of learning. Paralyzed, my mind a blur of requirements I
struggled to meet, I colored in Eduardo's self-portrait myself, using
my left hand in an effort to mimic his developing small motor skills.
I hung the work high on the bulletin board, half-hidden behind the
process chart—betrayal of myself, of Eduardo, and of our relationship. I had literally crafted him for my benefit. The following day,

when my principal and district observers came to check the boards, they did not notice anything amiss about Eduardo's picture.

Lynne Strieb: Parents supported curriculum: They brought and sent animals, plants, and objects for science; brought babies for the children to observe; shared origins of their children's names. They made, taught, and played math games. They prepared paints and clay; supervised sewing, tie dying, weaving; made clay objects alongside the children; taught how to make Ukrainian and Yugoslavian Easter eggs.

Parents cooked with the children. They supervised children using knives to cut apples, pumpkins. They cooked and baked: peanut butter fudge, cookies, breads, tomato sauce from our class garden, potato latkes, chapatti, stir-fried string beans, spring rolls, stone soup, gingerbread sleds, sweet potato pie. They lent me equipment.

Parents shared their cultures and backgrounds. They taught written and spoken words; dances; songs and stories in Swahili, Chree, Hebrew, Russian, Serbian, Japanese, Spanish, Chinese, Malay, French, German, Urdu, American Sign Language. They shared foods, rituals, family customs and celebrations of Ireland, Pakistan, India, China, Yugoslavia; of African American families, Jews of Eastern Europe.

Sherri Wu: As a teacher of English in Taiwan, I was always able to surprise my students in one way or another in our first class— youngish appearance, casual way of talking, integration of some innovative techniques, and tolerant when being "authority challenged," etc. Yet no matter how we started, what we normally ended up doing was "following the script" given the condition that, whatever you do, just make sure the test results are good. In consequence, when the "honeymoon" was over and the sense of curiosity wore off, the students and I realized we did not go very far from where we were (supposed to be). Regardless of all the novelty, in the end we would find ourselves remaining in a traditional classroom, dissecting English, transmitting knowledge, and polishing test-taking skills. Not this time. This time I was determined to ride with a critical literacy curriculum and see where it would lead us.

Thus, even though there were still rows of desks and chairs, a blackboard, and an altar in the front, and even though I still took a roll call on the first day as I used to in the traditional classroom, my college writing students knew they were going to experience something different as soon as they realized that I was serious about my questions for them, to which I did not have ready-made answers. Questions such as "Why do people write? Why do *you* write? Who do you write to/for? Under what circumstances?" that opened the class were not rhetorical questions but inquiries that did not (and could not) require single "correct" answer. Questions like those continued to remind us why we were in this class, doing what we were doing.

Lynne Strieb: Parents demonstrated and described their own work and interests in great depth: sign painter and carpenters, pathologist, pediatrician, internist, ophthalmologist's assistant, secretaries, homemaker, computer expert, union organizer, musicians, filmmaker, architects, artist, Fairmount Park team leader, teacher, nurse, truck driver, and barber.

Parents gave me suggestions: about homework, for end-of-year picnics, about African American history activities, about my tension, about things their children wanted to do, about handling difficult kids.

Parents helped the children in the classroom: with writing conferences, reading, math, handwriting, project time. They walked children to the bathroom, stopped fights, calmed a child having a tantrum, noted who seemed to need help. They helped make things go smoothly. They calmed me.

Stage Directions: Maria and Lynne sit down. Sherri stays standing at microphone #1.

Stage Directions: Sherri stands at microphone #1. Sarah stands at microphone #2. Miriam stands at microphone #3.

Miriam Fife: Names—whose and in what proximity—are a big deal for these 1st-grade writers. There are a plethora of stories developing in which a child who has helped a fellow writer with spelling soon has his or her name added to the story as a character. Recently, Lisa wrote about planting daisies in a pool in her front yard. As the daisies grew, so did the words on her paper, physically representing the flowers outside her home. She included everyone in her family who helped plant the flowers, and soon added all the classmates at her writing table and with whom she's discussed her piece, in her planting daisies story. Is it that they helped her write about the daisies, and thus became a central part of her story? What significance does adding classmates' names to a story have for students?

And then there is the relevance among students concerning the proximity of names on paper. One morning during my first days working with students, the children sitting with me at a writing table asked me to spell my name and then to write their names as they spelled them. They asked me to add class members sitting at other tables, spelling the names for me that they had suggested and explaining their relationship (friends, cousins). I wrote their names in a simple line down the sheet of paper. Students from neighboring tables wandered over to see. Pretty soon Mari, who started the activity, was grinning, with two front teeth missing, and shouting: "Look! My name is closest to hers!" Mari pointed to her name next to mine on the paper as proof, an observation that the other 6-year-olds greeted with furrowed brows and frowns. A heated conversation ensued about whose name was second and third closest—and here I'd thought I'd been engaged in a simple name-spelling, getting-to-know-each-other exercise. Do names together imply friendship, favoritism, or some mix of each? Or was it simply a bother that Mari had pointed out this fact with a grin, enough of a bother to prompt an argument over the placement of names on paper?

Sarah Hobson: It was a slow morning. I was tired. The students were tired. We were seated in a circle, and I had planned to have them perform the poems they had written for one another. No one wanted to share. "OK," I said, "you don't have to." And then we just sat and looked at each other. "What would you like to do instead?" They just looked at me, still not quite awake. I waited and waited. Finally, one student said, "Someone else can read mine." Another student agreed to read. She stood and read it quickly, not capturing its rhythm, not enunciating so that we could really hear the words. She sat back down. "OK," I said. "Did anyone notice anything in that poem that they would like to know more about?" A few students pointed out two lines that were back to back that had particular appeal. "OK," I said, "would two students be willing to just read those two lines together?" Two girls came forward. I asked them to use their bodies and their voices and to develop a relationship with each other so that they were truly performing together. They did. The rest of the class began to smile. I asked the rest of the class to direct the two performers, to try the words in different ways, to use different gestures, different emphasis on the words, a different rhythm. We looked at where the breaks in ideas were, what kind of beat was in play, and how the meaning of the poem might change with each reading. We practiced collectively responding to moments in their performance. "Who wants to go next?" I asked. Almost every hand went up as students vied to be the next performer.

Sherri Wu: When I returned to Taiwan to conduct my practitioner research study, I was not sure what kind of composition teacher I would become. I was anxious about the way my students and I would approach each other and come to know each other (better). So the first assignment for everybody in this class, including me, was a sketch of our own literacy autobiographies. I wasn't confident about defining the term *literacy,* so I read to the class "My Name" from Sandra Cisneros's *The House on Mango Street,* with its eloquent narrator Esperanza, and Leah's essay from Elizabeth Cantafio's doctoral dissertation. Hopefully, the students would "get" the kind of autobiographical writing I was looking for.

When I stopped, the class was quiet, which was unusual and even a bit scary because, after all, it was a class of 50 students. And then when I looked up I saw some sad faces and watery eyes. "This is good," I said to myself, not only because it was the first time in our first class that I seemed to get everybody's attention, but also because from their reactions, I was glad that I didn't have a group of students who would perceive expository essay as the only thing worth doing in a writing class. Nevertheless, in our second class I got almost 50 identical sketches, which all followed a certain format, one that is usually adopted for a job interview. I couldn't say I was not disappointed, but I decided not to show my feelings, at least not before I found out what was going on. So I began our third class by asking the students to share experiences of writing their first assignment. Dan stood up and said it was difficult because "how can you write an autobiography as worth reading as Leah's when your life is just not as interesting?" Many nodded in agreement. It was at that moment that I realized: They did "get" it. They knew what I was looking for. Yet they were not ready to "give," perhaps because to some writing like Esperenza and Leah was beyond their familiar realities, while to the others, it meant making themselves vulnerable.

Stage Directions: Sherri, Miriam, and Sarah sit down.
Stage Directions: Gerald stands at microphone #3.

> *Gerald Campano:* There is a physical, material component to
> teaching, an emotional and bodily strenuousness. There is no sepa-
> ration between contemplation and "menial" labor, between intel-
> lectual inquiry and social responsibility. We are literally "on the
> ground" with our students, spending countless hours planning,
> completing paperwork, organizing our rooms, sitting in meetings,
> performing for evaluators, attending to emotional needs, comfort-
> ing children with asthma, visiting homes, participating in commu-
> nity events, administering tests, and responding to children's work
> long into the night. These are daily facts.
>
> Sometimes we are resolving conflicts, breaking up fights, pro-
> testing misguided policies, spending hours in the office trying not
> to have a child suspended or tracked. After the bell rings, we meet
> with former students trying to figure out what happened, why they
> are so disaffected when once so excited about school. We continue to
> advise students who have gone on to college or ones who have found
> themselves in the criminal (in)justice system. We pay our respects
> at funerals and try our best to counsel children about death and loss.
> In one year, three of my students' caretakers passed away due to
> poverty-related causes. These realities of the heart and body are in-
> dispensable to the nature of our inquiries and the very material from
> which we theorize our practice and shape our political stance.
>
> Sometimes this resistance takes an overt political form and
> is aligned with larger activist movements. Other times it is more
> subtle, but resistance nonetheless; for example, our efforts to dilate
> time and open opportunities for reflection, creativity, and bonding
> with our students may radically interrupt the institutional drive for
> efficiency and standardization.
>
> One of the most urgent challenges for urban teacher researchers
> may be to reformulate a progressive language that has political effica-
> cy because it is grounded in the actual lives of children and is persua-
> sive about what is required for urban students to flourish. We need to
> communicate the complexity of our work with pragmatic effects.

Stage Directions: Gerald sits down.
Stage Directions: Gill stands at microphone #5.

Gill Maimon: June 15, 2004. On this last day, it all goes so fast. The children suggest that center work for today be a time for them to make things for me and for each other, and I gladly agree. Manuel makes me a card that says, "Thank you for teaching us," and it is the first of many instances of teariness for me. At lunchtime, Lola's mother and father bring pizza to celebrate her birthday, which is tomorrow, so we have one last meal together. I present the memory books and the farewell gifts that I have purchased for the children. I load them down with the work they have produced over the course of the year, and then we are done.

And so we go on from here as different people than we were on a day as warm as this one when we met 9 months ago. That a school year lasts exactly as long as a gestation period seems fitting somehow. From here, there will be summer camp, and trips down South to see the relatives, and long afternoons at the public pool, and scorching sidewalks, and incessant ice-cream truck jingles, and opened-up fire hydrants. Then, for most, there will be second grade. Many in rooms just across the hall from mine, but some farther away than that. Quanice and her sister will be going to a charter school in the fall. Adam has already left our city for Boston. Taeshawn is back for today, but beyond now, who knows? Maybe the new 3rd-grade teacher will come back, maybe she won't. Maybe the principal will move on to a better-paying job in a district not quite as insane as ours. Maybe our student teacher will find a classroom where she can share all of herself with her students. Maybe our district will find a leader who knows as much about education as he or she does about business. Maybe the scripting of curriculum and the testing of babies will be recognized as obscenity. Maybe I will prevail, and maybe I will be worn down. Maybe I will be lucky enough to stay right in this room for the rest of my career.

Eventually the yard clears out, it is quiet, and that's when I know that it's done. The teachers will be back tomorrow for an inservice day, but it will likely be more a day for celebration than for work. Summer starts now. I gather my presents into a bag and walk out of the building. There is far greater treasure than the loot that I carry in my hands.

I knew these children.

Rebecca Akin and Gerald Campano

What is the phenomenology of teaching? How do teachers make sense of their work? How is teaching political? How does teaching involve both the messiness and joys of human relationships? How can the ever-evolving intellectual and ethical deliberations of teaching be captured in research? As teacher researchers ourselves, we know that writing from the location of the classroom entails the often ill-fitting task of freezing in text perceptions and understandings that in reality are fluid, continually changing, and often contradictory. While teaching is highly interpretive "cultural work" (Freire, 1998), its understandings are in a continual process of (re)vision. This is particularly true when teachers adopt an inquiry stance that frames the work through questions rather than certainties.

The genre of readers' theatre is uniquely suited for capturing what the philosopher Maria Lugones (2003) might call the "subordinate world of sense" of schools, or an alternative world of value, creativity, and perception that is largely invisible to dominant instrumental views of teaching and learning. In positioning multiple representations of teaching side by side, this format allows the reader to enter into a space where teaching is experienced as moving, changing, contradictory, and fluid—an "ontological multiplicity" (Lugones, 2003) rather than the impression of homogeneity and stability. This is not to suggest that the robust diversity of perspectives represented in the script is ungrounded and floating; the vignettes are in fact grounded in the realities of classroom life. The varied "practitioners' voices" are also motivated by a shared understanding that current educational arrangements are too often inequitable and that the process of creating more just classrooms involves critically working through uncertainty, self-doubt, and conflict rather than dogmatically clinging to preconceived ideas.

It is in this spirit that we invite readers to engage the script. Often, when audiences encounter representations of practice, a first impulse is either judgmental critique or uncritical affirmation. While both reactions have their value, we caution against them as the place either to begin or end. A more productive way of encountering this script might be with a focus on the questions it raises. How do the social locations of the authors shape their readings of the situations represented? What resonates with you? What seems remote? What interpretive frameworks are the authors using? Which ones are you using? How do the vignettes reflect the structural constraints of teaching? How do the various practitioners enact agency within these constraints? Certainly readers of this script will have their own pressing questions that relate to their local contexts. The script, therefore, becomes something of a "writerly text" (Barthes, 1970/1974) requiring readers to adopt an inquiry stance themselves: to read with as well as against the script, all the while keeping in mind that what might be most generative about engaging with it is not simply critique but the opportunity it affords to raise new questions and gain alternative perspectives. An essential part of the work of reading this script is to fill in the gaps with one's own experience.

It's important to note that the actual written text of a reader's theatre, as opposed to the performance, loses something of the interplay of varied perspectives. At a performance, the audience moves between readers and therefore among different scenes, classrooms, perspectives, locations, contexts, and understandings. There are different voices, literally, and varied tempos and tones. They carry their regional, class, and ethnic dialects as well as the idiosyncrasies of individual personality. At times the voices are in solidarity; at times they are in tension with each other. What is powerful about the actual performance is that it embodies the immediate emotions and visceral struggles of classroom life. We therefore recommend that the text be rendered in multiple voices. We also hope that other communities of teachers and teacher educators are inspired to create their own readers' theatre.

As editors who have given the text a close reading and heard it performed, we are struck by the humility in the words. While the script invokes the "I," it is not an omniscient "I," but rather a dialogical one that invites response. We are also struck by how the ensemble of voices, though varied, conveys a "resistant intentionality" (Lugones, 2003) against dehumanizing readings of teachers, students, and schools. The juxtaposed voices defy a "unitary and reductive logic" (Lugones, 2003) that too often informs educational policy and practice. Although there are ways in which the writing here is critical, the script is not a treatise on critical pedagogy. It is not another "how-to" on teaching. The script is unavoidably political while at the same time deeply personal.

Resistance to hegemonic understandings extends to the research process itself, which is too often conducted "on" rather than "with" those in educational settings. The script grew organically out of classroom inquiries, whether as part of formal dissertation studies, in the context of local or national teacher inquiry communities, or through self-initiated research. Regardless of where they fall in the spectrum of practitioner inquiry, these voices illustrate the relational nature of being an "observant participant" (Florio-Ruane & Walsh, 1980). Although we had (and raised) some questions about representation with several of the authors, we realize that the teachers were not representing abstract "others" but individuals with whom they worked and advocated for daily and whose lives were in many ways intertwined with their own. Unlike research where the researcher makes his or her appearance primarily to extract data, teacher researchers have developed methodologies for listening to and learning from students. The script illustrates how teaching from an inquiry stance is about shared knowledge construction with one's students and colleagues. While the authors work to expose this process, they also make themselves vulnerable to scrutiny. They partake in this "risky business" (Lytle, 1993) because of their greater commitment to illuminating the true complexity and value of teaching.

REFERENCES

Alexander, M. (1984). Spilled salt. In M. Alexander (Ed.), *Speaking for ourselves: Women of the South*. New York: Pantheon.

Barthes, R. (1974). *S/Z: An essay*. New York: Hill & Wang. (Original work published 1970)

Britzman, D. (1991). *Practice makes practice: A critical study of learning to teach*. Albany: State University of New York Press.

Cantafio, E. (2002). *What we would perish without: Response and responsibility in developmental education*. Unpublished doctoral dissertation, Philadelphia: University of Pennsylvania.

Cisneros, S. (1984). *The house on Mango Street*. New York: Vintage.

Cochran-Smith, M., & Lytle, S. (2001). Beyond certainty: Taking an inquiry stance on practice. In A. Liebermann & L. Miller (Eds.), *Teachers caught in the action: Professional development that matters* (pp. 45–58). New York: Teachers College Press.

Edwards, J. A. (1996). *Last of the really great Wangdoodles*. New York: HarperCollins.

Florio-Ruane, S., & Walsh, M. (1980). The teacher as colleague in classroom research. In H. Trueba, G. Guthrie, & K. Au (Eds.), *Culture in the bilingual classroom: Studies in classroom ethnography* (pp. 87–101). Rowley, MA: Newbury House.

Freire, P. (1998). *Teachers as cultural workers: Letters to those who dare teach* (D. Macedo, D. Koike, & A. Oliveria, Trans.). Boulder, CO: Westview.

Greene, M. (1988). The dialectic of freedom. New York: Teachers College Press.

Henks, K. (2003). *Olive's ocean*. New York: HarperCollins.

Hughes, L. (1994). *The collected poems*. New York: Knopf.

Jones, D. W. (2003). *Cart and cwidder*. New York: Oxford University Press.

Keats, E. J. (1964). *Whistle for Willie*. New York: Viking Juvenile.

Keats, E. J. (1976). *The snowy day*. New York: Puffin.

Lankshear, C., & McLaren, P. L. (1993). Critical literacy and the postmodern turn. In C. Lankshear, M. Greene, & P. L. McLaren (Eds.), *Critical literacy: Politics, praxis, and the postmodern* (pp. 379–420). Albany: State University of New York Press.

Lugones, M. (2003). *Pilgramages/Peregrinajes: Theorizing coalition against multiple oppressions.* Lanham, MD: Rowman & Littlefield.

Lytle, S. L. (1993). Risky business (teacher research). *Quarterly of the National Writing Project and the Center for the Study of Writing and Literacy, 15*(1), 20–23.

Naylor, P. R. (2001). *Jade green: A ghost story.* New York: Simon & Schuster.

Rich, A. (1986). North American time. In A. Rich (Ed.), *Your native land, your life* (pp. 33–36). New York: Norton.(Original work published 1983)

Simon, R. D., & Alnutt, B. (2007). Philadelphia, 1982–2007: Toward the postindustrial city. *Pennsylvania Magazine of History and Biography, 131*(4), 395–444.

Index

About the Authors

MARILYN COCHRAN-SMITH holds the John E. Cawthorne Chair in Teacher Education for Urban Schools and directs the doctoral program in Curriculum and Instruction at Boston College's Lynch School of Education. A frequent keynoter on issues of teacher education and teacher quality, Dr. Cochran-Smith was the 2005 president of the American Educational Research Association and received AERA's 2007 Relating Research to Practice Award for her book *Practice, Policy and Politics in Teacher Education*. She was co-editor (with K. Zeichner) of AERA's report *Studying Teacher Education*, which received the American Association of Colleges of Teacher Education's (AACTE) 2005 best publication award. For 6 years, Dr. Cochran-Smith has chaired Boston College's Evidence Team, which is part of the Carnegie Corporation's Teachers for a New Era project. This interdisciplinary group, which has constructed "teaching for social justice" and "inquiry" as legitimate outcomes of teacher education, has published and presented this work in many places in the United States and internationally.

SUSAN L. LYTLE is Associate Professor and Chair of the Language and Literacy in Education Division as well as director of the master's and doctoral programs in Reading/Writing/Literacy at the Graduate School of Education, University of Pennsylvania. She is also the Founding Director of the 22-year-old Philadelphia Writing Project (PhilWP), a site of the National Writing Project and an urban school–university collaborative network focused on teacher-to-teacher professional development and practice-based research on teaching, learning, and schooling. Dr. Lytle has a long-standing commitment to working with urban K–12 teachers, community college/university faculty, and adult educators to design and document a variety of inquiry-based collaborative research programs and projects. She has published widely on topics related to literacy education, practitioner inquiry, teacher learning and leadership, and school–university partnerships. Dr. Lytle is a past president of the National Conference on Research in Language and Literacy (NCRLL) and the National Council of Teachers of English's (NCTE) Assembly on Research.

Dr. Cochran-Smith and Dr. Lytle have been writing together about teacher research and practitioner inquiry for the last 20 years. Their first book, *Inside/Outside: Teacher Research and Knowledge*, won AACTE's best publication award in 1994 and was translated into Spanish (Ediciones Akal, 2002). In addition, they have co-authored more than 20 articles and chapters related to practitioner research. They also co-edit the Teachers College Press Practitioner Inquiry Series, which includes nearly three dozen books about practitioner research and/or written by practitioner researchers in school and other educational settings. *Inquiry as Stance: Practitioner Research for the Next Generation* is the 37th book in the series.